The Presidential-Congressional
Political Dictionary

THE PRESIDENTIAL-CONGRESSIONAL POLITICAL DICTIONARY

Jeffrey M. Elliot
Sheikh R. Ali
North Carolina Central University

ABC-Clio Information Services
Santa Barbara, California
Denver, Colorado
Oxford, England

104138

Index by R. Reginald

This book is printed on acid-free paper to meet library standards

Library of Congress Cataloging in Publication Data

Elliot, Jeffrey M.
  The Presidential-Congressional political dictionary.

  (Clio dictionaries in political science ; 9)
  Includes index.
  1. Presidents—United States—Dictionaries.   2. United States. Congress—Dictionaries.   3. United States—Politics and government—Dictionaries.   I. Ali, Sheikh Rustum.   II. Title.   III. Series
JK9.E4 1984   320.473′03′21   84-6316
ISBN 0-87436-357-8
ISBN 0-87436-358-6 (paper)

10   9   8   7   6   5   4   3   2   1

ABC-Clio Information Services
2040 Alameda Padre Serra, Box 4397
Santa Barbara, California 93103

Clio Press Ltd.
55 St. Thomas Street
Oxford OX1 1JG, England

Manufactured in the United States of America

"The legislative and executive branches may sometimes err, but elections and dependence will bring them to rights."

—THOMAS JEFFERSON

Clio Dictionaries in Political Science

SERIES STATEMENT

Language precision is the primary tool of every scientific discipline. That aphorism serves as the guideline for this series of political dictionaries. Although each book in the series relates to a specific topical or regional area in the discipline of political science, entries in the dictionaries also emphasize history, geography, economics, sociology, philosophy, and religion.

This dictionary series incorporates special features designed to help the reader overcome any language barriers that may impede a full understanding of the subject matter. For example, the concepts included in each volume were selected to complement the subject matter found in existing texts and other books. All but one volume utilize a subject matter chapter arrangement that is most useful for classroom and study purposes.

Entries in all volumes include an up-to-date definition plus a paragraph of *Significance* in which the authors discuss and analyze the term's historical and current relevance. Most entries are also cross-referenced providing the reader an opportunity to seek additional information related to the subject of inquiry. A comprehensive index, found in both hard cover and paperback editions, allows the reader to locate major entries and other concepts, events, and institutions discussed within these entries.

The political and social sciences suffer more than most disciplines from semantic confusion. This is attributable, *inter alia,* to the popularization of the language, and to the focus on many diverse foreign political and social systems. This dictionary series is dedicated to overcoming some of this confusion through careful writing of thorough, accurate definitions for the central concepts, institutions, and events that comprise the basic knowledge of each of the subject fields. New titles in the series will be issued periodically, including some in related social science disciplines.

—Jack C. Plano
Series Editor

CONTENTS

A NOTE ON HOW TO USE THIS BOOK

The Presidential-Congressional Political Dictionary is organized so that entries and supplementary data can be located easily and quickly. Items are arranged alphabetically within subject-matter chapters. The one exception is Chapter 3 on the presidency, where the presidents are listed chronologically. Terms relating to limits on the president's powers, like The War Powers Act or Impoundment of Funds, can be found in the chapter titled "Powers of the President." When doubtful about which chapter to look up, consult the general index. Page numbers for entries appear in the index in heavy black type; subsidiary concepts discussed within entries can be found in the index identified by page numbers in regular type. For study purposes, numerous entries have also been subsumed under major topical headings in the index, giving the student access to broad classes of related information.

The student can also more fully explore a topic by using the extensive cross-references provided in most entries. These may lead to materials included in the same chapter or may refer him or her to the subject matter of other chapters. Page numbers have been included in all cross-references for the convenience of the reader. A few entries can be found as subsidiary concepts in more than one chapter, but in each case the item is related to the subject matter of the chapter in which the term appears.

The authors have designed the unique format of this book to offer the student a variety of useful applications in the quest for information. These include its use as (1) a *dictionary* and *reference guide* to the language of the presidency and Congress; (2) a *study guide* for the introductory course in American government or for the more specialized courses in Congress and the presidency; (3) a supplement to the *textbook* or to a group of paperback monographs adopted for use in the above courses; (4) a *source of review material* for the political science major enrolled in advanced courses; and (5) a *social science aid* for use in cognate fields in such courses as electoral politics, political elites, and public policy.

PREFACE

The Presidential-Congressional Political Dictionary derives from the authors'
20-plus years of study, teaching, research, and writing on the related
subjects of the presidency and Congress. The volume that has emerged
is intended to serve as a guide to the rich technical language of American politics and government. It emphasizes those concepts, theories, and
facts which the authors believe to be essential to a basic understanding
of these two important institutions.

This book is organized in a format uncommon in dictionaries. Entries
are grouped into subject-matter chapters that parallel chapter topics in
most current textbooks in these areas. In addition to a definition or
description, each entry contains a paragraph of *Significance* so that the
historical roots and contemporary meaning of a term can be studied.
Furthermore, an extensive cross-reference system is used throughout
the volume, providing opportunities for the reader to seek additional
information.

In the world of scholarship, precise language is truly the first scientific
tool. The authors believe that the ability to communicate in a technical
language is fundamental to the mastery of any academic field of study.
The orientation of this book reflects the classroom experiences of its
authors and their belief that emphasis should be placed on learning the
basics in every introductory course. The basics in the fields of the
presidency and Congress include those concepts, theories, and facts that
contribute to an understanding of how the American political system
functions.

The entries in this work have been systematically selected and organized to complement the subject matter typically found in leading
textbooks and course materials. Thus, the instructor or student can use
the Dictionary as a teaching/learning supplement to a textbook or as a
tool for unifying courses developed around individual readings. The
authors have tried to incorporate relevant data accurately, but we would
appreciate it if readers alert us to any sins of omission or commission.
However, please note that the authors have been discriminating rather
than exhaustive; we selected only those terms that we consider to be
most pertinent to an understanding of the presidency and Congress.

We wish to express our appreciation to the many students who over the years have challenged and excited our interest in the field of American politics and government. We hope that this excitement and interest proves contagious. *The Presidential-Congressional Political Dictionary* grew out of our recognition of the need for such a tool, made obvious by these classroom interactions. We extend our appreciation to the Clio Books staff, with special thanks to Gail Schlachter, Vice President; Cecelia A. Albert, Clio Books Editor; and Ann L. Hartman, Director of Marketing and Sales. In addition, we wish to thank Jack C. Plano, Series Editor, who read the manuscript in its entirety and made many valuable comments and suggestions, and whose helpful and encouraging words stimulated our interest and determination. Finally, we wish to thank J. Dante Noto for his tireless research efforts, as well as his grace and good humor, and Rina Ali, for her unflagging cooperation and painstaking assistance in preparation of the final manuscript.

—Jeffrey M. Elliot
—Sheikh R. Ali
North Carolina Central University

The Presidential-Congressional
Political Dictionary

1. The President and the Electorate

Availability Factor   The sum total of the qualifications and electability of a potential candidate as evaluated by party members. Availability factor particularly refers to a candidate's ability to attract and influence voters. It may include such special factors as having no large, well-organized groups of voters opposed to the candidate on social, political, racial, religious, and economic grounds. The concept of availability developed because a party needs to evaluate the qualifications of a potential candidate to make certain it is supporting a possible winner. The Constitution requires only three formal criteria for the presidency: minimum age of thirty-five, fourteen-year residence in the United States, and citizenship as a native-born American. The availability factor implies that a presidential candidate must meet certain requirements beyond the constitutional demands in order to be elected. These include experience in holding important political offices such as senator or governor, exposure in foreign affairs, and popular appeal. Ultimately, availability refers to all those qualities that are likely to enhance a candidate's chances for electoral victory. *See also* PRESIDENTIAL CANDIDATE, p. 20; PRESIDENTIAL ELECTION, p. 22.

Significance   Availability is usually the critical factor considered in nominating a candidate. Regional considerations are one of the most important of such factors. The nomination of Jimmy Carter, a former southern governor, by the Democratic party in 1976, is an example of such regionalism. Another key factor is whether the candidate comes from a large state. This consideration influenced the 1980 Republican nomination of Ronald Reagan, a former California governor. The personal popularity and family background of the candidate are also relevant. Many presidential candidates have been wealthy persons and have contributed part of their personal fortunes to the campaign.

3

Politics is what politicians make it. Personal character, honesty, and integrity are all American traits. Senator Edward M. Kennedy's marital status and the Chappaquiddick incident are often cited as detriments to his presidential candidacy. Personal health is another key factor for securing the nomination. A candidate must have charm and good looks, given the impact of television. The media domination of presidential politics demands that a hopeful candidate possess a dignified and stately appearance; availability depends on a good television image. Incumbency is considered one of the most crucial availability factors. An incumbent's record, party influence, and presidential visibility may add up to electoral success.

Campaign Funding   Money collected and spent in furthering the election of a candidate for public office. Campaign funding is a crucial element in winning an election. Money and politics have always been intertwined to a great extent because of the high stakes involved in winning. The 1980 presidential election was one of the costliest in history, with total spending for the primary and general election campaigns totaling $300 million. The two major candidates, Jimmy Carter and Ronald Reagan, each received approximately $30 million in federal funds. Money for the public financing of presidential elections comes mostly from the reserve created by the one-dollar income tax check-off, private and corporate donations, and the candidate's personal fund. State and local party agencies are free to raise and spend unlimited sums from their respective national committees. *See also* PUBLIC FINANCING, p. 23.

Significance   Campaign funding is not the only resource necessary for electoral victory. But money can, to a great extent, make up for the inadequacy of other resources. It has been said that American politics is a politics of, by, and for money. Electoral campaigns are highly professional affairs. It has become so expensive to run for the presidency that candidates must seek large public contributions. This raises questions about the candidate's honesty and independence from influence while serving in office. A government that money can buy could be the worst government for the people.

Congress enacted a comprehensive measure regulating federal campaign finance and attached it to the Revenue Act of 1971. The presidential election of 1972 was partially governed by the provisions of this act. However, the Watergate scandal (in which President Richard M. Nixon and several high administration officials were charged with criminal misconduct) showed the inadequacies of this act and the undue influence of money in politics. A Senate committee investigated the irregularities in President Nixon's 1972 campaign and submitted its report calling for far-reaching reforms, resulting in the Federal Election Campaign Act of 1974. First, it set limits on campaign contributions and expenses by candidates. Second, it made the provisions regarding financial disclosure more stringent. Third, it provided for the public financing of presidential elections. In passing this act, Congress hoped to reduce a presidential candidate's dependence on large donors and discourage illegal contributions. The Campaign Finance Act guarantees the continual domination of politics by the two major parties, because minor party candidates are required to garner 5 percent of the total vote to qualify retroactively for federal funds. The Supreme Court has declared unconstitutional those provisions of the act which attempted to impose limitations on the amount of personal money candidates and their families could spend in elections. The High Court in *Buckley* v. *Valeo* (1976) held that the 1974 Campaign Finance Act violated the First Amendment because it imposed undue restrictions on an individual's right to participate in the election process.

Coattail Effect   The apparent ability of a strong candidate who heads a ticket or is a party leader to affect the outcome of other elections by influencing the vote. Literally, it means to take shelter under the coattail of a person. The coattail effect implies that a lesser known person or weaker candidate will profit by the presence on the ticket or in the party of a stronger, more popular person. This often occurs when electors cast their votes for congressional candidates of the president's party because they like and support the presidential incumbent. It is assumed that the margin by which incumbents lead the ticket is a reflection of their popularity and ability to strengthen the chances of candidates for lesser offices. Metaphors used in the media such as "hide under the coattail," "hang onto the coattail," and "ride on the coattail," show evidence of a president or a presidential candidate's power to gain the support of voters. *See also* PRESIDENTIAL CANDIDATE, p. 20.

Significance   The coattail effect suggests that voters who support a party's presidential candidate will also back other candidates of that party. Voting for a presidential aspirant and that party's ticket is a product of different motivations. The coattail effect depends on the personality, policy, philosophy, and ability of a presidential candidate to influence the voters. If the public is content with the president, they may vote for the candidates of the president's party. If they are unhappy, they may vote against the party. In a presidential election year, the fortunes of congressional candidates are frequently linked with the presidential candidate. After President Richard M. Nixon's resignation in 1974, thirty-six incumbent Republicans lost their seats in Congress. When Jimmy Carter lost the presidential election in 1980, thirty-three Democrats were also defeated. A popular presidential candidate may help elect the candidates running on the same party ticket, but this may not be possible in an off-year when presidential candidates are not up for election. In 1980 President Ronald Reagan's victory helped produce a gain of twelve senators and thirty-three representatives. However, a correlation between presidential and congressional elections has not been empirically established.

Various studies show that incumbency is a dominant factor, particularly in the election of representatives. In recent years, it has also been found that the coattail effect has become less important in congressional, state, and local elections. In the eight presidential elections from 1952 through 1980, Republican candidates were elected to the presidency five times. However, they only had full control of Congress for four of those years. Democratic candidates for the presidency have received fewer votes than their congressional candidates, except in 1964. Today, most congressional candidates and other office seekers need to marshal their own resources and cultivate their own following, as there is seldom blind acceptance of presidential leadership.

Dark Horse   Popular name for a compromise candidate, relatively unknown or not seriously considered until the campaign is well under way. A dark horse is a noncandidate or, at best, a marginal one. In a presidential nominating convention, a dark horse is a politician who, with little or no advance notice, suddenly is given consideration as the party's candidate. *See also* FRONT RUNNER, p. 11.

Significance   Dark horse was a racing term until it invaded the political vocabulary when James K. Polk was nominated as the first dark horse presidential candidate in 1844. The strategy of a dark horse is to become acceptable to all contenders, to avoid primaries, and to wait until a deadlock occurs in the selection of candidates. When all else fails, the party may turn to the dark horse, in an attempt to displease no one and unite the party with a neutral person.

The two major political parties are based on diverse philosophies, interests, and outlooks. There are divergent factions within each party, often reflecting liberal/conservative differences. Deadlocks over the selection of presidential candidates have arisen on several occasions. After a protracted stalemate, the Republican party turned to dark horse Warren G. Harding in 1920. In 1960 Stuart Symington (D-Mo.) was a dark horse candidate but failed to secure his party's nomination. In 1968 Ronald Reagan also proved unsuccessful when he adopted a dark horse strategy. The presidency is too great a prize for the parties to wait for a "Johnny come lately" to be nominated.

Delegate Selection Process   Process of delegate selection by party members to their national convention. The delegate selection process varies with different state laws. Two principal methods are the party convention and party primary. The number of convention or primary votes allotted to each state is determined by the major parties. In 1980, thirty-four states, the District of Columbia, and Puerto Rico used direct primaries to choose about three-quarters of the delegates. In the remaining states, delegates were chosen by state or county conventions, party committees, or a combination of these various processes. The method of selection begins with indirect election at the precinct level. Delegates are elected to the county convention and finally to the state convention. State conventions pick the party delegates. Owing to complicated formulas based on population and party strength within each state, the number of party delegates differs significantly. In 1980 the Republicans had 1,194 delegates at their convention, while the Democrats had 3,331 delegates. Each party also selects alternate delegates. *See also* PRESIDENTIAL CAMPAIGN, p. 19; PRESIDENTIAL CANDIDATE, p. 20; PRESIDENTIAL ELECTION, p. 22.

Significance   The delegate selection process is one of the first steps toward nomination of a candidate. The primary is the most common device for choosing delegates to a national convention. This method was first used in Wisconsin in 1905. Since then, thirty-four states have used this system to select delegates. Primaries take the selection of delegates out of the direct control of party leaders. Still, political considerations dominate the delegate selection process. In the case of the Democrats, there are factional conflicts between the North and South, labor, farm groups, and old-line party members. Republicans also have strong underlying conflicts between northeasterners and midwesterners, moderates and conservatives. In general, the influential and affluent members of the party are selected as delegates, such as senators, members of Congress, governors, state legislators, and major fund-raisers and donors.

Many objections have been raised concerning the weaknesses in the delegate selection process. The two parties have recently instituted a number of reforms. The Democrats have sought to broaden their base by increasing the number of women, youths, blacks, and ethnic groups. They tend to favor larger, more urban states where the presidential votes are greatest. Republicans have reduced the number of delegates from the heavily populated states and increased the number from less populous states. Both parties seek means to democratize the delegate selection process. The 1980 convention rules called for each party to make a good faith effort to select an equal number of male and female delegates.

Direct Primary   A party election in which candidates are chosen by party members. The direct primary constitutes the preliminary selection of a party's nominees. Nomination allows candidates to run for office with party labels. The two major political parties, the Democrats and Republicans, dominate the nominating process. The state primary system has largely replaced the convention process; only about a dozen states use conventions to select candidates. (A convention is a meeting of either appointed or elected members of a party that nominates candidates for elective office.) State laws regulate primaries as well as general elections. Primaries are used to nominate candidates for the Senate and House of Representatives, the governorship, and various state and local offices.

There are two kinds of direct primaries: closed and open. A closed primary is closed to voters who are not registered members of that party. In an open primary all voters, irrespective of their party affiliation, may take part in the primary. Alaska, Louisiana, and Washington use a so-called blanket primary in which voters receive a ballot containing the names of both major party candidates. For example, a voter may choose a Democratic candidate for senator and a Republican for governor. When no candidate receives a majority of the vote in a primary, a second or runoff primary is held. A runoff primary is a contest between the two candidates who receive the highest number of votes in the first primary. Minor party candidates may not be required to take the primary route. *See also* DELEGATE SELECTION PROCESS, p. 7; NATIONAL CONVENTION, p. 14; NATIONAL PRESIDENTIAL PRIMARY, p. 15.

Significance   The direct primary has waxed and waned in American politics. The primary is a unique American election process; no other nations use this system. In other countries, the selection of party nominees is reserved to party members. In many countries, party membership entails payment of dues and other party obligations. Critics contend that primaries represent democracy gone mad, yet there is some method in this madness. The parties select the nominees through internal caucuses. The rules concerning primaries vary from party to party and state to state. The direct primary system democratizes nominations at the grass roots level. The system gives rank and file voters a greater voice in party affairs and in the selection of candidates. Primaries allow some degree of popular control over nominations.

A large segment of the electorate does not participate in primaries. One reason is that many primaries are not exciting contests. The system is complex and not well understood by people; it takes too long and costs too much. It invites factionalism. Although turnout is relatively low at primary elections, those participating are usually older and more experienced, affluent and better educated. Despite their shortcomings, primaries have had a great effect on parties, particularly in terms of nominating and electing candidates.

Electoral College   A special group of electors who vote for the president and the vice president in an indirect election. The electoral college represents the collectivity of voters. It is organized under a constitutional provision for presidential elections: electors chosen in each state by popular vote in turn elect the president and the vice president. This system was designed by the framers of the Constitution as a compromise between the popular election of the president and selection by the Congress. Under the electoral college system, each state is allotted electoral votes totalling the number of its senators and representatives. This ensures that each state has at least three electoral votes. The electoral college consists of 538 electors: 100 (corresponding to the number of senators), 435 (the number of representatives), and 3 (for the District of Columbia). To win the presidency, a candidate must secure a majority of the electoral votes (270).

Each state determines how its electoral votes will be cast. Both parties run a slate of electors pledged to the party's presidential candidates. The names of these electors do not appear on the ballots. All of the electoral votes from a state go to the candidate who receives the largest popular vote from that state. In this winner-take-all system, the loser receives no electoral votes. The members of the electoral college, who are chosen in November of the presidential election year, go to their state capitals in December of that year to cast their ballots. The electors are not constitutionally bound to vote for the candidate to whom they are pledged. However, since the founding of the nation, only twelve electors have defected and voted for the losing candidate. The electoral votes are listed, certified, sealed, and transmitted to the President of the Senate, who opens the certificates on January 6 and counts them in the presence of the Senate and House members. This completes the presidential election process. (Refer to the Appendix, Figure 1 for a map of the electoral college vote.) *See also* POPULAR VOTE, p. 17; PRESIDENTIAL ELECTION, p. 22; WINNER-TAKE-ALL RULE, p. 24.

Significance   The electoral college system is based on two principles: federalism and elitism. It reflects the federal compromise formula reached at the Constitutional Convention of 1787, creating a bicameral legislature based on equal territorial representation and proportional representation on the basis of population. The concept of elitism evolved because of the aristocracy that surrounded the making of the Constitution in the late eighteenth century. The framers of the Constitution felt that the presidential electors should be men of superior intelligence who may prove more adept at selecting the president than the masses. The masses were considered not only ignorant but also incapable of deciding the great political issues; the architects of the Constitution believed that deciding the election of the most powerful and prestigious office in the country could not be left with the masses.

Critics contend that this system violates the very spirit of a democratic society. Under this system three presidents—John Quincy Adams, Rutherford B. Hayes, and Benjamin Harrison—were elected even though they received fewer popular votes than their opponents. An additional problem arises when no candidate wins a majority of electoral votes, in which case the House of Representatives chooses the president from among the three leading candidates. It is possible for a minority of the House members to elect the president since voting is by states, each state having one vote. Owing to the complexity of the electoral college system, many proposals have been made to amend or abolish it. Those favoring the electoral college system believe it is important for the states to play a crucial role in deciding the presidential election. Their opponents argue that the popular vote has a much deeper meaning in a democracy and should be recognized as such.

Favorite Son Candidate   A prospective candidate for the presidency or other national office who is strongly supported by leaders of the candidate's home state or its delegates. A favorite son candidate is not considered a serious prospect. Sometimes it is merely a means of honoring a distinguished citizen of the state by offering the nomination for high office. It is also used as a dilatory tactic where there is a lack of consensus on the nominee. Favorite sons are mock candidates to be traded off later in negotiations between leaders, having the support of their own delegation and no one else. They may bargain with a leading contender who needs their votes in order to win the nomination. *See also* NATIONAL PRESIDENTIAL PRIMARY, p. 15; PRESIDENTIAL CANDIDATE, p. 20; PRESIDENTIAL ELECTION, p. 22.

Significance   The term favorite son candidate was first applied to George Washington in 1788, but without explicit political meaning. The frequency with which favorite sons are brought forward with no possible chance to secure the nomination, but as a means of drawing attention to a state delegation, leads to occasional satire in electoral politics. Favorite son candidacy serves much the same purpose as an unpledged slate of delegates, except that it puts control of state delegations directly into the hands of the favorite son. Favorite sons usually fail to win the primaries because they lack the necessary broad base appeal and financial resources. In 1970 the Democratic party adopted a rule that requires a favorite son candidate to secure the support of fifty delegates. Favorite son nominations allow citizens an opportunity to participate directly in national politics on the local level that they might not be able to do otherwise. They can join in parades, carry banners, and chant slogans for their favorite candidate.

Front Runner　　A leading contender for the presidential nomination. The term front runner literally means to "show early foot." As applied to a horse race, it means that the horse (candidate) is capable of getting out of the starting gate early and setting the pace for the others. A candidate who does so may garner media attention and support from delegates ahead of others. Many candidates engage in fund-raising, planning, and campaign organizing. A front runner needs to gain sufficient strength to be one of the leaders on the first ballot and have enough strength in reserve for the psychologically important second ballot. The contender moves through the early stages of the campaign and then attempts to pick up sufficient delegates to ultimately win at the convention. A front runner has a greater chance of victory than does a dark horse, a relative unknown that wishes to be nominated as a compromise candidate. A front runner remains active for months or even years before the convention gets underway. *See also* DARK HORSE, p. 6.

Significance　　A front runner has certain advantages as well as disadvantages. Occasionally, a front runner becomes unsurpassable, as the nomination of Barry M. Goldwater (R-Ariz.) in 1964 showed. Jimmy Carter's early lead in 1976 helped him to capture many delegates in advance of the primaries. In 1980 Ronald Reagan was the acknowledged front runner of the Republican party. Throughout the primary season, Reagan's task was to avoid losing his early lead, as he had twice been defeated in the past. He had the advantages of a national reputation and prior campaign experience. Despite the hazards of being the front runner, political parties prefer such candidates to dark horses, as they stand a greater chance of success in the general election.

There are also several disadvantages. For example, the nature of preconvention strategy is such that the front runner often becomes a target of criticism and jealousy within the party, as well as the target of other candidates, real and potential. Another disadvantage is that the front runner's every word is politically interpreted and becomes the subject of early criticism. Favorite son candidates have little or no support beyond their own state delegations and attempt to keep their delegations out of the front runner column so long as there is advantage in doing so.

National Chairman   The head of the national committee of a political party. The national chairman is generally the choice of the presidential candidate with nominal approval of the national committee. As the official director of the political campaign and a full-time executive officer of the party, the chairman's main task is to coordinate the convention and raise sufficient money for the ensuing presidential campaign. The chairman supervises the campaign staff and manages the campaign from the party headquarters in Washington, D.C. Prior to and during the national convention, the chairman negotiates with domestic and foreign news media for coverage of the convention. *See also* NATIONAL COMMITTEE, p. 13; NATIONAL CONVENTION, p. 14; NATIONAL PRESIDENTIAL PRIMARY, p. 15.

Significance   The national chairman makes sure that the activities of the national committee center almost exclusively around him. A chairman's role depends upon the outcome of the presidential election. If the party's candidate wins, the chairman's role is subordinate to the president who acts as chief party leader. If the candidate loses, the chairman is more prominent, often becoming the chief party spokesman. He is frequently unable to speak candidly because of the coalition nature of party politics. He is the personal representative of the candidate or the president if his party is in power. The national chairman must take a neutral stance toward the candidates seeking the nomination and remain as objective as possible in selecting the convention location and assigning space to various delegations. The chairman appoints all the working committees of the convention. Through these committees, he manages the convention and recommends measures to resolve conflicts among contenders. Much depends on his ability to manage.

The chairman assumes added responsibility when party control of government changes and a new president is elected. Before a president recommends the top positions to the Senate for approval, applicants for these patronage jobs are usually cleared through the office of the national chairman. The chairman, in consultation with the president, dispenses these favors in a way that maintains party harmony, attempting to reward the party faithfuls whenever possible. The president may seek the chairman's cooperation in maintaining party discipline in the states and Congress on important issues. In 1980 Republican Chairman

William Brock launched an aggressive campaign and fund-raising drive aimed at defeating the Democrats. Even before the convention was held, the Republican National Committee had raised $23.8 million. The GOP used electronic techniques as part of a direct-mail campaign and developed a close relationship with the news media and major campaign firms. The Republicans won the presidency.

National Committee   A committee of each major political party composed of one man and one woman representative from each state, territory, and the District of Columbia. The national committee is the capstone of the formal party organization. The Republican National Committee includes a third member, the state party chairman. The Democratic committee consists of representatives from Congress, as well as the Democratic governors. Both national committees include representatives from the Young Democrats and Young Republicans organizations. National committees are standing committees; they act for the party between presidential election years and direct party activities during the intervening years. The national committee sets the time and place for the national convention and carries on publicity, usually under the direction of a chairman. It is largely inactive during nonpresidential election years. The national committee serves as the governing body when the delegates are not in session. It also issues pronouncements of party policy analogous to the party platform. The national committee represents states, not people. *See also* NATIONAL CHAIRMAN, p. 12; NATIONAL CONVENTION, p. 14; NATIONAL PRESIDENTIAL PRIMARY, p. 15.

Significance   The national committee meets only infrequently. It does not make policy. It is charged with choosing the convention site and preparing a temporary roll of convention delegates. The first national committee was established in 1848, when the Democrats decided to organize an efficient party structure to coordinate the upcoming primary and general election campaigns. In 1856 the Republicans organized their own national committee. Both parties had an equal number of male members. Women were added to their national committees in 1920. The national committee is temporary and lacks vitality. Party stalwarts, such as an incumbent presidential candidate, totally overshadow the committee. Membership on the national committee entails costs both in time and money. The members are mostly big businessmen, lawyers, and professional politicians who are willing to pay for stature. The national committee meeting brings together party leaders from all over the country. This gives the members an opportunity to rise in national politics. The party chieftains float in the news media and grow as national leaders.

The national committee is very much an election year phenomenon. Presidential nominees largely ignore the apparatus of the national committee and build their personal organizations to raise funds and manage their campaigns. Many states have placed a variety of complex laws regulating the activities of party organizations on the books, the real meaning of which is not even clear to the experts. At the state level, these regulations vary enormously and sometimes create tremendous problems. Although the power and influence of the national committees are not great, certain penalties for members who bolt the party may be imposed by the committee. The national committee of both parties may declare vacant the seat of any member who deserts the party to support the candidate of the opposition.

National Convention   A national meeting of a political party, composed of delegates from the states, territories, and District of Columbia for the purpose of nominating a presidential candidate. The national convention is also responsible for the party platform, the party's statement of general policy. The quadrennial national convention is the final arbiter of the nomination of a presidential candidate. The selection of a vice presidential candidate is also made at the national convention by the presidential nominee and is typically approved by the convention. Delegates to the convention are selected on the basis of state representation, with bonus delegates for states having voted for the party in the last presidential election. After the delegates have been selected in the primaries, the parties hold their national conventions. Candidates are nominated by an absolute majority vote. The first national conventions were held in 1932. (Refer to the Appendix, Figure 2 for a diagram of the nomination process.) *See also* FAVORITE SON CANDIDATE, p. 10; FRONT RUNNER, p. 11; PARTY PLATFORM, p. 16; PRESIDENTIAL ELECTION, p. 22.

Significance   The national convention is a historic American institution. It provides the nation with pageantry and political excitement. However, behind the fanfare, serious deliberation goes into the nomination of candidates. There is nothing quite like this system anywhere else in the world. The political parties of other countries organize their assemblies and conventions, but in ways which differ markedly from the American party system. After the preliminaries, the convention moves to its main business with a series of nominating and seconding speeches in which the names of the various candidates are proposed. The delegations are called by states in alphabetical order. A spokesman for each delegation rises and either offers the name of a candidate or yields to another state for that purpose. Once the roll call is complete and the oratory is over, the convention proceeds to vote. The number of ballots required is a measure of conflicts within the party. The national convention attempts to resolve these conflicts. Many nominations, however, are decided on the first ballot. In 1980, when the Republican National Convention opened, Ronald Reagan had already captured the required number of delegates. Former representative George Bush (R-Tex.) was the last to quit the race, but unlike Senator Edward M. Kennedy (D-Mass.) in the Democratic party, he did not press his fight to the convention. The Republican platform exhibited a cautious move toward the right, calling for American military superiority. The platform reflected a basically conservative tone. In the case of the Democrats, it was clear that Jimmy Carter had locked up the nomination unless Kennedy could wean away a large bloc of delegates.

Winning a nomination is not exactly like winning an election, but it is an indispensable first step. The shape and substance of modern conventions have been indelibly altered by television. The entire nomination procedure, from start to finish, is stage managed and timed not so much for the delegates in the hall as for the multitude of viewers watching the proceedings on television. Much criticism has been directed at the convention system for its circus atmosphere. Many Americans do not participate in the nomination process. In 1980 only about one-fourth of the American voting public participated in the primaries; perhaps it is difficult for many Americans to grasp the full essence of the convention system.

National Presidential Primary   A national party primary election in which delegates are selected to represent the voters of that party and help select its presidential and vice presidential candidates. National presidential primaries are of two types: The simplest form is when the voters elect delegates to the party's national convention. The other type is a preferential primary, when voters express their preferences among the various presidential contenders. Primaries are usually held in many states in the spring and summer of the election year. The Constitution makes no provision for the nomination of presidential candidates. To give the citizen a voice in the selection process, the first primary was instituted in 1904. No two states are alike in the way in which they conduct their primary. This complex system is built around national party rules, state and local rules, and various court rulings. *See also* DIRECT PRIMARY, p. 8; NATIONAL COMMITTEE, p. 13; NATIONAL CONVENTION, p. 14.

Significance   The national presidential primary is notable for many reasons. It is closely watched by the parties and the electorate for indications as to the relative strength of the candidates. The party leaders, delegates, and news media scrutinize the candidates for their potential electability. The United States is an election-happy country, and the presidential primary is an example of this. Presidential candidates use the primaries to test their popularity. Dwight D. Eisenhower in 1952, John F. Kennedy in 1960, and Ronald Reagan in 1980 had to demonstrate that being a retired general, a Catholic, and a twice-defeated presidential candidate would not stand in the way of winning the presidency. Primaries are also used to build popularity by lesser-known candidates such as Jimmy Carter in 1976. The primaries are interstate testing grounds of candidates in the only national election in the country, but they are not always considered essential or crucial to the nomination of a candidate. Already famous candidates may prefer not to risk primaries, resting on their standing with the voters. Hubert H. Humphrey won the Democratic nomination in 1968 without entering a single primary.

For some time, the primary system was in a state of decline. However, it gained new life with the passage of the Federal Election Campaign Act of 1974. The new law provides public funds for candidates in the primaries as well as the general election. In 1980, thirty-seven states and territories used primaries to select three-fourths of the delegates. A dozen candidates in these primaries spent more than $100 million in the course of campaigning. Good standings in the primaries help prospective candidates impress the electorate.

Party Platform   A political party or candidate's statement of principles, policies, and promises adopted at its national convention. The party platform is presented by the platform committee to the national convention. It consists of a series of policy statements on important national and international issues. Each of these statements is called a plank. To win voter support, parties make promises to various diverse interests and compromise many contending claims. The party in power makes resounding references to its record and pays glowing tribute to the president. The other party usually includes criticism of the record of the incumbent in its platform. *See also* NATIONAL CONVENTION, p. 14.

Significance   The party platform is basically a set of vague generalities about past, present, and future issues confronting the country, the candidate, and the party. A comparison of the platforms of the two major political parties reveals some differences in their philosophies and programs. Party platforms are electioneering devices, not blueprints for action. A party does not dictate a candidate's views, but it does provide a basic philosophical foundation. The candidate is expected to behave and act within the general guidelines set down in the platform.

However, few candidates consider themselves bound by platforms once elected. They may supplement or modify platform commitments. The platform is open to interpretation. Ultimately, the candidate must interpret its meaning. The leading contender usually exercises a controlling voice in the platform. Many party professionals look with distaste upon platform battles. However, the party activists consider platform battles healthy because they bring to the fore policy differences within the party and seek to resolve those differences. The winning presidential candidate tends to enact much of the party's platform. There are important similarities and differences between the platforms of the two major parties. Political scientist Ross K. Baker compares this situation with that of automobile manufacturers, "who produce cars that are very similar to one another as they seek to capture the mass market. Yet . . . car buyers find differences between Fords and Chevys" (Baker 1983, 255).

Popular Vote   Ballots cast by registered voters in a presidential election. The popular vote is cast directly by the voters for the electoral college candidates who represent the presidential candidate of their choice. The presidential election is held in November. For all practical purposes, the election is decided in November every four years (the voters in the fifty states, territories, and District of Columbia cast their ballots for their favorite candidates), even though the winner is formally certified in early January by a joint session of Congress when the electoral ballots are opened and counted. In 1980, 84 million people voted in the presidential election. Voter turnout fell to 52.4 percent from 54.3 percent in 1976, continuing the steady decline that developed after a 63.4 percent turnout in the 1960 presidential election when President John F. Kennedy was elected. In 1980 Republican candidate Ronald Reagan won 43.2 million popular votes, or 51 percent of the total; Democratic incumbent Jimmy Carter received 34.9 million, or 41 percent; and independent candidate John Anderson received 5.6 million, or 7 percent. It was the lowest popular vote turnout in a presidential election since 1948. *See also* ELECTORAL COLLEGE, p. 9; PRESIDENTIAL ELECTION, p. 22; WINNER-TAKE-ALL RULE, p. 24.

Significance   The popular vote resolves conflicts and does so peacefully. Presidential candidates seek to garner the support of the greatest number of people. A democracy is a government of, by, and for the people. The people must have the power to select their rulers in free elections. Democracy is meaningless if people do not have the right to choose from competing candidates for public office. Citizens must be free to express their self-interest and to disagree with their government, party, and leaders. The outcome of an election is determined by the total number of votes a candidate receives. An election, if it is fair and free, is an objective means of determining the popularity of the winning candidate. It not only ensures that the loser will accept the results gracefully but also assures a smooth transition.

The framers of the Constitution did not favor the popular election of the president because they took the Aristotelian view that democracy was a perverted form of government. Implicit in such ideas is the profound suspicion that the masses are not qualified to decide the great issues of government and should not be allowed to choose the president by popular means. The architects of the Constitution provided safeguards against mass rule, including the establishment of the electoral college. Many reforms have been proposed as far as the electoral college is concerned. These proposals have failed to move forward, however, because they pose a threat to the powers that be. Those in power believe that such reforms would jeopardize their interests, as well as the two-party system.

President-Elect   The candidate who receives a majority vote by the electoral college. The president-elect is also known as the president-designate. Once the election is decided, the unofficial results are made known. From that point the winner is referred to as the president-elect, until the electoral college convenes and officially selects the president, early in the following year. The president-elect is then inaugurated as president on the constitutionally designated date and time; under the Twentieth Amendment, this occurs at noon on January 20. At this time, he recites the oath of office and delivers his inaugural address to the nation. Should the president-elect die, the vice president-elect is sworn in as president. *See also* PRESIDENTIAL ELECTION, p. 22.

Significance   The president-elect spends the time between the election and inauguration preparing for the transition. For all practical purposes, he enjoys the privileges of the office of president. The president-elect is briefed by the outgoing president, executive departments, and others on official matters, consulted on long-term negotiations in foreign affairs, and taken into confidence by the president in matters relating to peace and war. These consultations and briefings enable the president-elect to adequately prepare for the assumption of presidential duties. He is like an intern receiving training. The president-elect receives Secret Service protection and is entitled to other perquisites, such as official transportation. The president-elect enters into discussion with party leaders and trusted confidants to select top appointees, often leaking the names of potential cabinet members as a way of paying off campaign debts by enhancing the prestige of those considered.

To ensure a smooth transition from one administration to another, these new officials will also be briefed by those departments to which they will be assigned. The president-elect drafts the new budget and works on a legislative program. With the noise, turbulence, and pressure of the campaign now over, the president-elect prepares to lead. He is usually portrayed by the news media and public as soberly cautious in making decisions, almost above criticism. He is at the center of power and gravity in Washington without having to assume any direct responsibility for the affairs of the nation. The president-elect is like a rising sun, slowly acquiring the power and confidence of the country and the world without having the concomitant responsibilities.

Presidential Campaign   The steps taken by presidential candidates to influence voters and garner sufficient votes to win the election. An American presidential campaign is one of the most hotly contested and closely watched political events in the world. Presidential elections have been held since 1788, but candidates did not participate personally in such campaigns for many years because it was considered unbecoming to the status of the presidency. Instead, the candidate's supporters and party stalwarts appealed to the voters. In 1896 Democratic nominee William Jennings Bryan actively campaigned by traveling around the country and addressing the voters. But his Republican opponent, William McKinley, who campaigned from his home and talked to throngs of visitors, won the election. A new era in presidential election campaigning began in 1952 when the two major party candidates used television as a campaign device.

Because presidential campaigning is complex and time-consuming, the candidates follow certain well-planned and calculated strategies and logistics. They hire campaign managers, staff, fund raisers, pollsters, counsels, consultants, and press secretaries.

One of the most important strategies is to gain sufficient electoral college votes by concentrating campaign appearances and visits to the largest states: California (47 electoral votes), New York (36), Texas (29), Pennsylvania (25), Illinois (24), Ohio (23), Florida (21), Michigan (20), New Jersey (16), Massachusetts (13), North Carolina (13), and Indiana (12), for a total of 279 votes; 270 electoral votes are needed to win. Another aspect of campaign strategy is to capitalize on the demographic characteristics and political attitudes of the electorate. Presidential candidates focus their campaigns on important national issues, such as inflation, unemployment, and interest rates, as well as major issues in foreign policy, including military preparedness, foreign aid, and nuclear disarmament. *See also* CAMPAIGN FUNDING, p. 4; DIRECT PRIMARY, p. 8; NATIONAL PRESIDENTIAL PRIMARY, p. 15.

Significance   The presidential campaign is a major development in American political history. Basic to success is a campaign strategy. The potential candidate must formulate an overall plan that establishes a theme, sets a schedule of places and times for campaigning, and determines the techniques to be used. An important strategic factor for a presidential campaign is whether the incumbent is seeking reelection. Incumbents usually emphasize their record, defend it, and try to impress upon the American public that their reelection is vital to continued peace and prosperity. Challengers attack the incumbent and seek to convince the electorate that a change is desirable. If no incumbent is involved, candidates emphasize that they can best serve the country and fill the vacant position.

The most active persons in campaigns are the candidates and their staff. The staff includes professional campaigners who offer services to candidates on a contract basis. This trend in campaigning is natural in a business-oriented society such as the United States, with its highly mobile and dispersed population. A presidential candidate must also utilize organizational resources. These include the support of the candidate's own party, as well as various interest groups in the country. One of the most important tasks of any major campaign is garnering effective news coverage; a friendly press is critical. Money is one of the most indispensable resources to a successful campaign. The political parties raise funds for their nominee through such events as rock concerts, celebrity appearances, and other kinds of entertainment. This type of campaign activity exposes the candidate to possible political and economic misadventure for the sake of winning the election at any cost. However, reforms have eliminated some of the pitfalls of campaigning, most notably the shortage of funds.

Presidential Candidate   One who seeks election to the office of president. A presidential candidate is usually a professional politician. In order to qualify under the Constitution to be president, a person must be a natural-born American citizen, must have resided in the United States at least fourteen years, and must be at least thirty-five years old. Individuals who run for the highest office in the country are interested in politics and may have a high level of political awareness. They may also be dedicated people, anxious to serve their country. For many candidates, an important factor is the support of party, friends, and family. The personal wealth of John F. Kennedy and Ronald Reagan may have influenced them to enter the presidential race. Still others may

be attracted to the power, prestige, and glamor of the office. *See also*
AVAILABILITY FACTOR, p. 3; FAVORITE SON CANDIDATE, p. 10; FRONT RUN-
NER, p. 11.

Significance   Presidential candidates fascinate the American public.
Traditionally, the electorate has valued certain characteristics in a presidential candidate. They expect the candidate to be strong, assertive,
competent, knowledgeable, and statesmanlike. The candidate is considered a father figure by many Americans. People expect a candidate to be
capable of solving the nation's problems and defining its interests at
home and abroad. Both incumbent and nonincumbent alike try to
impress upon the voters that they can deal with national and international crises, as well as cope with the myriad problems facing the nation.
Many times presidential candidates will cite facts and figures to exhibit
their knowledge on a given subject. In his debate with President Gerald
R. Ford, Jimmy Carter quoted, without notes, a series of figures on the
economy, taxes, and the military preparedness of the United States. His
objective was to equalize the information advantage that an incumbent
president has. This paid him high dividends, as the election results
illustrated. An adroit candidate seeks to project an image consistent
with public expectations. Personal charm, candor, demeanor, and integrity emerge as important attributes for a presidential candidate. It is also
good politics for a candidate to make gracious references to his opponent. Most candidates try to harmonize their position with the popular
will of the country. This is part of a calculated strategy to appeal to the
broad middle of the American electorate.

Presidential Debate   Head-to-head discussion by presidential
candidates on television and radio. Presidential debates attract huge
audiences and have a significant impact on the election. Television first
came into use in presidential races in the 1950s. It was with the 1960
presidential campaign, however, that television took a new turn, when
the two major party candidates agreed to debate the issues. They held
four one-on-one, 60-minute debates. No other debates took place until
1976, when incumbent Republican President Gerald R. Ford faced his
Democratic opponent, Jimmy Carter, on television. In 1980 Jimmy
Carter and Ronald Reagan appeared in a single debate. *See also* PRESI-
DENTIAL CAMPAIGN, p. 19; PRESIDENTIAL ELECTION, p. 22.

Significance   A presidential debate is probably the most important
political debate on television. With some 125 million television sets in
America, the visual impact of television has created new dimensions of
political communication and election campaigning. It is estimated that

more than half the adult population in the United States view the presidential television debates. With nearly one-half of the nation watching, the debates hopefully provide the public with a close-up view of the candidates' personalities, behavior, knowledge, and ability to manage the affairs of the country. As part of their ongoing voter education program, the League of Women Voters has sponsored many of these televised debates. Studies show that although the debates change few votes, they do stimulate interest in the candidates and their positions on the various issues. Although the elections of recent presidents have been aided by the technological miracle of television, the presidential debate system is not without its flaws. The format resembles a television press conference: reporters ask questions, the candidates respond, and then each candidate makes a closing statement. It remains to be seen whether recent television debates have set any precedent that future presidential candidates will follow.

Presidential Election   The process of nominating and electing the president. The presidential election takes place on the first Tuesday after the first Monday in November, every four years. The procedures for nominating a presidential candidate in the United States differ from state to state. The primary is the most common device for selecting delegates to the party conventions. Each political party determines the total number of delegates to attend the national convention. In the 1980 presidential election, there were 3,331 delegates at the Democratic convention, while 1,994 attended the Republican convention.

The most crucial step is, of course, securing the nomination. To do so, a presidential candidate must obtain a majority of the convention votes. Once nominated, the two major party contenders do battle in the general election. The victor is ultimately determined in the electoral college. The president is elected for a four-year term of office and may not serve more than two consecutive terms. *See also* ELECTORAL COLLEGE, p. 9; FAVORITE SON CANDIDATE, p. 10; FRONT RUNNER, p. 11; PRESIDENTIAL CANDIDATE, p. 20.

Significance   A presidential election in the United States is perhaps the most complex and yet popularly based method of selecting the chief executive of any nation in the world. At the outset of the 1980 Republican convention, Ronald Reagan was already the clear choice of a majority of delegates. Except for George Bush (R-Tex.), all other rivals had already withdrawn from the race. Bush decided not to take his fight to the convention and was later selected as Reagan's vice presidential running mate. In the Democratic party, Jimmy Carter had the nomination sewn up unless, by some miracle, Edward M. Kennedy (D-Mass.)

could win over a sizable number of his delegates. Once nominated, Reagan and Carter shared one thing in common throughout the campaign: each tried to take advantage of the other's weaknesses and shift the voters' attention to the shortcomings of his opponent. They took diametrically opposite positions on such issues as the Equal Rights Amendment, abortion, welfare, taxation, foreign aid, and defense. The 1980 election took place in the shadow of the Iranian hostage crisis. Many observers of the election scene believe that the frustration and disillusionment Americans suffered in this crisis contributed to Carter's defeat. The Reagan-Bush ticket swept the country from coast to coast, capturing 44 states with 51 percent of the popular vote, and a total of 489 electoral votes. The Carter-Mondale ticket carried only 6 states and the District of Columbia with 41 percent of the popular vote, and only 49 electoral votes. The independent candidacy of Representative John B. Anderson (R-Ill.) had no measurable effect on the election outcome. The magnitude of Reagan's victory astonished many political pundits who, up until midday of the election, viewed the race as too close to call. The Republican victory was momentous in two respects: the enormous majority secured by Reagan in the electoral college and the significant Republican gains in the Senate. But the landslide for Reagan was not quite as impressive in terms of the popular vote. Reagan's 51 percent reflects the traditional balance between the major parties—it offers no guarantee of future success.

Public Financing   A method of financing the presidential election through public funds. Public financing is controlled by the Federal Election Campaign Act of 1974. In the early days of the Republic, candidates could capture the presidency by spending small sums of money. As the population increased and campaign costs steadily escalated, it became necessary for candidates to spend more and more money in order to win. The increased use of expensive electronic media to reach the electorate has been primarily responsible for the increase. Public financing has thus become essential. *See also* CAMPAIGN FUNDING, p. 4; PRESIDENTIAL CAMPAIGN, p. 19.

Significance   Public financing encourages many qualified citizens to run for the presidency who could not do so otherwise. In recent years, presidential candidates of both major parties have turned to large donors—the so-called fat cats—for money. The 1972 presidential election, with its illegal contributions, generated public and congressional support for enactment of legislation to prevent the recurrence of such abuses. In 1974, 1976, and 1979, Congress passed laws designed to bring contributions into the open and to prevent their undue influence on candidates. This legislation placed limits on contributions, controlled expenses, and subsidized the cost of campaigns. By so doing, Congress hoped to make the election process more fair and equitable. Congress also established a Federal Election Commission to oversee compliance and prosecute offenders. This legislation has achieved some but not all of its intended goals. Designed to ensure that candidates have wide national support, it has reduced the importance of fat cats and increased the importance of having a large number of small donors.

The Supreme Court upheld the constitutionality of public financing as consistent with Article I, Section 8 of the Constitution (the power of Congress to tax the public and use that money to promote the general welfare). The High Court maintained that the law was further designed to safeguard the honesty and integrity of the electoral system. However, the Court declared as unconstitutional some provisions of the Campaign Finance Act, most notably those that sought to impose limitations on the amount of personal money candidates and their families could spend.

Winner-Take-All Rule　　An election rule in which the candidate who receives the largest number of votes wins the contested office. The winner-take-all rule is based on securing a plurality of the vote: in all elections for president, senator, representative, governor, and other officials, the winner is the person that garners the largest vote. Losers, regardless of the size of their vote, receive nothing. All electors in every state, with the exception of Maine, are chosen by the winner-take-all method. This principle is personified in the electoral college. A presidential candidate who wins the largest vote in a state receives all of the electoral votes of that state. In the 1980 presidential race, the Reagan-Bush ticket won 51 percent of the popular vote in 44 states. This gave them a total of 489 electoral votes. Their rivals received nothing in those states. The Carter-Mondale ticket won 6 states and the District of Columbia, securing 49 electoral votes. Their opponents received no electoral votes in those states. *See also* ELECTORAL COLLEGE, p. 9.

Significance　　The winner-take-all rule favors populous states like California, New York, Pennsylvania, Michigan, Illinois, Texas, Ohio, Florida, New Jersey, Massachusetts, and North Carolina. Presidential candidates concentrate their campaigns in these states. Winning in California, even by a single vote, assures forty-seven electoral votes for a candidate, while an overwhelming victory in Nevada brings only four. Since the twelve largest states control a majority of the electoral votes, a candidate may be elected by these states' electoral votes only, while the rival candidate may have received a majority of the popular votes in the country as a whole.

Many proposals have been advanced to either change or abolish the winner-take-all system, including the elimination of electors, proportional voting, single-member districts, and direct popular election. The system is unlikely to be abolished, as it enjoys widespread support. It maintains the stability of the two-party system and enhances the power of the states in the decision-making process. This has served to make third and fourth parties less attractive. To vote for minor party candidates, some critics argue, is to throw away one's vote. This successfully eliminates minor parties as competitors.

2. Powers of the President

Appointment Power   The authority of an administrative official or agency to fill a nonelective position in an organization. The appointment power for almost all top positions in the United States government is vested in the president, under Article II, Section 2 of the Constitution, subject to the advice and consent of the Senate. All of the president's noncareer appointments, except those of the White House staff, must be confirmed by the Senate. The president heads the largest governmental organization in the world, with approximately 3 million civilian and 2 million military employees. As chief executive, the president is responsible for appointing all heads of executive departments and agencies, undersecretaries and assistant secretaries, members of regulatory commissions, foreign ambassadors, and federal judges. About 4,000 positions are filled by the president.

It is rare for the Senate to reject the president's choice for a position within the executive branch of government. Only eight cabinet nominees in history have been rejected. On twenty-six occasions, however, the Senate has refused to confirm United States Supreme Court nominees. The president's power to appoint federal officials within a state is limited by senatorial courtesy. This unwritten rule requires that the president clear any nominations with the senior senator of the state if they are of the same party. If neither of that state's senators are from the president's party, the president will usually seek advice from party leaders in that state. The president may make interim appointments between Senate sessions. *See also* CHIEF EXECUTIVE, p. 31; CHIEF LAWMAKER, p. 33; CHIEF OF PARTY, p. 35; CONSTITUTIONAL POWERS, p. 39; SENATORIAL COURTESY, p. 209.

Significance   The appointment power is one of the most important constitutional powers of the president. It carries the authority to choose officials who are personally loyal as well as able to administer and supervise the operations of government. When the Constitution was framed, the United States was so thinly populated and had so few high officials that it was assumed the president would know personally most of the officials to be appointed. This would assure a greater chance of gaining control over the administration. This was probably the best thing to do when there were no political parties. With the development of political parties, however, presidents solicit recommendations from their party before nominating top officials for key patronage jobs. When John Adams became president in 1797, the political parties had already been established, and the appointment of high officials became partisan.

In exercising their appointment power, presidents typically act as party leader and chief executive. Appointments are often made for party loyalty, with minimal concern for merit. There have been numerous scandals involving these political appointees. In 1883 a permanent Civil Service Commission was set up to recruit middle and lower level officials on a merit basis. High ranking officials are frequently appointed by the president and serve at his pleasure. At the same time, they will not last long or perform their job well without support from the civil servants (recruited by the Civil Service Commission) and congressional leaders (who fund their departments or agencies). Environmental Protection Agency (EPA) Administrator Anne M. Burford was forced to resign her post as a result of congressional investigations in 1983. Conversely, congressional support and public image may keep an agency head in office even though a president may want that person removed. Although he lost the confidence of several presidents, the late Federal Bureau of Investigation (FBI) Director J. Edgar Hoover served the country for forty-eight years, until his death at age seventy-seven. To remove top level officials, the president usually acts with caution, so as to avoid political embarrassment. Instead of firing them outright, they are asked to resign in order to avoid adverse reaction and publicity.

Chief Defender of Law   The highest authority in the country to defend and execute the law. The chief defender of the law is the president. The president's oath of office includes a promise to execute not merely the law as enacted by Congress, but also to "preserve, protect, and defend the Constitution of the United States" (Article II, Section 1). The executive authority of the president includes the duty to "take Care that the Laws be faithfully executed" (Article II, Section 3). This does not give the president the power to determine what laws shall be executed, although some presidents have refused to enforce laws that they viewed as unconstitutional. However, most presidents have taken the position that they have no alternative but to enforce the law.

During the Civil War (1860–1865), President Abraham Lincoln took the position that he had "no choice but to call out the war power" and enforce federal laws in the seceding southern states. President Harry S Truman, in his attempt to enforce the law by a means that Congress had not clearly authorized, exceeded the judicial limits of constitutionality when he seized most of the nation's steel mills in 1953. In 1957 President Dwight D. Eisenhower nationalized the Arkansas National Guard and used it to enforce a court order to integrate Little Rock Central High School. *See also* CHIEF EXECUTIVE, p. 31; CHIEF LAWMAKER, p. 33; CHIEF NATIONAL LEADER, p. 34; COMMANDER IN CHIEF, p. 38; CONSTITUTIONAL POWERS, p. 39; EMERGENCY POWERS, p. 41; WAR POWERS ACT, p. 49.

Significance   The chief defender of law, in the task of enforcing and executing the law, is assisted by the thirteen executive departments, as well as many independent agencies and regulatory commissions. The president is theoretically responsible for the conduct of these officials as they carry out the laws enacted by Congress. While most of these officials are responsible to the president, they enforce laws made by Congress. This underscores the fact that federal officials are not responsible exclusively to the president, which often creates divided loyalties and sometimes conflicts between officials. In this regard, the congressional power of the purse, the procedure of hearing and confirmation of presidential nominees by the Senate, and the oversight functions of the Congress create mixed loyalties for many federal officials.

Congressional investigations into the actions of the Environmental Protection Agency (EPA) and its administrator, Anne M. Burford, and several others in 1983 resulted in a series of firings and resignations of the officials involved. President Ronald Reagan's administration struggled to control an expanding congressional probe into allegations of conflict of interest, political manipulation, and agency mismanagement at the EPA, but failed. It is principally through the Congress that powerful lobbying groups and individuals bring pressure to bear on the executive branch of government, and laws are often "faithfully executed" in a manner beneficial to vested interests. This raises the question: How can presidents be held personally responsible for enforcing the law by officials who may not be responsible to them?

Chief Diplomat   The top diplomat who determines the official position of a nation concerning negotiation, recognition, treaties, and exchanges of diplomatic representatives with other countries. As chief diplomat, the president directs negotiation of treaties with other nations and enters into executive agreements. (Agreements made by the president, unlike treaties, do not require Senate approval.) The president establishes foreign military bases and signs agreements on the reduction of tariffs with legal authority given by Congress. Treaty negotiations, such as in the United Nations (UN), the North Atlantic Treaty Organization (NATO), and the Strategic Arms Limitation Talks (SALT), are conducted under the direction of the president, and national commitments are made subject to ratification by the Senate.

Many officials in the State Department and other agencies of government assist the president in this diplomatic task. The president also appoints special envoys and diplomats who possess the skills necessary to conduct highly technical and complicated negotiations, such as the 1982–1983 disarmament talks with the Soviet Union. Sometimes the president's personal involvement in the negotiations helps in resolving differences and reaching consensus on an agreement. President Jimmy Carter's personal interest and involvement in the Camp David Accord in 1978, which established peace between Egypt and Israel, is an example of the president's role as chief diplomat. *See also* CHIEF EXECUTIVE, p. 31; CHIEF FOREIGN POLICYMAKER, p. 32; EXECUTIVE AGREEMENT, p. 42; TREATY-MAKING POWER, p. 47; WAR POWERS ACT, p. 49.

Significance   The president as chief diplomat has considerable leeway in the conduct of the nation's foreign policy. Since the power to make treaties is subject to ratification by the Senate, the president, as chief diplomat, enters into executive agreements with foreign heads of state. Many of these agreements typically involve the establishment of American military bases and the granting of diplomatic recognition or its withdrawal.

Many political scientists view President Richard M. Nixon's involvement in the Watergate scandal as less important than the changes he brought about in the United States's relations with the Soviet Union and China. Aided by the diplomatic skills of Secretary of State Henry A. Kissinger, Nixon resumed diplomatic contact with the Chinese. He also launched new cooperative endeavors with America's number one adversary, the Soviet Union. The prospects for survival in a nuclear age may depend on the wisdom and diplomatic sagacity of the president. Since the Vietnam War, the people and Congress have been reluctant to see the president extend American military commitments abroad. Yet presidential supremacy in diplomacy remains because many constitutional provisions and court decisions recognize the executive's responsibility in foreign affairs, where immediate actions may be required.

Chief Executive   The president's role as head of the United States government. The chief executive oversees the executive branch of government and carries out the laws passed by Congress. According to the Constitution (Article II, Section 1), "The executive Power shall be vested in a President...." The president "shall take Care that the Laws be faithfully executed" (Article II, Section 3). The chief executive can veto legislation, call Congress into special session, and make treaties with the advice and consent of the Senate. He has the power of pardon in all federal cases except impeachment. The chief executive wields power over a bureaucracy of about 5 million employees, serving in some 1,900 federal agencies. Over 4,000 top-level officials of the United States government are nominated and appointed by the president, with the advice and consent of the Senate (except for the White House staff). The chief executive has broad powers to remove these officials, with the exception of federal judges and members of the regulatory agencies.

The president must devote considerable energy, thought, and time to manage the federal government and to offer leadership and incentive to the bureaucracy. Because presidential control over the administration is limited by Congress and the courts, the chief executive's leadership also depends on the ability to influence the nation at large. As chief executive, the president administers an annual budget of more than $800 billion. *See also* CHIEF DEFENDER OF LAW, p. 28; CHIEF LAWMAKER, p. 33; CHIEF NATIONAL LEADER, p. 34; CONSTITUTIONAL POWERS, p. 39; EXECUTIVE AGREEMENT, p. 42; EXECUTIVE PARDON, p. 43.

Significance   The chief executive is charged with seeing that the laws be faithfully executed. The constitutional grant of power to the chief executive is made in general language, but the realities of presidential power are best seen in the history of what chief executives have actually done with this constitutional authority. George Washington established early precedents when he asserted presidential responsibility for suppressing domestic disorder in the Whiskey Rebellion. Thomas Jefferson initiated the Louisiana Purchase without advance congressional approval. Abraham Lincoln greatly expanded the chief executive's power by blockading ports, summoning militia, and freeing the slaves, all without congressional approval. Theodore Roosevelt regarded the chief executive as subject only to the people and the constraints of the Constitution. He believed he had the power to act unless the Constitution or law expressly forbade him from doing so. Harry S Truman reasserted civilian control of the military and removed General Douglas MacArthur as American Commander in Korea in 1951 for disobeying orders. Truman exceeded the limits of his constitutional power when he seized the steel mills, at the height of the Korean War, without congressional authorization. Dwight D. Eisenhower used federal troops to enforce school integration in Little Rock, Arkansas, when the governor refused to carry out the law. These examples show how the powers of the chief executive have increased in response to such factors as war, popular demand, and the failure of Congress to act in times of crisis. An effective chief executive possesses powers of persuasion that enhance his constitutional and legal authority.

Chief Foreign Policymaker   The main authority in formulating and implementing foreign policy. As chief foreign policymaker, the president has the upperhand in foreign affairs. The voice of the president is the voice of the United States. Article II, Section 2 of the Constitution gives the president specific powers related to foreign affairs: the power to make treaties, appoint ambassadors and other diplomats (with the advice and consent of the Senate), receive foreign ambassadors, and recognize foreign governments. In 1933 a far-reaching instance of diplomatic recognition occurred when President Franklin D. Roosevelt recognized the Soviet Union, sixteen years after the Bolshevik Revolution. Likewise, President Jimmy Carter accorded diplomatic recognition to the People's Republic of China in 1979, thirty years after the Communist takeover of mainland China. The president's position in foreign affairs is further strengthened by access to information through the Departments of State, Defense, and the Central Intelligence Agency, which work directly under him. The president can enter into executive agreements with other nations without senatorial approval. *See also* APPOINTMENT POWER, p. 27; CHIEF DIPLOMAT, p. 29; CHIEF OF STATE, p. 37; CONSTITUTIONAL POWERS, p. 39; EXECUTIVE AGREEMENT, p. 42; TREATY-MAKING POWER, p. 47; WAR POWERS ACT, p. 49.

Significance   The chief foreign policymaker's role varies from one administration to another. President Woodrow Wilson gave little importance to departments and agencies working under him and went so far as to type some of his diplomatic messages himself. President Dwight D. Eisenhower gave his Secretary of State, John Foster Dulles, almost unlimited power in conducting foreign policy. President John F. Kennedy relied more on his White House aides than he did on the secretary of state. President Richard M. Nixon considered himself chief foreign policymaker but relied heavily on Secretary of State Henry A. Kissinger. President Ronald Reagan depends both on the secretary of state and White House aides. So great is the president's power to influence foreign affairs that President Carter, who accomplished relatively little at home, nonetheless secured the Panama Canal Treaty, a Strategic Arms Limitation Treaty (SALT), and the Camp David Accord.

Although Congress plays an important role in foreign policy, it tends to be mostly negative rather than positive. The Senate can reject treaties, or it can require changes in them. Should a foreign policy initiative call for the spending of money, the consent of both the House and Senate is required. Sometimes presidents win, other times they lose, when they present treaties to the Senate. The Senate has rejected nineteen treaties since the nation's founding, the most famous being the Treaty of Versailles, which created the League of Nations at the end of World War I. Other than this negative power of the Senate, the president is truly the chief foreign policymaker.

Chief Lawmaker   The president's role as chief legislator. The chief lawmaker presents a legislative program to Congress through the State of the Union message, public speeches, and written communications. The Constitution mandates that the president annually send to Congress a message assessing the State of the Union. Two other annual presidential messages are also concerned with lawmaking: the National Budget, and the Economic Report. President Woodrow Wilson was the first president in modern times to deliver his State of the Union message personally. Since World War II, both the Budget and Economic Messages have been submitted by the president to the Congress. Taking advantage of prime time television, presidents communicate their legislative ideas not only to Congress, but also to the American public.

The president's role as legislative leader has evolved into one of his principal sources of power. Major legislative programs are identified with the president and not with Congress. President Franklin D. Roosevelt, not the Seventy-third Congress, is given credit for the New Deal. Many presidents have sought to arouse public support for their legislative programs by giving them titles, such as Theodore Roosevelt's Square Deal, Woodrow Wilson's New Freedom, John F. Kennedy's New Frontier, Lyndon B. Johnson's Great Society, and Richard M. Nixon's New American Revolution. In these legislative programs, presidents are assisted by highly trained professionals, such as the members of the Congressional Liaison Office. The Constitution gives the president the power to veto congressional legislation. The veto is an effective tool; it is extremely difficult to override a veto, because a two-thirds majority vote of Congress is required. Other constitutional powers give the president the authority to adjourn Congress (never used) and to call Congress into special session (seldom used). *See also* CHIEF DEFENDER OF LAW, p. 28; CHIEF EXECUTIVE, p. 31; CHIEF FOREIGN POLICYMAKER, p. 32; CONSTITUTIONAL POWERS, p. 39; VETO POWER, p. 48.

Significance   The chief lawmaker, as a term, is an invention of textbook writers; it is not used in the Constitution. But the president's role as chief legislator has developed out of the constitutional power to advise Congress on the State of the Union and to sign or veto legislation. The development of this law-making power can also be traced to the fact that the president is the one leader (other than the vice president) elected by the entire country. Many presidents use this fact to gain public support for their programs. They confer personally with top congressional leaders to solicit support for their legislative initiatives. The president's ability to persuade Congress to support the administration's programs often rests on personal popularity and reputation. To influence passage of a bill, many times presidents may use their power of patronage, as well as their position as head of their party. In some cases, where there is widespread congressional resistance, the president may appeal directly to the people through the use of radio and television addresses, presidential press conferences, and carefully timed speeches to select groups and organizations. He may also seek to persuade recalcitrant members of Congress in telephone conversations or at meetings with congressional leaders in the White House over breakfast, lunch, or dinner.

Congress expects the president to propose a complete legislative program at the opening of each session. Political scientist Richard E. Neustadt contends that the Congress has come to demand that the president exercise this function. The president is expected to set the national agenda. In the last two decades, 80 percent of the major laws passed by Congress were initiated in the executive branch. A president who does not propose a legislative program will be considered a failure by many people and regarded as indifferent to the wishes of the people. The ability of the president and the executive branch to gather information in support of or in opposition to a bill is considerable. Not only can the president overwhelm Congress with information, but he may also withhold it.

Chief National Leader   The preeminent position as national spokesman and decision maker. The chief national leader is usually the president, who plays the dominant role in national and world affairs. Presidents are expected to stir hope, confidence, and a sense of unity and purpose among the people. They honor the nation's traditions and set an example for others to emulate. Because the president is the highest official in the country, elected by the voters of the entire nation, he is regarded as the chief national leader and is supposed to transcend partisanship in performing this ceremonial role. The symbolic nature of the office is reflected in the numerous events in which the president is called upon to participate: dedication ceremonies, patriotic festivals, and other nonpartisan national occasions. Sometimes presidents use symbolism to shape public opinion and galvanize public support for their programs and policies. President Lyndon B. Johnson turned off the lights in the White House in 1964 to dramatize the need for national austerity. President Jimmy Carter joined marchers in his own inaugural parade in 1977 to stress his style of plain living. The president is a moral leader who helps to shape voter attitudes on national and international issues, and his success depends on the ability to alter the nation's behavior in socially significant ways. *See also* CHIEF EXECUTIVE, p. 31; CHIEF OF PARTY, p. 35; CHIEF OF STATE, p. 37; COATTAIL EFFECT, p. 5; EXECUTIVE PARDON, p. 43.

Significance   The chief national leader must be a skillful politician. After winning the election, a president does not cease being a politician. The regularity with which candidates from the president's party seek to "ride his coattails" is a measure of his popularity and influence as a national leader. By contrast, many candidates seek to avoid identification with an unpopular president for fear of losing the election.

The president's success as the top national leader depends mostly on a good relationship with the people and Congress. Frustrated by congressional politics and unable to win a legislative victory, many presidents take the issues directly to the people. Having failed to win senatorial approval on the Versailles Treaty incorporating the League of Nations after World War I, President Woodrow Wilson toured the country from coast to coast to seek public support but lost the fight. President Franklin D. Roosevelt's famous fireside chats in the 1930s won him public support against Congress on many issues. Several recent presidents, such as Lyndon B. Johnson and Richard M. Nixon, have not been as effective in winning public support because of what political observers call their false humility. By contrast, President Ronald Reagan is successful in exerting leverage on Congress by mobilizing interest groups and appealing to the public. Presidents are considered successful national leaders if they are able to gain public support and articulate the ideals of the nation to the people. The president as chief national leader is expected to be both a partisan and nonpartisan political leader.

Chief of Party   The head of a political party. Although the role of chief of party is one of the most important functions of the president, it is not mentioned in the Constitution. After receiving the party's presidential nomination, it is customary for the presidential candidate to name a party chairman and begin to function as chief of that party. A president who commands overwhelming support within the party can expect to win renomination and impose major changes in national policy. The president plays a major role in mobilizing public support for the party, as its principal spokesman. The president is literally the Chief

Republican, or Chief Democrat. The national committee of the president's party reports to him, and he attempts to carry out his party's platform. The president is expected to raise campaign funds for party candidates and select most of his political appointees from among the party faithful.

Although parties began to evolve in President George Washington's time, he abstained from functioning as the chief of party, deeming it divisive and parochial and incompatible with his duty as founding father and president. The first major shift in party politics occurred in the 1820s when Jacksonian democracy established the president as the chief of party. The power of the party chieftain stems largely from the fact that officeholders are often beholden to him for their nomination and electoral success, as well as their future careers. Usually, the party chief leaves less important routine matters to other officials. But sometimes an assertive and powerful president may intervene in the party's primaries, seeking the nomination of candidates who support the president. President Franklin D. Roosevelt attempted to expand his voting base by replacing foes of the New Deal within his party with those who promised support, but this effort ended in failure. *See also* APPOINTMENT POWER, p. 27; CHIEF EXECUTIVE, p. 31; CHIEF NATIONAL LEADER, p. 34.

Significance   Chief of party is one of the many roles that the president plays. No other political leader can rival the president in party influence. Yet he does not have the kind of power within his party comparable to that of the British prime minister. Unlike the latter, the president cannot dissolve Congress if the members of his party refuse to support the administration's major legislative actions. Still, the president is the nation's foremost political leader.

No president can escape party politics. President Theodore Roosevelt thoroughly enjoyed party politics, whereas President Dwight D. Eisenhower announced flatly, "I do not like politics." Whether they like it or not, they are chosen by their party and are expected to lead it and serve it. As chief of party, the president is supposed to be the nation's top professional politician. A president who is unable to lead the party will have difficulty in running the country and securing support for administration policies through the party apparatus. However, a president who has an overwhelming command over the party and enjoys its support can impose major changes in national politics. The ability to manipulate party resources, distribute patronage, and dispense favors is a key to the success of a party chief. Being president requires political acumen and skill.

Chief of State   Ceremonial title of the president of the United States, a role that transforms the office into the symbol of unity. The president receives foreign heads of state and ambassadors, makes goodwill tours, throws out the first baseball of the season, lights the White House Christmas tree, reviews parades, confers medals of honor, and proclaims national holidays. Elected by the people of the nation as a whole, the president is the leader of all the people and thus represents the entire country. It is for this reason that, particularly on ceremonial occasions, the president is not addressed by name, but only as "Mr. President." The president, like the Queen of England, serves as a symbol of unity and continuity of the nation. To add to the stature, influence, and prestige of the office, some of these responsibilities are delegated to the vice president, cabinet officers, and congressional leaders. In most foreign countries, there are two persons who perform as ceremonial leader and as governmental leader. In the United States, both of these functions are combined in the president as chief of state and government.

The president's role as chief of state enhances the image of a magnanimous leader. The president is empowered by the Constitution to grant pardons "for offenses against the United States, except in Cases of Impeachment," and he may grant amnesty to an entire group of people. President Abraham Lincoln pardoned most secessionists in 1863. President Gerald R. Ford pardoned President Richard M. Nixon in 1974 by absolving him of any guilt in Watergate crimes, thus avoiding a trial. Presidents Ford and Jimmy Carter granted amnesty to Vietnam draft evaders. *See also* CHIEF NATIONAL LEADER, p. 34; CONSTITUTIONAL POWERS, p. 39; EXECUTIVE PARDON, p. 43.

Significance   A parliamentary government has a head of state and a head of government. In the British parliamentary system, the head of state is the monarch. The framers of the American Constitution disliked the monarch for obvious reasons, as the American colonies were ruled by a despotic king. So the framers of the Constitution proposed a presidential government in which the president assumed both roles— head of state and head of government. The United States is virtually the only country in the world that has a combined chief of state and government. Other nations take the view that the chief of state must be a nonpartisan and noncontroversial figure who stands above the normal conflict of politics. The presidency should be an office "most above politics." But in the United States, the Constitution fused a monarch's decorum and dignity and a prime minister's prestige and power into one office: the presidency.

In a parliamentary system, a prime minister can be forced out of office by a vote of no confidence. But the American president has a constitutionally guaranteed tenure. Because of this provision, the president can maintain the continuity of the administration, independent of Congress, while a parliamentary system requires a titular head of state to do so. Who the president is does not matter; it is the office that embodies the entire nation, in a nonpartisan manner. Still, people confuse the chief executive's policies with the presidential role as chief of state. Although a good case can be made for a separate ceremonial chief of state, most Americans accept the dual role of the president. Many people honor and respect the president as chief of state, while often criticizing his performance as chief executive.

Commander in Chief   The role of the president as supreme leader of the armed forces of the United States. The commander in chief receives this authority from Article II, Section 2 of the Constitution. As commander in chief, the president has the ultimate responsibility for the conduct of American military policy. In consultation with the secretary of defense, secretary of state, National Security Council, Joint Chiefs of Staff, and military advisers, the president appoints military officers. The authority of the president over the armed forces guarantees civilian supremacy. Civilian control of the armed forces has been exercised by many presidents, although they may delegate some of the powers to the defense secretary, national security advisers, and Joint Chiefs of Staff. During the Whiskey Rebellion in 1794, for example, President George Washington led the troops into Pennsylvania. During the Civil War in the 1860s, President Abraham Lincoln often visited army camps to instruct the officers.

Modern presidents do not personally lead the troops during wartime, but they make decisions on deployment of the armed forces, as well as the strategy to be followed. Presidents Woodrow Wilson, Franklin D. Roosevelt, Harry S Truman, Lyndon B. Johnson, and Richard M. Nixon all authorized the use of American armed forces abroad without a congressional declaration of war. A dramatic example of presidential authority over the armed forces is illustrated by President Truman's removal of General Douglas MacArthur as American and United Nations commander in Korea in 1951 for publicly disobeying orders. For the same reason, President Jimmy Carter relieved a top general from his duties in Korea. In war as well as in peace, the president is the commander in chief. The constant reminder of this role is the locked briefcase stuffed with nuclear codes, sometimes called the "football" or "black box." The box is always kept near the president, who could use it to order nuclear retaliation. *See also* CHIEF DEFENDER OF LAW, p. 28; CHIEF EXECUTIVE, p. 31; CHIEF FOREIGN POLICYMAKER, p. 32; CONSTITUTIONAL POWERS, p. 39; EMERGENCY POWERS, p. 41; WAR POWERS ACT, p. 49.

Significance   The commander in chief may not only deploy the armed forces in support of American foreign policy, but may also take the nation into war. The power of the commander in chief is a major instrument of the president's foreign and war policy, with control over a military establishment of over two million people. American bases and fleets are scattered all over the world and stand as a constant reminder of presidential supremacy in world affairs. Although the Constitution is clear in terms of civilian control over the military, it is debatable today whether the president is empowered to send troops into battle without congressional authorization. Of the nearly 200 wars and military actions undertaken by the United States in its history, only five wars have been formally declared. These include the War of 1812, the Mexican War in 1846, the Spanish-American War in 1898, and World Wars I and II (1914–1918 and 1939–1945).

Since Japan's surprise attack on Pearl Harbor in 1941, presidents have ordered large-scale combat forces into Korea (1950–1953), Vietnam (1962–1973), Cambodia (1975), and many small-scale incursions. Americans suffered 137,000 military casualties in Korea and 200,000 in Southeast Asia. These costly military actions initiated by presidents underscore the fact that the country's war policy lays in their hands as commanders in chief. Realizing that presidential authority as commander in chief comes close to dictatorship in military matters, Congress passed the War Powers Act of 1973. This act limits presidentially ordered foreign combat to sixty days and requires the president to report to Congress within forty-eight hours of this decision to send troops into action. The president and Congress frequently clash over authorizing and funding wars and weapons systems, although the president prevails in most such cases. These battles with Congress, however, are not always easily won by the commander in chief.

Constitutional Powers   The powers of the president as enumerated in Article II, Section 1 of the Constitution. The Constitution states: "The executive Power shall be vested in a President of the United States of America" (Article II, Section 1). This Article also requires the president to "take Care that the Laws be faithfully executed" (Article II, Section 3). Out of these constitutional skeletons has grown a set of roles for the president: chief of state, commander in chief, chief executive, chief lawmaker or legislator, and chief diplomatic leader. Two other roles, manager of the economy and party chieftain, stem from additional responsibilities. (The role of party chieftain is not mentioned in the Constitution.)

Presidential powers, as found in the Constitution, include: First, chief of state. As ceremonial head of government, the president performs many symbolic functions. The chief of state receives visiting dignitaries, confers honors, presents awards, proclaims holidays, undertakes good-will tours, and grants pardons. Second, commander in chief. As supreme commander of the armed forces, the president can order armed conflict abroad, in most cases without congressional approval. The War Powers Act of 1973, enacted with an override of President Richard M. Nixon's veto, curtailed the president's power as commander in chief. The president can now only commit American troops abroad for sixty days unless Congress grants an extension. Third, chief executive. As head of the administration, the president is responsible for administering the affairs of the country. Fourth, chief lawmaker. The president assumes the role of principal legislator through the power to shape the congressional agenda as well as veto legislation. Fifth, chief diplomat. The president holds the preeminent position as head of the foreign policy establishment, responsible for formulating and implementing foreign policy with the advice and consent of the Senate. Sixth, manager of the economy. The president is the general manager of the economic welfare of the country and must deal with problems of inflation, interest rates, unemployment, strikes, and economic shortages. Seventh, party chieftain. This function is not mentioned in the Constitution. Yet, the success of a president depends on the ability to lead his party and articulate its philosophy. *See also* CHIEF DEFENDER OF LAW, p. 28; CHIEF DIPLOMAT, p. 29; CHIEF EXECUTIVE, p. 31; CHIEF FOREIGN POLICYMAKER, p. 32; CHIEF LAWMAKER, p. 33; CHIEF OF STATE, p. 37; COMMANDER IN CHIEF, p. 38.

Significance   The constitutional powers of the president have expanded in recent years. The presidency has grown in policy-making authority because of what was written into the Constitution and because of what was omitted from it. Many powers are specifically stated in the Constitution, while others are subject to interpretation. Controversy exists over the interpretation of the first sentence in Article II, Section 1, usually referred to as "the vesting clause" or "the delegatory clause." This clause enumerates the powers of the president. The vagueness of the Constitution has contributed to the growth of presidential power. A great deal of the president's power derives not from constitutional authority, but from skillful political leadership. The presidency was tailor-made for George Washington, and he broadly defined his powers and functions. Each subsequent president has redefined these roles and duties. Political scientist Richard E. Neustadt states it well: "A President is many men or one man wearing many 'hats,' or playing many 'roles'" (Neustadt 1960, viii). Many of the president's powers are derived today from extraconstitutional sources such as congressional legislation, precedents set by earlier presidents, and court rulings. Some of these relate to each other and often overlap.

Emergency Powers   Those powers that the President of the United States may exercise on extraordinary occasions. Emergency powers are exercised on such occasions as wars, rebellions, labor strikes, epidemics, and natural disasters. Article II, Sections 2 and 3 of the Constitution grant the president powers as commander in chief of the armed forces and as crisis manager respectively. In times of conflict and danger, presidents must have the power to respond quickly and decisively. As commander in chief, the president may take personal command of the armed forces in the field. President George Washington did precisely that during the Whiskey Rebellion in 1794. During the Civil War (1860–1865), President Abraham Lincoln combined the power of commander in chief with his constitutional duty to execute the law when he expanded the size of the army and navy beyond authorization, spent money without congressional approval, suspended the *writ of habeas corpus*, and ordered the blockade of the South. President Rutherford B. Hayes sent troops into ten states during the railway strikes of 1877. During the bitter Pullman strike of 1894, President Grover Cleveland authorized troops in Chicago over protests from the governor. In 1942, invoking his war powers, President Franklin D. Roosevelt authorized commanders on the West Coast to round up and place in detention camps over 100,000 Japanese, two-thirds of whom were Americans by birth. President Harry S Truman seized control of the strike-bound steel industry during the Korean War in 1950. Presidents Dwight D. Eisenhower, John F. Kennedy, and Lyndon B. Johnson have dispatched federal troops into service to enforce the laws and to protect black students in their right to attend public schools and colleges. Congress may enact special legislation giving the president power to establish emergency agencies and to carry out unusual functions. *See also* CHIEF DEFENDER OF LAW, p. 28; CHIEF DIPLOMAT, p. 29; CHIEF EXECUTIVE, p. 31; CHIEF FOREIGN POLICYMAKER, p. 32; CHIEF LAWMAKER, p. 33; COMMANDER IN CHIEF, p. 38; CONSTITUTIONAL POWERS, p. 39.

Significance   Emergency powers are derived from constitutional and congressional sources, as well as various Supreme Court and lower court rulings. After the Civil War, the Supreme Court declared that "the government, within the Constitution, has all the powers granted to it which are necessary to preserve its existence." From this time onward, many national crises have called for the exercise of governmental powers that many constitutional experts believe are unconstitutional. However, the authority of the vesting clause in the Constitution is complicated by domestic wartime emergencies or exigencies in which the president is forced to take drastic action to defend the country and preserve order. In the landmark case of *ex parte Milligan* (1866), the Supreme Court held that suspension of *habeas corpus* should be made by the president only with the approval of Congress. The Supreme Court, in light of the war emergency, found President Roosevelt's action in removing large numbers of American citizens of Japanese origin into relocation camps a permissible exercise of his powers as commander in chief. Although the High Court has upheld emergency powers in wartime, in the case of *Youngstown Sheet and Tube Co.* v. *Sawyer* (1952), the court denied President Truman's assertion that the inherent emergency powers of the president justified the seizure of the steel mills.

Although the concept of national emergency does not originate in the Constitution, its invocation is considered compatible with the president's constitutional power. The enhanced power which Congress gives the president for coping with economic or military crises derives from the broad interpretation of Article I, Section 8 of the Constitution, which deals with commerce, tax, and defense matters. Approximately sixty statutes, or portions of them, are applicable during emergencies which the president so determines. Public support for the president peaks during emergencies. A president may try to stimulate crisis situations in order to engender support or enhance executive powers.

Executive Agreement   A presidential agreement entered into with other nations or heads of state. An executive agreement, unlike a treaty, does not require Senate approval. Such agreements cover a broad range of activities, from routine business like international mail delivery to diplomatic, political, and economic issues. The first executive agreement, which provided for mail delivery, was promulgated by President George Washington. President Franklin D. Roosevelt's "destroyer deal" with Britain in 1940, as well as other undertakings such as his Lend Lease agreement (1941), was based solely upon executive authority and committed the United States to World War II. Executive agreements reached by Presidents Dwight D. Eisenhower, John F. Kennedy, and Lyndon B. Johnson involved the United States in a prolonged war in Vietnam. In January 1981, shortly before leaving office, President Jimmy Carter signed an executive agreement with Iran. The agreement provided for the release of the fifty-two American hostages and established a basis for resolving financial problems between the two nations. Although such agreements do not have formal constitutional status, they do have the force of law. These agreements have become the standard method for dealing with international relations. As of January 1, 1981, there were

967 treaties and 6,188 executive agreements in force. *See also* CHIEF DIPLOMAT, p. 29; CHIEF EXECUTIVE, p. 31; CHIEF FOREIGN POL-ICYMAKER, p. 32; COMMANDER IN CHIEF, p. 38; EMERGENCY POWERS, p. 41; EXECUTIVE PRIVILEGE, p. 44; TREATY-MAKING POWER, p. 47.

Significance   Executive agreements, though they are not expressly provided for in the Constitution, are often used by presidents. There are six times more executive agreements than treaties in force. Congress may or may not be taken into confidence by the president in such executive agreements. A president may not have time in a crisis to consult Congress. There is a tendency for the public to rally around the president in times of peril, yet Congress has insisted that understandings with other countries take the form of treaties or agreements reached with the advice and consent of the Senate. Congress and the president often differ on what constitutes an agreement and precisely what forms of executive undertakings with foreign nations are subject to senatorial approval. An executive agreement has many inherent advantages, such as speed in handling vital matters, secrecy, and efficiency.

The legally binding effect of executive agreements has been upheld by the Supreme Court. They have the same force as treaties. Both are supreme laws under the supremacy clause of Article VI of the Constitution. A bitter controversy over the treaty-making power of the president, as well as the use of executive agreements, developed in the mid-1950s. To safeguard the constitutional system against abuse through treaties and executive agreements, Senator John W. Bricker (R-Ohio) proposed an amendment in 1954 known as the Bricker Amendment. The proposed amendment was an attempt to curb the president's treaty and executive agreement powers. Although the amendment had strong Democratic backing, it was defeated by one vote short of the required two-thirds majority. The defeat of the amendment shows how difficult it is to develop acceptable limitations on presidential power in foreign affairs.

Executive Pardon   Presidential clemency shown toward those accused or convicted of federal crimes, except impeachment. The executive pardon is granted under Article II, Section 2 of the Constitution, which states that the president "shall have Power to Grant Reprieves and Pardons for Offenses against the United States, except in Cases of Impeachment." A president may even grant amnesty to an entire group of people. In 1863 President Abraham Lincoln pardoned most of the secessionists in the South. President Andrew Johnson pardoned most Confederate soldiers after the Civil War. President Gerald R. Ford was the first American president to grant a pardon to a former president, Richard M. Nixon, for any crime that he "committed or may have committed or taken part in" while he was president. On September 16, 1974, President Ford offered a conditional amnesty to Vietnam draft evaders and deserters.

The power of clemency extends not only to pardons, but also to reprieves. Under this authority, a president can postpone or reduce criminal sentences. Invoking this power, President John F. Kennedy released 104 prisoners, Lyndon B. Johnson 227, Nixon 63, Ford 27, and Jimmy Carter 5 (one of whom was Patricia Hearst, who was kidnapped by the Symbionese Liberation Army and convicted of bank robbery in 1979). President Carter did not pardon his nephew who was sentenced to a long prison term in California for two armed robbery convictions. *See also* CHIEF DEFENDER OF LAW, p. 28; CHIEF EXECUTIVE, p. 31; CHIEF LAWMAKER, p. 33; CHIEF NATIONAL LEADER, p. 34; CHIEF OF STATE, p. 37; CONSTITUTIONAL POWERS, p. 39.

Significance   An executive pardon often produces public controversy. Until the 1970s, this power was used mainly to release convicted prisoners. When President Nixon pardoned former Teamsters Union President Jimmy Hoffa shortly before that union endorsed Nixon for reelection in 1972, it produced a storm of public controversy. The Watergate tapes revealed that Nixon wanted to grant clemency to the Watergate defendants in return for their silence concerning their ties with the administration. The most dramatic example of the executive pardon was President Ford's pardon of former President Nixon in 1974. Although Nixon was not convicted of any crime, this pardon absolved him of any alleged criminal activity. Characterizing the Nixon family's ordeal as "an American tragedy," Ford decided to put the issue behind the nation and proceed with the business of governing America. This pardon is considered constitutional because Nixon had not been impeached, although Congress was threatening such action. The news of the pardon evoked shock and outrage in the country. Many Americans believed it represented a grave miscarriage of justice to permit Nixon to escape possible criminal prosecution. Some commentators went so far as to speculate that the pardon was part of a deal between Ford and Nixon, reached before the latter's resignation. Nixon left the White House in disgrace, and Ford's standing with the public suffered serious damage. His judgment on many issues was called into question, and his relations with Congress and the press deteriorated. Ford's nomination of former New York Governor Nelson A. Rockefeller to be vice president encountered unexpected difficulties. Gerald R. Ford, the first unelected president in history, lost his election bid to Jimmy Carter in 1976.

Executive Privilege   The right of the president to withhold information or to refuse to appear before congressional panels. Executive privilege is used by the president to withhold information from Congress and the courts that might jeopardize national security or embarrass the government. This alleged right has also been extended to cabinet members and presidential advisers. The Constitution makes no provision concerning executive privilege, but many presidents have acted as if they had the privilege. Beginning with George Washington, presidents have withheld documentation of certain executive actions and decisions from Congress and the courts. Presidents contend that the doctrine of separation of powers protects presidential decision making from congressional and judicial scrutiny. Executive privilege is justified mainly on two grounds. First, certain top-level decisions are sensitive and critical to the interests of the country and, as such, they cannot be made public. Second, presidents must guarantee confidentiality of information from their subordinates, otherwise such information could not be obtained.

During the Watergate scandal in 1972–1974, President Richard M. Nixon made claims in the name of executive privilege. His administration asserted that every presidential communication and every employee in the executive branch of government was covered by executive privilege. The Nixon administration also argued that former employees of the White House were also covered by executive privilege. However, Nixon's claim was rejected by the Supreme Court. *See also* CHIEF EXECUTIVE, p. 31; CHIEF FOREIGN POLICYMAKER, p. 32; CHIEF LAWMAKER, p. 33; CHIEF OF STATE, p. 37; CONSTITUTIONAL POWERS, p. 39; EMERGENCY POWERS, p. 41.

Significance   Executive privilege is based on custom, rather than law. Under this privilege, the Congress cannot require the president or other officials of the executive branch to appear before congressional committees to testify without the consent of the president. In 1948 President Harry S Truman claimed that executive privilege included every executive officer responsible to him. President Nixon often invoked the doctrine of executive privilege during the Watergate era. On July 23, 1973, he refused to release certain tapes as requested by the federal prosecutor, citing the principle of separation of powers.

Can a president refuse to provide Congress with any information it seeks? In the case of *United States* v. *Nixon* (1974), the Supreme Court ruled that executive privilege was not absolute. The court said: "Neither the doctrine of separation of powers, nor the need for confidentiality of high level communications ... can sustain an absolute, unqualified, presidential privilege of immunity from judicial process under all circumstances." President Nixon released three tapes as ordered by the High Court. This ruling became an instrument in bringing about the first presidential resignation in history. We do not know what a popular and strong president, unencumbered by such scandals as Watergate, would do if challenged. Until the Supreme Court decides to prohibit the use of executive privilege, which is highly unlikely, presidents will continue to invoke this privilege.

Impoundment of Funds   The refusal of the president to spend funds, temporarily or permanently, that Congress has allocated. Impoundment of funds may produce a bitter controversy between the president and Congress. During the nineteenth century only two presidents, Thomas Jefferson and Ulysses S. Grant, made use of impoundment; since the 1930s it has become more common. Presidents Franklin D. Roosevelt, Harry S Truman, Lyndon B. Johnson, and John F. Kennedy used it frequently. But President Richard M. Nixon's impoundment of $18 billion far exceeded the amount impounded by any other president. The Constitution is not clear whether the president must spend the money that Congress appropriates. Article I, Section 9 states: "No Money shall be drawn from the Treasury, but in Consequence of Appropriations made by Law. . . ." This congressional appropriation is viewed by presidents as a ceiling on expenditures, not as a mandate to spend. The president impounds funds by ordering the Treasury not to release money.

In 1974 Congress passed the Impoundment Control Act, whereby either house of Congress can stop temporary impoundment of funds by adopting a simple resolution. By tradition, a simple resolution passed by one house of Congress cannot be vetoed by the president. The act further sets up procedures for dealing with impoundment. The president may ask Congress for a rescission of funds, or a deferral, to impound funds. Unless Congress rescinds the appropriation within forty-five days, the money must be spent. *See also* CHIEF EXECUTIVE, p. 31; CONSTITUTIONAL POWERS, p. 39; EMERGENCY POWERS, p. 41; VETO POWER, p. 49.

Significance   The impoundment of funds affords the president an additional control over the policy of the nation. The Congress maintains that such action represents a direct challenge to their fiscal authority. Congress tries to maintain its control over the president in three ways (1) it sets spending targets in the budget; (2) it authorizes federal expenses; and (3) it passes appropriation bills. When funds are impounded, relations between the president and Congress become strained, especially if they are from different parties.

Republican President Richard M. Nixon was involved in a major impoundment controversy with the Democratic-controlled Congress (1969–1974). In 1972 Nixon proposed that Congress give him the authority to reduce federal spending, but Congress refused. Nixon exercised his veto power twelve times to kill various money bills. When Congress appropriated funds over his veto, he impounded them. Many state and local governments, as well as Congress, objected to such actions by the president. Thirty federal court cases challenged the president's right to withhold appropriated funds. The Nixon administration lost all but five of the cases. In the most important case, *Train v. City of New York* (1975), the Supreme Court unanimously ruled that the president is obligated to spend the money that Congress appropriates.

Treaty-Making Power　　The authority of the president to negotiate and enter into treaty obligations with other nations. The treaty-making power is provided by the Constitution, which states in Article II, Section 2 that the president "shall have Power, by and with the Advice and Consent of the Senate, to make Treaties, provided two-thirds of the Senators present concur. . . ." The president does not normally negotiate a treaty; it is done by presidential representatives or diplomats in the State Department or American embassies. Usually the Senate approves treaties negotiated by the administration, but there have been important exceptions. Nineteen treaties, including the Treaty of Versailles in 1919, which would have established the League of Nations, have been rejected by the Senate since the nation's founding. The Senate took an active role in ratifying the Panama Canal Treaty in 1977; debate in the Senate continued over two months. Nearly 200 amendments, reservations, and declarations were proposed to the original treaty before it was ratified by the Senate by a vote of 68 to 32 (67 votes are required when all senators are present).

Duly ratified treaties are the law of the land, and they have the force of law. Article VI of the Constitution places "all Treaties made, or which shall be made, under the Authority of the United States" on the same level with the laws of the land. Article I, Section 10 implicitly recognizes agreements made between the head of state (the president) and foreign nations, without formal Senate approval. Although these executive agreements are less formal and explicit than treaties, they are equally legal and valid. To circumvent the Senate's role in the treaty process, many presidents have resorted to this kind of agreement. In 1981 there were 967 treaties and 6,188 executive agreements in force between the United States and other nations of the world. *See also* CHIEF EXECUTIVE, p. 31; CHIEF FOREIGN POLICYMAKER, p. 32; CHIEF LAWMAKER, p. 33; CHIEF OF STATE, p. 37; COMMANDER IN CHIEF, p. 38; CONSTITUTIONAL POWERS, p. 39.

Significance　　The treaty-making power is considered one of the most dramatic and legally binding powers of the president. Treaty making involves two stages: negotiation and ratification. Although the Senate can refuse to ratify a treaty, it cannot force the president to negotiate or decline to negotiate one. But the historic role of the Senate cannot be characterized as one of rubber stamping treaties. President George Washington took the advising and consenting role of the Senate quite seriously. He personally appeared before the Senate in order to secure approval of a treaty with the Indian tribes in 1793 but failed to gain the support of the majority of the twenty-six senators. In 1794 Washington negotiated the Jay Treaty with England without involving the Senate in the process. Many subsequent presidents have sought to involve the Senate in the negotiating process, while others have ignored it.

The constitutional provision that the president make treaties with the advice and consent of the Senate has evoked controversy throughout the nation's history. Until the 1960s, the Senate's role in treaty making was considered rather passive, but the Vietnam War changed that. Many Americans blamed the tragedy in Vietnam on presidential war-making, which was often done without congressional approval. The senators asserted their prerogatives to set limits on the president's power to negotiate such treaties as the Panama Canal Treaty (1977) and the Soviet-American Strategic Arms Limitation Treaty (SALT, 1979). Under growing pressure from Congress and the people, President Jimmy Carter's administration wisely decided to involve the Senate more directly in the treaty-making process.

Veto Power   Authority of the president to disapprove a bill passed by Congress. The veto power is a mechanism used by presidents against legislation that threatens their policies or constitutional rights. The Constitution states in Article I, Section 7 that any bill passed by Congress shall be presented to the president for approval or disapproval. The president must sign or veto a bill within ten days. This is called a regular or messaged veto, as the president returns the bill to Congress with a message. A two-thirds vote in both houses of Congress is needed to override this veto. Many bills are passed in the rush of the closing days of a congressional session. By law, a president has ten days to act on a bill. When given less than ten working days to act, the president may refuse to act at all, in which case the bill is automatically killed. This is called a pocket veto. It is more effective than a regular veto, because Congress has adjourned and cannot meet in time to override the veto. A bill that is not vetoed or signed within ten days while the Congress is in session becomes law automatically.

Unlike most governors, presidents do not have an item veto. They must either approve a bill in its entirety or reject it wholly. To take advantage of this rule, Congress attaches riders to a bill. A rider is a legislative addition. If the president approves a bill, the rider is accepted as well. Many presidents have used their veto power. President Franklin D. Roosevelt exercised the highest number of vetoes (631) between 1933 and 1945. The second highest was President Grover Cleveland, who vetoed 414 bills between 1885 and 1889. He was followed by President Harry S Truman, who vetoed 250 bills between 1945 and 1953. President Ronald Reagan has used his veto power 8 times between January 1981 and December 1982. (Refer to the Appendix, Figure 3 for a table of presidential vetoes.) *See also* CHIEF EXECUTIVE, p. 31; CHIEF LAWMAKER, p. 33; CONSTITUTIONAL POWERS, p. 39.

Significance   The veto power is used increasingly to punish or reward individual members of Congress on private bills. Many presidents have compromised with Congress on important legislation. All presidents have formal and informal contacts with Congress. However, President Harry S Truman was the first to assign a White House staff to maintain continuous liaison with Congress. Since then, other presidents have maintained this practice. The threat of a veto is often a more effective weapon than the actual use of the veto itself. From 1961 to 1981, presidents vetoed 196 bills, and Congress overrode only 20 of them. A mere hint of a veto is sometimes enough to convince Congress to change its mind in favor of the president. Winning a two-thirds majority to override a veto is very difficult. Therefore, presidents have been more successful in using the veto power or the threat of it than Congress in overriding the veto.

Although the pocket veto has fallen into disuse because of longer and longer congressional sessions, President Richard M. Nixon claimed that he could exercise such a veto even when Congress temporarily adjourned for Easter, or other short breaks. Senator Edward M. Kennedy (D-Mass.) instituted court action to overturn Nixon's use of the pocket veto. Both the district and circuit courts held Nixon's action to be unconstitutional. Instead of appealing to the Supreme Court, where the issue could be finally settled, Nixon's successor, President Gerald R. Ford, continued to use the pocket veto. As Senator Kennedy said, the administration wanted to have it both ways: ignore the court decision and continue to use the pocket veto. Often a president whose party is in the congressional minority, like Ford, will use the veto power to carry out his policies and run the country the way he wishes.

War Powers Act   Power of the president to wage and conduct war against other nations. The War Powers Act grants the president authority to raise, organize, equip, and command the armed forces. Although the Constitution expressly vests in Congress the power to declare war, only five of the eleven major wars fought by the United States were declared by Congress. Yet in each of these five wars—the War of 1812, the Mexican War, the Spanish-American War, and World Wars I and II—Congress declared war only in response to the president's request. The first and the second War Powers Acts were passed in 1941 and 1945 respectively, giving the presidents additional powers to deal with war situations. The third War Powers Act, enacted in 1973, is the most significant in limiting the president's power. This resolution imposes a duty on the president: In the absence of a declaration of war by Congress, the president must report to Congress within forty-eight hours after American armed forces have been dispatched into conflict. Additionally, the president must recall all troops within sixty days after the report unless Congress declares war or approves the military action. The Congress can take action to recall the armed forces at any time during the sixty-day period. *See also* CHIEF EXECUTIVE, p. 31; COMMANDER IN CHIEF, p. 38; CONSTITUTIONAL POWERS, p. 39; EMERGENCY POWERS, p. 41.

Significance   The War Powers Act of 1973 recognizes emergency situations in which the president must have power to act quickly and decisively to protect the nation from foreign attack. In recent years, presidents have had to respond to such crises as the Soviet intervention in the Middle East, the Cambodian seizure of the American merchant ship *Mayaguez* in 1975, or Libya's attempt to intercept United States Air Force jets in 1982. The War Powers Act has not served to undermine the president's authority as commander in chief. Rather, it is a recognition of the broad interpretation of presidential power as the supreme commander of the armed forces. The act clarifies and further legitimizes the president's authority to commit American troops abroad without a formal declaration of war or authorization by Congress.

The heart of the act is the provision that the president must terminate the use of military action within sixty days, if during this period Congress has not declared war, or granted the president an extension of the use of the armed forces, or is unable to convene as a result of an armed attack upon the United States. The act limits the power of the president to infer executive authority to send troops abroad, as Presidents Lyndon B. Johnson and Richard M. Nixon did during the Vietnam War. In vetoing the act, President Nixon asserted that it was blatantly unconstitutional. However, Congress overrode the veto. The act has not really been tested in a situation in which the president deployed American troops on a large scale and for a long period of time. It remains to be seen whether Congress will refuse to approve the president's use of the armed forces and authorize such use beyond sixty days.

3. The Presidents

George Washington   First president, born in Pope's Creek, Westmoreland County, Virginia, on February 22, 1732. Washington's father was Augustine Washington, his mother, Mary Ball. Washington attended school irregularly from his seventh to fifteenth year but evidenced early a facility in mathematics and surveying, so marked as to suggest a gift for practical affairs. In 1752 he became the manager of a sizable estate, when he inherited Mount Vernon on the death of his half-brother Lawrence. Washington's military service began in 1753 when the Virginia governor sent him on missions into the Ohio Valley to assert British claims against France's determination to control the valley. In 1759 he married Martha Dandridge Custis.

As a member of the Virginia House of Burgesses from 1759 to 1774, Washington opposed the Stamp Act, which imposed heavy taxes on the colonies for the support of the British army. He also opposed taxes levied on tea, paper, lead, glass, and painters' colors. Along with other Virginia burgesses, he proposed that a Continental Congress be held and was elected one of the delegates to the first Continental Congress. Washington opposed British exactions and took command of the Virginia troops. In 1775 he was named commander in chief of the American revolutionary forces by the Continental Congress. Washington's military record during the Revolution was most distinguished, and under his leadership a Declaration of Independence was promulgated on July 4, 1776. Washington became the founding father and the *de facto* president of the country. He served as president of the Constitutional Convention which met in Philadelphia to draft a constitution for the country and to secure its ratification. The Constitution contained many of his ideas. Washington was unanimously elected president by the electoral college and was inaugurated on April 30, 1789, in New York

51

City's Federal Hall. In 1792 he was unanimously reelected by the electoral college. (Refer to the Appendix, Figure 4 for a chart of major parties' popular and electoral vote for president.)

Significance   George Washington created and consolidated the first nation in the new world. As the first president, he established many precedents, among them the president's power to select, nominate, appoint, and remove executive officers. He regarded himself as standing aloof from party divisions and believed that the head of the nation should be nonpartisan. In legislative matters, Washington moved quickly to establish presidential prerogatives. Through various bills and executive orders, he laid the economic foundation of the new nation. When armed resistance against the excise tax broke out in Pennsylvania, known as the Whiskey Rebellion (1794), Washington himself led the troops to suppress it. Under his leadership, a federal judiciary was created. In foreign affairs, Washington aimed at keeping the country at peace and issued a proclamation of neutrality during the Anglo-French war in 1793. He received foreign emissaries, establishing the precedent that the president, as head of state, had the right to receive ambassadors and accord diplomatic recognition to other nations. When the Senate failed to render advice on treaty negotiations, Washington vowed not to seek its counsel on further treaties. Since then, despite the constitutional requirement that the president shall make treaties with the advice and consent of the Senate, no subsequent president has sought that body's advice on treaty negotiations.

By 1795 Washington's creative work was done, and he was exhausted. As his health declined, President Washington's Republican opponents alleged that Alexander Hamilton was ruling the country as the virtual president. They accused him of deserting France, a faithful ally of the United States, and of trying to reinstitute the British monarchy. Washington's second term was stormy, and he was troubled by the mounting controversy in party matters and in the press. However, his decision not to seek a third term quieted his opponents and established a tradition which has been broken only once, when Franklin D. Roosevelt was elected to four terms.

Washington believed that the federal government should be strengthened and given adequate powers to deal with the problems of the nation. A forceful figure, he favored a strong central government that could unite the thirteen disunited states into a single powerful United States of America. In his farewell address (September 17, 1796), Washington urged the people to cherish the Union, support public credit, respect the Constitution, and abide by the election results. At a time when conditions were ripe for the monarchical and dictatorial rule that prevailed in most of the world, Washington's administration was, as political scientist

Clinton Rossiter suggests, "nothing if not painfully constitutional." Robert K. Murray, Professor of History at Pennsylvania State University, after surveying and sampling 970 other historians in the country in 1983, ranked Washington as the third greatest president, after Abraham Lincoln and Franklin D. Roosevelt. Other historians have rated him as the second greatest, after Lincoln.

John Adams   Second president, born on October 30, 1735, in Braintree (Quincy), Massachusetts. Adams's father was also named John Adams, his mother, Susanna Boylston. In 1755 he graduated from Harvard College, taught school for a time and studied law, and was admitted to the Boston bar in 1758. He began his career writing wills and deeds and authored many anonymous articles for the *Boston Gazette*. In 1764 he married Abigail Smith. He argued against taxation without representation before the British governor. Adams expressed his views in political forums, assailing the Stamp Act as an unnecessary burden upon the people. This became a model for demonstrations and protests against the act in New England. Adams was an advocate of liberty and defended the British soldier accused of murder in the Boston Massacre. As a member of the first Continental Congress, he signed the Declaration of Independence. Later, he was a commissioner to France and the first American minister to England. In 1788 he was elected vice president and in 1796 elected president, barely defeating Thomas Jefferson.

Significance   John Adams declared his faith in republicanism in his inaugural address and called upon the people to end partisan wrangling. His administration was marked by controversy; he tried to reach an accord with Jefferson but failed. Adams decided to keep George Washington's cabinet in order to reconcile the Federalists. His four-year term as president was marked by a succession of political intrigues, which were a source of personal embitterment. Four bills to control subversion were passed, as well as the Alien and Sedition Acts of 1798, and these brought discredit to the Federalist party. One of the acts imposed severe penalties on those who criticized the government. Many journalists were punished for their attacks on the administration.

At this time, the United States was drawn into complications with European powers. As relations with France worsened, Adams recommended war preparations while negotiations for peace continued. Adams wanted to take reprisals against French seizures of American ships, but he had advice from Europe that France would resume negotiations. Finally he secured peace with France, much against the wishes of his cabinet, which led to defeat when he ran for reelection. Less elevated than President George Washington in the nation's regard,

Adams caught the full blast of Republican opposition at the end of his presidency. Although he failed to maintain the euphoria of independence and further consolidate the nation, historians rate him as a near great president.

Thomas Jefferson   Third president, born at Shadwell in Albemarle County, Virginia, on April 13, 1743. Jefferson's father was Peter Jefferson, his mother, Jane Randolph. Jefferson attended the College of William and Mary and was admitted to the Virginia bar in 1767. He inherited a considerable fortune from his father and augmented it by marrying Martha Skelton in 1772. Jefferson became a justice of the peace, a member of the House of Burgesses, and a delegate to the Continental Congress in Philadelphia. In 1776 he was chosen to draft the Declaration of Independence. His revolutionary philosophy is reflected in that document. It proclaimed, among other things, that "all men are created equal," and that government is the servant, not the master, of the people. In 1779 he became governor of Virginia, and when the state was overrun by British expeditions, he was blamed for its ineffectual resistance. In the Continental Congress in 1783, Jefferson drafted an ordinance for the Northwest Territory forbidding slavery after 1800. In 1785 he was sent to France as minister. George Washington appointed him secretary of state in 1789. A Republican candidate for president in 1796, he was defeated by John Adams and subsequently became vice president. In 1800 Jefferson received the same number of electoral college votes for president as his own vice presidential candidate, Aaron Burr. The House of Representatives, controlled by Federalists, ultimately elected Jefferson president. To avoid this situation in the future, Congress adopted the Twelfth Amendment to the Constitution in 1804.

Significance   Thomas Jefferson was the first president inaugurated in Washington, D.C. His accession to the presidency marked the end of Federalist supremacy in the country, and despite Federalist obstructionism, the transition of power from conservatism to liberal rule was effected peacefully. This peaceful transfer of power, from one party to another, set a precedent that has since been retained in American political history. Jefferson was the undisputed leader of his party and labored long and hard to develop a loyal opposition. Many scholars believe that his election as president removed the threat of counterrevolution, thus saving the country for democracy. Jefferson restored party balance in the civil service but failed to balance the judiciary along party lines, because his predecessor, John Adams, reinforced it by fresh Federalist appointees. He treated as null and void late appointments by Adams, and the new Republican Congress repealed the Judiciary Act of 1801. Chief Justice John Marshall rebuked Jefferson in the famous case of *Marbury* v. *Madison* (1803) for withholding the commission of an Adams appointee. Jefferson's efforts to remove partisan judges by impeachment was also a failure. However, all this had one result: judges became less partisan.

Jefferson's failure to restore party balance in the judiciary was compensated by the most notable accomplishment of his presidency and one that helped secure his reelection in 1804: the Louisiana Purchase from France. So potent was his leadership that he did not exercise a single veto during his eight years in office; in fact, no bill that he seriously opposed was passed by Congress. Jefferson enlarged the power of the presidency, as evidenced by his ability to guide the Embargo Act of 1807 through both houses of Congress in one day. In both domestic and foreign affairs, Jefferson encountered greater difficulties during his second term. The conspiracy to seize power by former Vice President Aaron Burr was foiled. Relations with France and Britain improved considerably, but Jefferson failed to avert war with the latter. Opinions differ about his conduct of the presidency; however, Jefferson has generally been hailed as a man of the people, because he sought to conduct the government in the interests of the people. Robert K. Murray, in a landmark survey of the strengths and weaknesses of American presidents, rated Jefferson as the fourth greatest, following Abraham Lincoln, Franklin D. Roosevelt, and George Washington, in that order (*Durham Morning Herald*, February 21, 1983, 2A).

James Madison   Fourth president, born at Port Conway, King George County, Virginia, on March 16, 1751. Madison's father was also named James Madison, his mother, Eleanor Rose Conway. In 1771 he graduated from the College of New Jersey (now Princeton University). He was chosen a delegate to the Virginia Constitutional Convention in 1776. As a member of the Continental Congress, he drafted the United States Constitution and was its chief recorder. Madison was elected a member of the House of Representatives in 1789. In 1794 he married Dorothea (Dolley, incorrectly Dolly) Dandridge Payne Todd.

While in Congress, Madison proposed nine amendments to the Constitution that were the basis of the Bill of Rights embodied in the first ten amendments. In 1798 he joined Thomas Jefferson in opposing the Alien and Sedition laws. Madison became secretary of state upon Thomas Jefferson's accession to the presidency in 1801 and was instrumental in negotiating the purchase of Louisiana from France. Madison and Albert Gallatin, the secretary of the treasury, were confidants of

Jefferson; these three Republicans ran the affairs of the nation for eight years. In 1808 Madison was elected president.

Significance   James Madison's administration was foreshadowed with difficulties. Federalist opposition thwarted administration policies. To placate party opposition, he reluctantly appointed several ineffectual cabinet officers. The renewed war between France and Britain became the major crisis for Madison's administration. Both warring nations inflicted heavy damage on American shipping, but Madison's devotion to democratic ideals prevented him from seizing emergency powers. Under mounting pressure from the "hawks" in Congress, Madison decided to go to war against England. The American army was not adequately prepared for war, nor was the country united behind Madison's war policy; the war ended in a stalemate. Following his reelection in 1812, Madison grew increasingly unpopular. However, with the peace declaration between England and the United States, the president gained some popularity. With the threats of disunion ended, his last years as president proved successful.

Madison proposed a series of wide-ranging domestic programs to guide and stimulate the economy and recommended defense measures sufficiently strong to deter potential enemies. During the last years of his administration, Madison cast aside personal dogma, believing that the people should use government to fulfill national objectives. Madison tried to maintain the effectiveness of Jefferson's administration, but he was notably unsuccessful. Toward the end of his administration, Madison succumbed to opposition demands and approved many measures supported by the Federalists. As the last survivor of the founding fathers, Madison's place in history reveals his weakness as a chief executive.

James Monroe   Fifth president, born in Monroe's Creek, Westmoreland County, Virginia, on April 28, 1758. Monroe's father was Spence Monroe, his mother, Elizabeth Jones. Monroe attended the College of William and Mary but left in 1776 to enlist in the Third Virginia Regiment. As a lieutenant, he saw action in the battles of New York and Trenton, where he was seriously wounded. In 1780 he returned to Virginia and began the study of law under Governor Thomas Jefferson. Monroe's career was greatly influenced by Jefferson. In 1782 Monroe was elected to the Virginia House of Delegates and served in the Congress under the Articles of Confederation. Monroe married Elizabeth Kortright in 1786. On retiring from Congress, he established a law practice in Virginia. Monroe was again elected a member of the Virginia House of Delegates in 1787, and the following year a member of the state convention that ratified the United States Constitution (although he opposed it because the Constitution lacked a bill of rights). In 1790 he was chosen a United States Senator. Monroe was an opponent of George Washington, but the latter nevertheless nominated him a minister to France.

From 1799 to 1802, Monroe served as governor of Virginia, demonstrating great administrative ability and winning high praise for his action to suppress a slave uprising. President Thomas Jefferson sent Monroe to France in 1803 as a special envoy to assist in negotiating the Louisiana Purchase. This established Monroe as a national figure. He then served as minister to Britain. Monroe was appointed secretary of state under James Madison. In 1814, after the capture of Washington, D.C., by the British, he was appointed secretary of war, thus holding two cabinet posts. In 1816 Monroe was elected president.

Significance   James Monroe's administration heralded an "era of good feeling," which was marked by calm and prosperity. His greatest achievements as president lay in foreign affairs. Monroe obtained Florida from Spain, settled boundaries with Canada, and recognized the new Latin American states. Enacted in 1823, the Monroe Doctrine includes three essential elements (1) no further European colonization in the new world; (2) abstention of the United States from the political affairs of Europe; and (3) nonintervention of Europe in the governance of the Western Hemisphere.

Monroe's domestic policies received less attention. He supported the antislavery position that led to the Missouri Compromise of 1820. Another Monroe achievement was the construction of a network of coastal fortifications to prevent future invasions. Monroe was so popular during his first term that he was reelected in 1820 with all but one electoral vote. The sole dissenter, William Plumer from New Hampshire, cast his vote for John Quincy Adams in protest against a unanimous election. Monroe's second term was less successful, owing to bitterness created by the Missouri debates and the rivalry of the various aspirants to succeed him as president. Weak as he was, Monroe attempted to achieve the revolutionary ideal of a representative government based on free institutions, but he failed. Historians rank Monroe as an average president.

John Quincy Adams   Sixth president, born in Braintree (Quincy), Massachusetts, on July 11, 1767. Adams was the only son of a president (John Adams) to become chief executive; his mother was Abigail Smith. As a boy of ten, he accompanied his father on diplomatic missions in Europe. Adams learned French in a private school in Paris and entered the University of Leiden in 1780. The following year he traveled with Francis Dana, American envoy to Russia, as his private secretary and interpreter of French. Returning home, he graduated from Harvard College in 1787 and was admitted to the Boston bar in 1790. He served as American foreign minister in various European capitals. In 1797 he married Louisa Catherine Johnson in London.

Adams was chosen as a United States Senator in 1803 and was appointed secretary of state by President James Monroe in 1817. Adams negotiated the cession of Florida from Spain and helped formulate the Monroe Doctrine. As President Monroe's second term drew to a close, a number of his official advisers, including Adams, wanted to succeed him. In the contest that followed, no candidate secured the required majority of electoral votes. Adams was selected president by the House of Representatives in 1825, receiving the second highest number of votes (84) while Andrew Jackson received 99, William Crawford 41, and Henry Clay 37. The House selected from among the three candidates who received the largest vote and chose Adams over Jackson.

Significance   John Quincy Adams's career was notably successful until his election as president. It was during his presidency that irreconcilable differences developed between Jackson and himself. Jackson's followers accused Adams of being partner to a corrupt bargain to obtain Clay's support in the election and then appoint him secretary of state. The judgment of historians is that there was a bargain and Adams benefitted from this political deal with Clay, but no evidence of corruption. Like his father, Adams's lack of political sense and inability to garner public support spelled defeat for his policies and displayed weakness. Opposition arose to his proposals for the creation of a national university, and government support for the arts and sciences. Adams fought many losing battles with Congress but failed to exercise the veto, another sign of weakness. Adams did little or nothing to develop a personal following; with no real political party behind him in 1828, he lost his reelection bid to Jackson, his archenemy. An Arthur M. Schlesinger, Jr. poll taken in 1948 ranked him as an average president.

Andrew Jackson   Seventh president, born on March 15, 1767, at a settlement on the banks of Crawford's Branch of Waxhaw Creek in South Carolina. Jackson's father was also named Andrew Jackson, his mother, Elizabeth Hutchinson. He studied law in Salisbury, North Carolina and was admitted to the bar in that state in 1787. The next year, Jackson arrived in Nashville, Tennessee, where he was appointed public prosecutor of the western district of North Carolina. Jackson prospered in slave speculations. In 1791 he married Rachel Donelson Robards. Her formal divorce from her previous husband was not granted until after her wedding to Jackson; they were officially married in 1794. In 1796 he became a member of the convention that drafted a constitution for Tennessee. Jackson was elected to the United States Senate in 1797, but financial difficulties led him to resign from the Senate and accept an appointment as a judge of the Tennessee Superior Court.

In 1802 Jackson became major general of the Tennessee militia. During the War of 1812 with Britain, he raised 50,000 volunteers from Tennessee to invade Canada. The federal government looked askance at this action, but his services were later used against the Creek Indians, who were allied with the British. Jackson crushed the Creeks at the Battle of Tohopeka in Alabama, and he was named commander of the southern district. Jackson's occupation of parts of Florida hastened its acquisition from Spain by the United States. In 1821 Jackson became the governor of Florida and was elected president in 1828.

Significance   Andrew Jackson's election is a turning point in the political history of the United States; he was the first president to be elected both by the electoral college and the American public through a direct appeal to the mass of voters. The success of Jackson appeared to be a vindication of the new democracy and, as he was the central figure in this movement, it is often called Jacksonian Democracy.

His first term was dominated by a contest between Martin Van Buren, his secretary of state, and John C. Calhoun, the vice president. Jackson removed from office many of his political opponents, including long time civil servants. Jackson destroyed the Bank of the United States by depositing federal funds with the state banks. In foreign affairs, he ended a long dispute with Britain by reopening the British West Indian ports to American ships. Jackson profoundly affected the development of the presidency by concentrating presidential power through wide use of the veto and insisting that the president alone represented the will of the nation. The widespread approval of his actions exercised a profound effect on the character of American politics for decades to follow. A United States Historical Society poll, taken in 1977, rated Jackson as one of the ten greatest presidents.

Martin Van Buren   Eighth president, born in Kinderhook, New York, on December 5, 1782. Van Buren's father was Abraham Van Buren, his mother, Maria Van Alen. He studied in the Kinderhook Schoolhouse and the Village Academy. At the age of fourteen, he began to study law under a local attorney and was admitted to the bar at the age of twenty-one. In 1807 he married a distant cousin, Hannah Hoes. In 1812 he was elected to the New York State Senate; in 1821 elected to the

United States Senate; and reelected in 1827. Van Buren became governor of New York in 1828 but resigned the governorship to accept the post of secretary of state in President Andrew Jackson's cabinet. In 1831 he was appointed minister to Britain and, while working in England, he learned that his nomination as minister to England had been defeated in the Senate by the tie-breaking vote of Vice President John C. Calhoun. This ensured Van Buren's nomination for the vice presidency by the first Democratic national convention in 1832. He became the vice president and in 1835 was elected president.

Significance   Elected as Andrew Jackson's protégé, Martin Van Buren became president while a financial panic spread throughout the nation. Soon after taking office, he summoned a special session of Congress and was instrumental in securing passage of a bill to deposit federal funds with state banks. On this issue, many Democrats deserted to the Whig party. Although Van Buren showed statesmanlike courage, bitterness among the Democratic party born of the financial panic of 1837 continued to mount against him, and many conservative Democrats defected to the Whig party. A bitter war with the Seminole Indians in Florida and his failure to support the proposed annexation of Texas made Van Buren unpopular with the voters. In foreign affairs, he had problems with Britain arising out of the U.S.S. *Caroline* incident (an American steamer that had been transporting supplies to Canadian insurgents). A territorial dispute between the inhabitants of Maine and Canada resulted in a series of armed clashes. The dispute was halted through negotiation, and a threatened war by Britain was also averted. Because of his failure to achieve tangible results in domestic and foreign affairs, historians view Van Buren as a weak and average president.

William Henry Harrison   Ninth president, born at Berkeley plantation on the James River in Charles City County, Virginia, on February 9, 1773. Harrison's father was Benjamin Harrison, his mother, Elizabeth Bassett. Harrison was privately tutored to meet the entrance requirements at Hampden-Sydney College in 1787 and later entered the College of Physicians and Surgeons in Philadelphia. He gave up his study to enter the army as an ensign in the First Infantry Regiment. Harrison remained in the army until 1798, rising to the rank of captain. He married Anna Tuthill Symmes in 1795. (Their grandson, Benjamin Harrison, became the twenty-third president.)

In 1798 President John Adams appointed Harrison secretary of the Northwest Territory. The following year, the territorial legislature elected him its delegate to Congress. In 1800 President Adams appointed him governor of the Indian territory and as governor,

Harrison led the army and won an important victory against the Indians. This gained him national recognition and prestige. During the war with Britain in 1812, he was appointed a major general in the Kentucky militia and was later made a brigadier general in the United States Army. In this capacity, Harrison commanded all troops in the Northwest. Harrison was elected president in 1840.

Significance   William Henry Harrison was the first candidate to conduct a vigorous campaign for the presidency. He delivered twenty-three speeches, ranging from one hour to three hours in length. On March 4, 1841, in one of the longest inaugural addresses ever delivered, he pledged not to run for a second term. Harrison appointed an able cabinet headed by Daniel Webster as secretary of state and called a special session of Congress to enact Whig economic legislation. At age sixty-eight, then the oldest president to be inaugurated, he was also the first to die in office (Ronald Reagan is the oldest of all presidents, having taken office at the age of sixty-nine). It is generally believed that Harrison died of pneumonia, which he caught during his inauguration. His illness was complicated by the fatigue brought on by the hundreds of opportunity seekers who called upon him constantly. Harrison is credited with no notable achievements, as he served in office for only one month, too short a period for any kind of assessment.

John Tyler   Tenth president, born at Greenway, Charles City County, Virginia, on March 29, 1790. Tyler's father was also named John Tyler, his mother, Mary Marot Armistead. He attended local schools and at age twelve entered the College of William and Mary, from which he graduated in 1807. Tyler studied law in his father's office and was admitted to the bar in 1809. Beginning in 1811, he was elected to the Virginia state legislature for five consecutive terms. Tyler was twice married, first to Letitia Christian in 1813, and then to Julia Gardiner in 1844. In 1816 he was elected to the Council of State and one year later to the United States House of Representatives. As a member of the House, he steadfastly opposed the Missouri Compromise as an unconstitutional restriction on slavery. Tyler was elected governor of Virginia in 1825 but resigned to enter the United States Senate in 1827. As a member of the Virginia Constitutional Convention of 1829–1830, he opposed democratic reform of suffrage, representation, and court procedure. In 1840 he was elected vice president and, on President William Henry Harrison's death, succeeded him as president.

Significance   John Tyler was the first president to succeed a president. The opposition party (the nationalist Whigs) proposed to recognize him as acting president, but Tyler nonetheless exercised all of his powers and privileges as president. The Whigs tried hard to force him to accept their negative programs against his will, but he adamantly refused. During his administration, Congress passed two bills to create a new bank of the United States that Tyler vetoed as unconstitutional. In an apparent attempt to force him out of office, all but one of his cabinet officers (Daniel Webster) resigned; however, Tyler reorganized his cabinet within two days. The congressional Whigs, under the leadership of Senator Henry Clay, opposed the president. Tyler, in turn, defeated the enactment of Clay's American System. After Tyler twice vetoed the bill rechartering a national bank, Clay declared him a party outlaw. Clay seized upon every difference with the president as an occasion to charge him with authoritarianism and usurpation of power. Tyler became a president without a party and was denounced and repudiated by both the Whigs and Democrats.

Yet his administration accomplished a great deal. Tyler reorganized the United States Navy, established a naval observatory depot, developed a magnetic telegraph, annexed Texas, and established the weather bureau. He guided successful negotiations to secure the Webster-Ashburton Treaty, which settled the Maine border dispute with Canada. In 1842 he extended the Monroe Doctrine to Hawaii to thwart British interests there. His administration brought the Seminole War to an end, quieted the Dorr rebellion, and negotiated a treaty with China. Historians consider Tyler a weak figure and a below average president.

James Knox Polk   Eleventh president, born in Mecklenburg County, North Carolina, on November 2, 1795. Polk's father was Samuel Polk, his mother, Jane Knox. Polk was unable to attend school as a youngster because of poor health but passed the entrance requirements for the University of North Carolina. In 1820 he was admitted to the bar in Columbia, South Carolina. He was elected to the lower house of the Tennessee legislature in 1823. The next year he married Sarah Childress. In 1825 Polk was elected to the United States House of Representatives and held that position for fourteen years, until he left the House to become governor of Tennessee. Polk's nomination for the presidency in 1844 was unsought by him. The first dark horse candidate for the presidency (chosen because he championed control of Oregon and the annexation of Texas), Polk was elected president.

Significance   James K. Polk, elected when less than fifty years of age, was the youngest president to occupy the office. His administration was marked by large territorial gains. Texas was annexed as a state; Mexico ceded California and much of the Southwest to the United States as a consequence of the two-year war. The Mexican-American War coincided with the Oregon crisis with Britain, finally resolved when Britain accepted a compromise boundary along the forty-ninth parallel. During Polk's administration, the northwest boundary of the United States became fixed by treaty, and the continental United States emerged as a reality. The expansion of the country resulted in the creation of the Department of the Interior. Polk concluded a treaty with Colombia clearing a right-of-way for United States citizens across the Isthmus of Panama. The reenactment of an independent treasury system helped to solve some of the nation's financial problems. Polk established the United States Naval Academy at Annapolis, Maryland.

One of the strongest presidents in American history, Polk proved successful in settling a trade dispute with Great Britain, increasing the size of the United States armed forces, enacting the Tariff Act of 1846, reenacting the independent treasury system, and expanding foreign trade. Polk refused to share information with Congress on the grounds that it was incompatible with the public interest. Indeed, he displayed great leadership in administration that gave weight to his influence over Congress and impressed upon it that national welfare should predominate over narrow and parochial interests. Historians rate him as a near great president.

Zachary Taylor   Twelfth president, born in Oregon County, Virginia, on November 24, 1784. Taylor's father was Richard Taylor, his mother, Sarah Dabney Strother. Taylor grew up on a farm near Louisville and had practically no formal schooling. President Thomas Jefferson appointed him as first lieutenant in the Seventh Infantry. He married Margaret Mackall Smith in 1810. Taylor fought in the War of 1832 and the second Seminole War of 1837. His victory made him brigadier general the next year, and he commanded all United States troops in Florida. In 1845 he was sent to the Rio Grande and there defeated the Mexican army. The news of these victories was received with great joy in Washington, D.C., and elsewhere in the country. Many Whig politicians were convinced of his potential as a leader and a presidential candidate. President James K. Polk appointed him a major general. The Whig party nominated Taylor as its presidential candidate in 1848, and he was elected president.

Significance   Zachary Taylor entered the presidency with less knowledge of government than any president before him. He served only about sixteen months, yet he influenced many important political events. Although a slaveholder, Taylor recommended that California be admitted to the Union as a free state. When southern congressmen protested because California had prohibited slavery, Taylor refused to back down. The Congress, which had a Democratic plurality in both the House and Senate, fought hard to discredit the Whig president. With congressmen brandishing firearms and even involved in fistfighting, there was danger of civil war.

As a renowned soldier and a dedicated unionist, Taylor made it clear that he would use troops if necessary to carry out the antislavery law. His congressional speeches over the extension of slavery are among the most famous in history. During his sixteen-month administration, Taylor became a "doughface" in reverse—a southerner with northern principles. Considered by historians an inexperienced, weak, and below average president, Taylor is credited with few achievements in domestic affairs. One notable achievement in foreign affairs was the Clayton-Bulwer Treaty with Britain, which provided for control over canal routes in Central America.

Millard Fillmore   Thirteenth president, born in a frontier cabin in Cayuga County, New York, on January 7, 1800. Fillmore's father was Nathaniel Fillmore, his mother, Phoebe Millard. Fillmore was largely self-educated until the age of eighteen, when he received six months of formal schooling. He obtained a clerkship in a court in Montville, New York, where he studied law. Fillmore taught school and worked in a law firm in Buffalo. In 1823 he was admitted to the New York bar and established his law practice near Buffalo. In 1826 he married Abigail Powers. In 1828 he was elected to the New York Assembly, where he served three terms. He was elected to the United States House of Representatives in 1836 and went on to become chairman of the powerful Ways and Means Committee. Fillmore was nominated as the Whig candidate for governor of New York but lost the election by a narrow margin. However, in 1847 he was elected by a large margin as the first comptroller of New York State. In 1848 he was elected vice president and, on the death of President Zachary Taylor, became president on July 10, 1850.

Significance   Millard Fillmore showed a marked lack of leadership as president, although earlier he had displayed considerable ability as chairman of the Ways and Means Committee and as comptroller of New York. As for presidential accomplishments, he favored the Compromise of 1850 and signed the Fugitive Slave Law. But Fillmore pleased neither expansionists nor slaveholders; he had been a moderate antislavery man and believed the issue should be settled by compromise and not by force. However, the enactment of the Fugitive Slave Law divided the Whig party.

Fillmore took great interest in the nation's economic development. He arranged the first federal land grants for railroad construction and expanded foreign trade. Fillmore was one of the first leaders to recognize the importance of extending America's influence in the Far East. In 1853 he authorized Commodore Matthew C. Perry's expedition to Japan, which resulted in the opening of trade and diplomatic relations between the two nations. He was not a dramatic leader and was handicapped by divisions in the Whig party. Fillmore was a candidate for the Whig presidential nomination in 1852 but failed in his effort. Although a weak and below average president, Fillmore maintained the dignity, integrity, and magnanimity of the office.

Franklin Pierce   Fourteenth president, born at Hillsboro Lower Village, New Hampshire, on November 23, 1804. Pierce's father was Benjamin Pierce, his mother, Anna Kendrick. Pierce was educated at Hillsboro Center, Hancock Academy, and Bowdoin College. In 1827 he was admitted to the New Hampshire bar. Pierce was elected to the New Hampshire House of Representatives in 1829 and served as Speaker of that body. In 1833 he was elected a member of the United States House of Representatives. Pierce married Jane Means Appleton in 1834. In 1837, at the age of thirty-three, he became the youngest United States Senator. In 1846 he enlisted in the Mexican War and became brigadier general. At the close of the war, Pierce returned to his law practice in Concord. Pierce became a dark horse Democratic nominee for president in 1852, when the national nominating convention was unable to choose from among four other prominent candidates. Pierce won the election for president.

Significance   Franklin Pierce was the youngest man, at age forty-eight, to be elected president at that point in time. In his inaugural address, delivered from memory, he dwelt on the theme of Young America, demanding a program of territorial expansion and promising to develop an adventurous foreign policy. An opponent of slavery, he attempted to turn the nation's attention away from the slavery issue by proposing an ambitious foreign and domestic program. His domestic policy consisted of reducing the Treasury surplus by lowering customs rates and paying off the national debt. Pierce obtained congressional support for building a railroad to the Pacific Coast. He pursued an aggressive but mostly unproductive foreign policy. Pierce wished to force Britain out of Central America, to obtain Cuba from Spain, Alaska from Russia, and to seize Hawaii, but failed. During his administration, Commodore Matthew C. Perry inaugurated diplomatic and trade relations with Japan. However, it was Pierce's inability to handle rising agitation over the slavery issue that made him unacceptable as a candidate for a second term. A United States Historical Society poll of 1977 shows that Pierce received no vote on his rating, although Arthur M. Schlesinger, Jr.'s 1962 poll shows him as a below average president.

James Buchanan   Fifteenth president, born in Cove Gap near Mercersburg, Pennsylvania, on April 23, 1791. Buchanan's father was James Buchanan, his mother, Elizabeth Speer. He grew up in a frontier trading post near their home and learned the business from his father. In 1809 he graduated with honors from Dickinson College; he then studied law and was admitted to the bar in Lancaster in 1813. The following year he was elected to the lower house of the state legislature, while maintaining his law practice. His engagement to Ann Caroline Coleman ended, and he never married.

Buchanan was elected to the United States House of Representatives for five terms. As chairman of the House Judiciary Committee, he conducted the impeachment trial of Judge James Peck in 1830. Buchanan represented the United States at the Court of St. Petersburg from 1832 to 1833. Upon his return in 1834, he became a United States Senator, serving as chairman of the Foreign Relations Committee. President James K. Polk named him secretary of state in 1845. After the dissolution of the Federalist party, he became a Democrat. Following his failure to secure the Democratic nomination for president in 1852, he was sent by President Franklin Pierce as minister to Britain. On his return from England in 1856, he was nominated by the Democratic party for president and was elected.

Significance   James Buchanan became the only bachelor president. He took office at a time when the nation was headed toward civil war, and he could not avert it. He wrote: "The great object of my administration will be to arrest ... the agitation of the slavery question" (*Encyclopedia Americana* 1981, 674). Buchanan failed to silence slavery agitation but excluded extremists from his cabinet, selecting instead conservative politicians. On the slavery issue, he favored a popular referendum and a choice by state constitutions. Buchanan denied the right of states to secede. The Democratic party split in two, paving the way for the election of Abraham Lincoln. Buchanan, a lame duck president, urged President-Elect Lincoln to join him in a call for a constitutional convention in order to gain time, but Lincoln rejected the proposal. The seven states of the Deep South formed the confederacy on February 4, 1861. Buchanan succeeded in keeping eight of the fifteen states in the Union. Yet Buchanan, whose domestic and foreign policy fell victim to the slavery controversy, was a convenient scapegoat for the incoming Lincoln administration. Nothing of consequence that Buchanan attempted in domestic and foreign policy succeeded. Historians rate him at the bottom of the weak and below average presidents.

Abraham Lincoln   Sixteenth president, born in a log cabin near Hodgenville, Kentucky, on February 12, 1809. Lincoln's father was Thomas Lincoln, his mother, Nancy Hanks. Lincoln occasionally attended school in a log schoolhouse near their home. His entire schooling amounted to no more than one year. But he could read and write, had a desire to learn, and borrowed countless books from friends and acquaintances. Lincoln worked as a ferryman on the Ohio River. In 1830 his family moved from Indiana to Illinois. Lincoln enlisted as a volunteer in the Black Hawk War of 1832. Aspiring to be a politician, he lost his first election to the Illinois General Assembly but went on to win four terms beginning in 1834. He taught grammar and mathematics and began to study law books. In 1836 he passed the bar examination and set up practice in Springfield. Four years later he married Mary Todd.

In 1847 he was elected to the United States House of Representatives. Lincoln opposed the Mexican War, and the Kansas-Nebraska Act of 1854, which sanctioned the extension of slavery. In 1858 he failed in his bid for the United States Senate but gained national recognition in the process. The Republican party nominated him for president in 1860, on an antislavery platform. A split in the Democratic party resulted in the nomination of two candidates, Stephen A. Douglas and John C. Breckinridge. Another candidate, John Bell, was nominated by the Constitutional Union party. In a four-way contest Lincoln won the presidency. In 1864 Lincoln was reelected, carrying every state except Kentucky, Delaware, and New Jersey. On April 14, 1865, Lincoln was shot by actor John Wilkes Booth in Ford's Theater in Washington and died the next day.

Significance   Abraham Lincoln entered the presidency at a critical juncture in American history, just prior to the Civil War. Even before his inauguration, South Carolina had seceded from the Union. Lincoln stated decisively in his inaugural address that he would not accept a divided nation. He soon faced a crisis over Fort Sumter in Charleston Harbor: the Sumter garrison, unless supplied or withdrawn, would shortly be starved out. When notified of the approach of the federal supply fleet, the confederated authorities bombed the fort on April 12, 1861 and thus began the Civil War.

Because Congress was in recess, Lincoln mobilized the Union by executive order. He requisitioned 75,000 volunteers from the states, precipitating the secession of Virginia, North Carolina, Tennessee, and

Arkansas. Washington, D.C. was cut off from communication with the North. To maintain law and order, Lincoln exercised presidential war powers and directed that the *writ of habeas corpus* be suspended. He ordered an increase in the size of the regular army and navy and spent money without congressional authorization. As commander in chief, Lincoln supervised the commanders in the field and, on many occasions, he overruled the generals. By the summer of 1862, it was evident that military action alone would not prove successful; political action was required. In response to antislavery sentiments, Lincoln came forth with an emancipation plan. On September 22, 1862, after the battle of Antietam, Lincoln announced that slaves in territories in rebellion would be freed on January 1, 1863. Although his cabinet opposed it, the Emancipation Proclamation was issued on that date without congressional approval. Because Lincoln was uncertain whether his action would be sustained by the United States Supreme Court, he urged the Congress to adopt the Thirteenth Amendment to the Constitution, forever abolishing slavery in the nation; the amendment was ratified on December 19, 1865. He became the first president to be assassinated.

Lincoln is adjudged almost universally by historians and political scientists as the greatest and strongest president in American history, owing to his ability to use, seize, and expand power. The power of influence and the influence of power worked hand in hand with Lincoln. Robert K. Murray's survey of American presidents ranks Lincoln as the greatest and most powerful president in American history. Arthur M. Schlesinger, Jr.'s 1962 poll and the United States Historical Society poll of 1977 also rank Lincoln as America's greatest president. Yet his critics claim that he was an absolute dictator: Lincoln did not hesitate to censor newspapers and mail, confiscate private property, and try civilians in military courts, all in the name of preserving the Union. However, Lincoln's success rested on the fact that neither the Congress nor the Supreme Court curtailed his power.

Andrew Johnson   Seventeenth president, born on December 29, 1808, in Raleigh, North Carolina. Johnson's father was Jacob Johnson, his mother, Mary McDonough. He had no schooling but learned the basics of reading and writing from the foreman of a tailor shop. In 1826 he moved with his family and settled in Greeneville, Tennessee, where he opened another tailor shop. In 1827 he married Eliza McCardle, an educated woman, who taught Johnson writing and mathematics. Johnson soon turned to politics and organized a workingman's party that elected him alderman in 1828 and mayor of Greeneville in 1830. He served in the Tennessee House of Representatives and State Senate from

1835–1843. In 1843 he was elected to the United States House of Representatives and became a United States Senator in 1857.

Johnson worked to prevent Tennessee from joining the secession movement, the only southern senator to refuse to support his state's position. This forced him and his family to flee Tennessee, but he became a hero in the pro-Union North. Johnson allied with the Whigs and also maintained close relations with the Republicans. When Union forces occupied Tennessee, President Abraham Lincoln appointed Johnson military governor. In 1864 he was Lincoln's running mate and was elected vice president. Johnson became president on April 15, 1865, following Lincoln's assassination.

Significance   Andrew Johnson's administration faced the most vexing problems of the post–Civil War era. A strict constructionist, Johnson wanted to reconstruct the former confederate states. In a controversy with Congress over the president's power related to these states, Johnson proclaimed on May 26, 1865, an amnesty to most confederates if they would ratify the Thirteenth Amendment abolishing slavery, an offer that enraged Congress. Over his veto, the radicals in Congress passed a series of acts setting up a "radical reconstruction" plan based upon suffrage for blacks. Congress also restored military control over the South. Johnson suspected his secretary of war, Edwin M. Stanton, of working secretly with the radicals in Congress. When Johnson removed this untrustworthy adviser without Senate approval, as required by the Tenure of Office Act (passed earlier, over his veto, and later declared unconstitutional by the Supreme Court in 1925), the House of Representatives impeached him. The Senate acquitted him by one vote on May 26, 1868. Johnson quietly served out the remainder of his term.

One major achievement of his foreign policy was the purchase of Alaska from Russia in 1867, at a nominal cost of $7.2 million. While most historians rate Johnson as a weak and average president, some consider him a failure because of his controversial Reconstruction policy aimed at restoring the Union following the Civil War. Standing almost alone, Johnson faced the complexities of Reconstruction and became the only president ever to be impeached, although he was subsequently acquitted.

Ulysses Simpson Grant   Eighteenth president, born at Point Pleasant, Ohio, on April 27, 1832. Grant's father was Jesse Root Grant, his mother, Hannah Simpson. Although he attended grammar school, Grant had little interest in education. However, he won an appointment to the West Point Military Academy, graduated in 1843 as a second lieutenant, and was assigned to the United States Fourth Infantry. In 1848 he married Julia Boggs Dent. Grant resigned in 1854, after serving in the Mexican War. In 1860 he moved to Galena, Illinois, and went to work as a clerk in his father's store.

When the Civil War broke out, Grant offered his services to the United States government. President Abraham Lincoln named him brigadier general of volunteers. He won Forts Henry and Donelson, fought at Shiloh, and took Vicksburg. After his victory at Chattanooga, President Lincoln promoted Grant to major general in the Union army. On April 9, 1865, Grant accepted General Robert E. Lee's surrender. Grant was brought to Washington to receive a gold medal voted by Congress, as well as the newly created rank of lieutenant general, and the command of the entire United States Army. In 1866 he was given the rank of full general (newly created). Grant was appointed secretary of war by President Andrew Johnson but failed to win confirmation. In 1868 he received the Republican nomination for president and was elected.

Significance   Ulysses S. Grant came to the presidency with little experience, and he made many political mistakes. He picked personal friends, often cronies, for his cabinet. His halfhearted efforts to enforce the Fourteenth and Fifteenth Amendments proved futile. Most blacks had been driven from the polls, and the southern states voted Democratic. Grant, however, suspended the *writ of habeas corpus* in parts of South Carolina where the Ku Klux Klan was terrorizing blacks. Grant was reelected in 1872, but railroad scandals involving several prominent Republican congressmen and high government officials dominated public attention during his second term. His secretary of war received bribes, and his private secretary was involved in a whiskey ring. Although none of these scandals involved the president personally, many other officials in his administration were involved in corrupt activities. This resulted in a declining confidence in government; hence Grant has been universally rated a weak president who miserably failed in the performance of his duties.

Rutherford Birchard Hayes   Nineteenth president, born in Delaware, Ohio, on October 4, 1822. Hayes's father was Rutherford Hayes, his mother, Sophia Birchard. Hayes attended a private school in Delaware, an academy at Norwalk, and a preparatory school in Middletown, Connecticut. In 1842 he graduated from Kenyon College and from Harvard Law School in 1845. In 1852 he married Lucy Ware Webb. He served four years in the army during the Civil War, was wounded five times, and achieved the rank of major general. In 1864 he was elected to the United States House of Representatives where he supported Reconstruction and the impeachment of President Andrew Johnson. Hayes resigned from Congress, was elected governor of Ohio in 1867 and reelected in 1869. In 1876 he became Ohio's favorite son candidate for the Republican presidential nomination. Hayes went to sleep thinking he had lost the election to his Democratic opponent, Samuel J. Tilden, as early returns showed him running behind. The Republicans contested Democratic claims in South Carolina, Florida, Louisiana, and Oregon, and submitted two sets of electoral votes to Congress. An electoral commission was created, composed of fifteen members representing the Republican Senate and Democratic House, and the Supreme Court had to decide which set of electoral votes should be counted. The commission awarded all disputed votes to Hayes, giving him 185 electoral votes to Tilden's 184. The popular vote in the election was as follows: Hayes, 4,035,924; Tilden, 4,287,670. This election demonstrated that it is quite possible to have a minority president, one who receives a majority of the electoral vote even though garnering fewer popular votes than the opponent.

Significance   Rutherford B. Hayes was inaugurated on March 5, 1877, although the vote counting was completed on March 2. Keeping a promise to his southern supporters, Hayes withdrew troops from areas still occupied in the South. He also fulfilled his promise to appoint southerners to his cabinet (David Key, who had been a confederate colonel, was appointed postmaster general).

In addition to this reconciliation with the South, his administration resulted in two other notable achievements: resumption of specie payments of paper currency and civil service reform. The railroad strikes of 1877 required Hayes to send federal troops into ten states to preserve law and order. His presidency was noted for banning alcohol in the White House, in deference to the wishes of his wife. In foreign affairs, Hayes announced that an American-controlled canal across Panama was a goal of his administration. Hayes reached an agreement with the Chinese government regulating Chinese immigration. Historians generally view Hayes as an average president, although a highly principled politician who kept his pledge to serve only one term. By trying to heal the nation's Civil War wounds, Hayes elevated the image of the presidency.

James Abram Garfield   Twentieth president, born on November 19, 1831, in a log cabin on a farm in Orange, Cuyahoga County, Ohio. Garfield's father was Abram Garfield, his mother, Eliza Ballou. After attending the neighborhood school, Garfield enrolled in the seminary. In 1856 he graduated from Williams College with distinction. Garfield taught at Hiram College and later became principal. In 1858 he married Lucretia Rudolph. Garfield showed an early interest in politics and actively opposed slavery. In 1859 he was elected as a Republican to the Ohio Senate. At the start of the Civil War, he recruited a regiment consisting of many of his former students at Hiram College. Garfield became colonel of the Forty-second Ohio Infantry and then brigadier in 1862. He fought at the battle of Shiloh and was promoted to major for his gallantry.

Garfield resigned his commission to become a member of the United States House of Representatives and served in the Congress from 1863 to 1880. He sided with the radical Republicans in supporting black suffrage, Reconstruction, and the impeachment of President Andrew Johnson. He helped elect President Rutherford B. Hayes, serving on the commission that settled the disputed election. During the Hayes' administration, he became the minority leader of the House. In 1880, when he was senator-elect, he was nominated for president. Garfield was elected with a margin of only 10,000 popular votes.

Significance   James A. Garfield was a competent president, but in his brief stint of less than four months in office he had little opportunity to evidence his talents. A bitter struggle ensued over the confirmation of a customs nominee in New York and developed into a personal clash between Garfield and Senator Roscoe Conkling (R-N.Y.). Garfield won this political battle, and his victory strengthened his power. During his brief administration, Garfield laid the foundation for improved relations with Latin America.

On July 2, 1881, Garfield was shot by a disgruntled office seeker, Charles J. Guiteau, in a Washington rail station. His long disability raised for the first time the problem of presidential succession. For eighty days the president was able to sign only one official paper (an extradition document). Political scientists and constitutional experts agree that in such cases, the vice president is empowered to assume the duties of the president. However, ambiguity existed in the pertinent provision of the Constitution (Article II, Section 1). This anomaly has been clarified by the adoption of the Twenty-fifth Amendment to the Constitution in 1967. Garfield's four-month presidency is remembered for its struggle over patronage and the beginning of "good neighbor" relations with Latin America. Had Garfield not served as president, he probably would have earned a place in American history as a distinguished congressman.

Chester Alan Arthur   Twenty-first president, born in Fairfield, Vermont, on October 5, 1829. Arthur's father was William Arthur, his mother, Malvina Stone. Arthur graduated from Union College with honors in 1848, became a school teacher, and studied law at the same

time. In 1853 he joined a law office in New York and was soon admitted
to the bar. The next year he married Ellen Herndon. Arthur participated in local politics in New York City and joined the state militia. At
the time of the Civil War, he was engineer in chief in the New York
governor's office. Later, he became the state's assistant quartermaster
general. In 1862, when President Abraham Lincoln requested 300,000
additional troops, Arthur was promoted to the position of quartermaster general. President Ulysses S. Grant appointed him collector of
customs in New York in 1871. Arthur was delegate-at-large to the
Republican National Convention in 1880. In the midst of the conflict
over the presidential nomination, James A. Garfield was selected as the
nominee for president, and Arthur was nominated for vice president.
The Garfield-Arthur ticket won the election, and when President Garfield died on September 19, 1881, Arthur took the oath of office on the
following day.

Significance   As president, Chester A. Arthur showed great responsibility, and his inaugural address was reassuring. Contrary to general
expectations, Arthur filled federal offices with competent persons. He
developed a moderate legislative program and asked Congress for tariff
revision and reduction of excise taxes. Despite a huge revenue surplus,
Congress refused to pass his bill. He was very concerned about national
defense and secured increased appropriations for the navy. Arthur
authorized the construction of the navy's first steel cruisers and vetoed a
huge pork barrel appropriations bill for the improvement of rivers and
harbors. Both vetoes were overridden. Arthur also vetoed a Chinese
exclusion bill barring Chinese nationals from admission as immigrants,
but he signed into law the reformed Civil Service Act of 1883, which
established a merit system for appointments. Another law passed during
his administration was the Anti-Polygamy Act. Reputed to be a fac-
tionalist and party opportunist, Arthur assumed the presidency at a
time of intense factional controversy following the assassination of President Garfield. Although he surprised the country with an honest
administration, Arthur has been rated an average president because of
his limited achievements at home and practically none abroad.

Grover Cleveland   Twenty-second and twenty-fourth president,
born in Caldwell, Essex County, New Jersey, on March 18, 1837.
Cleveland's father was Richard Falley Cleveland, his mother, Ann Neal.
The family moved to New York, where Cleveland attended the town
academy. Cleveland worked in a general store and taught at the New
York Institution for the Blind. He studied law, clerked in a Buffalo law
firm, and was admitted to the bar in 1859. During the Civil War,

Cleveland was drafted but hired a substitute under the commutation provision of the law. After the Civil War, he became the sheriff of Erie County, New York. Elected mayor of Buffalo in 1881 to rid the city administration of corruption, he thoroughly reorganized the various departments and introduced corporate methods for running the administration. In 1883 he became the governor of New York. The Democrats nominated Cleveland for president in 1884, while the Republicans nominated James G. Blaine. In one of the most bitter campaigns in American political history, Cleveland won the election. In 1892 Cleveland ran for his second nonconsecutive term against incumbent Benjamin Harrison, whom he defeated.

Significance   Grover Cleveland is the only president to have served two nonconsecutive terms. He has been ruled the twenty-second and twenty-fourth president by the Department of State because his two terms were not consecutive. Cleveland's first victory ended twenty-four years of unbroken Republican control of the presidency. His first term was characterized by firmness and fair play. Cleveland made extensive use of the veto power, refusing to sign 413 bills (some records show 414 bills). Until that time, this was the highest number of vetoes exercised by any president. Many of these bills involved imaginary private pensions for Civil War veterans. To stop scandals and raids on the Treasury, Cleveland was the first president to veto private pension bills. In 1887 there was a large revenue surplus because of high tariff duties on imports. This protective tariff contributed to higher prices for consumers, and Cleveland took the initiative to lower the tariff. He was the first president to devote his entire annual message to Congress to a single topic: the dangers of the high tariff. However, he was unable to secure an effective law to solve the problem.

His second term proved to be stormier. A severe depression and labor trouble struck the country, followed by financial crises. He sent federal troops to break the bitter Pullman strike of 1894, which had interrupted railroad and mail service. Although he saved the nation from abandoning the gold standard, his efforts to improve the economy bore no results. In the absence of unemployment compensation and other social welfare benefits, many of the nation's 4 million unemployed (out of a total population of 65 million) suffered severe hardship.

Cleveland partially recovered his popularity by successful foreign policy negotiations. At his initiative, the boundary dispute between British Guiana and Venezuela was arbitrated. He stood by his anti-imperialistic convictions and refused aid to rebel movements in Hawaii and Cuba. His greatness as a president rests more on his character than on his accomplishments. Cleveland is judged as a strong and near great president—for his decency, integrity, and courage—by historians, especially Allan Nevins, who has made an extensive study of Cleveland.

Benjamin Harrison   Twenty-third president, born at North Bend, near Cincinnati, Ohio, on August 20, 1833. Harrison's father was John Scott Harrison (the son of William Henry Harrison, the ninth president of the United States), his mother, Elizabeth Irwin. He was prepared for college by private tutors, went to the Farmer's College, near Cincinnati, and graduated from Miami University at Oxford, Ohio. In 1853 Harrison married Caroline Scott. The next year he studied law and was admitted to the bar. Later, Harrison moved to Indianapolis, set up his law practice, and was elected city attorney not long thereafter. In the Civil War, he fought at various places, including Nashville and Atlanta. In recognition of his ability, he was promoted to the rank of brigadier general.

Although he failed to be elected governor of Indiana, the campaign won him national prominence. President Rutherford B. Hayes appointed him to the Mississippi River Commission in 1879. The following year he was elected to the United States Senate, where he gained a reputation as an eloquent speaker and a skillful legislative draftsman. He was a favorite son candidate for the Republican presidential nomination in 1888. Harrison conducted his campaign mostly from his home, delivering eighty speeches to more than 300,000 people who visited him. In the ensuing election, he defeated Grover Cleveland. The Republicans renominated Harrison in 1892, and once again he ran against Cleveland, but this time he was defeated.

Significance   Benjamin Harrison was inaugurated 100 years after the election of George Washington and the adoption of the American Constitution. He came from a most distinguished family and further distinguished himself as the Centennial President. Although his administration was marked by a deteriorating domestic situation, he adopted new ventures in foreign policy. Harrison attempted to solve the nation's pressing economic problems by recommending several important measures, among them the Sherman Antitrust Act, the Sherman Silver Purchase Act, the McKinley Tariff Act, and the Dependent Pension Act. During his presidency, the United States participated in the Pan-American Conference in Washington in 1899; was represented at the Berlin Conference on the Samoan islands; called an international monetary conference; concluded commercial treaties with many nations; and resolved a bitter controversy between Chile and Britain. However, his administration failed to annex Hawaii. Ranked today as an average president, in his era Harrison demonstrated marked leadership that enabled the United States to approach world power.

William McKinley   Twenty-fifth president, born at Niles, Ohio, on January 29, 1843. McKinley's father was also named William McKinley, his mother, Nancy Allison. McKinley received his secondary education at an academy in Poland, Ohio. He entered Allegheny College, where his studies were cut short by illness. McKinley taught school briefly before joining the Twenty-third Ohio Volunteer Regiment at the outset of the Civil War. In 1865 he distinguished himself in action and was appointed a major. After studying law in Ohio and New York, McKinley was admitted to the Ohio bar. He practiced law in Canton, Ohio and was elected prosecuting attorney of Stark County. In 1871 he married Ida Saxton.

In 1876 he was elected to the United States House of Representatives, where he served six terms. McKinley was elected and reelected governor of Ohio in 1891 and 1893. In 1896 he received the Republican nomination for president and won the election by defeating his Democratic opponent, William Jennings Bryan. He was reelected in 1900, once again defeating Bryan, but by a more sizable margin the second time. On September 6, 1901, McKinley was assassinated by Leon Czolgosz, an anarchist, and he died eight days later.

Significance   William McKinley's one major accomplishment in domestic policy was that he called a special session of Congress to revise customs duties. Congress enacted the Dingley Tariff, which provided for the highest average duties yet established. McKinley was an ardent proponent of the gold standard.

McKinley's administration was dominated by foreign policy conflicts. Spain relinquished Cuba and ceded Puerto Rico, Guam, and the Philippines to the United States. The United States annexed Hawaii in 1898. McKinley's administration won a landmark agreement, an Open Door policy for Chinese trade. During the consequent Boxer Rebellion, led by Chinese opposed to the West, McKinley sent 5,000 American troops to China to safeguard Western interests. This was done without congressional approval. McKinley looked forward to a second term focused on domestic rather than on international issues. Less than six months after his inauguration, he was felled by an assassin. Although the expansion of presidential power so characteristic of the twentieth century began during his term, contemporary historians unkindly rank McKinley as an average president because he offered no permanent solutions to problems.

Theodore Roosevelt   Twenty-sixth president, born in New York City on October 27, 1858. Roosevelt's father was also named Theodore Roosevelt, his mother, Martha Bullock. Roosevelt was fifth cousin to Franklin D. Roosevelt, the thirty-second president, and uncle to Franklin's wife Eleanor. His parents provided him with an early education through private tutoring. During his undergraduate years at Harvard College, Roosevelt wrote a book entitled *The Naval War of 1812*, which was published upon his graduation in 1880. The same year he married Alice Hathaway Lee. In 1881 he was elected to the New York Assembly. President Benjamin Harrison appointed him a member of the United States Civil Service Commission, and President William McKinley named him assistant secretary of state. Roosevelt resigned the latter office during the Spanish-American War in 1898 to join the First United States Volunteer Cavalry as a lieutenant colonel. While serving in Puerto Rico, he was promoted to colonel. His heroic battle exploits at San Juan established his reputation throughout the United States. Roosevelt was later elected governor of New York. He campaigned vigorously for the vice presidency with incumbent President McKinley in 1900 and was elected on the Republican ticket. Following McKinley's death on September 14, 1901, Roosevelt took the oath of office. In 1904, he was elected president to a full term.

Significance   Theodore Roosevelt took the oath of office at age forty-two, the nation's youngest president. He fought political corruption by special interests; dissolved Northern Securities for violating antitrust laws; intervened in a celebrated coal strike; and secured passage of the Elkins Law, a measure prohibiting rebates to corporations. Roosevelt was an outspoken proponent of the navy, each year asking Congress for larger and larger appropriations. He built the navy into one of the major sea forces in the world. In 1903 he bought a French company's rights to construct a canal through Panama. Roosevelt withdrew American troops from Cuba and warned the Germans not to intervene in Venezuela. To expand America's influence in the world, he ordered the United States Navy around the globe as a show of military might. During his second term, he won passage of the Hepburn Act, which gave the Interstate Commerce Commission (ICC) power to regulate railroad rates and prohibited discrimination among shippers. In 1906 he won approval of the now-heralded Pure Food and Drug Act.

Roosevelt mediated peace between Japan and Russia; his skillful diplomacy won him the Nobel Peace Prize. His administration sought to cultivate friendly relations with Japan and recognized its suzerainty in Korea. Roosevelt forced the San Francisco school board to allow Japanese children in public schools. The United States also recognized Japan's ascendancy in Manchuria, while Japan reaffirmed an Open

Door policy in China. Roosevelt is the most widely published president; he wrote over 2,000 works, including 40 books. Historians rate him as a near great president, because he was popular and at the same time controversial. Roosevelt was a strong president, greatly expanding presidential power abroad, thereby making the United States a major force in world affairs. He did much to inspire the nation's confidence in the presidency; many presidents from Abraham Lincoln to Roosevelt had been lackluster and ineffective leaders, and during these years the presidency declined in prestige and influence.

William Howard Taft   Twenty-seventh president, born in Cincinnati, Ohio, on September 15, 1857. Taft's father was Alphonso Taft, his mother, Louise Torrey. In 1878 he graduated with distinction from Yale University and, within two years, graduated from Cincinnati Law School and was admitted to the bar. Taft became assistant prosecuting attorney of Hamilton County. In 1886 he married Helen Herron. The next year, Taft was appointed a judge of the superior court of Ohio and was later named solicitor general of the United States. President Benjamin Harrison named him to the Sixth United States Circuit. In 1900 President William McKinley appointed him head of a commission to terminate United States military rule in the Philippines. The following year, he became the first civil governor of the Philippines. In 1904 President Theodore Roosevelt appointed Taft the secretary of war. Taft was in direct charge of the construction of the Panama Canal. In 1906, in the face of an impending revolution in Cuba, he effected a peaceful settlement. Taft improved Japanese-American relations, despite the abuse of immigration laws. These achievements gave Taft the Republican nomination for president in 1908, and he was elected.

Significance   William Howard Taft vigorously enforced the Sherman Antitrust Act, bringing twice as many antitrust suits against large corporations as had the previous administration of President Theodore Roosevelt. Taft's administration inherited widespread demands for a lower tariff; he accepted the compromise Payne-Aldrich Act of 1909, providing downward revision of the tariff. This angered the progressive Republicans and big business. His administration dissolved the Standard Oil Company, established the Labor Department, proposed a federal income tax, and drafted an amendment providing for direct election of senators. Taft saw the creation of a postal savings system and the admission of Arizona and New Mexico to the United States. The last year of his administration was clouded by a quarrel with his predecessor (Roosevelt) that culminated in the disruption of the Republican party. Taft has been ranked as a weak and average president because of his restrictive use of power; he was so timid that he even viewed himself as a constrained actor in his relations with Congress. He once said: "The President can exercise no power which cannot be fairly and reasonably traced to some specific grant of power or justly implied." Taft was afraid of taking risks and bold action.

Woodrow Wilson   Twenty-eighth president, born in Staunton, Virginia, on December 28, 1856. Wilson's father was Joseph Ruggles Wilson, his mother, Janet Woodrow. He briefly attended Davidson College in North Carolina before entering the College of New Jersey (now Princeton University) in 1875. After graduation from Princeton, he studied law at the University of Virginia in 1897 but had to withdraw because of poor health. Wilson continued his studies at home and then opened a law office in Atlanta. Following an unsuccessful attempt at legal practice, he pursued graduate studies in government and history at Johns Hopkins University in Baltimore and received his Ph.D. degree in 1886. In the meantime, he married Ellen Louise Axson. In 1888 Wilson accepted a professorship at Connecticut Wesleyan University. Within two years, he became a professor of jurisprudence and political economy at Princeton University and was chosen president of Princeton in 1902. As a professor, and later as president of Princeton, Wilson achieved national recognition owing to his scholarly publications and innovative programs. In 1911 he was elected governor of New Jersey. The next year, Wilson was nominated for president by the Democratic party and was elected.

Significance   Woodrow Wilson worked hard to follow through on his campaign promises. Reviving President George Washington's idea of a personal appearance before Congress, Wilson delivered his State of the Union message to Congress, breaking a century-old precedent. He called Congress into a special session to redeem his promise of tariff reform. The new tariff act was followed by a measure aimed at currency reform. The Federal Reserve Act was signed into law in 1913, and the federal income tax was instituted. The following year the Federal Trade Commission was established. In foreign affairs, Wilson protected American interests in revolutionary Mexico and defended American rights on the high seas.

However, foreign affairs were dominated by the outbreak of World War I in Europe. At the beginning of the war the United States proclaimed neutrality, but ultimately joined on the Allied side. This proved to be politically beneficial and helped Wilson win a second term as president. In his famous Fourteen Points address of January 8, 1918, President Wilson reiterated his call for world peace and the establishment of a postwar international organization, the League of Nations, dedicated to international cooperation. The Germans accepted his armistice plan, and Wilson himself attended the peace conference in Paris. Wilson was stunned when the United States Senate refused to ratify the Versailles Treaty which would have created the League of Nations. To salvage the treaty, he traveled 8,000 miles across the country and delivered 40 addresses to create public support for the League of Nations. As a result of his contributions to world peace, Wilson was awarded the Nobel Peace Prize in 1919. Later, personal exhaustion resulted in a severe stroke and paralysis. He remained incapacitated for an extended period of time and was unable to discharge his official duties. Most historians rank Wilson as a great and strong president because he enlarged presidential power, owing to the events of World War I. Wilson took control of the vast new problems of military and industrial mobilization, and his dynamic leadership brought the war to a successful conclusion, ensuring victory to the Allied powers. He not only directed the armed forces effectively as commander in chief but also managed the wartime economy well and rallied the American people to the war effort.

Warren Gamaliel Harding   Twenty-ninth president, born on November 2, 1865, in Blooming Grove, Morrow County, Ohio. Harding's father was George Tyron Harding II, his mother, Phoebe Elizabeth Dickerson. After attending local schools, he went to Ohio Central College. He found employment on a weekly newspaper, the *Marion Democratic Mirror* and, soon thereafter, the *Marion Star*. In 1891 Harding married Florence Kling De Wolfe, who took charge of the paper. From 1900 to 1904, he was an Ohio state senator and served as lieutenant governor from 1904 to 1906. In 1914 he was elected United States senator, and in 1920 he received the Republican presidential nomination. Imitating President William McKinley, Harding conducted a front porch campaign, as well as a speaking tour. He was the beneficiary of the nation's war weariness, and the electorate welcomed his promise of a return to normalcy. Harding won the election for president.

Significance   Warren G. Harding's landslide victory in the election was more negative than positive; it was a repudiation of President Woodrow Wilson's policies, coupled with postwar frustrations. Under Harding, the White House took on a lax atmosphere. Harding called a special session of Congress and recommended the retrenchment of government, lowering of taxes, repeal of wartime excess profits tax, reduction in railroad rates, a national budget system, and a department of public welfare. His major accomplishment was the creation of the

Bureau of the Budget. He appointed several distinguished figures to his cabinet, among them Secretary of State Charles Evans Hughes, Secretary of Commerce Herbert Hoover, and Secretary of Agriculture Henry A. Wallace.

Corruption was rampant in his administration. The most sensational scandal during his presidency centered around Teapot Dome, Wyoming, and the California oil reserves. Secretary of the Interior Albert B. Fall transferred jurisdiction over these oil reserves from the Department of the Navy to the Department of the Interior and then leased them to oil interests in exchange for a bribe, for which he was eventually incarcerated in a federal penitentiary. Harding called for political, economic, and educational equality of the races—a bold step at that time. In the field of foreign affairs, he convened an international conference on the Limitation of Armaments in 1921. Harding is rated at the bottom of failures as president because the Teapot Dome scandal is linked with him as a symbol of corruption.

Calvin Coolidge   Thirtieth president, born at Plymouth, Vermont, on July 4, 1872. Coolidge's father was John Calvin Coolidge, his mother, Victoria Moor. After being educated in local schools, Coolidge graduated from Amherst College in 1895. He studied law and was admitted to the bar at Northampton, Massachusetts, in 1897. The next year he was elected as a city councilman. In 1905 he married Anna Goodhue. In 1906 Coolidge was elected to the Massachusetts House of Representatives, and later mayor of Northampton, state senator, and then lieutenant governor for three terms, beginning in 1916.

In 1918 Coolidge was elected governor of Massachusetts. Although he began his administration with moderation, Coolidge attained national prominence by calling out the state militia in the Boston police strike, which contributed to his reelection. At the 1920 Republican national convention, Coolidge was among a number of minor candidates for the presidential nomination, but the party nominated Warren G. Harding and selected Coolidge for vice president. The Harding-Coolidge ticket won. As vice president, Coolidge broke tradition by attending cabinet meetings. Upon the death of President Harding, Coolidge became president on August 2, 1923.

Significance   Calvin Coolidge was sworn in by his father at the family's rural home in Vermont when President Harding died. Coolidge created a precedent by taking the oath of office from his father. Initially, he set out to establish a working relationship with key officials in the Harding administration but slowly brought about a reformation in the administration. Coolidge gained sufficient control of the divided Republican party to be nominated for president. Rampant dissention in the Democratic party helped to secure his election as president.

During his full term, he decreased the national debt by $2 billion. He reduced income taxes, making more money available for consumer spending. Coolidge took a laissez-faire attitude toward business and industry, minimizing governmental intervention in economic affairs, but he sought to provide relief to financially troubled farmers. In foreign affairs, he pursued a policy of nonintervention, and his administration opposed the League of Nations. Pursuing his "good neighbor" policy toward Latin America, he restored diplomatic relations with Mexico. The most notable foreign policy accomplishment of his administration was the negotiation of the Kellogg-Briand pact in 1927 to renounce war. However, the pact was rendered irrelevant at the outbreak of World War II. Coolidge has been rated by historians as a below average president. His accomplishments in the domestic realm, debt and tax reduction, were temporary and later forgotten by the nation.

Herbert Clark Hoover   Thirty-first president, born on August 10, 1874, in West Branch, Iowa. Hoover's father was Jesse Clark Hoover, his mother, Hulda Randall Minthorn. Hoover attended the public school at West Branch. Upon the death of his mother when he was eight (his father died earlier), Hoover moved to Newberg, Oregon, to live with his uncle. There Hoover attended a Quaker academy and in 1891 entered Stanford University as a special student in its first freshman class. He defrayed his college expenses by typing and delivering newspapers until his graduation as an engineer in 1895. Hoover began his career by doing odd jobs and later became a mining engineer in Colorado. In 1897 he went to work for the British mining firm of Bewick, Moreing and Company as chief of its gold mining operations in Australia. Hoover engaged in mining activities throughout the world, maintaining offices in New York, San Francisco, and London. The Chinese government offered him the position of chief engineer of the Chinese Engineering and Mining Company, where he directed food relief for victims of the Boxer Rebellion. Before leaving for China, he married Lou Henry in 1899. Hoover established himself as a world renowned engineer and acquired considerable wealth. During World War I, he directed the American Relief Committee in London. After the war, President Woodrow Wilson appointed him United States Food Administrator, charged with feeding people in defeated nations. Hoover served as secretary of commerce under Presidents Warren G. Harding and Calvin Coolidge. In 1928 he won the presidency, defeating Democratic candidate Alfred E. Smith.

Significance   Herbert Hoover began his administration under auspicious circumstances. He called Congress into special session to consider farm relief and changes in the tariff. His administration was dominated by one major development: a nationwide depression. In 1929 the stock market plummeted and the economy collapsed, leaving 12 to 14 million people unemployed. On his recommendation, Congress appropriated $500 million and established the Reconstruction Finance Corporation (RFC) in 1932. The RFC provided indirect relief to the unemployed and offered financial assistance to insurance companies, banks, farms, railroads, and state, county, and city governments to stimulate the economy. This inaugurated the first program of government assistance to the needy.

In foreign affairs, Hoover opposed the League of Nations but supported disarmament. The only tangible achievement of his administration in foreign affairs was the signing of the London Naval Treaty of 1930, which placed limits on the number and type of naval vessels, battleships, and cruisers that each nation might build. Hoover's presidency was dominated by the Great Depression, which proved a bitter disappointment for him. People held Hoover responsible for their plight, and he was soundly defeated for reelection. He is considered an average president; historians have accused him of limiting presidential power.

Franklin Delano Roosevelt   Thirty-second president, born at Hyde Park, New York, on January 30, 1882. Roosevelt's father was James Roosevelt, his mother, Sara Delano (she was sixth cousin to his father, and President Theodore Roosevelt was Franklin's fifth cousin). Roosevelt received his early education from governesses and private tutors. At age fourteen he entered Groton School in Massachusetts. This school, modeled after the public schools of England, emphasized Christian ethics and the virtues of public service. In 1904 he graduated from Harvard University, entered Columbia Law School, and was later admitted to the bar. Roosevelt married his fifth cousin, Ann Eleanor, in 1905. He was elected a New York state senator in 1910 and 1913 and was later named assistant secretary of the navy by President Woodrow Wilson. Roosevelt ran unsuccessfully for vice president in 1920 after which he then returned to his law practice. Soon polio paralyzed his legs, forcing him to walk with braces and cane. In 1928 Roosevelt was elected governor of New York. During his two terms as governor, he acted vigorously to mobilize the state government, particularly when the depression became catastrophic. In the 1932 presidential election, he directed his campaign against the depression and promised to repeal prohibition; he was elected president.

Significance   Franklin D. Roosevelt inherited a desperate economic situation in the country. As many as 14 million people were unemployed, with some 2 million wandering the country looking for jobs. Many panic-stricken depositors, hoping to withdraw their money, found the banks closed in thirty-eight states. Roosevelt asked Congress for emergency powers, proclaimed the New Deal, and adopted major administrative changes. Two key recovery measures were the Agricultural Adjustment Administration and the National Industrial Recovery Act. He quickly introduced a banking reform. The Federal Deposit Insurance Corporation (FDIC) was created, guaranteeing bank deposits. The powers of the Federal Reserve System were increased. The United States went off the gold standard. The Securities and Exchange Commission regulated the stock exchanges. The Federal Emergency Relief Administration was established, and Congress appropriated $500 million in relief grants to state and local governments. Public funds were appropriated for public works programs, administered by the newly created Public Works Administration. Congress also approved funding for the Civilian Conservation Corps, which employed large numbers of people in reforestation and flood-control work. To help home buyers, the Home Owners Loan Corporation and the Federal Housing Administration were established. Roosevelt consolidated existing farm credit agencies into the Farm Credit Administration.

Although his policies did not go so far as to embrace the socialism that Karl Marx had advocated, they were seen by some people (particularly those on the political right) as moving in that direction. He alienated conservatives, but he was reelected with the support of farmers, laborers, and the underprivileged. On January 20, 1937, he became the first president to be sworn in under the Twentieth Amendment to the Constitution. (Before this amendment was adopted, a president elected in November did not take office until the following March.) During his second term, Roosevelt vigorously pressed his earlier case for public housing, fair labor standards, and aid to tenant farmers. He was the first president to use radio to speak directly to the American people. His famous fireside chats proved extremely popular and effective.

By 1939 Roosevelt was spending considerable time on foreign affairs, as World War II threatened Europe. Roosevelt eschewed the isolationist sentiments rampant in the country but hoped to avoid entanglement in war. Many Americans were opposed to giving the president an unprecedented third term, yet he won the election against a relatively progressive Republican, Wendell Willkie. During his third term, Roosevelt secured passage of the Lend-Lease Act, enabling the United States to offer financial aid to Britain and later to the Soviet Union. When a German submarine fired a torpedo at the American destroyer *Greer*, Roosevelt ordered United States warships to shoot German ships on sight. When Japan attacked Pearl Harbor, Hawaii, in 1941, Roosevelt requested Congress to officially declare war. During the war, he concentrated on strategy and negotiation, conferring with Allied leaders at Casablanca, Quebec, Tehran, Cairo, and Yalta. On January 1, 1942, the United States and the Allies signed the Declaration of the United Nations. With the war still in progress, Roosevelt became the only president to have been elected to a fourth term. His hope to bring the war to an early close and to attend a conference in San Francisco to draft a United Nations Charter was not fulfilled because of his sudden death. Historian Robert K. Murray's survey of 970 fellow historians in 1983 ranked Roosevelt as the second greatest president after Abraham Lincoln, because he was not afraid of using power and expanding it for the public's welfare. Roosevelt was a charismatic leader whose bold initiatives in domestic and foreign affairs helped sustain the morale of the Americans during the greatest crises of their history—economic depression and world war.

Harry S Truman   Thirty-third president, born in Lamar, Montana, on May 8, 1884. Truman's father was John Anderson Truman, his mother, Martha Ellen Young. The middle name *S* in Truman's name is not an abbreviation. It is used because both of his grandfathers had names beginning with the letter *S*. Truman graduated from high school at age 17 and did not attend college because of financial difficulties. He was employed as a bank clerk in Kansas City, Missouri. Although poor eyesight prevented him from attending West Point, World War I provided an opportunity for a career in the army, and he served in France as a captain. After returning home in 1919, he married Elizabeth Bess Wallace and established a haberdashery in Kansas City. The business failed, leaving him with a debt of $20,000. Truman became a judge of Jackson County Court in 1922 and entered Kansas Law School the following year. In 1934 Truman was elected United States Senator and reelected in 1940. In 1944, with the support of President Franklin D. Roosevelt, he was nominated and elected vice president. When President Roosevelt died, on April 12, 1945, Truman was inaugurated as president. He was elected president in 1948, defeating his opponent, Thomas E. Dewey.

Significance   Harry S Truman's legislative agenda, which he called the Fair Deal, included many far-reaching reforms. But the pressure of the last days of World War II forced him to abandon many of these programs. Truman attended the Potsdam summit conference with British Prime Minister Winston Churchill and Soviet Premier Joseph Stalin, in order to resolve postwar problems. Truman brought to fruition the plans for the surrender of Germany and the establishment of the United Nations. In 1945 he authorized detonation of the first atomic bomb against Japan. He proclaimed the Truman Doctrine, intended to aid nations that were threatened by communism, such as Greece and Turkey. Truman was responsible for creating the North Atlantic Treaty Organization (NATO) to combat aggression. His administration instituted the Marshall Plan to help restore Europe's shattered economy. Truman broke the Soviet blockade of West Berlin by ordering a massive airlift. In 1950 he won United Nations approval for military intervention in Korea and sent United States troops there under the command of General Douglas MacArthur. The next year he removed MacArthur for publicly disobeying orders by expanding the war into North Korea. Truman seized the steel industry to end a strike, but his action was ruled unconstitutional by the United States Supreme Court. He decided not to seek reelection. Among recent presidents, Truman has been ranked a near great chief executive, although some historians have attacked his record at home and abroad. Many political scientists consider him an architect of the cold war that heralded the beginning of his presidency.

Dwight David Eisenhower   Thirty-fourth president, born on October 14, 1890, in Denison, Texas. Eisenhower's father was David Eisenhower, his mother, Ida Elizabeth Stover. Nicknamed Ike in his boyhood, Eisenhower distinguished himself in athletic competition through grade school and high school. In 1911 he entered the United States Military Academy at West Point and graduated in 1915. The following year he married Mamie Geneva Doud. In 1917 he was appointed captain in the United States Army and was promoted to major in 1920. Eisenhower served in the Panama Canal Zone from 1922 to 1924. He graduated first in a class of 275 from the army's command and general staff school in 1926 and graduated from the Army War College in 1928. From 1929 to 1933, Eisenhower served in the office of the assistant secretary of war. As an assistant to the chief of staff, he was associated with the founding of the Army Industrial College, and he devised an industrial mobilization plan for use in case of war. Eisenhower spent four years in the Philippines, assisting General Douglas MacArthur to build up the defenses of the islands.

During World War II, he was commander of the Allied forces landing in North Africa in 1942. The next year he was promoted to a full general. In 1943 he became supreme Allied commander in Europe. When he took over the Supreme Headquarters of the Allied Expeditionary Force, he found himself in command of the largest single military operation ever attempted. On June 6, 1944, he led the Normandy invasion, and on May 7, 1945, he received the surrender of the Germans at Rheims.

Eisenhower returned home to serve as chief of staff. In 1948 he was appointed president of Columbia University. President Harry S Truman appointed him commander of the newly created Supreme Headquarters for the North Atlantic Treaty Organization (NATO). Eisenhower resigned from the army and was nominated for president in 1952, defeating Adlai E. Stevenson.

Significance   Dwight D. Eisenhower was more popular than his party. The domestic objectives of his administration were to balance the budget and reduce the agricultural surplus by lowering the price support for farmers. He achieved these goals within three years. Eisenhower kept government out of labor disputes and promoted military preparedness. His administration organized and supported a network of defense organizations, such as the Southeast Asia Treaty Organization (SEATO) and the Central Treaty Organization (CENTO). In 1956 he supported Egyptian nationalization of the Suez Canal. That same year he was reelected, defeating Stevenson once again. Eisenhower faced increasing repercussions from the 1954 school desegregation decision of the United States Supreme Court. In 1957 he sent United States troops to Little Rock, Arkansas, to enforce a federal court order to integrate Little Rock Central High School. He ordered Marines into Lebanon in 1958 to defend the Lebanese government.

Eisenhower suffered a setback in foreign relations when the downing of an American U-2 plane in the Soviet Union became the pretext for the break up of the Paris summit conference between himself and the Soviet premier. An era of cold war dawned; hostilities erupted in Cuba and the Congo, among other places, which became theaters for this cold war between the two superpowers. Among contemporary presidents, historians and political scientists rank Eisenhower as an above-average president. He is credited with having ended the Korean War, but his presidency is remembered more as a period of racial unrest in the country. His two terms produced few legislative achievements, although he institutionalized the president's legislative role by creating processes to assist him through the Bureau of the Budget and the White House staff.

John Fitzgerald Kennedy   Thirty-fifth president, born on May 29, 1917, in Brookline, Massachusetts. Kennedy's father was Joseph Kennedy, his mother, Rose Fitzgerald. He attended private elementary schools and later spent a year at Canterbury Catholic Boarding School in Connecticut. Kennedy enjoyed sports, especially football. In 1935 he spent the summer studying at the London School of Economics and entered Princeton University in the fall of that year. However, his freshman year was cut short by an attack of jaundice. The next year he transferred to Harvard University where he injured his back playing football. He graduated *cum laude* from Harvard in 1940. Kennedy briefly attended the graduate school of business at Stanford University and traveled to various foreign countries. From 1941 to 1945 he served in the navy, commanded a PT boat, and won a medal for bravery. Kennedy won a Pulitzer prize for his book *Profiles in Courage*.

In 1947 he was elected to the United States House of Representatives. Representing a low-income district, he supported President Harry S Truman's Fair Deal social programs. In 1952 he was elected to the United States Senate. The following year, he married Jacqueline Bouvier. Kennedy was reelected to the United States Senate in 1958, where he identified with liberal and internationalist positions. In 1960 he was nominated for president. Kennedy appeared in a unique series of televised debates with the Republican nominee, Richard M. Nixon. He was elected by a narrow margin of 150,000 of the nearly 70 million popular votes cast. On November 22, 1963, he was assassinated in Dallas, Texas, by a self-styled Marxist, Lee Harvey Oswald.

Significance   John F. Kennedy was the first Roman Catholic to become president. At forty-three, he was the youngest person elected president, although Theodore Roosevelt was younger when he became the chief executive after President William McKinley's death. Kennedy devoted most of his inaugural address to world affairs; it was acclaimed a classic inaugural speech. Kennedy exhorted the nation: "Ask not what your country can do for you—ask what you can do for your country." He chose people of high caliber for his cabinet. Kennedy made the steel industry rescind an inopportune price increase, championed civil rights legislation, expanded medical care for the aged, and supported mental health programs. Kennedy was criticized for nepotism when he appointed his brother Robert F. Kennedy as attorney general and his brother-in-law Sargent Shriver as director of the newly created Peace Corps.

In foreign affairs, his administration engaged in a test of strength with the Soviet Union on the question of Berlin and the Cuban missile crisis. His most acclaimed act was the successful demand, on December 22, 1962, that the Soviets withdraw from Cuba and dismantle their bases. Kennedy announced a naval and air quarantine on all offensive weapons bound for Cuba. He resumed underground nuclear tests and greatly expanded the space program. Although the Kennedy family name is a household word in the country, President Kennedy is ranked by historians as a strong but only an above-average president, because his mission remained unfulfilled. The nation respected his courage in times of crisis and his ability to handle his duties with skill and grace.

Lyndon Baines Johnson   Thirty-sixth president, born on August 27, 1908, on a farm near Stonewall, Texas. Johnson's father was Sam Ealy Johnson, his mother, Rebekah Baines. The family moved to Johnson City, a Texas town founded by Johnson's grandfather, where Johnson attended public school and graduated from Johnson City High School in 1924. He entered Southwest Texas State Teachers College in San Marcos and graduated in 1930. Johnson then became a teacher at Sam Houston High School in Houston. From 1932 to 1935 he served as secretary to United States Congressman Richard M. Kleberg (D-Tex.) and took night courses at Georgetown University Law School. Johnson married Claudia Alta Taylor (known as Lady Bird). In 1938 he was elected to the United States House of Representatives and served in that body until he became a United States Senator in 1948. In 1951 he became the Democratic party whip and was elected majority leader in 1954. The next year, he was reelected to the Senate. Johnson was elected vice president in 1960 and became president upon the death of President John F. Kennedy in 1963.

Significance   Upon becoming president, Lyndon B. Johnson asked all members of the Kennedy cabinet to remain in their posts. He pressed Congress for enactment of Kennedy's proposals on civil rights and tax reduction, and Congress passed the most comprehensive civil rights bill since the Reconstruction era. During his first year in office, Johnson declared a War on Poverty, which proved to be one of his most successful undertakings. Johnson received an overwhelming mandate from the public when they elected him to a full term in 1964. However, his landslide victory was overshadowed by the Vietnam War, which required his constant attention. Johnson maintained a middle ground between those who advocated a unilateral withdrawal and those who called for intensification of the war effort. His administration was also confronted with other international crises. When the elected president of the Dominican Republic was overthrown, Johnson intervened with more than 20,000 United States troops.

At home, he organized a series of task forces to build a Great Society and sent to Congress a number of messages and bills; but Congress did not respond readily. He was the first president to name a black American (Thurgood Marshall) to the United States Supreme Court as an associate justice. Johnson was also the first president to appoint a black cabinet officer, Robert C. Weaver, as secretary of housing and urban development. By these actions he was trying to elevate the political status of black Americans, whose importance in national politics was growing rapidly. Faced with increasing national division over his handling of the Vietnam War, Johnson decided not to seek reelection. Many historians rate Johnson as only an above-average president, because his popularity and ability to control events declined as he escalated the Vietnam War. Moreover, his Great Society program received quick response neither from Congress nor the American public.

Richard Milhous Nixon   Thirty-seventh president, born in Yorba Linda, California, on January 9, 1913. Nixon's father was Francis Anthony Nixon, his mother, Hannah Milhous. He went to local public schools and at age seventeen entered Whittier College. In 1937 he graduated from Duke University Law School and then practiced law in Whittier for five years. In 1940 he married Thelma Patricia Ryan. He served as an attorney in the Office for Emergency Management in Washington in 1942. Nixon then joined the navy, served in the South Pacific, and was discharged as a lieutenant commander in 1946. That same year he was elected to the United States House of Representatives, and he returned to Congress unopposed in 1948. Two years later, he became a United States Senator.

As a running mate to Dwight D. Eisenhower, he was elected vice president in 1952. Nixon became a leading spokesman of the Eisenhower administration and traveled throughout the world. When the president was ill, Nixon presided over cabinet meetings and the National Security Council. During his two terms as vice president, Nixon visited fifty-six countries and was the target of mob violence in Venezuela in 1958. Because Nixon also faced hostile demonstrations in other Latin American countries, President Eisenhower sent troops to the Caribbean to protect him. Nixon lost his bid for president in 1960 to John F. Kennedy. In 1962 Nixon ran for governor of California but was defeated by the incumbent Edmond G. (Pat) Brown. Following his defeat, Nixon moved to New York and set up law practice. In 1968 he won the presidency, narrowly defeating Hubert H. Humphrey.

Significance   Richard M. Nixon inherited a country at war in Vietnam and beset by domestic and campus protest. He intensified the bombing of Vietnam and Cambodia and devoted much of his time to foreign affairs. In 1972 Nixon became the first American president to visit China and the Soviet Union. Henry A. Kissinger, his secretary of state, sought detente with the communist bloc. In 1973 Nixon signed a Strategic Arms Limitation Treaty (SALT I) with the Soviet Union. Congress dealt Nixon a setback when it approved, over his veto, legislation to limit presidential war-making powers. During his tenure in office, Nixon appointed four Supreme Court justices, including Chief Justice Warren E. Burger. Despite his narrow victory in 1968, Nixon sought reelection and, with little effort, was successful in 1972. Nixon completed the troop withdrawal from Vietnam, but the shaky peace he engineered was shattered when Vietnam united under a communist regime.

The greatest setback of his administration was a series of scandals beginning with the burglary of the Democratic party national headquarters in the Watergate office. Nixon and his top aides sought to cover up White House involvement in the scandal. Under questioning by Congress, it was revealed that many of Nixon's conversations and phone calls had been secretly recorded, but he claimed executive privilege to keep the tapes secret. Nixon removed the Watergate special prosecutor when he demanded these tapes, and the attorney general resigned in protest. The situation worsened as seven of Nixon's former aides were found guilty of participating in a cover-up and conspiracy and were sentenced to prison. On July 24, 1974, the United States Supreme Court ruled that Nixon had to submit the tapes to the special prosecutor. The House Judiciary Committee recommended adoption of three articles of impeachment, charging Nixon with obstruction of justice, abuse of power, and contempt of Congress. Nixon wavered, and on August 8, 1974, he resigned effective at noon on August 9. Nixon became the first president to resign from office in disgrace. He was a strong president and a skilled negotiator who possessed a broad understanding of world affairs. This aided his efforts to improve America's relations with China and the Soviet Union. Nixon's presidency was shattered by the Watergate break-in and cover-up; he remains the most controversial president in American history. Although some historians rate Nixon as a below-average president, Robert K. Murray views him as a failure, equating Nixon with Warren G. Harding and Ulysses S. Grant, the two presidents who failed most miserably.

Gerald Rudolph Ford   Thirty-eighth president, born in Omaha, Nebraska, on July 14, 1913. Ford's father was Leslie King, his mother, Dorothy Gardner. Ford was christened Leslie King, Jr., but when his parents divorced and his mother remarried, he adopted the name of his stepfather, Gerald R. Ford. He grew up in Grand Rapids, Michigan. After finishing high school in 1931, he went to the University of Michigan and graduated in 1935. While working as assistant football and boxing coach at Yale University, he earned an LL.B. degree and was admitted to the Michigan bar in 1941. The next year he joined the navy and served in the Pacific. Ford was elected to the United States House of Representatives in 1948 and that same year married Elizabeth (Betty) Bloomer Warren. Ford served in the House of Representatives for twenty-five years, eight years as Republican minority leader. President Lyndon B. Johnson named Ford to the Warren Commission to investigate the assassination of President John F. Kennedy. Ford made an unsuccessful attempt in 1970 to instigate impeachment against the late Supreme Court Justice William O. Douglas. When Vice President Spiro T. Agnew resigned on October 10, 1973, President Richard M. Nixon nominated Ford to succeed Agnew under the provision of Section 2 of the Twenty-fifth Amendment to the United States Constitution. The Senate approved the nomination by a vote of 92–3 on November 27, and the House of Representatives by 387–35 on December 6. When Nixon resigned on August 9, 1974, Ford became president.

Significance   Gerald R. Ford was the first president to succeed to the presidency because of the resignation of a president. He was the first president to serve without being elected vice president or president. Ford tried to restore public confidence in government and America's leaders. His nomination of former New York governor Nelson A. Rockefeller to serve as vice president was applauded by many people. However, public approval for President Ford waned when he pardoned President Nixon on September 8, 1974, for all federal crimes he might have committed while in office. This action produced shock and outrage in the country; people believed it was part of a political bargain between Ford and Nixon. Ford offered a conditional amnesty to Vietnam draft evaders and deserters. His only appointment to the United States Supreme Court was that of Associate Justice John Paul Stevens. He replaced all but three members of the Nixon cabinet. Ford vetoed 48 bills in his 29 months in office, contending that most would prove inflationary. He brought inflation down to an annual rate of 4.8 percent, but it created recession and more unemployment.

After the fall of Cambodia, the new Cambodian government seized an American ship, the *Mayaguez*. Ford ordered limited marine and air action to free the ship and its crew. He visited China, Japan, and the Soviet Union. His administration's efforts to provide aid to anti-Soviet factions in the Angolan civil war failed to produce the desired results. Ford was nominated for president in 1976 to oppose Democratic candidate Jimmy Carter but was defeated. Historians rate Ford as an average president. He became president at a time when public confidence in government and political leaders was low. Yet, through integrity and strength of character, he was able to heal the wounds of the Watergate scandal in a period of a little over two years.

Jimmy (James Earl) Carter   Thirty-ninth president, born at Plains, Georgia, on October 1, 1924. (He prefers the nickname Jimmy.) Carter's father was James Earl Carter, his mother, Lillian Gordy. He attended school in Plains and studied at Georgia Technical Institute. In 1946 he graduated from the United States Naval Academy at Annapolis and in that year married Rosalyn Smith. Carter served on battleships and did submarine duty. He studied nuclear physics at Union College in Schenectady, New York. Following the death of his father, Carter resigned from the navy to administer the family business of peanut farming, fertilizer production, and cotton ginning. Carter became chairman of the Sumter County school board and president of the Plains Development Corporation and the Crop Development Association. In 1962 he was elected to the Georgia State Senate and became governor in 1970. As governor, he demonstrated fiscal conservatism and social liberalism. Carter called for an end to racial discrimination, appointed increased numbers of blacks in state agencies, and placed a portrait of Martin Luther King, Jr. in the state capitol. Carter won the nomination for president in 1976 and defeated incumbent President Gerald R. Ford by a narrow margin.

Significance   Jimmy Carter was the first president elected from the Old South since before the Civil War. After his inauguration, Carter and his family walked to the White House to show his way of simple living. He sold the presidential yacht to demonstrate his disdain for an imperial presidency. Carter severely criticized his predecessor, President Ford, for his failure to control inflation and reduce unemployment. However, the economic situation worsened during his administration, and the inflation rate rose to 12 percent from less than 5 percent when Ford left office. The value of the dollar eroded in the world market. Carter advanced a long-term program to solve the energy problem and created a Department of Energy. He also established a Department of Education.

In foreign affairs, Carter undertook to establish human rights as a principle of policy. He signed the Strategic Arms Limitation Treaty (SALT II) in 1979. After much debate, the Senate ratified the Panama Canal Treaty. Full diplomatic relations were opened with the People's Republic of China. The greatest achievement of his presidency was his role in the successful negotiation resulting in the Camp David Accord between Egypt and Israel on March 29, 1979. Carter reacted to the Soviet invasion of Afghanistan by imposing a grain embargo and boycotting the 1980 Moscow Olympic games. But the greatest crisis of his administration occurred on November 4, 1979, when Iranian terrorists occupied the United States embassy in Tehran and took the embassy staff hostage. His abortive attempt to rescue the remaining fifty-two hostages caused irreparable damage to his presidency and plagued him to the end of his term; he lost his bid for reelection in 1980 to Ronald Reagan. Carter has been rated as an average president because he was not able to fulfill his promises to balance the budget, reduce inflation, enact a comprehensive energy program, and reform the tax system.

Above all, his failure to resolve the Iranian hostage crisis during his term of office made him a weak and indecisive president.

Ronald Wilson Reagan   Fortieth president, born in Tampico, Illinois, on February 6, 1911. Reagan's father was John Edward Reagan, his mother, Nellie Wilson. He showed interest in acting in high school. After graduating from Eureka College in 1932, Reagan began working as a sports announcer for radio station WOO in Davenport, Iowa. While covering baseball spring training in California in 1937, he signed a contract with Warner Brothers as a radio announcer for a film called *Love Is on the Air*, which began his career in motion pictures and television. In 1940 he married actress Jane Wyman. Reagan joined the army air force as a captain during World War II. In 1952 he divorced his first wife and married Nancy Davis. Once a liberal Democrat, his politics reversed, and he became a conservative Republican. In 1966 he was elected governor of California and reelected in 1970. Reagan lost the Republican nomination for president twice but received his party's nomination in 1980 and this time won a landslide victory over the incumbent Jimmy Carter. Early in his presidency, he narrowly survived an attempted assassination.

Significance   Ronald Reagan, at age sixty-nine, became the oldest person ever to be elected to the presidency. The resolution of the Iranian hostage crisis on his first day of office won Reagan considerable praise, though critics claim that credit actually belonged to his predecessor, President Jimmy Carter. No sooner had he taken office than he began to press Congress for his supply side economic policy, which placed greater emphasis on encouraging production in the private sector and less emphasis on encouraging consumption. Reagan forged a bipartisan coalition in Congress that led to the enactment of some of his economic programs, including the largest budget and tax cut in American history. His administration argued that this combined approach would result in lower federal deficits and a balanced budget. However, many budget analysts disagreed, contending that revenue losses caused by the tax cut were not likely to be offset by spending cuts or stimulation of the economy. Reagan dominated the Congress like no president since perhaps Franklin D. Roosevelt. Huge deficits of billion of dollars were forecast. In his 1982 State of the Union message, Reagan proposed the New Federalism, a sweeping transfer of many social programs to state and local governments. After three years in office, Reagan could claim, with some satisfaction, reductions in the annual inflation rate from 13.1 to 4.8 percent and interest rates from 21 to 11.5 percent. However, the slowdown in economic growth resulted in a recession and an unemployment rate of 10.8 percent, the highest level since 1940. The country has not yet fully recovered from the recession. The Congress reacted negatively to the massive deficit contained in Reagan's proposed budget deficit for 1983–1984. After an earlier defeat in Congress on the proposed MX missile, Reagan's status increased on May 24, 1983, when the House of Representatives passed a resolution for development of the missiles and provided $625 million for that purpose. The Senate approved the measure the next day.

His administration scored a minor victory when American F-14 jets shot down two Russian-built Libyan jets. Reagan ordered limited marine and naval action in Lebanon to help the Lebanese government establish control over various warring factions. Citing the need to protect the lives of Americans living on the Caribbean island of Grenada, to foil Cuban and Soviet military schemes, and to help establish a democratic government, President Reagan ordered the invasion of that island on October 25, 1983. Critics charged that the Grenada invasion was calculated to win an easy victory against a tiny island in an effort to boost the morale of his disspirited conservative supporters and divert public attention away from the Lebanese suicide bomb explosion, in which more than 240 marines were killed and many injured just two days prior to the invasion of Grenada. It is too early to rate Reagan; yet critics claim that his economic policy is aiding the rich at the expense of the poor. Reagan, they charge, has created a situation in which the rich have grown richer, and the poor have become poorer. Reagan remained optimistic that the economy would moderate, although he was unable to balance the budget by 1984 as he had promised; instead he ended the fiscal year with the largest budget deficit in American history. It remains to be seen whether historians will judge Reagan as a great or an average president.

4. Presidential Leadership

Budget Message   United States government receipt and expenditure estimates for the next fiscal year presented by the president to the Congress. The Budget Message is prepared by the Office of Management and Budget (OMB), with the assistance of the Council of Economic Advisers and other federal agencies. The message presents an overview of the president's budget proposals. It includes explanation of spending programs in terms of national needs, agency missions, and a discussion of the president's tax proposals, if any. The document also contains a description of the budget system. The Budget and Accounting Act of 1921 and the Budget Act of 1974 require all departments and federal agencies to submit their proposals to the president, who in turn submits a consolidated statement to Congress in January of each legislative session. The Budget Message is not usually delivered in person but sent to Congress in writing. The federal budget includes all three branches of government: legislative, executive, and judicial. In 1974 Congress established special budget committees in both houses to examine more closely the president's proposals and estimate their financial impact before approval and appropriation. *See also* COUNCIL OF ECONOMIC ADVISERS, p. 118; ECONOMIC MESSAGE, p. 98; OFFICE OF MANAGEMENT AND BUDGET, p. 133.

Significance   A Budget Message is a policy document that starts with the assumption that all of the president's proposals will be adopted. However, once budget negotiations are underway, demands typically are adjusted downward, rarely upward. It is a well-established tradition that appropriated money must be spent before the new fiscal year begins on October 1. There is widespread apprehension in the bureaucracy that if money is not spent, Congress will cut the following year's budget accordingly. This results in many wasteful expenditures in the final months of a fiscal year.

While Congress is the ultimate authority on the appropriation of funds, the president has the power to control the spending process. As political scientist Louis Fisher maintains, "Billions of dollars are impounded, transferred, reprogrammed, or shifted in one way or another by the president and his assistants" (Fisher 1975, 3). Many presidents have adopted a cost-benefit system to analyze budgetary policy. President Jimmy Carter favored a zero-based budget system: every federal agency had to justify its budget each year starting from zero. President Ronald Reagan's use of cost-benefit analysis favors business interests over social goals such as health and human welfare. Contending interests fight budget battles to ensure their share of national funds, seeming to prove Harold D. Lasswell's concept of politics as "who gets what, when, and how" (Lasswell 1958).

Economic Message   The annual report from the president on the national economy submitted each January to the Congress. The Economic Message is prepared for the president by the Council of Economic Advisers and the Office of Management and Budget. The Employment Act of 1964 requires the president to submit to Congress a statement of trends in the nation's economy, employment levels, production, purchasing power, inflation, interest rates, and taxing and spending policy. The president also makes projections and presents future plans and policies for implementation.

The Economic Message delineates the monetary and fiscal policy of the government. Through monetary policy, the government attempts to influence the growth of the economy by controlling interest rates, regulating the availability of credit, and controlling the supply of money. Fiscal policy is another major tool of economic management that emerges out of the Economic Message. This policy is largely established by the president with the cooperation of Congress through taxing, spending, and borrowing policies. *See also* BUDGET MESSAGE, p. 97; COUNCIL OF ECONOMIC ADVISERS, p. 118; OFFICE OF MANAGEMENT AND BUDGET, p. 133; STATE OF THE UNION MESSAGE, p. 111.

Significance   The Economic Message reflects the health of the economy. In submitting the annual report, the president looks backward and forward: backward to problems in the economy and forward to policy adoption. It is a statement proclaiming the current economic realities and presenting the alternatives under consideration. Traditionally, government has been conceived as an umpire with respect to the economy.

However, since the Great Depression in the 1930s, it has clearly become an economic player as well. Increasingly, the federal government has assumed the responsibility of maintaining stability in the economy. Like the president's State of the Union message, the Economic Message adds to the presidential role of chief lawmaker. Through it, presidents initiate and recommend many of their legislative programs involving the economy. After President Ronald Reagan took office, he initiated a policy of supply side economics that placed greater emphasis on encouraging production in the private sector and less emphasis on encouraging consumption. Through a bipartisan coalition in Congress, he managed to enact many of his key economic programs, including major budget and tax cuts.

First Lady   The president's spouse. The first lady is the right arm of the president and an important personal confidant. She has an office, staff, and other facilities in the east wing of the White House. Since most presidents to this date have been married men (except for bachelors James Buchanan and Grover Cleveland during the first two years, and widowers Thomas Jefferson, Andrew Jackson, Martin Van Buren, and Chester A. Arthur), their wives have functioned as first lady. Beginning with Martha Washington, wife of George Washington, the first president, first ladies have acted as hostess on celebrated state occasions. Eleanor Roosevelt, wife of President Franklin D. Roosevelt, set the pattern for modern first ladies, acting as his liberal conscience. She spoke out publicly on many issues. Bess Truman, wife of President Harry S Truman, and Mamie Eisenhower, wife of President Dwight D. Eisenhower, were less publicly active. Rosalyn Carter, wife of President Jimmy Carter, emerged as an adviser to her husband on important issues. Nancy Reagan, wife of President Ronald Reagan, is primarily involved in hosting social events. *See also* PRESIDENT, p. 103.

Significance   First ladies sometimes influence national trends in culture and lifestyle. When Jacqueline Kennedy, wife of President John F. Kennedy, moved into the White House, there was a revival of interest in period furniture and pillbox hats, which she liked and used. Some first ladies are known for austerity: Sarah Childress Polk, wife of President James K. Polk, forbade card playing and dancing in the White House. Lucy Ware Webb Hayes, wife of President Rutherford B. Hayes, banned alcohol in the White House. Some first ladies were known for extravagance and were the subject of criticism. Mary Todd Lincoln, wife of President Abraham Lincoln, ordered 300 pairs of gloves in four months, paid $500 for a single shawl, and spent $5,000 for three evening gowns. After sharp criticism that Nancy Reagan was "socially chic," resulting from large expenditures on high fashion clothes, on refurbishing the White House, and on purchasing new china, she tried to counteract the criticism and divert public attention away from her by launching a campaign against teenage drug abuse. Nevertheless, her role as first lady has remained primarily ceremonial. She is known to have a strong private influence on President Reagan. The lifestyles of most of the first ladies have influenced the social lives of the presidents, and sometimes of the nation.

Inauguration   The formal installation of the president into office. The inauguration is largely a ceremonial affair: the president pledges to discharge the duties of the office and to uphold the Constitution. Prior to the adoption of the Twentieth Amendment to the Constitution in 1933, presidents were inaugurated on March 4 of the year following their election. Under the Twentieth Amendment, a newly elected president is inaugurated at noon on January 20 in the year following his election. Article II, Section 1 of the Constitution requires that the president recite the following oath of office: "I do solemnly swear (or affirm) that I will faithfully execute the Office of President of the United States, and will, to the best of my Ability, preserve, protect, and defend the Constitution of the United States." George Washington, the first president, added the phrase "so help me God." A president is usually sworn in by the chief justice of the Supreme Court. It is a common practice to conduct the swearing in on Capitol Hill with the Bible in the hand of the president's spouse. The swearing in is followed by an inaugural address. The day ends with an inaugural ball in the evening in which legions of political and diplomatic officials participate. *See also* PRESIDENT, p. 103.

Significance   The inauguration of the president has come to be a gala festival in Washington, D.C. It is not a constitutional requirement to swear by the Bible; presidents do so perhaps because they recognize the awesome powers and duties of the presidency and the Judaeo-Christian heritage of the nation. However, if a person of another religious heritage were elected to the presidency, the practice of swearing in by the Bible would probably be discontinued.

The inaugural address sets the theme of the administration and attracts international press coverage, because it gives clues to the incoming president's foreign and domestic policy plans. Sometimes presidents demonstrate their personal style of living on this ceremonial day. After his inauguration in 1977 at Capitol Hill, President Jimmy Carter and his family walked to the White House to demonstrate his simple and austere way of living. In contrast to Carter, President Ronald Reagan brought pomp and grandeur to his inauguration in 1981, culminating with an inaugural ball in which his wife wore a gown (privately donated) valued at $10,000.

Kitchen Cabinet   An informal group of trusted personal advisers, friends, and well wishers of the president. The term kitchen cabinet originated during the administration of Andrew Jackson, the seventh president, who met with a group of informal advisers in the White House kitchen. His kitchen cabinet was composed of four persons who held no official positions in the White House but had worked hard for his election in 1828. Jackson, largely ignoring his official cabinet, relied upon these four persons for confidential advice. Since then many presidents, such as Abraham Lincoln, Theodore Roosevelt, Woodrow Wilson, Franklin D. Roosevelt, Dwight D. Eisenhower, John F. Kennedy, Richard M. Nixon, and Ronald Reagan, have formed kitchen cabinets in their search for loyal advisers and confidants. Some presidents choose the members of their kitchen cabinet from the White House staff; others pick the members of this cabinet from political associates, friends, and academics. *See also* PRESIDENT, p. 103; WHITE HOUSE STAFF, p. 138.

Significance   The kitchen cabinet serves as an inner circle to the president. It has developed because most presidents cannot find sufficient selflessness and candor among cabinet members. President Lincoln, for example, issued the Emancipation Proclamation in consultation with his kitchen cabinet, ignoring the wishes of his formal cabinet. President Wilson met with his kitchen cabinet for major decisions regarding World War I. President Franklin D. Roosevelt relied on his kitchen cabinet for issues involving the depression of the 1930s and World War II. The quasi-official kitchen cabinet serves many useful purposes, but it could act as sycophant and isolate the president from his official advisers. Often this body creates unnecessary rift and division in the administrative hierarchy. President Nixon, for example, was accused of undercutting his secretary of state, William P. Rogers, by seeking advice from his presidential assistant, Henry A. Kissinger. Ultimately, Rogers resigned, and Kissinger was appointed to his position.

Lame Duck President   An incumbent who is not eligible for, is not seeking, or has lost reelection, but is still exercising authority for the remainder of an unexpired term. The lame duck period for the outgoing president was reduced by the Twentieth Amendment, which changed the date for beginning the presidential and vice presidential terms from March 4 to January 20. This so-called Lame Duck

Amendment also provides that if a president-elect dies before taking office, the vice president-elect shall become president; if a president-elect has not been chosen or fails to qualify by January 20, the vice president-elect shall act as president until a president is chosen; if neither qualifies, then Congress shall decide who shall act as president until a president or vice president qualifies; and if the election of the president and vice president is to be decided by the House of Representatives and the Senate, and a candidate dies, Congress shall determine by law what shall be done. Congress has provided for this eventuality in the Presidential Succession Act of 1947 and later amendments to this act. *See also* PRESIDENT, p. 103; PRESIDENT-ELECT, p. 18; PRESIDENTIAL SUCCESSION, p. 110.

Significance   A lame duck presidency has its advantages and disadvantages. A lame duck president maintains continuity and keeps the administration running until the president-elect is sworn in at noon on January 20 following the year of election. It gives the president-elect a chance to consult with the lame duck president and receive briefings on administrative and policy matters. In this sense, the lame duck president "trains" the president-elect. Constitutionally speaking, there is no president-elect until the electoral votes have been counted and certified by Congress or, in the event that no person receives a majority of the electoral votes, until the House and Senate make their choices. Therefore, a lame duck president may have a short or long period to serve depending upon the circumstances. A lame duck president may have other problems, too. James Buchanan, while a lame duck president in 1859, urged President-Elect Abraham Lincoln on the eve of the Civil War to join him in a call for a constitutional convention in order to gain time, but Lincoln rejected the idea. As a lame duck president, Buchanan was unable to exercise his power against the rising tide of secession; he proved to be a convenient scapegoat for the incoming Lincoln administration.

Patronage   Public jobs in the form of political appointments when a party comes into power. Patronage, as applied to politics, is the practice of rewarding persons for past services rendered to the grantor, or for future expected services. Many of these jobs are distributed to the party faithful. At the national level, the patronage powers are vested primarily in the president, who, for example, may reward a generous campaign donor with an appointment to a high government position. Patronage appointments are of three kinds (1) appointments authorized by statute, such as cabinet and subcabinet officers, ambassadors, judges, and members of the various commissions; (2) jobs of a confidential or policy-determining nature, such as aides and assistants; and (3) noncareer executive assignments offered to civil service personnel. There are no accurate figures on the number of federal patronage jobs today, but estimates range as high as 3,200. The most prestigious ones are White House staff appointments. *See also* APPOINTMENT POWER, p. 27; CHIEF EXECUTIVE, p. 31.

Significance   Patronage is a two-edged sword. While an appointment pleases some, it may irritate others. Many historians believe that a disappointed officeseeker assassinated President James A. Garfield in 1881. In the early days of the Republic, virtually every job in the federal government was filled by patronage. In 1885 Democratic President Grover Cleveland replaced 40,000 Republican postal employees with his party followers. As a result of public outrage over the abuses of a president's patronage power, a merit system of hiring federal employees has developed in the country. Many federal jobs, especially at the lower and middle levels, have been made competitive through civil service examinations. The patronage system worked best when campaigning was done face-to-face. Today, fewer patronage jobs exist, owing to a number of important court decisions. In *Branti* v. *Finkel* (1980), the United States Supreme Court virtually declared party patronage to be unconstitutional.

President   The chief executive of the United States. The president plays many roles, but the formal powers of the office relate to only a few constitutional prerogatives. Article II, Section 1 of the Constitution states: "The executive Power shall be vested in a President of the United States of America." The president's constitutional tasks can be conveniently grouped under six categories: chief executive, commander in chief of the armed forces, director of foreign policy, chief lawmaker and executor of law, and head of state. As chief executives, presidents are responsible for administering the affairs of the country. As commanders in chief, they can order armed conflict abroad. They are responsible for formulating and implementing the foreign policy of the nation. As chief lawmakers and executors of law, they shape the congressional agenda as well as veto legislation. As ceremonial heads of state, they receive visiting dignitaries, confer honors, present awards, proclaim holidays, undertake goodwill tours, and grant pardons. Many other roles are not mentioned in the Constitution but are derived from statutory laws and precedents set by earlier presidents. Among these roles are party leader and manager of the economy. The president plays a major role in determining political strategy, often lending influence and campaigning for supportive candidates of the same party. Presidents use patronage to reward party faithfuls. They may appeal to the people against the action of Congress, and create public opinion in support of their policies. *See also* CHIEF EXECUTIVE, p. 31; CHIEF OF STATE, p. 27; COMMANDER IN CHIEF, p. 38; CONSTITUTIONAL POWERS, p. 39.

Significance   The president represents the government for millions of Americans; he is the most powerful political figure in the nation and one of the most powerful in the world. Among the various duties and functions that the president performs is the demanding one of serving as the general manager of a vast civilian and military establishment employing nearly 5 million people, who serve in some 1,900 federal agencies, and spend over $800 billion annually.

To faithfully discharge the duties of the office, the president must coordinate the activities of the thirteen executive departments and more than fifty major agencies. The administrative task of the president alone has become an impossible one. As political scientist Richard E. Neustadt maintains, "From outside or below, a president is many men or one man wearing many 'hats,' or playing many 'roles'" (Neustadt 1960, viii). Although assisted by millions of federal employees, the president is responsible for running the administration and receives credit or blame for the actions of the federal government. Americans revere their presidents but hate them as well. This is evidenced by the fact that four presidents have been assassinated, while attempts were made on the lives of another four, an unusual rate of assassination and attempted assassination for an American political office.

Presidential Accountability   The extent to which a president is held answerable to the people. Presidential accountability is based on the concept that elected officials, including the president, must be responsible to the electorate for their actions. The prevailing view in the country is that the president is too powerful and that he must become more accountable to the people and the Congress. In actuality there is a paradox: The president has too much power and also too little power. For example, a president has the authority to wage a nuclear war, which may be catastrophic, but has insufficient authority to solve unemployment and other economic problems facing the nation.

Presidents are considered accountable not only for their own deeds and actions, but also for the federal government and many inherited agreements reached by their predecessors. The framers of the Constitution devised a system of shared power between Congress and the president as a means of checking excessive use of power by the president. Under Article I, Section 9 of the Constitution, the Congress maintains its control over the president by exercising its authority to appropriate money for governmental programs, and by overseeing the activities of the government. As a last resort, impeachment is one of the most potent checks on presidential action (Article II, Section 4). *See also* IM-PEACHMENT, p. 201; PRESIDENTIAL GOVERNMENT, p. 108; STRONG PRESIDENTS, p. 113.

Significance   Presidential accountability implies that the people must be given an opportunity to pass judgment on their president. This requires frequent elections, recall, and impeachment. Public opinion plays a most effective role in making a president answerable to the people. While the parliamentary system provides for a vote of no-confidence against the prime minister or president, the American presidential system provides for impeachment. Only one president has been impeached: Andrew Johnson. Impeachment proceedings were also initiated against President Richard M. Nixon, following the mounting public pressure at the height of the Watergate scandal (in which he and several top aides were charged with criminal misconduct), but he resigned before Congress voted to impeach him. The fear of impeachment is always present, and it works as an ultimate check upon presidential authoritarianism. Presidential elections, held every four years, hold the president accountable to the voters; thus many incumbent presidents, such as Gerald R. Ford and Jimmy Carter, lost their bids for reelection. An effective opposition, particularly in the Congress, is another means of making the president responsible. The best insurance to prevent presidential autocracy is to strengthen citizen interest and involvement in the political process.

Presidential Character   A theory of variations in presidential performance based on two broad dimensions: active-passive and positive-negative. Presidential character is further divided into four main types: active-positive, active-negative, passive-positive, and passive-negative. James David Barber, a well-known political scientist, postulates this theory on presidential character in his book entitled *The Presidential Character: Predicting Performance in the White House* (1972). According to Barber, an active-positive president "tends to show confidence, flexibility, and a focus on producing results through rational mastery." An active-negative president "tends to emphasize ambitious striving, aggressiveness, and a focus on the struggle for power against a hostile environment." A passive-positive type "tends to be receptive, compliant, agreeable, and cooperative." A passive-negative president "tends to withdraw from conflict and uncertainty." Barber has classified the following presidents as active-positive: Franklin D. Roosevelt, Harry S Truman, John F. Kennedy, Gerald R. Ford, and Jimmy Carter. According to Barber, active-negative presidents include Woodrow Wilson, Herbert Hoover, Lyndon B. Johnson, and Richard M. Nixon. He cites William Howard Taft and Warren G. Harding as passive-positive; Calvin Coolidge and Dwight D. Eisenhower are termed passive-negative. *See also* STRONG PRESIDENTS, p. 113; WEAK PRESIDENTS, p. 116.

Significance   Presidential character analyzes the relationship between personality and politics. One writer, Garry Wills, describes Barber's analysis as an example of "games academics play" (Wills 1982, 186). If there are lessons to be learned from Barber's classification of presidential character it is that the country is better off when the president is active-positive, meaning decisive and assertive. Barber has attracted the attention of political scientists, as well as politicians, many of whom are influenced by the above typology. Others argue that his predictions are vague and unscientific. His judgment of Carter as an active-positive president has been criticized as incorrect. To the critics, Carter more resembles an active-negative president. In his evaluation of the thirteen most recent presidents, Barber reveals a bias toward many of the Democratic presidents, as well as Republican President Ford. There are many opinions of course, but no single answer as to what type of personality makes for a successful president.

Presidential Compensation   Benefits and emoluments to which the president is entitled. Presidential compensation in 1984 includes an annual salary of $200,000 (taxable), an annual expense account of $50,000 (taxable), an annual travel budget of $100,000 (tax-free), and a pension, on retirement, of $63,000 per year (taxable). The president is also entitled to a free furnished residence and office (the White House). The presidential family receive Secret Service protection during and after the term of office. After retirement, the president is provided with a skeleton staff, free office space, free mailing privileges, and up to $90,000 a year for office help. Upon the president's death, the surviving spouse receives an annual pension of $20,000.

Nearly 600 people work as assistants and aides in the White House and in the Executive Office of the president. In addition to the seventy-five full-time staff who maintain the White House and the compound, the president is provided with five maids, two chefs, two cooks, two kitchen helpers, a pantry assistant, two laundry workers, a seamstress, two storekeepers, a linen supervisor, four doormen, and five housemen. Air Force Number One is the official presidential plane and is equipped with instant communication facilities to any part of the world. In addition, the president has the use of five Boeing 707s, eleven Lockheed jets, sixteen soundproof helicopters, and four additional jets on order. Some

200 people, including the press corps, travel with the president on trips abroad. The Air Force clears the air lanes and flies sorties to ensure the safety of the presidential entourage. The Secret Service is charged with maintaining surveillance. The bullet-proof limousines that the president uses each costs over $500,000, but the manufacturer leases them to the president at $15,000 a year. The president has been provided with four "doomsday" jumbo jets. These are windowless planes which will fly the president and top aides above the atmosphere in the event of nuclear attack. In this regard, several mountain hideouts have been built in the country to protect the president and aides from nuclear attack. *See also* CHIEF EXECUTIVE, p. 31; PRESIDENT, p. 103; SECRET SERVICE, p. 153.

Significance   Presidential compensation has been criticized by many. Former Vice President Walter F. Mondale observed: "Unfortunately, the world's greatest democracy has allowed the trappings of monarchy to overgrow the office originally intended to be a protection against monarchical rule" (Mondale 1975, 67). Although many doctors, lawyers, engineers, scientists, entertainers, movie stars, and corporate executives make more money than the president, no one else in government service receives as much compensation and perquisites as the president. The Constitution, in Article II, Section 1 prohibits decreasing the compensation of a president while in office, in order to prevent a hostile Congress from doing so. However, many abuses of presidential benefits and facilities have been alleged. Presidential aides have been found using official vehicles for personal use. President Richard M. Nixon flew his dog King Timahoe to Camp David by official helicopter. As a result of generous benefits, many presidents became richer when they left the White House than when they entered it.

Presidential Disability   The inability of the president to discharge the duties of the office. The issue of presidential disability is addressed by the Twenty-fifth Amendment, Section 3. It provides that the vice president shall become the acting president if the president transmits to "the President Pro Tempore of the Senate and the Speaker of the House of Representatives his written declaration that he is unable to discharge the powers and duties of his office." The president can also be considered disabled if the majority of the cabinet and the vice president certify in writing that the president is unable to perform the duties of office. The Congress must determine by a two-thirds vote of both houses whether the president can reclaim the post. *See also* PRESIDENTIAL SUCCESSION, p. 110.

Significance   Presidential disability has occurred several times, but until the Twenty-fifth Amendment, Congress had never established the actual procedures to be followed. Whether or not presidents are unable to discharge their duties has caused many problems: when President James A. Garfield suffered a lingering illness; when President Woodrow Wilson had a physical breakdown; when President Franklin D. Roosevelt had a fatal attack; and when President Dwight D. Eisenhower had a stroke. Now it is clear at what point the vice president shall act as president, and Congress is empowered to make laws to deal with these situations. Yet those who are apprehensive point to the role that suspicion and ambition play in politics. Can an overly ambitious vice president conspire with the majority of the cabinet officers to certify that the president is unable to perform official duties, even though this is not true? With human beings there is no guarantee against intrigue and caprice. The present disability rule may have unwittingly perpetuated such failings.

Presidential Government   A form of government in which the chief executive is elected by the people and serves a fixed term of office. A presidential government is representative and one in which the president may serve as both chief of state and chief executive of the government. The president is the one official, elected nationwide, who is charged with representing the interests of the entire country. The president serves as the chief administrator, commander in chief, chief lawmaker, chief diplomat, and chief of party. The president may not be removed from office by the Congress upon a vote of no-confidence. The president is entitled to serve a full term unless removed by impeachment. (Refer to the Appendix, Figure 5 for a diagram of the government of the United States.) *See also* CHIEF EXECUTIVE, p. 31; CONSTITUTIONAL POWERS, p. 39; PRESIDENT, p. 103.

Significance   Presidential government does not (at least in theory) represent the narrow view of any one group, region, or interest. Simply put, the president is the national leader around whom the country's affairs move, the symbol of the nation who is expected to speak for all Americans. Presidential government possesses many intrinsic advantages. It ensures a stable national government. Moreover, presidential primacy in domestic and foreign affairs has stimulated the growth of presidential power and influence. The president can, in the event of an emergency, deal swiftly and effectively with various crises and disasters. The president is the paramount political figure and wherever the president is, there the government is thought to be. The inherent stability of this form of government has enabled the United States to retain the same political system for over 200 years. America is the oldest of the new nations in the world, and the strength and vitality of its institutions spring directly from presidential government. As a result, many newly independent nations have eschewed parliamentary government and embraced the presidential model because of its great unifying force.

Presidential Press Conference   A means to inform the public and mold citizen opinion through the news media. The presidential press conference is a formal function, usually broadcast live on television and radio. The president relies on the news media to reach the people, and the press depends on the White House for information, since many executive decisions are made behind the scenes. The first twentieth century president, Theodore Roosevelt, innovated the press conference. President Woodrow Wilson addressed the press in his office for a question and answer exchange. President Franklin D. Roosevelt made wide use of the news media by setting up two press conferences a week. President Dwight D. Eisenhower introduced televised press conferences; the broadcast was made with minor editing. President John F. Kennedy permitted the media to broadcast his televised press conferences without editing. Each press conference is preceded by days, sometimes weeks of research by the presidential aides to brief the president on possible questions and answers. The president and aides seek to manage and control information in a way favorable to the administration. *See also* WHITE HOUSE PRESS SECRETARY, p. 137; WHITE HOUSE STAFF, p. 138.

Significance   Presidential press conferences involve the art of news management. Success or failure of a president depends in many respects on the use of this art. Presidents Franklin D. Roosevelt and John F. Kennedy used this art with great imagination, and they became highly successful. President Roosevelt is accused of employing the media to create a personality cult. President Ronald Reagan has used witticism to evoke interest in his press conferences. The presidential press conference serves mutual needs. The president needs to reach the public in order to predispose them favorably toward the administration's policies. The press, in turn, wishes to gather as much information as possible to feed their clientele—the public.

The presidential press conference can be considered a rough equivalent to the question period in the British parliament, when the prime minister answers questions posed by members of parliament. Since American presidents address Congress only on special occasions and do not attend congressional debates nor answer questions, frequent press conferences offer them the opportunity to reach the public. The press conference has become an extraconstitutional tool of presidential leadership in the legislative process. Presidents use such press conferences to check Congress and generate pressure for or against various programs and policies.

Presidential Qualifications   The formal eligibility requirements of a presidential candidate to hold that office. There are only three presidential qualifications: a native-born citizen, at least thirty-five years of age, and a resident of the United States for at least fourteen years (Article II, Section 1). A person born to American parents in a foreign country is also eligible. Originally, restrictions were imposed by the Constitution upon the president but not upon the vice president, until the Twelfth Amendment was ratified in 1804. However, a candidate for the vice presidency was never selected who did not meet the presidential qualifications. *See also* AVAILABILITY FACTOR, p. 3; CHIEF EXECUTIVE, p. 31; PRESIDENT, p. 103; PRESIDENTIAL CANDIDATE, p. 20.

Significance   Presidential qualifications distinguish between natural-born and naturalized citizens. The constitutional provision in Article II, Section 1 seems to conflict with the Fourteenth Amendment, which states: "All persons born or naturalized in the United States, and subject to the jurisdiction thereof, are citizens of the United States. . . ." Many naturalized citizens maintain that their rights have been unfairly abridged because they are barred from seeking the office of the president. A presidential candidate is required to be at least thirty-five years of age, because it is felt that a person must be sufficiently mature to run the affairs of the country. Prior to the election of President Herbert Hoover, there was some question about the residence requirement, as he did not reside in the country for fourteen consecutive years prior to his election. Hoover's election as president settled the issue. In addition to the formal qualifications, a presidential candidate is expected to meet certain political standards, usually referred to as the availability factor. A strong character, previous political experience, and nationwide popular appeal as demonstrated by opinion polls are considered some of the major requirements.

Presidential Succession   The order in which officials assume the office of the president in the event of vacancy. The Constitution provides for the succession of the vice president when a vacancy occurs in the presidency. The Presidential Succession Act of 1947 with its amendments stipulates that, after the vice president, the order of succession is as follows: the Speaker of the House of Representatives, the President pro tempore of the Senate, and then cabinet officers in order of the establishment of their departments, beginning with the secretary of state. Currently, the last to succeed would be the secretary of education, since that department is the newest. Under the act, however, cabinet officers would serve only until a Speaker or President pro tempore was selected.

There are five major documents relating to the presidential succession (1) Article II, Section 1, of the Constitution; (2) the Presidential Succession Act of 1792; (3) the Presidential Succession Act of 1886; (4) the Presidential Succession Act of 1947; and (5) the Twenty-fifth Amendment to the Constitution. Until John Tyler assumed the presidency upon the death of President William Henry Harrison in 1841, anyone succeeding to the presidency was merely an acting president. Since then it has been assumed that anyone other than the vice president succeeding to the presidency would be an acting president. This rule has not been tested, as no one other than a vice president has ever succeeded to the presidency. *See also* PRESIDENTIAL DISABILITY, p. 107.

Significance   The Presidential Succession Act of 1886 recognized the importance of the executive branch and made provision for unelected cabinet officers to succeed to the presidency. The statement made by former Secretary of State Alexander M. Haig after the attempted assassination of President Ronald Reagan on March 30, 1981, that "I have taken charge" of the administration, was an incorrect interpretation of law, since the Vice President, Speaker of the House of Representatives, and President pro tempore of the Senate would have succeeded, in that order, had Reagan died. Under Section 2 of the Twenty-fifth Amendment, whenever there is a vacancy in the vice presidency, the president shall nominate a vice president. Accordingly, President Richard M. Nixon nominated Gerald R. Ford to become the vice president when Vice President Spiro T. Agnew resigned on October 10, 1973. Later, when President Nixon resigned on August 9, 1974, Ford succeeded to the presidency, thus becoming the first unelected president in American history. President Ford then nominated his potential successor, Nelson A. Rockefeller, to assume the vice presidency. The most unsettling aspect of the Twenty-fifth Amendment is that it effectively bars the American public from participation in the process of presidential succession, by keeping the line of succession among appointed (not elected) officials within the executive branch.

State of the Union Message   An annual message of legislative programs proposed by the president to a joint session of Congress. The State of the Union message sets the agenda of Congress. Article II, Section 3 of the Constitution requires that the president "shall from time to time give to the Congress Information of the State of the Union, and recommend to their Consideration such Measures as he shall judge necessary and expedient...." Although the president may choose to transmit the message to Congress at any time, it has become customary to deliver it at the beginning of each congressional session. President George Washington appeared in person before Congress to deliver his State of the Union address. Presidents John Adams and Woodrow Wilson also delivered their messages to Congress in person. All recent presidents have delivered personally their State of the Union messages. *See also* BUDGET MESSAGE, p. 97; CHIEF LAWMAKER, p. 33; CONSTITUTIONAL POWERS, p. 39; ECONOMIC MESSAGE, p. 98.

Significance   The State of the Union message offers to presidents an unparalleled opportunity to highlight and dramatize their legislative agenda. Typically, these messages focus on major problems facing the country (and sometimes the world) and recommend statutory solutions. Throughout the message, the president documents promises and substantiates past performance. It is a formal occasion in which not only the members of Congress are present, but also the Supreme Court justices, the president's cabinet, and the Washington diplomatic corps. The State of the Union message receives wide publicity at home and abroad through radio and television. The president is empowered to call Congress into special session to act on legislative recommendations. The president's message consists of a list of legislative initiatives that stand a good chance of passage. The State of the Union message gives the president preeminence in legislative matters; the executive branch initiates about 90 percent of the legislation. The message is often followed by intensive lobbying by White House aides and administration supporters to ensure the passage of as many bills as possible. The Constitution does not require Congress to approve the president's legislative recommendations, but in most cases it does.

State of the World Message   A brief annual review of the world situation by the president. The State of the World message also deals with the role that the United States should play in world affairs. President Richard M. Nixon initiated the practice of delivering the State of the World message in 1971. Employing radio, television, and satellite communications, he reported the shape and objectives of American foreign policy. The problems facing America in the world are described by the president. The message is prepared with the assistance of the National Security Council and the Department of State. *See also* DEPARTMENT OF STATE, p. 128; NATIONAL SECURITY COUNCIL, p. 132; STATE OF THE UNION MESSAGE, p. 111.

Significance The State of the World message is not a constitutional requirement, yet presidents send this message to Congress to outline the state of the world and the shape of things to come in foreign affairs. The message gives some hints of foreign policy aims and concerns. President Nixon, in his initiation message to Congress, said that the United States was "at the end of an era" in its relations with other nations. Since then, the policies of Presidents Gerald R. Ford, Jimmy Carter, and Ronald Reagan have defined two sharply divergent responses to fundamental changes in the international environment. Their messages reflect America's relative decline in military and economic power and a growing interdependence between nations. Increasingly, the United States has become aware that it faces critical situations in a world in which more than three-quarters of the population live in dire conditions in the Third World. Presidential rhetoric is attuned to the politics of scarcity and limits of power. Presidents' economic and security policies are part of an implicit adjustment to what these leaders see as the end of American preeminence in world affairs. Modern-day presidents have argued that as the world changes, American foreign policy must change with it. The message is primarily designed for foreign consumption and serves as a propaganda device to win over other nations in favor of American foreign policy.

Strong Presidents Those who extend their power in domestic and foreign policy arenas. Strong presidents feel they are limited only by explicit checks and balances provided by the Constitution and statute. Whether a president is strong or weak depends on personality. Presidents Woodrow Wilson, Franklin D. Roosevelt, and Harry S Truman adopted bold domestic and foreign policy initiatives in conducting war. Those presidents who are rated as great are usually strong presidents who attempt to overshadow Congress and effectively persuade it to enact legislation favorable to their policy. Strong presidents are usually of the active-positive type. *See also* PRESIDENTIAL CHARACTER, p. 105; WEAK PRESIDENTS, p. 116.

Significance Strong presidents are power oriented and assertive leaders. Richard E. Neustadt, a former adviser to President John F. Kennedy, contends that strong presidents frequently attempt to aggrandize personal power. They identify with the power and prestige of the office and defend it against all criticism. Strong presidents relish power and its use. According to several writers, Theodore Roosevelt was the first twentieth century president that could be described as strong. In his autobiography, President Roosevelt said of power: "I did not usurp power, but I did greatly broaden the use of executive power.... I did not care a rap for the mere form and show of power; I cared immensely for the use that could be made of the substance" (Roosevelt 1913, 357). Political scientist James David Barber takes the view that strong presidents are active-positive and are usually successful because they are decisive and assertive. Most modern presidents have defined bold political and economic goals and have been active in eliciting public support. With the possible exception of Presidents Dwight D. Eisenhower, Gerald R. Ford, and Jimmy Carter, all chief executives since Franklin D. Roosevelt have jealously guarded presidential prerogatives and exercised broad powers. They were all strong and activist presidents, sometimes in spite of their lack of personal charisma.

Summit Conference   A conference between two or more heads of state or heads of government. The term summit is somewhat inexact. Often known as personal diplomacy, such discussions take place between monarchs, presidents, and prime ministers. Summit diplomacy is broadly interpreted as meaning the determination and management of foreign policy at the head of state level. It encompasses at least five principal elements (1) presidential policy formulation; (2) presidential communication; (3) presidential participation; (4) state visits; and (5) summit negotiation. World War II and its aftermath evoked an unusual number of summit conferences. President Franklin D. Roosevelt attended many conferences with Allied heads of state at Casablanca, Quebec, Tehran, Cairo, and Yalta. President Harry S Truman attended a summit conference at Potsdam; John F. Kennedy at Vienna; Lyndon B. Johnson at Glassboro; Richard M. Nixon at Moscow and Beijing; Gerald R. Ford at Helsinki; Jimmy Carter at Vienna; and Ronald Reagan at Cancun. *See also* CHIEF DIPLOMAT, p. 29; DEPARTMENT OF STATE, p. 128; PRESIDENT, p. 103.

Significance   Summit conferences represent the highest level of diplomatic activity. Beginning with Franklin D. Roosevelt, summit diplomacy by American presidents has become the most dramatic manifestation of their role as chief diplomat. Some of the most notable summit conferences were held by President Nixon in 1972 with Soviet President Leonid I. Brezhnev and Chinese Communist Party Chairman Mao Tsetung. Nixon's meeting with the Soviet leader was soon followed by the first major grain trade deal between the United States and the Soviet Union. His meeting with the Chinese leader was a major step forward in the process of normalization of Sino-American relations.

President Carter's peace talks with Egypt and Israel and his persistent prodding resulting in the Camp David Accord (1979) is another illustration of the president's diplomatic role. President Reagan's summitry at

Cancun was marked by rhetoric rather than any concrete achievement, as evidenced by his statement: "History demonstrates that time and time again, in place after place, economic growth and human progress make their greatest strides in countries that encourage economic freedom." By this statement, he created more enemies than friends among the Third World leaders that attended the conference; not every nation subscribed to Reagan's "get tough" policy with poor countries. A summit conference is a risky undertaking, for when heads of state fail to resolve a dispute, there is no higher government authority that an issue can be referred to. Whether they succeed or not, American presidents (like many other heads of state) relish summit meetings because these events offer pageantry, grandeur, and entertainment.

Textbook Presidency   An idealized model of the cult of presidency that is extensively nurtured in textbooks. The textbook presidency is a concept built around exaggerated and unrealistic interpretations of presidential power, competence, and beneficence. Many textbook writers try to create the impression that what is good for the president is good for the nation. These writers idealize the presidency and presidents. President George Washington is portrayed as the creator and consolidator of the new Republic. President Abraham Lincoln is credited with saving the Union. President Franklin D. Roosevelt is depicted as the rescuer of the nation. The textbook authors also emphasize the need for strong presidents and a strong America. *See also* STRONG PRESIDENTS, p. 113; WEAK PRESIDENTS, p. 116.

Significance   Textbook presidency describes the chief executive as the central figure in the American government, around whom the nation revolves. The president is symbolized as a godfather who is benevolent and omnipotent. The president may not be all-powerful, but there is no denying the fact that Americans prefer strong, powerful, and active-positive presidents. Few authors criticize particular presidential policies, and most believe that the chief executives tend to be competent and effective. Not only the writers, but the public in general, have short memories and quickly forget about such scandals as Watergate, which involved flagrant misconduct by a powerful president, Richard M. Nixon. Many American government courses center around the presidency and are offered at almost all levels of education. Students and instructors are often convinced that this simplistic model reflects reality, and they believe in the precision of the textbook view of the presidency. They forget that, in fact, several presidents failed miserably in their performance, and all have exhibited various weaknesses of human nature.

Weak Presidents   Those who are unable to use their authority and consciously limit their power. Weak presidents are not motivated by the desire to be successful at any cost. They are afraid of taking risks and bold action. Their administrations are characterized by a "no risk, no gain" approach. They are not power hungry like strong presidents. *See also* CHIEF EXECUTIVE, p. 31; PRESIDENTIAL CHARACTER, p. 105; STRONG PRESIDENTS, p. 113.

Significance   Weak presidents are timid persons. President William Howard Taft was typical of this group. He said: "The President can exercise no power which cannot be fairly and reasonably traced to some specific grant of power or justly implied." His view was that the president could exercise only the specific powers given him by the Constitution or statute. By contrast, Theodore Roosevelt, a strong president, declined to adopt the view that "what was imperatively necessary for the nation could not be done by the President. . . ." The list of weak presidents includes William H. Taft, James Buchanan, Warren G. Harding, Calvin Coolidge, Ulysses S. Grant, and Herbert Hoover. According to political scientist James David Barber's psychobiological analysis of the presidency, weak presidents are passive-negative and are usually unsuccessful.

Americans still face the same question that the framers of the Constitution did nearly 200 years ago. How powerful should a president be? There is no consensus on this, but generally, people feel that too strong a president usurps power and works against the interests of the people. A weak president worries about constraints on the use of power. Since the Vietnam War and the Watergate scandal, presidents have become vulnerable to criticisms of abuse of authority. As a result, they are unable to use their power for fear of public criticism. Former President Gerald R. Ford has expressed the view that the presidency has changed from an "imperial" to an "imperiled" one. A president who is too weak is unable to perform the presidential duties effectively. Political analyst Arthur M. Schlesinger, Jr. maintains that "the American democracy must discover a middle ground between making the President a Czar and making him a puppet." A middle ground is preferred by many: a president who is neither too strong nor too weak.

5. The Presidential Establishment

Cabinet   A body of principal presidential advisers selected by the president and confirmed by the Senate. The cabinet serves as a vehicle for coordinating and implementing government policy. It is a creation of custom and tradition dating back to the first president, George Washington. The cabinet consists of the heads of the thirteen executive departments, as well as several other top officials, including the vice president and the ambassador to the United Nations. Presidents choose their cabinet officers for a variety of reasons: some are selected as a result of their expertise or special qualifications, others are chosen for political or personal reasons. Individually, the cabinet members head various executive departments. *See also* KITCHEN CABINET, p. 101; WHITE HOUSE STAFF, p. 138.

Significance   Cabinet members are not elected by the people, and as such, they are not directly responsible to them. In appointing individuals to cabinet positions, however, presidents give special consideration to certain key factors, including the nominees' party affiliations and service to the party; their personal philosophies; their state or regional backgrounds; their race, religion, and sex; and their standing with the American public. The Constitution does not expressly mention the cabinet, let alone establish it. Nonetheless, presidents have found many important uses for the cabinet.

One of the president's most difficult tasks is to maintain cordial relations with the Congress. In this regard, the cabinet can be of inestimable value. Cabinet members advocate the president's position on Capitol Hill, perform various liaison functions, and bring their expert knowledge to bear on the intricacies of executive-legislative relations. The cabinet also affects the standing of the president, either positively or negatively. By recruiting distinguished persons into the cabinet,

117

presidents can partly overcome their personal weaknesses or limitations in certain areas. For instance, President John F. Kennedy's appointment of C. Douglas Dillon as secretary of the treasury, and President Richard M. Nixon's selection of Henry A. Kissinger as secretary of state, greatly strengthened their respective administrations. Many presidents have tended not to rely on the cabinet for advice; instead, they have sought advice from their kitchen cabinet.

Council of Economic Advisers   A staff agency that analyzes the national economy and recommends fiscal policy to the president. The Council of Economic Advisers advises the president on measures to maintain the nation's economic stability. It analyzes trends in the economy and recommends to the president policies for economic growth and stability. Established by the Employment Act of 1946, the council consists of three members appointed by the president with Senate approval. The president designates one of the members as the chairman of the council. The council assists in the preparation of the annual economic report of the president to the Congress and helps the president make policies regarding inflation, unemployment, and taxation. The members of the council are economists who are sympathetic to the president's political and economic goals. *See also* EXECUTIVE OFFICE OF THE PRESIDENT, p. 131; OFFICE OF MANAGEMENT AND BUDGET, p. 133; STATE OF THE UNION MESSAGE, p. 111; WHITE HOUSE STAFF, p. 138.

Significance   The Council of Economic Advisers gathers statistics and other forms of data from various government agencies—national, state, and local—and from private sources, in order to keep abreast of economic conditions in the country. It is concerned with forecasting levels of investment, inflation, and unemployment. The council has made major fiscal recommendations to overcome post–World War II recessions. Its recommendations are included in the president's State of the Union message to the Congress.

Over the years, the council's role in economic planning has varied. Disagreement with the president or among the members and outside economists has weakened the influence of the council. It is expected to give objective and professional advice to the president. However, since the members are part of the administration, they sometimes become partisan and controversial. During a presidential election year, the council may express optimism about the economy in general, and inflation and unemployment in particular, in order to help the incumbent win reelection. The council's reputation as a group of professional economists may diminish if it tailors its recommendations to fit the administration's policies.

Department of Agriculture   A major cabinet-level department that provides numerous services for farmers and maintains farm income. Created in 1862, the Department of Agriculture regulates various aspects of agriculture and expands markets abroad for American agricultural products. Headed by the secretary of agriculture, who is appointed by the president with Senate approval, the department helps to curb poverty, hunger, and malnutrition. It subsidizes agriculture by purchasing and storing food surpluses. Some of the operational units of the department include (1) Farmers Home Administration; (2) Rural Electrification Administration; (3) Federal Crop Insurance Corporation; (4) Agricultural Cooperative Service; (5) Animal and Plant Health Inspection Service; (6) Federal Grain Inspection Service; (7) Food and Nutrition Service; (8) Agricultural Stabilization and Conservation Service; (9) Agricultural Research Service; (10) Forest Service; (11) Soil Conservation Service; and (12) Economic Research Service. The department assures standards of quality in the food supply. *See also* DEPARTMENT OF COMMERCE, p. 120; DEPARTMENT OF HEALTH AND HUMAN SERVICES, p. 123.

Significance   The Department of Agriculture is the sixth ranking executive department of the United States government. It is responsible for maintaining stability in the farm economy, controlling agricultural surpluses, and expanding agricultural markets. Many of its services grew out of emergencies occasioned by plant and animal diseases, insect infestations, droughts, floods, and famines at home and abroad. The department administers the school lunch and food stamp programs and numerous food distribution programs overseas. It inspects meat, poultry, and food products for wholesomeness. The department also establishes standards of quality for every major agricultural commodity. Through the grading system, it safeguards and assures standards of quality in the food supply.

Under the leadership of the department, an agricultural revolution has occurred in the United States: in recent years, productivity in agriculture has grown faster than in industry. This increase in output has not been achieved by cultivating more land, but through intensive scientific methods. The agricultural abundance has been a blessing to the consumer. The United States has one of the lowest food costs in the world and a rich and nutritious diet. The United States donates food to many hungry nations in the world. In addition, the department sells grains to other nations, notably the Soviet Union and China. In 1983 a $10 billion five-year pact with the Soviet Union provided a tremendous boost to farm production and the economy. Politically, the grain sale may improve Soviet-American relations and make President Ronald Reagan more popular with farmers, who desperately need to better their lot through market expansion. Ironically, the success of the department in increasing farm productivity has contributed to the massive glut of farm products that costs the department billions of dollars each year in subsidies.

Department of Commerce   A cabinet-level department that promotes international trade and exports of American products and encourages technological advancement and economic growth. The Department of Commerce awards patents, registers trademarks, and administers programs to prevent unfair foreign trade competition. It administers the Census Bureau and National Weather Service. It assists in the maintenance and development of the United States Merchant Marine. The department provides research and support for the use of scientific, engineering, and technological development. It offers assistance and information to help increase exports and provides social and economic statistics and analyzes them for business and government planners. It encourages domestic economic development and promotes travel in the United States by foreigners. The department assists in the growth of minority businesses. Originally created as the Department of Commerce and Labor in 1903, it was redesignated in 1913. It is headed by the secretary of commerce, who is appointed by the president with Senate approval. *See also* DEPARTMENT OF AGRICULTURE, p. 119; DEPARTMENT OF LABOR, p. 127; DEPARTMENT OF STATE, p. 128.

Significance   The Department of Commerce is the seventh ranking executive department of the United States government. It is assigned to foster and promote domestic and foreign trade and develop manufacturing industries. It is a veritable storehouse of aids for business. It helps businesses to export their wares and protects patents. The department collects data on products and markets through the Census Bureau. The bureau conducts the decennial census of population and housing and quinquennial censuses of agriculture and industry. Other operating units of the department prepare and analyze measures of business activity, such as surveys of investment outlays, business planning, and major economic indicators. This data is invaluable for policy planning by various agencies of the government and private organizations. Typically, the secretary of commerce is a former businessman and the department maintains friendly relations with the business community at home and abroad. This is done mainly to promote foreign trade in order to reduce deficits and create a favorable balance of trade, if possible.

Department of Defense   The agency charged with responsibility to defend the country against aggression and to provide the military forces needed to deter war. The Department of Defense coordinates logistics and the general administration of the armed forces; supervises the Joint Chiefs of Staff; and awards military contracts. The department includes the separately organized military departments of Army, Navy, and Air Force. The major elements of the armed forces are the Army, Navy, Marine Corps, and Air Force, consisting of about 2 million persons on active duty. They are backed, in case of emergency, by 2.5 million members of the reserve components. With about 1 million civilian employees, the department is the Western world's largest employer. The headquarters of the department is located at the Pentagon. It is headed by the secretary of defense, who is appointed by the president with Senate approval and serves as a member of the cabinet. The National Security Act of 1949, as amended in 1974, unified the armed forces under the control of the secretary of defense. As commander in chief, the president is responsible for the overall operations of the Department of Defense. It oversees three important agencies, including International Security Affairs, the Defense Intelligence Agency, and the National Security Agency. The latter intercepts the codes of other nations and conducts electronic espionage. *See also* COMMANDER IN CHIEF, p. 38; DEPARTMENT OF STATE, p. 128; JOINT CHIEFS OF STAFF, p. 131; NATIONAL SECURITY COUNCIL, p. 132.

Significance   The Department of Defense is the third ranking executive department of the United States government. It is the largest department in number of employees and amount of money spent. The principle of civilian control over the military establishment is deeply rooted in American tradition. The president is the commander in chief of the armed forces, and the secretary of defense, by law, must be a civilian. Yet many people have questioned the effectiveness of civilian supremacy over a vast and powerful military establishment. Since World War II, the department has maintained military bases around the world and has coordinated military programs with many nations. The department is involved in a massive research and technological weapons race with the Soviet Union. As it is difficult to distinguish between military and foreign policy, the Department of Defense has often developed rivalries with the Department of State. Many times these interdepartmental conflicts over policy and personality have been resolved by the president.

Department of Education   A major agency that seeks to unify administration of federal activities in the field of education and coordinate educational assistance programs. Created in 1979, the Department of Education administers most federal assistance to education. Existing and newly legislated programs of the department include Arts in Education, Women's Educational Equity, Basic Skills, Environmental Education, Consumer Education, Teacher Centers, Metric Education, Law-Related Education, Civic/Citizenship Education, Marine-Aquatic Education, and Library Resources. The department is responsible for the four federally aided corporations: the American Printing House for the Blind, Gallaudet College, Howard University, and the National Institute for the Blind.

The department maintains ten regional offices to disseminate information and provide technical assistance to state and local educational institutions, agencies, and individuals. The department provides support for programs, activities, and management initiatives that meet the special educational needs of bilingual populations. It provides financial and technical assistance to meet special needs incident to the elimination of racial segregation and discrimination. It offers grants for the education of neglected and delinquent students. The department is responsible for ensuring that programs and activities receiving financial assistance and employers holding federal contracts comply with federal laws and guidelines. The department is headed by the secretary of education, who is appointed by the president with Senate approval. *See also* DEPARTMENT OF HEALTH AND HUMAN SERVICES, p. 123; DEPARTMENT OF JUSTICE, p. 126.

Significance   The Department of Education is the thirteenth ranking executive department of the United States government. It is the smallest and the newest of the departments. Formerly a part of the Department of Health, Education, and Welfare, now called the Department of Health and Human Services, the Department of Education was established as a separate major agency in 1979 by President Jimmy Carter. Its opponents question whether the department deserves separate status, since education falls primarily under the jurisdiction of state and local governments. During the presidential election debate in 1980, presidential candidate Ronald Reagan promised to abolish the Department of Education and to end intervention in local government matters. After becoming President, however, Reagan failed to fulfill this promise.

Department of Energy   A major agency that promotes energy conservation and research, regulates gas and electric power rates, and manages nuclear waste. Created in 1977, the Department of Energy provides the framework for a comprehensive energy plan through coordination and administration of energy programs of the federal government. It is responsible for long-term, high risk research and development of energy technology; the marketing of federal power; the development of nuclear power; and a central energy data collection and analysis program. The Energy Organization Act of 1977 consolidated the major federal energy functions into one department, including within its jurisdiction the responsibilities of the Energy Research and Development Administration; the Federal Energy Administration; the Federal Power Commission; and the Alaska, Bonneville, Southeastern, and Southwestern Power Administrations. Also transferred to it were certain functions of the Interstate Commerce Commission, the Department of Commerce, and the Department of Housing and Urban Development. The department is headed by the secretary of energy, who is appointed by the president with Senate approval and serves as a member of the cabinet. *See also* DEPARTMENT OF COMMERCE, p. 120; DEPARTMENT OF HOUSING AND URBAN DEVELOPMENT, p. 124; INTERSTATE COMMERCE COMMISSION, p. 151.

Significance   The Department of Energy is the twelfth ranking executive department of the United States government. It was created to consolidate federal energy research and development, energy regulation, and policy formulation. It has sought to promote consumer interests in energy conservation, encourage competition in the energy industry, and protect human health and environment. Prior to the Arab oil embargo of 1973–1974, responsibility in energy matters was fragmented among several agencies. After the oil embargo, two federal agencies were created, the Energy Research and Development Administration and the Federal Energy Administration. These intermediate steps proved inadequate and led to President Jimmy Carter's creation of the Department of Energy to make energy independence from unreliable foreign sources of oil a national priority. Because of the lack of any consensus on a national energy policy, efforts to stimulate alternatives to oil are sources of continual controversy.

Department of Health and Human Services   A major agency that administers social security pensions, medicare and medicaid programs, pure food and drug laws, and public health research. Of all executive departments, the Department of Health and Human Services is most concerned with people and most involved with human welfare. It issues social security checks to recipients and makes health services available to deserving people. The department is headed by the secretary of health and human services, who is appointed by the president with Senate approval and has cabinet status. The main operating units of the department are (1) Human Development Services; (2) Public Health Service; (3) Health Care Financial Administration; (4) Social Security Administration; (5) Child Support Enforcement; and (6)

Community Services. The department administers the Office of Civil Rights which enforces laws prohibiting discrimination. It is also responsible for protecting public health through the Food and Drug Administration programs. The former Department of Health, Education, and Welfare was divided into the Department of Health and Human Services and the Department of Education in 1979. *See also* DEPARTMENT OF EDUCATION, p. 121; FOOD AND DRUG ADMINISTRATION, p. 148.

Significance   The Department of Health and Human Services is the ninth ranking executive department of the United States government. It reflects the commitment of the government to protect the health, welfare, and dignity of the public through its various programs. Many of these programs, such as social security, medicare, and medicaid, have been highly controversial and the subject of severe criticism because they are sometimes viewed as socialistic in nature. However, many Americans and the two major political parties accept the fact that without such programs the problems of hunger, poverty, and disease will worsen. The department's budget and number of employees is second only to the Department of Defense. The department disburses hundreds of billions of dollars annually, with about 80 percent of it in social security payments and medicare benefits.

Department of Housing and Urban Development (HUD)   A major agency that offers public housing assistance, urban renewal financial grants, and government guaranteed home purchase loans. The Department of Housing and Urban Development is responsible for overseeing America's housing needs, promoting fair housing opportunities, and improving the nation's communities. The department was established in 1965 to assist the federal government in achieving maximum coordination of the various activities that affect communities; to encourage the solution of housing problems through local initiative; and to encourage private homebuilding. It is headed by the secretary of housing and urban development, who is appointed by the president with Senate approval and has cabinet rank. HUD administers mortgage insurance programs; rental subsidies for low income people; anti-discrimination laws in housing; and neighborhood rehabilitation programs. It also protects the home buyer and develops programs that stimulate the housing industry. The main operating units of the department are (1) Housing Production and Mortgage Credit; (2) Federal Housing Commission; (3) Federal Insurance Administration; (4) Community Development; (5) Fair Housing and Equal Opportunity; and (6) Equal Opportunity. *See also* DEPARTMENT OF HEALTH AND HUMAN SERVICES, p. 123.

Significance   The Department of Housing and Urban Development is the tenth ranking executive department of the United States government. In 1937 President Franklin D. Roosevelt proclaimed that one-third of the nation was "ill-housed, ill-clad, and ill-nourished." A great many of these people still live in cities and suburbs that are fast decaying and require assistance. The Department of Housing and Urban Development, as the name indicates, has the mission of reversing the factors that make American cities into prisons for many urban residents.

Among the programs launched by the department have been those involving public housing, urban renewal, college housing, housing for the elderly and the handicapped, inner city open space, demonstration and rehabilitation housing, community renewal, rent subsidies, and urban public facilities. Many of these programs have commanded public support; however several programs, such as rent subsidies and demonstration housing, have been hotly debated. With more than 70 percent of Americans living in cities that boast the nation's highest percentage of major crimes, arrests, disease, delinquency, fires, broken homes, drug addiction, prostitution, gambling, and unemployment, the department has become the principal federal agency charged with seeking answers to the problems of urban decay.

Department of the Interior   The major agency that administers public lands, the Bureau of Indian Affairs, mine safety laws, national parks, overseas territories, and mineral resources. The Department of the Interior also conserves water resources and administers various hydroelectric power facilities. It owns one-third of the public lands in the country and is responsible for management of these lands. This jurisdiction includes direct management of over 500 million acres of federal land and trust responsibility for an additional 50 million acres, consisting mostly of Indian reservations. The department leases land and offshore areas for oil exploration and drilling. It ensures that the development of resources is in the best interest of the people and the nation. Some of the major operating units in the department are (1) Fish and Wildlife Service; (2) Bureau of Mines and Geological Survey; (3) Bureau of Indian Affairs; (4) Bureau of Land Management; (5) National Park Service; (6) Bureau of Outdoor Recreation; and (7) Bureau of Reclamation. The department was established in 1849. The secretary of the interior, who heads the department, is appointed by the president with Senate approval and has cabinet rank. *See also* DEPARTMENT OF AGRICULTURE, p. 119.

Significance   The Department of the Interior is the fifth ranking executive department of the United States government. It consists of thirty bureaus and offices that carry out an extensive variety of managerial regulation, planning, and research functions. Fish, wildlife, and other resources are protected against abuses and environmental damage. A nation's strength depends, in part, on its natural resources. By preserving and conserving America's natural resources, the department assures the continued greatness of the United States.

Not only is the department the custodian of the nation's resources, it is also the administering agency for Guam, the Virgin Islands, American Samoa, and the Pacific trust territories. The department is sometimes at the center of conflicts and controversies over the management of public lands, as competing interest groups put pressure on the department for more liberal policies allowing exploitation of federal land. The department often adopts policies to satisfy divergent interests within the country, policies that are partisan in their origin and controversial in their administration.

Department of Justice   The principal law enforcement agency of the United States. The Department of Justice administers the Federal Bureau of Investigation (FBI), enforces acts of Congress, prosecutes court cases for the United States government, and maintains federal prisons. It investigates violations of federal antitrust and civil rights laws and supervises immigration. The department files lawsuits in the court in which the United States is involved. It represents the government in legal matters and renders advice and opinions to the president and the executive departments. The department is responsible for the enforcement of all statutes affecting civil rights, including the Civil Rights Acts, slavery cases, election fraud, and obstruction of justice. Headed by the attorney general, who is appointed by the president with Senate approval, the department supervises and directs the activities of United States attorneys and marshals. The department's six divisions are (1) Antitrust Division; (2) Civil Division; (3) Civil Rights Division; (4) Criminal Division; (5) Land and Natural Resources Division; and (6) Tax Division. In addition, it has two bureaus, the Federal Bureau of Investigation and the Bureau of Prisons. The department includes a Board of Immigration Appeals. *See also* FEDERAL BUREAU OF INVESTIGATION, p. 144.

Significance   The Department of Justice is the fourth ranking executive department of the United States government. It is the largest law office in the world, with a staff of about 30,000 persons. Through these attorneys, investigators, and agents, the department makes decisions about who will be prosecuted for alleged federal law violations and who will not. During the Watergate scandal (which involved President

Richard M. Nixon and several top officials, who were charged with criminal misdeeds), public suspicion grew over the willingness of the department to prosecute high officials of President Nixon's administration.

Although law enforcement is primarily the responsibility of state and local authorities, the department is playing an increasingly larger role in civil rights issues. The Civil Rights Division of the department has underscored the government's concern in enforcing federal civil rights laws which prohibit discrimination on the basis of age, race, sex, religion, national origin, and handicap in the areas of voting, education, employment, housing, credit, public accommodations, and public facilities. The department plays a key role in protecting citizens through crime prevention and detection, and prosecution and rehabilitation of offenders.

Department of Labor　　A major agency that enforces minimum wage and occupational safety laws. The Department of Labor fosters and promotes the welfare of laborers and workers in the United States. It administers unemployment compensation and compiles cost-of-living statistics. The department administers more than thirty labor laws guaranteeing workers' rights, minimum wage, overtime pay, freedom of employment, unemployment compensation, and protects workers from discrimination. Its responsibilities include manpower and job training programs, and enforcement of safety and health standards for workers. It also seeks to protect workers' pension rights. The department is headed by the secretary of labor, who is appointed by the president with Senate approval and has cabinet rank.

The department is divided into seven major operating units (1) Employment and Training Administration; (2) Labor Management Services Administration; (3) Employment Standards Administration; (4) Occupational Safety and Health Administration (OSHA); (5) Mine Safety and Health Administration; (6) Bureau of Labor Statistics; and (7) Veteran's Employment Service. Although a Bureau of Labor existed under the Department of the Interior since 1884, the Department of Labor was not established until 1913. *See also* DEPARTMENT OF COMMERCE, p. 120; DEPARTMENT OF THE INTERIOR, p. 125.

Significance　　The Department of Labor is the eighth ranking executive department of the United States government. It has expanded considerably, and its operations now extend throughout the world. Since it has the task of promoting the cause of labor, the department is considered one of the main clientele agencies of the federal government. (A clientele agency maintains special ties with the groups it serves, such as trade unions.) The Bureau of Labor Statistics, for example, issues monthly reports on unemployment figures and other data essential to government monitoring of the national economy. As the department seeks to assist people who need jobs, efforts are made to meet the job market problems for older workers, minority groups, women, youth, handicapped, and migrant workers.

Department of State   The major agency that advises the president in the formulation and execution of American foreign policy. The Department of State is headed by the secretary of state, who is appointed by the president with Senate approval and has cabinet rank. The department supervises diplomatic personnel and administers foreign aid. Its primary objective is to promote the long-range security and well-being of the United States. The department analyzes the facts relating to American interests abroad and recommends future action. It consults with the public, Congress, and other departments in the formulation of policy. The department maintains embassies and consulates in almost all the independent nations of the world. It represents the United States in more than fifty international organizations and more than 800 international conferences annually. The department negotiates treaties with foreign governments. It issues passports to Americans. The American consular officers, working under the department, grant visas to foreigners to visit the United States.

The department has five regional bureaus that are responsible for the various regions of the world: the Bureaus of African Affairs; European Affairs; East Asian and Pacific Affairs; Inter-American Affairs; and Near Eastern and South Asian Affairs. These bureaus help devise policy and supervise its implementation. The bureaus are assisted by "country desks" headed by some fifty country directors. In addition, the department has eleven functional bureaus and offices. They are (1) Economic and Business Affairs; (2) Intelligence and Research; (3) International Organization Affairs; (4) Legal Adviser; (5) Public Affairs; (6) Consular Affairs; (7) Politico-Military Affairs; (8) Oceans and International Environment and Scientific Affairs; (9) Protocol; (10) Human Rights and Humanitarian Affairs; and (11) Refugee Programs. Other instruments of the department include the Agency for International Development, the International Communication Agency, the Peace Corps, and the Arms Control and Disarmament Agency. *See also* DEPARTMENT OF COMMERCE, p. 120; NATIONAL SECURITY COUNCIL, p. 132.

Significance   The Department of State is the oldest and the highest ranking executive department of the United States government. It is responsible for protecting the lives and properties of American citizens and government agencies abroad. The traditional functions of the department (representation, reporting, and negotiation) are supplemented today by a wide variety of activities. As foreign and domestic policy become enmeshed, as interdependence of nations grows, and as the United States assumes wider international responsibilities, the role of the department in foreign policymaking becomes more complex. The department couriers personally carry diplomatic documents 10 million miles annually between Washington and 143 American embassies abroad. The department can communicate with any embassy in two minutes.

Despite these facilities, its level of efficiency has been criticized by many. Among the chief problems associated with its operation is the overlap of functions with other departments and agencies of the United States government, and the possible conflicts between these departments because of their related functions. Also, it has been difficult to establish a close identification between the American public and the department's elite officer corps, a problem attributable to the fact that these officials deal with the external affairs of the country and prefer to remain aloof from people at home.

Department of Transportation   A major agency that establishes the overall transportation policy of the United States government. The department is headed by the secretary of transportation, who is appointed by the president with Senate approval and has cabinet rank. The Department of Transportation administers interstate highway programs, air safety standards, automotive safety laws, and the Alaska railroad. The components of the department are the United States Coast Guard, Federal Aviation Administration, Federal Highway Administration, Federal Railroad Administration, Urban Mass Transportation Administration, Saint Lawrence Seaway Development Corporation, and National Highway Traffic Safety Administration. The department was established in 1966; more than thirty agencies were subsumed under it. Its jurisdiction includes highway planning, development, and construction; urban mass transit; the safety of waterways, ports, and highways; and oil and gas pipelines. The air traffic controllers of the Federal Aviation Administration operate airport towers across the country. The Clear Air Act of 1970 charged the department with responsibility of reducing automobile emissions. *See also* DEPARTMENT OF ENERGY, p. 122.

Significance   The Department of Transportation is the eleventh ranking executive department of the United States government. It is charged with developing national transportation policies to achieve fast, safe, efficient, and convenient transportation at low cost. In order for the department to be successful, it must possess and exercise power to evaluate safety in all forms and improve allocation of its resources, while avoiding undue interference by various interest groups, such as the automobile industry. For years, tough battles have raged between the automakers and the department about how stringent auto exhaust pollution requirements should be. The department claims that the automakers are delaying compliance with pollution standards in hopes that Congress will relax the requirements. Congress has done so many times. Decisions made by the department affect programs such as land planning, energy conservation, resource allocation, and technological change.

Department of the Treasury   The agency that is charged with formulating fiscal policies for the United States government. The Department of the Treasury is headed by the secretary of the treasury, who is appointed by the president with Senate approval and has cabinet rank. The department serves as the financial agent for the United States government. Important units of the department include (1) Bureau of Alcohol, Tobacco, and Firearms; (2) Office of the Comptroller of the Currency; (3) United States Customs Service; (4) Bureau of Engraving and Printing; (5) Federal Law Enforcement Training Center; (6) Bureau of Government Financial Operations; (7) Internal Revenue Service; (8) Bureau of the Mint; (9) Bureau of the Public Debt; (10) United States Savings Bonds Division; and (11) United States Secret Service. The department is responsible for designing, engraving, and printing paper currency, bonds, and other securities. It oversees the Secret Service, which protects high government leaders and their families. It is concerned with making studies and recommendations on financial matters. The department is charged with collecting income tax and duties on imported goods. The department maintains a watchful eye on the importation of illegal commodities into the United States. *See also* INTERNAL REVENUE SERVICE, p. 150; OFFICE OF MANAGEMENT AND BUDGET, p. 133; SECRET SERVICE, p. 153.

Significance   The Department of the Treasury is one of the original departments established in 1789, and it is the second ranking executive department of the United States government. It formulates and recommends domestic and international financial and economic policy to the president. By law, the department is required to submit periodic reports to the Congress on the fiscal operations of the government. It maintains the central accounts for all receipts, expenditures, and appropriations for the United States government. The department is authorized to protect the person of the president, the president-elect, the vice president, their immediate families, major presidential and vice presidential candidates, and many others.

Executive Office of the President   A collection of top agencies that serve the president by advising him in carrying out his duties and responsibilities. The components of the office have changed over time. Today, they include the White House office, Office of Management and Budget, Council of Economic Advisers, National Security Council, Office of Policy Development, Office of the United States Trade Representatives, Council on Environmental Quality, Office of Science and Technology, Office of Administration, and Office of the Vice President. Among the most important components of the Executive Office are the White House Office, National Security Council, Office of Management and Budget, and Council of Economic Advisers. Created by President Franklin D. Roosevelt in 1939, the Executive Office provides the president with specialized assistance, advice, and coordinated effort in various policy matters. (Refer to the Appendix, Figure 6 for a diagram of the executive office of the president.) *See also* COUNCIL OF ECONOMIC ADVISERS, p. 118; NATIONAL SECURITY COUNCIL, p. 132; OFFICE OF MANAGEMENT AND BUDGET, p. 133; WHITE HOUSE OFFICE, p. 137.

Significance   The Executive Office of the President was established during the Great Depression of the 1930s, amid the additional challenge of World War II. It has since grown with each emergency that the nation has faced. In 1915 President Woodrow Wilson was assisted by only three aides, and he often answered his own telephone. By 1977 about 500 persons assisted the president. Today the Executive Office has about 1,500 employees who facilitate and maintain communications with the Congress, cabinet departments, information media, and the general public. These officials include persons with such titles as counselor to the president, assistant to the president, special consultant to the president, and so forth. They provide indispensable help in the performance of presidential duties. Many experts believe that these individuals insulate the president and create for him an unreal sense of his own significance and that of his policies and programs.

Joint Chiefs of Staff   The principal military advisers to the president, along with the secretary of defense and the National Security Council. The Joint Chiefs of Staff include the senior military officers of the army, navy, air force and, when marine matters are considered, the Commandant of the Marine Corps. The chairman and other members of the Joint Chiefs of Staff are appointed by the president with Senate approval. The chairman serves two years, and the others serve four-year terms. The chain of command runs from the president to the secretary of defense and through the Joint Chiefs of Staff to the commanders of combined and specified commands. Orders to such commands are issued by the president or the secretary of defense, or by the Joint Chiefs of Staff. The commanders have operational control over all forces assigned to them. *See also* COMMANDER IN CHIEF, p. 38; DEPARTMENT OF DEFENSE, p. 120; NATIONAL SECURITY COUNCIL, p. 132.

Significance   The Joint Chiefs of Staff are responsible for the conduct of daily military operations as well as long-term planning. They are assisted by some 400 officers selected about equally from the three services. Although they advise the president on military matters, the president may choose to disregard such advice. During the Cuban missile crisis of 1962, the late Attorney General Robert F. Kennedy believed that the Joint Chiefs of Staff wanted to use nuclear weapons in Cuba. According to Kennedy, the military advisers seemed to believe that war was in the national interest. President Lyndon B. Johnson put it more succinctly: "The generals know only two words—spend and bomb."

Today, foreign policy and military policy are closely linked. The top military brass have reputations as hawks in foreign policy matters. However, not every military officer is a hawk. Many generals, such as George C. Marshall, Omar N. Bradley, and Maxwell D. Taylor, view foreign policy in its broadest implications. Several studies show that the Joint Chiefs of Staff are slightly more hawkish than civilian advisers.

National Security Council (NSC)   The agency that serves as the major adviser to the president on domestic, foreign, and military policies involving national security. The National Security Council is composed of the president, vice president, and secretaries of state and defense; others may be invited by the president to participate. The chairman of the Joint Chiefs of Staff is the military adviser to the council, and the director of the Central Intelligence Agency (CIA) is its intelligence adviser. The president is the chairman of the council. The president's national security adviser directs the council. The agency was created in 1947 in the wake of World War II to coordinate the policies and operations of the domestic and military services and their intelligence-gathering departments. Two of these intelligence agencies, the CIA and the National Security Agency, are attached to the council.

The NSC integrates foreign and domestic policy and often deliberates on action to be taken in cases of national emergency. It runs the White

House Situation Room, the emergency headquarters equipped with advanced communications gear. The Situation Room is the president's crisis control center. The council's main role is to assess the risks of the United States in the area of national security and to recommend measures to be taken by the president. The NSC is an advisory body; the responsibility for the nation's security always rests with the president. *See also* CENTRAL INTELLIGENCE AGENCY, p. 142; DEPARTMENT OF STATE, p. 128; EXECUTIVE OFFICE OF THE PRESIDENT, p. 131.

Significance   The National Security Council was created under the National Security Act of 1947, when the United States emerged as a superpower after World War II. President Harry S Truman, the first chairman of the National Security Council, maintained that it "added a badly needed new facility to the government." Although President Truman praised the council, he seldom used it. By contrast, Presidents Dwight D. Eisenhower, John F. Kennedy, and Richard M. Nixon expanded the role of the council beyond its original purpose.

One obvious result of the establishment of the council is the awkward position of the Department of State, which is bypassed by the national security adviser on many occasions. This adviser is appointed by the president without Senate confirmation. The council adviser becomes the *de facto* secretary of state. The NSC often not only runs the foreign policy of the country but sometimes greatly influences the presidency itself, as did Henry A. Kissinger, council adviser to Presidents Nixon and Ford. Kissinger became as prominent as President Nixon and possibly more prominent than President Ford. Although the Department of State denied it, reports persisted that Secretary of State George P. Shultz lost considerable influence over policymaking in Central America and the Middle East to William P. Clark, President Ronald Reagan's former national security adviser. Perhaps the only time the NSC and Department of State worked in close cooperation was when Kissinger headed both offices.

Office of Management and Budget (OMB)   An advisory body that prepares the national budget and reviews agency requests for congressional appropriations. Formerly known as the Bureau of the Budget, the functions of the Office of Management and Budget include the following: (1) assist the presidential program to develop and maintain efficient coordinating mechanisms to implement government policies; (2) prepare the national budget; (3) supervise and control the administration of the budget; (4) help the president propose legislation; (5) develop regulatory reform; (6) assist in the preparation of proposed executive orders; (7) plan and develop information systems; (8) promote evaluation efforts in the assessment of program objectives; and (9) keep the president informed of the overall activities of the government. The OMB is headed by a director, who is appointed by the president with Senate approval. (Since 1974 Senate confirmation is required.) *See also* COUNCIL OF ECONOMIC ADVISERS, p. 118; EXECUTIVE OFFICE OF THE PRESIDENT, p. 131; WHITE HOUSE OFFICE, p. 137.

Significance   The Office of Management and Budget was inspired by the British practice to collect, collate, and correlate the spending plans of the United States government. Under the Budget and Accounting Act of 1921, its director is authorized to increase or reduce the budget estimates from executive departments. Since 1939, when the Bureau of the Budget was transferred from the Department of the Treasury to the Executive Office of the President, the OMB has become a major clearinghouse for legislative proposals and staff agencies in iscal matters. Its role is not only administrative and financial but often highly political, since it is constantly in a position of negotiation with departments and agencies. The president, as an individual, is not capable of preparing a national budget of more than $800 billion or knowing how money is spent and must depend on the OMB for the operation of the government. By creating this office, President Richard M. Nixon attempted to gain control over how the departments actually spent money, but he failed. A determined president and a capable OMB director can ensure the passage of most budget requests by Congress.

Office of Policy Development (OPD)   An agency that assists the president in the formulation, coordination, and implementation of domestic policy. The Office of Policy Development serves as the policy staff for the president's Cabinet Council. The OPD oversees the writing of bills in executive departments and resolves interdepartmental conflicts. President Richard M. Nixon created a Domestic Council in 1970 to establish a counterpart to the National Security Council. In 1977 President Jimmy Carter renamed the Domestic Council the Domestic Policy Staff. After taking office in 1981, President Ronald Reagan redesignated the Domestic Policy Staff as the Office of Policy Development. The OPD is responsible to the assistant to the president for policy development. It is administered by a director. The OPD includes the president, who serves as the chairman, the vice president, members of the cabinet (excluding the secretaries of defense and state), the three counselors to the president, and the director and deputy director of the Office of Management and Budget. *See also* EXECUTIVE OFFICE OF THE PRESIDENT, p. 131; NATIONAL SECURITY COUNCIL, p. 132; OFFICE OF MANAGEMENT AND BUDGET, p. 133.

Significance   The Office of Policy Development has the same position in domestic affairs as that of the National Security Council on national security matters. The OPD was established to advise the president on interdepartmental problems. However, from its inception, the OPD began to dictate policies to the departments, rather than consulting with them. Although created as a counterpart to the National Security Council in the domestic field, the OPD has been unable to assume such a role. As the Watergate scandal grew and John D. Ehrlichman (the first executive director of OPD) was forced to resign, the agency became inactive. Under President Gerald R. Ford, the OPD remained inactive until Vice President Nelson A. Rockefeller took charge of its operation. President Carter gave due importance to the OPD and cleared all domestic policy matters with it. Presidential administrations are not certain what the OPD's role should be. Various administrations have changed its nomenclature three times in trying to redefine its mission, making it a superfluous entity and creating confusion.

Vice President   The second highest executive in the nation. The vice president succeeds to the presidency upon the death, disability, resignation, or removal of the president. Nine vice presidents became president upon the death or resignation of presidents. In four of these cases, the presidents have been assassinated (Abraham Lincoln, James A. Garfield, William McKinley, and John F. Kennedy). The Constitution in Article II, Section 1 provides that the vice president shall assume the powers and duties of the president in the event of the removal, death, resignation, or inability of the president to discharge the official duties of the presidency. The vice president serves as presiding officer of the United States Senate but does not participate in Senate debate and votes only in the case of a tie. Under the Twenty-fifth Amendment of the Constitution, the vice president helps to decide whether the president is disabled, and if so, serves as acting president.

A vice presidential candidate is chosen by the presidential nominee to add regional, political, and ideological strength to the campaign, and in order to balance the ticket. All vice presidents, except three, have been elected. The first exception was Richard M. Johnson, who failed to secure a majority of electoral college votes, and was elected vice president by the Senate in 1836. The other two exceptions were Gerald R. Ford and Nelson A. Rockefeller, who were chosen under the Twenty-fifth Amendment by the president and received a majority vote in both houses of Congress. *See also* NATIONAL CONVENTION, p. 14; PRESIDENTIAL DISABILITY, p. 107; PRESIDENTIAL SUCCESSION, p. 110; VICE PRESIDENT, p. 231.

Significance   The vice president has few constitutional and legal powers and is not officially part of the cabinet. John Adams, the first vice president, described the office as "the most insignificant office that ever the invention of man contrived or his imagination conceived." There is little need for the vice president to preside over the Senate, and so this rarely occurs. Breaking tie votes in the Senate, is part of the vice president's constitutional role, but such ties are rare.

Contemporary presidents have assigned additional responsibilities to the vice president. President Dwight D. Eisenhower authorized Vice President Richard M. Nixon to call cabinet meetings and oversee the administration while he was ill. President Jimmy Carter involved Vice President Walter F. Mondale in complicated foreign policy negotiations. Since World War II, four of the eight presidents also served as vice president. Most recent vice presidents have been former senators or congressmen. Having experience in congressional politics, the vice presidents can become an important factor in the success or failure of a president's legislative program.

White House Chief of Staff   The principal aide to the president. The White House chief of staff serves the chief executive in such matters as the president may direct. The chief of staff facilitates and maintains communication with the Congress, executive departments, the information media, and general public, in an effort to make the president's performance easier. The president can appoint and remove the chief of staff without Senate approval. Presidents know their chiefs of staff well and count on their loyalty. They may have worked in the president's campaign and frequently are from the president's home state. They have direct access to the president as chief confidants and confer with him daily, if necessary. *See also* WHITE HOUSE OFFICE, p. 137; WHITE HOUSE STAFF, p. 138.

Significance   The White House chief of staff can become very powerful. He provides vital information and analyzes domestic and international problems. Many times the chief of staff is accused of taking over functions that should be performed by the cabinet. This was the case during President Richard M. Nixon's administration: according to his communications director, Herbert Klein, White House chief of staff H. R. Haldeman and other aides led the president down the path to disaster. "By substituting dishonesty and deceit for truth and openness, they built a wall around him—in the guise of a more efficient staff operation" (*New York Times*, August 25, 1974). The Nixon White House was not a typical one. President Jimmy Carter's chief of staff, Hamilton Jordan, and his secretary of health, education, and welfare, Joseph A. Califano, Jr., had acrimonious exchanges over policy matters. Conservative supporters of President Ronald Reagan blamed White House Chief of Staff James A. Baker for policy moderation.

The presidency is an institution, not a job for one person. Good and efficient staff are needed to run the administration smoothly. However, it is dangerous when top staff put up a wall around the president, shielding out criticism and opposing views that might reduce their influence. This may isolate the president and inhibit wise and informed decision making.

White House Office   The staff agency that serves the president in the performance of official duties. The White House Office is run by the president's personal staff. They include, among others, the assistants for national security, economic, domestic, and international matters. The office also includes such technical experts as a press secretary, communications director, and congressional liaison officer. These officials maintain close working relationships with the president, advising him on policy matters. They are trusted confidants of the president. They are appointed on a personal basis and do not require Senate confirmation. *See also* EXECUTIVE OFFICE OF THE PRESIDENT, p. 131; WHITE HOUSE CHIEF OF STAFF, p. 136; WHITE HOUSE STAFF, p. 138.

Significance   The White House Office has grown dramatically. It was not until 1857 that the president was allowed to have a paid secretary. Established in 1939, this staff agency grew dramatically during President Richard M. Nixon's administration: from 311 employees in 1970 to 606 in 1974, when President Nixon resigned. The upward trend was halted by Presidents Gerald R. Ford and Jimmy Carter.

The White House Office is molded by the personal preferences of the presidents. There are no general criteria to describe and evaluate it. Many observers have noted that the office has an intrinsic tendency to insulate the president from cabinet advisers and the public. Key staff members are chosen by the president according to their ability and loyalty. Necessarily, tension develops between these staff members and the cabinet. The infighting for power and privilege between these two groups of unelected officials suggests that the highest echelons of government are controlled, to a large extent, by an unrepresentative elite corps and not by the elected president.

White House Press Secretary   The president's key aide for dealing with the news media. The White House press secretary is the media spokesman for the president, acting as a conduit of information from the White House to the news media. The press secretary explains the needs of the media to the president; cultivates the news media to create a better image for the president; helps reporters gain access to the president and the White House; and provides reporters with texts and briefings on news originating in the White House. This is usually done in the White House Press Room. Press secretaries invite reporters to presidential press conferences and briefings. They are assisted by a deputy press secretary and a staff of fifty. They prepare daily summaries of important news events for the president and top White House aides. Ever since President Ronald Reagan's White House Press Secretary James S. Brady was incapacitated by assassin John W. Hinckley on March 30, 1981, the deputy White House press secretary has managed the press relations of the president. *See also* PRESIDENTIAL PRESS CONFERENCE, p. 109.

Significance   The White House press secretary is not involved in policy decisions, although he may give advice to the president. The press secretary tries to develop White House credibility with the news media. The press secretary helps prepare the president for news conferences and points out lapses to him. Beginning with President Theodore Roosevelt, all presidents have employed a press secretary. Some presidents have liked their press secretary, while others have not. President Lyndon B. Johnson did not trust his press secretary and was unwilling to share official secrets with him. President Richard M. Nixon was disappointed in his press secretary and demoted him in White House ranking. Presidents John F. Kennedy and Jimmy Carter liked their press secretaries and often shared secret information with them. The press secretary tries to court the media, inviting them to cocktails, receptions, and ceremonial occasions. The press secretary's friendly relations with the media help the president to cultivate a more positive and favorable image.

White House Staff   A group of top officials that give the president advice and assistance in carrying out official duties. The White House staff number approximately 5,000, many of whom are specialists of one kind or another. They staff the White House Office, which is one of the most important components of the Executive Office of the President. In recent years, a new phenomenon has arisen in the White House: the development of a massive public relations operation. In addition to the White House press secretary, more than 100 presidential aides are engaged in various forms of public relations. *See also* COUNCIL OF ECONOMIC ADVISERS, p. 118; EXECUTIVE OFFICE OF THE PRESIDENT, p. 131; NATIONAL SECURITY COUNCIL, p. 132; WHITE HOUSE CHIEF OF STAFF, p. 136.

Significance   The White House staff assists the president by collecting and disseminating information and serving as an instrument in the formulation and execution of presidential directives. The belief that critical national and international problems require that experts aid and assist the president has caused the White House staff to grow. Since the establishment of the White House Office by President Franklin D. Roosevelt in 1939, all presidents have endeavored to reduce the size and scope of their staff. However, personal and political pressures have not only forced presidents to expand the size of the White House staff but also to recognize their growing influence in presidential policymaking. This has created a number of new problems. For example, it is not uncommon for White House staff members to develop a great mistrust of, or strong disagreement with, various cabinet officers and executive department heads. Clearly, this creates a dilemma for the president, who must maintain an open line of communication between senior staff members and agency officials. It is unavoidable that conflicts of interest between the two groups will develop. However, because White House staff members have greater contact and work closely with the president, they frequently win such battles. Lately the White House staff has become less influential, as a result of President Ronald Reagan's increased reliance on his cabinet.

6. Agencies, Bureaus, and Commissions

Agency for International Development (AID)   The Agency charged with the main responsibility of managing American economic, technical, and military assistance in foreign countries. AID is headed by a director appointed by the president with Senate approval, who reports to the director of the International Development Cooperation Agency and to the president. Headquartered in Washington, D.C., AID maintains offices, attached to American embassies, all over the Third World. AID is a special agency within the Department of State, a semi-independent agency that carries out assistance programs designed to help Third World countries develop their human and economic resources. It is concerned with improving the quality of life in the developing nations and promoting their economic and political stability. Since the end of World War II, the United States has spent more than $175 billion in foreign aid; most of this money has been channeled through AID to Third World nations. AID was established in 1961, replacing the International Cooperation Administration. *See also* DEPARTMENT OF AGRICULTURE, p. 119; DEPARTMENT OF DEFENSE, p. 120; DEPARTMENT OF STATE, p. 128.

Significance   The Agency for International Development mainly administers two kinds of foreign economic assistance: development assistance and economic support funds. AID works in close cooperation with the Department of Agriculture to implement Public Law 480, which encourages economic development and assists in combating hunger and malnutrition in the poor countries. It also administers the donation of agricultural commodities to meet famine or extraordinary relief requirements for needy nations. This "food for peace" program is designed to meet the basic food requirements for the poor people in the

Third World. In recent years, the United States has placed more emphasis on foreign aid through multilateral financial institutions, such as the International Bank for Reconstruction and Development (World Bank) and the Asian Development Bank.

The agency is unpopular at home because many Americans consider it responsible for foreign "give away" programs. It is unpopular abroad because it is unable to provide sufficient aid to meet the demands of many needy nations. Moreover, AID programs have a "tying clause" that means poor recipient nations must use their AID funds to purchase expensive goods made in the United States. The supporters of foreign aid contend that to maintain peace and economic progress in the world, AID must step up its economic programs, especially to help counter the impact of the world debt crises of the 1980s.

Central Intelligence Agency (CIA)   A major agency that collects, researches, and analyzes foreign intelligence, and carries out clandestine operations abroad. The CIA is headed by a director who is appointed by the president with Senate approval and becomes a member of the president's cabinet. The CIA advises the National Security Council and the president in matters concerning intelligence activities of the departments and agencies of the United States government as they relate to national security. The CIA evaluates intelligence data supplied by the Departments of Defense and State. It makes recommendations to the National Security Council for the coordination of the intelligence activities of the government. The CIA engages in worldwide intelligence gathering and conducts counterintelligence activities outside the United States, as well as within the country. However, it is not permitted to assume or perform internal security functions within the United States. The agency conducts special activities approved by the president. The CIA was established under the National Security Act of 1947. *See also* CABINET, p. 117; NATIONAL SECURITY COUNCIL, p. 132.

Significance   The Central Intelligence Agency is a secret independent agency. It enjoys unique freedom from congressional budgetary controls and expenditure audits. The CIA's budget is secret, although its annual expenditures have been estimated at $10 billion. The agency has been accused of plotting against foreign governments and participating in various assassination attempts.

Although the CIA is expressly prohibited from engaging in any espionage activity within the United States, the Senate Select Intelligence Committee reported in 1976 that the agency has been spying on Americans at home since its creation. The committee found that 300,000 Americans were indexed in the CIA's domestic intelligence files. Further testimony before the committee revealed that the CIA engaged in research to control human behavior. Because the CIA had exceeded its legal authority, the United States Senate created a Permanent Committee on Intelligence with legislative and budgetary authority over the agency. The president is now required to approve all CIA clandestine operations. In spite of its failure to foresee developments such as the Iranian and Afghan crises, the CIA provides many reliable reports to the government that influence foreign policy decision making. Perhaps its most controversial role is that of developing and supporting antiregime rebels with the objective of overthrowing Communist governments, as in Cuba and Nicaragua.

Environmental Protection Agency (EPA)   The major agency that protects and enhances the present and future environment to the extent possible under the law. The EPA is headed by an administrator who is appointed by the president with Senate approval. The agency's mission is to control and abate pollution in the areas of air, water, solid waste, noise, radiation, and toxic substances. The EPA launches an integrated and coordinated attack on environmental pollution in cooperation with federal, state, and local authorities. Created in 1970, the EPA administers programs transferred to it from the Departments of Agriculture, Interior, and Health and Human Services; the Atomic Energy Commission; and the Federal Radiation Council. *See also* DEPARTMENT OF AGRICULTURE, p. 119; DEPARTMENT OF HEALTH AND HUMAN SERVICES, p. 123; REGULATORY AGENCIES, p. 152.

Significance   The Environmental Protection Agency is designed to serve as the public's advocate for a safe and healthy environment. The National Environmental Policy Act of 1970, which created the EPA, recognized that the federal government held the primary responsibility for the environment, not the states. The act also established a Council on Environmental Quality to oversee and evaluate EPA programs according to standards set by law. The agency is often called on to make difficult and controversial decisions: for example, whether or not to grant the automobile industry additional time to manufacture cars with cleaner engines.

However, the greatest crisis over EPA operations developed in 1983 when it was involved in a Superfund controversy of $1.6 billion. Established in the wake of the Love Canal disaster to help facilitate the cleanup of similar hazardous waste dumps, the EPA adopted a policy of seeking to negotiate settlements with chemical dumpers instead of taking them to court. Several House subcommittees investigated charges and subpoenaed documents on some of the cleanup sites, resulting in citations for contempt of Congress against EPA administrators, and other officials. Although the White House denied charges of favoritism, congressional subcommittees alleged that EPA officials manipulated the Superfund for political purposes. Finally, the EPA agreed to turn over all disputed documents to the House subcommittees. After months of turmoil, Anne M. Burford resigned as EPA administrator, and President Ronald Reagan surrendered the toxic waste cleanup records to Congress. As a result of congressional investigations, the administrator of hazardous waste programs was removed from her position, and evidence became public indicating that political considerations and unethical behavior were involved in managing EPA cleanup programs.

Federal Bureau of Investigation (FBI)   The principal bureau charged with responsibility to investigate all violations of federal laws except those assigned to other agencies by law. The FBI is headed by a director who is appointed by the president with Senate approval. The agency gathers and reports facts and compiles evidence in matters that may involve the United States government. Its jurisdiction includes a wide range of responsibilities in the criminal, civil, and security fields. Among these are: sabotage and espionage, kidnapping, extortion, bank robbery, interstate transportation of stolen property, interstate gambling, civil rights matters, fraud, and murder. The FBI cooperates with other law enforcement agencies in fingerprint identification, laboratory services, and police training. Established in 1908, the FBI has ten separate divisions at its headquarters in Washington, D.C. *See also* CENTRAL INTELLIGENCE AGENCY, p. 142; DEPARTMENT OF JUSTICE, p. 126.

Significance   The Federal Bureau of Investigation is the principal investigative arm of the Department of Justice. It does not express opinions concerning the guilt or innocence of subjects of its investigations nor does it assume the role of accuser, prosecutor, or judge. As the name suggests, the FBI is an investigating agency in federal matters. FBI officials have admitted, under pressure, that in the past the agency has engaged in illegal searches and seizures. The agency has infiltrated citizen organizations with paid informers to collect information on Vietnam protesters, civil rights activists, and leaders of the women's movement. FBI operatives have recruited prostitutes in an effort to harrass dissidents and arrest them on prostitution charges. Another practice involved posing as Arab sheikhs in order to entrap members of Congress in an illegal business scheme. This operation, known as Abscam, put several congressmen in jail.

The FBI has been accused of spying on Americans, opening mail, tapping telephones, bugging homes, offices, and hotels, and even kidnapping people. In the 1970s, the agency admitted to having compiled dossiers on more than 500,000 Americans. In 1974 Congress amended the Freedom of Information Act permitting individuals to obtain copies of their files from the FBI on payment of reproduction cost. However, if the file is classified owing to national security, access may be denied. However, the FBI has developed an improved public image through successful investigation and apprehension of criminals. Because the president and Congress are sensitive to public opinion, the FBI fares well in its demands for funds and facilities required for its operations.

Federal Communications Commission (FCC)   The agency that regulates interstate and foreign communications by radio, television, wire, and cable. Created by the Federal Communications Act of 1934, the FCC is headed by a chairman who is appointed by the president with Senate approval. The commission is assisted by a general counsel. The FCC is responsible for the orderly development and operation of broadcast services in the United States. It ensures nationwide telephone services at affordable rates and works in cooperation with other nations to maintain efficient telegraph services throughout the world. The FCC is an independent regulatory commission, composed of seven members.

The FCC grants licenses to broadcasters and enforces regulations prohibiting indecent language. It guarantees equal treatment on radio and television for political candidates under its fairness doctrine. The FCC was assigned additional regulatory jurisdiction under the Communications Satellite Act of 1962. The scope of this regulation includes cable television operation, two-way radio and radio operators, and satellite communication. *See also* REGULATORY AGENCIES, p. 152.

Significance   The Federal Communications Commission decides which broadcasters shall be licensed and on what terms. FCC hearings are hotly contested by various interest groups. When the FCC decides what a cable station can broadcast, it benefits either the cable companies or regular television networks. In granting a license to broadcast, the FCC may be awarding a company with a multimillion dollar asset. The commission's equal-time rule requires a broadcaster to make available equal advertising time to competing political candidates, but it does not protect the candidate who cannot afford to pay for equal time. The FCC requires broadcasters to present both sides of public issues; they must give opponents an opportunity to respond to editorial comments.

Although the FCC is forbidden by law from imposing censorship or control on the content of broadcasts, it does impose a variety of requirements. No one may operate a broadcasting station without a license granted by the commission. Critics complain that some broadcasters use indecent language and fail to comply with the equal-time and fairness doctrines. However, most broadcasters go out of their way to comply with FCC regulations. Few, if any, broadcasters have lost their licenses because they broadcast programs that contain obscenity or excessive violence. Although the FCC is supposed to regulate radio and television broadcasting, it has become subservient to the industry's wishes.

Federal Reserve System   The central banking regulatory system that influences the amount of credit available and currency in circulation. The Federal Reserve System is administered by a board of governors, with offices in Washington, D.C. It consists of seven members who serve fourteen-year terms, appointed by the president with Senate approval. The board is headed by a chairman who is appointed by the president for a four-year term and confirmed by the Senate. The board of governors determines general monetary, credit, and bank operating policies. The Federal Reserve System serves as the central bank of the United States. Through its supervisory and regulatory functions, the Federal Reserve helps to maintain the strength and integrity of the banking system.

It performs a number of other functions such as the transfer of funds, handling government deposits and debt issues, and regulating banks and interest rates. Created in 1913, the system consists of twelve Federal Reserve banks, each located in a Federal Reserve district. Membership in district federal banks is required of all national banks and may be obtained by state chartered banks. *See also* DEPARTMENT OF THE TREASURY, p. 130; OFFICE OF MANAGEMENT AND BUDGET, p. 133.

Significance   The Federal Reserve System is largely independent of both the White House and Congress. Federal Reserve banks are privately owned; they are sometimes called bankers' banks, because although they are owned by their members, they may borrow from the Federal Reserve.

Through its control of the flow of money and credit, the Federal Reserve System may circulate more money into the economy when a recession threatens or tighten the supply of money when inflation is high. If the prevailing economic trend is unfavorable for the country, the Federal Reserve System tries to reverse it, if possible. Whether it succeeds or fails, the system has the major responsibility of trying to control recession, inflation, and interest rates. Its goal is to stimulate the economy through effective monetary policies. The Federal Reserve System does so chiefly in four ways (1) it buys or sells government bonds; (2) it expands or contracts the total money supply by raising or lowering the discount rate it charges member banks to borrow; (3) it raises or lowers reserve requirements for member banks; and (4) it raises or lowers margin requirements for individuals buying securities. Since most of these decisions are made in secret, economists, speculators, observers, investors, and bankers try to outguess the Federal Reserve System but usually only discern its decisions after the fact.

Federal Trade Commission (FTC)   The agency that has the responsibility to promote free and fair competition affecting commerce through prevention of general trade restraints. The FTC has five members and a chairman, who are appointed by the president with Senate approval. The FTC safeguards the public interest by preventing dissemination of deceptive advertisements on consumer products; preventing illegal price fixing; and enforcing the Clayton Antitrust and Federal Trade Commission Acts of 1914. The operations of the FTC include, among others, making rules and regulations to establish a code of fair competition; holding hearings concerning alleged violations; advocating and enforcing truthful labeling of products; achieving true credit cost disclosure by consumer creditors; protecting consumers against credit reports; and making data concerning economic and business conditions in the country available to the president, Congress, and the public. *See also* DEPARTMENT OF COMMERCE, p. 120.

Significance   The Federal Trade Commission is, in a sense, an anomaly: it seeks to prevent competition in the private sector through governmental intervention and regulation. As a regulatory agency, it has the power to make rules covering areas in which there may be no specific laws. For example, the FTC has issued a rule stating that anyone paying for mail-order merchandise must receive it within 30 days or be allowed to cancel the order. To protect consumers from unscrupulous businesses, the FTC employs two kinds of professionals: lawyers, who draw up briefs and argue cases in courts; and economists, who analyze how a competitive economy is supposed to work. The FTC tries to obtain legal compliance through voluntary and cooperative action. Formal litigation is similar to that used in court.

The underlying purpose of the FTC is to maintain the free enterprise system by preventing corrupt practices. The FTC administers the Consumer Credit Protection Act, which requires that whenever people borrow money, they receive a statement showing the exact amount of interest they must pay. Often business firms influence the decision of the Antitrust Division of the commission. A recent study by consumer advocate Ralph Nader showed thirty-two such cases involving the Anti-trust Division of FTC. Critics have accused the FTC of being pro-business, but business critics charge that its regulatory activity tends to stifle much commercial activity. Actually, the intensity with which it pursues its role depends to a considerable extent on the ideological and practical perspectives of the administration in power.

Food and Drug Administration (FDA)   The major agency that works as protector of the health of the nation against impure and unsafe foods, drugs, cosmetics, and other potentially hazardous products. The FDA is headed by a commissioner who is appointed by the president with Senate approval. Created in 1906 and located originally within the Department of Agriculture, the FDA is now a part of the Department of Health and Human Services. The Food and Drug Act of 1906 prohibits interstate commerce in adulterated and misbranded foods and drugs. The FDA administers the regulations of biological products shipped in interstate and foreign commerce. The agency inspects manufacturers' facilities for compliance with standards, tests products submitted for release, and approves licenses of manufacturers of biological products. The FDA conducts research and develops standards on the composition, quality, nutrition, and safety of food, food additives and colorings, and cosmetics. The agency also conducts research designed to improve the detection, prevention, and control of contamination that may be responsible for illness or injury. The FDA carries out programs designed to reduce people's exposure to hazardous radiation. The major components of the FDA are the Bureau of Biologics, Bureau of Drugs, Bureau of Foods, Bureau of Radiological Health, Bureau of Veterinary Medicine, and Bureau of Medical Devices. *See also* DEPARTMENT OF AGRICULTURE, p. 119; DEPARTMENT OF HEALTH AND HUMAN SERVICES, p. 123.

Significance   The Food and Drug Administration has broad regulatory powers over the content, marketing, and labeling of food and drugs. The FDA must approve all drugs marketed in the United States. To cope with a national scandal in 1906 concerning adulterated meat and the improper processing and labeling of food and drugs, Congress established the FDA.

Any agency created as a result of scandal or entrepreneurial politics is likely to be vulnerable to the pressure of the industry it is supposed to regulate. Many times FDA has fallen victim to this kind of industry pressure and has appeared to develop a comfortable and uncritical attitude toward some drug manufacturers. In 1982 a drug known as Starch Blocker was marketed by the manufacturer without FDA approval. After dallying for a long period of time and only under the spur of public controversy, the FDA withdrew this product from the market and filed a lawsuit against the manufacturer. The FDA's refusal to approve the use of certain drugs has involved it in many legal battles. The intensity of its regulatory activities relates directly to the basic philosophy of the FDA commissioner, who in turn tends to reflect the views and positions of the president and the administration in power.

General Accounting Office (GAO)   The major congressional agency that audits government accounts and attempts to keep them within the prescribed policies established by Congress. The GAO is attached to Congress and is headed by a comptroller general who is appointed by the president with Senate approval for a fifteen-year term and can be removed only through impeachment or by a joint resolution of Congress. The Budget and Accounting Act of 1921 created the GAO to (1) prescribe an accounting system for federal agencies; (2) assist Congress in carrying out its legislative and oversight responsibilities; (3) carry out the accounting, auditing, and claims settlement functions of the federal government; and (4) recommend more efficient and effective government operations. The GAO has statutory authority to investigate all matters relating to the receipt, disbursement, and application of public funds. Its audit authority extends to the state and local governments, quasi-governmental bodies, and private organizations that receive federal aid. The comptroller general cooperates by law with the Department of the Treasury and the Office of Management and Budget to develop standardized information and data for use by the government. *See also* DEPARTMENT OF THE TREASURY, p. 130; GENERAL ACCOUNTING OFFICE (GAO), p. 314; OFFICE OF MANAGEMENT AND BUDGET, p. 133.

Significance   The General Accounting Office functions as an independent, nonpolitical agency within the legislative branch. Its audit authority extends to all departments, agencies, bureaus, and commissions, except for the Central Intelligence Agency. At its inception, the GAO primarily performed routine audits, but currently it investigates policies and makes recommendations on almost every aspect of government operations. The GAO has the power of preaudit authorization, meaning that no public monies may be spent except under warrants signed by the comptroller general. Critics maintain that the executive branch cannot be held responsible for spending activities if the GAO has to determine the validity of expenditures before they are made. The GAO also performs postaudits to ensure that the government has spent the money as Congress intended and conducts cost-benefit studies to assess the cost-effectiveness of government programs. The GAO is the only congressional watchdog agency that has subpoena authority. Under the law, the GAO reports not to the president but to Congress. The comptroller general is appointed for an extended term and therefore is not under obligation to any one president or influenced by either political party.

General Services Administration (GSA)   A major independent service agency that establishes policy and provides for an economical and efficient system to manage the federal government's property and records. The GSA is responsible for the construction and operation of government buildings; procurement and distribution of supplies; utilization and disposal of property; transportation and communications management; and stockpiling of strategic materials. It is headed by an administrator who is appointed by the president with Senate approval. The GSA provides information to businesses owned and operated by disadvantaged and handicapped persons. Its Consumer Information Center provides information and publishes catalogs listing more than 200 federal publications of interest to consumers. In addition, the GSA operates Federal Information Centers, clearinghouses for information about the government. It operates the National Archives, responsible for administering the presidential library system. The GSA publishes the *Federal Register, Statutes at Large*, and *The United States Government Organization Manual. See also* GENERAL ACCOUNTING OFFICE, (GAO), PP. 149, 314.

Significance   The General Services Administration is the government's main purchaser and landlord. It polices federal buildings. The GSA conducts independent reviews of agencywide programs to determine the effectiveness, efficiency, and economy of government operations. It controls and resolves audit objections from the General Accounting Office. The GSA is organized much like a large corporation doing business in a number of different areas. It works to avoid waste and duplication in the operation of the federal government. A housekeeping agency such as GSA is independent chiefly because it is a service agency for the entire government and cannot be placed under any one department.

Internal Revenue Service (IRS)   The major agency charged with responsibility to administer and enforce internal revenue laws, except those relating to alcohol, tobacco, and firearms. The IRS is responsible for the collection of all taxes, excluding custom duties. The main sources of revenues are personal income tax; social insurance and retirement taxes; and corporate income, excise, estate, and gift taxes. A unit within the Department of the Treasury, the IRS is headed by a commissioner who is appointed by the president with Senate approval. Its basic activities include providing taxpayer service and education; assessment and collection of federal income taxes; and determination of pension plan qualifications. The IRS issues rulings and regulations to supplement the provisions of the Internal Revenue Code. The IRS first received the authority to levy income taxes in 1913, pursuant to the Sixteenth Amendment to the Constitution. It is organized to achieve maximum decentralization and has seven regional offices throughout the country. *See also* DEPARTMENT OF THE TREASURY, p. 130.

Significance   The Internal Revenue Service is the largest tax collector in the world, collecting more than $450 billion annually. It is one of the few federal agencies that deals directly with American citizens. Its mission is to encourage and achieve voluntary compliance with the tax laws and regulations. The IRS conducts business in a professional manner, so as to warrant the highest degree of public confidence in the integrity of the service. To achieve this goal, the IRS advises taxpayers of their rights and responsibilities and assists them in complying with the laws. Where necessary, it takes enforcement action for effective tax administration.

The IRS receives about 125 million tax returns each year, subjecting each return to some scrutiny by an official or a computer. The agency decides how many income tax returns will be examined closely and how many of a violator's previous returns should be reopened. Furthermore, it decides whether the violations are deliberate, requiring criminal prosecution, or whether they are errors made in good faith. Taxpayers are entitled to hearings of their cases and may appeal IRS rulings to the United States Tax Court. The IRS has been struggling with a growing underground economy, wherein people demand payment in cash in order to avoid records of their transactions. According to political scientist Edward Greenberg, the IRS has a master index of persons and organizations considered to be engaged in subversive activities. Many of these dossiers are allegedly compiled through illegal electronic surveillance.

Interstate Commerce Commission (ICC)   An independent agency that regulates interstate surface transportation including trains, barges, trucks, buses, inland waterways, coastal shipping, freight forwarders, and pipelines. The ICC also regulates passenger rates and settles controversies over rates. Established in 1887, the commission is headed by a chairman who is appointed by the president with Senate approval. The ICC consists of eleven members appointed for seven-year terms. It ensures that interstate carriers provide the public with rates and services that are fair and reasonable, as guaranteed by law. Its regulations generally involve certification of carriers seeking to provide transportation for the public. In addition to interstate commerce, the commission's responsibilities include foreign commerce as it moves within the United States. *See also* DEPARTMENT OF COMMERCE, p. 120; REGULATORY AGENCIES, p. 152.

Significance   The Interstate Commerce Commission is designed to regulate the transportation sector in the public interest. The ICC was the first regulatory commission established by the government; only then did the federal government begin to regulate the economy to a major extent. At first the ICC had relatively few powers, but its authority has been strengthened and its jurisdiction broadened by many subsequent laws.

Scholars disagree as to the reasons for the creation of the ICC. One view is that railroad politics helped create the ICC, even though the ICC was designed to protect railroads. With the construction of highways and the advent of the trucking industry, the ICC found itself adjudicating the competing demands of truckers and railroads. The role of the ICC has become increasingly difficult as competition among the various carriers has intensified. Politics intrude as politicians and interest groups put pressure on the commission. For example, a favorable decision by the ICC to grant a new transportation route can mean millions of dollars to the licensee. Political, economic—even racial—interests may be involved in such decisions.

Regulatory Agencies   The independent agencies that control various areas of the American economy, largely independent of the president and Congress. The regulatory agencies were created for two principal reasons: a need for regulating the economy as society became increasingly complex and growing public pressure to protect consumers from unfair business practices. Beginning with the Interstate Commerce Commission (ICC) in 1887, about a dozen independent regulatory agencies have been created. Each of these agencies is governed by a small commission, usually composed of five to ten members. They are appointed (but cannot be removed) by the president, with Senate approval. These agencies are quasi-legislative, -executive, and -judicial bodies. They are empowered to make administrative laws. When violations take place, the agencies act as courts (subject to appeal to federal courts) and can impose penalties. Within broad guidelines established by Congress, these agencies control various aspects of economic life. For example, the Federal Power Commission sets natural gas prices, and the

Federal Reserve Board decides what the prime interest rate should be. *See also* FEDERAL RESERVE SYSTEM, p. 146; INTERSTATE COMMERCE COMMISSION, p. 151.

Significance   The regulatory agencies are described as independent because they do not report directly to the president or Congress. They are autonomous bodies and are supposed to function without hindrance or undue interference. The agency members are selected from the two major political parties. When President Franklin D. Roosevelt removed a member of the Federal Trade Commission, the United States Supreme Court ruled in *Humphrey's Executor* v. *United States* (1935) that disagreement with the president is not sufficient grounds for dismissal. A president may, however, remove members of the regulatory agencies for neglect of duty or criminal offenses. Unlike cabinet departments and other executive offices, regulatory agencies do not simply perform executive functions. They serve as legislator, investigator, prosecutor, judge, and jury—all in one. Congress has given the regulatory agencies broad powers to set policy and perform judicial tasks by settling disputes. Most of the regulatory agencies were created in the 1930s during President Roosevelt's administration to cope with the economic depression of that era.

Although these agencies have functioned well, critics point to the close relationship that has developed between the agencies and the interests they regulate. Marver Bernstein, in his classic study *Regulating Business by Independent Commission* (1977), points to the "capture" of the regulators by the regulatees. Indeed the agencies have, on numerous occasions, become captured by the very individuals and groups they were supposed to oversee. In the 1930s, regulatory agencies were created to regulate business competition. Beginning in the 1970s, a new political and economic elite adopted the view that competition can produce more efficient and less costly services in such areas as airlines, banks, oil, natural gas, and telephone industries. The deregulation movement, begun under President Jimmy Carter, was expanded and speeded up by President Ronald Reagan. Not all efforts at deregulation received the support of the affected industries. Major opposition came from the airlines, while the oil industry favored ending price controls. Despite opposition from some industries, many deregulation bills became law, although some were modified to meet industry objections.

Secret Service   The agency that protects the president, the vice president, the major presidential and vice presidential candidates, and their families. In addition, the Secret Service is authorized to detect and arrest any person who commits any offense against the laws of the

United States relating to coins, currency, and securities. The agency came into existence in 1901, prompted by the assassination of President William McKinley. Prior to that time, the president was not provided with a bodyguard. At the time of its formation, the Secret Service was primarily involved in the investigation of counterfeiting operations, but it also assigned several of its agents to act as bodyguards to the president. This situation changed in 1963, with the assassination of President John F. Kennedy. The Secret Service increased the number of bodyguards protecting the president to over 100 and expanded its activities to include similar protection for vice presidents, past presidents, major presidential candidates, cabinet officers, and potential presidential candidates. The Secret Service maintains surveillance against people suspected of plotting the assassination of federal officials and investigates threats made against the life of the president. *See also* DEPARTMENT OF THE TREASURY, p. 130.

Significance   Secret Service agents take an oath to protect those officials to whom they are assigned, and they are prepared to risk death to ensure the safety and well-being of those officials. At the White House, the president enjoys the services of more than 100 Secret Service agents and 300 uniformed White House police; on the road, 12 Secret Service agents accompany the president, as well as many personal aides. These agents have often performed heroic deeds, risking life and limb to protect America's leaders. Despite their valiant efforts, there is no foolproof way to prevent attempts on the lives of public officials, as witnessed by the assassinations and attempted assassinations of Presidents John F. Kennedy, Gerald R. Ford, and Ronald Reagan.

Securities and Exchange Commission (SEC)   An independent agency that provides the fullest possible disclosure of information concerning securities (stocks and bonds) and protects the interest of the public against malpractice in the financial markets. Headed by a chairman, the five-member commission is appointed by the president for five-year terms with Senate approval. The Securities and Exchange Act of 1934 assigns to the commission broad regulatory power over the securities markets and persons conducting business in securities. The SEC is responsible for the establishment of a national market for securities. It has broad policy-making authority over the activities of brokers, dealers, information processors, and transfer agents. The SEC requires companies selling securities to file an accurate registration statement and prospectus. In addition to the 1934 act, the SEC enforces the Public Utility Holding Company Act of 1935, under which it regulates mergers of utility companies. *See also* REGULATORY AGENCIES, p. 152.

Significance   The Securities and Exchange Commission protects stockholders' interests and polices corporate operations. In response to widespread reports of illegal campaign contributions, the SEC now requires corporations to report all donations to candidates. It also requires corporate executives to disclose their fringe benefits to shareholders. The SEC cannot guarantee the economic viability of any security; it only requires disclosure of information for public benefit. The SEC tries to prevent fraud and deception in the purchase and sale of securities by obtaining court orders to revoke the registration of brokers, dealers, and investment advisers.

The Great Depression of 1929 was at least partly attributable to the high degree of corruption in the stock and other securities markets that the SEC has attempted to bring under control. Today, the commission's authority is respected and felt in many areas of corporate financing and the securities markets; most investors place a high value on the regulatory efforts of the SEC. The SEC has been criticized as being more protective of the securities industries and large investors than the interests of small stockholders.

United States Arms Control and Disarmament Agency (USACDA)   The major agency charged with responsibility of formulating and implementing the arms control and disarmament policies of the United States. The USACDA (also known as ACDA) is headed by a director, appointed by the president with Senate approval, who arranges and oversees American participation in international arms control and disarmament negotiations and leads the American delegation in disarmament talks at Geneva. The USACDA is responsible for conducting long-range research on arms control methods and preparing position papers for consideration by the National Security Council. At present, the agency is participating in discussions and negotiations with the Soviet Union and other countries on such issues as strategic arms limitations, mutual force reductions in Europe, and prohibition of chemical weapons. The USACDA is concerned with preventing the spread of nuclear weapons to nations that do not now possess them and monitoring the flow of arms abroad. Established in 1961, the USACDA provides for a General Advisory Committee, not to exceed fifteen members, to advise the president and secretary of state. *See also* DEPARTMENT OF STATE, p. 128; NATIONAL SECURITY COUNCIL, p. 132.

Significance   The United States Arms Control and Disarmament Agency was established in response to congressional demands for greater efforts to create a central organization charged with primary responsibility for arms control and disarmament. Many of its research studies are conducted by individuals, private and public institutions, through contracts and agreements. The USACDA is not technically a division of the Department of State, but its director serves as an adviser to the president and the secretary of state because the USACDA is considered a presidential agency. (A presidential agency is one that is oriented more toward presidential control and does not directly affect important congressional constituencies.)

The agency played an active role in negotiations leading to the Senate ratification of the Antarctic Treaty of 1959 to demilitarize that continent; the Partial Nuclear Test Ban Treaty (1963) to prohibit all but underground nuclear tests; the Outer Space Treaty (1967) to bar weapons from outer space and celestial bodies; the Non-Proliferation Treaty (1967) to limit the "nuclear club" (those nations that now possess nuclear weapons) to its existing members; the Seabed Treaty (1971) to prohibit emplacement of nuclear weapons in the seabed outside territorial waters; and the Strategic Arms Limitation Treaties and agreements (SALT I and SALT II, negotiated during the 1970s) to curtail the arms race between the United States and the Soviet Union. Through these and other arms control efforts, the USACDA has endeavored to achieve a greater measure of arms control leading to eventual disarmament. Although the terms arms control and disarmament are used interchangeably, the former refers to restraining the arms race, while the latter aims at the complete elimination of arms.

United States Postal Service   An independent agency that processes mail and provides delivery services to individuals and businesses. The United States Postal Service is headed by the postmaster general, appointed by the nine governors of the Postal Service who, in turn, are appointed by the president with Senate approval. The Postal Service was created by the Postal Reorganization Act of 1970 to replace the Department of Post Office. From what was one of the oldest cabinet departments, it has become a government corporation: it performs a variety of public functions but bears certain similarities to segments of the private sector.

The Postal Service operates almost 40,000 post offices throughout the country. It handles 110 billion pieces of mail annually. The Postal Service maintains extensive processing and delivery systems to link every household and business in the country. Through its membership in the Universal Postal Union (a specialized agency of the United Nations), the Postal Service links every nation in the world. In addition to mail delivery, it runs a parcel service and sells government bonds and money orders. The Postal Service inspects mail and apprehends those who violate postal laws. *See also* REGULATORY AGENCIES, p. 152.

Significance   The United States Postal Service was created to replace a "sick postal department": to correct several weaknesses and inefficiencies that led to substantial annual deficits. It is similar to a private corporation but differs from government departments and agencies in at least two ways: it operates like a private corporation with a profit motive, and it charges the customer for its services. The Postal Service is the largest government corporation with approximately 670,000 employees. Its businesslike approach has resulted in earnings that have produced budget surpluses during several years in the early 1980s. Since its inception, the Postal Service has adopted remedial measures to balance its budget, requesting one rate hike after another. The charge for mailing a first class letter was 13 cents until December 31, 1975; 15 cents until May 29, 1978; 18 cents until March 22, 1981; and 20 cents currently. This rate is expected to be raised to 23 cents, effective October 1, 1984. Although there has been no appreciable improvement in its efficiency, the Postal Service continues to raise the pay and other benefits of its employees through collective bargaining. It is the only federal service whose employment policies are governed by a collective bargaining process. As a result, letter carriers often receive more pay and fringe benefits than many professionals.

Veterans Administration (VA)   The agency that coordinates the administration of various laws providing benefits for veterans and their dependents. The VA is headed by a director who is appointed by the president with Senate approval. Established in 1930, the VA is responsible for payment of compensation for disability or death related to military service. It decides pensions based on financial need for totally disabled veterans. The VA provides assistance for education, rehabilitation, home loans, and burial. It administers a comprehensive medical program involving 1,700 hospitals and medical centers, nursing homes, and clinics. The VA dispenses college benefits to veterans. Its loan guarantee programs provide credit assistance to veterans and active duty service personnel for home building. The VA operates an insurance program for veterans and administers the National Cemetery system. *See also* DEPARTMENT OF DEFENSE, p. 120; UNITED STATES POSTAL SERVICE, p. 156.

Significance   The Veterans Administration is an independent executive agency that reports to the president. Although the agency is not attached to any cabinet department, the VA director may be removed by the president. The VA represents the aftermath of war. It is the governmental arm of the American Legion and other veterans' groups. More than half of the American people are concerned directly or indirectly with the operation of this agency. In terms of number of employees, it is the largest independent agency and, among the entire federal establishment, the VA is the third largest employer (after the Department of Defense and United States Postal Service).

Attempts to make the VA a cabinet department have proven politically difficult as its clientele have fought strongly against the VA losing its privileged independent status. The VA exists as an independent agency because of the desire of veterans' lobbyists to reduce the influence of government departments on the agency and thus make it more receptive to their demands. Its responsibilities are likely to increase substantially as millions of veterans from World War II, the Korean War, and the Vietnam War reach the age when additional medical, death benefit, and other services will be required.

7. The Congress and the Electorate

Apportionment   The allocation of legislative seats among or within the states. Apportionment is based on the population in each district. Malapportionment describes an unequal, unfair distribution; reapportionment involves the reallocation of seats to establish equilibrium. Senate apportionment is set forth in Article I, Section 3 (which was superseded by the Seventeenth Amendment) to the Constitution, which declares that each state is guaranteed two senators, regardless of population, and that this representation cannot be abridged without the state's consent. In the House, the 435 seats are apportioned among the states mainly on the basis of population. There are also four nonvoting delegates serving the District of Columbia, Guam, Virgin Islands, and American Samoa, plus a resident commissioner representing Puerto Rico. Following each diennial census, the mathematical formula of the Method of Equal Representation is used to decide House apportionment. *See also* CONGRESSIONAL DISTRICT, p. 162; GERRYMANDERING, p. 169; NONVOTING DELEGATES, p. 174.

Significance   Apportionment has long been a matter before the courts. The landmark "one person, one vote" ruling of *Baker* v. *Carr*, followed by *Gray* v. *Sanders*, and *Reynolds* v. *Sims* in the 1960s, held that unequal apportionment violated the equal protection clause of the Fourteenth Amendment. In *Wesberry* v. *Sanders* (1964), the courts ruled that congressional districts must have approximately equal population. What amount constitutes "approximate" has been reduced consistently through recent Supreme Court decisions. The task of determining how many seats a state will be apportioned has also undergone variation over time. Beginning in 1790, a series of formulas was utilized that incorporated fixed ratios and fractions to arrive at the number of seats allotted

159

to a state based on its population. In 1941 the current Method of Equal Representation was adopted. Priority values are given to each state based on the results of this formula, in order to determine gains and losses. Before applying the reapportionment formula, however, each state receives one representative regardless of its population size. The test of fairness is whether the percentage difference in population per representative is the smallest possible for any pair of states.

Once congressional seats are apportioned, the process of drawing district lines begins. This process is intensely political. The courts have shied away from intervention in this process, as they have in the area of equal district population. The result has been gerrymandering—the drawing of district lines to partisan advantage. Redistricting is a sensitive political exercise, one which can be most threatening to a member. State parties seek to create safe districts for members of Congress of the majority party, by concentrating or dispersing voters in particular districts. So while true apportionment guarantees "one person, one vote," political districting frequently guarantees "one person, one Democrat or Republican vote."

Campaign Finance   The raising of funds to support a political campaign. Campaign finance was regulated in large part, prior to 1971, under the Federal Corrupt Practices Act of 1925. This act set limits on campaign expenditures by candidates. In the 1970s campaign finance laws were strengthened under the Federal Election Campaign Acts of 1971, 1974, and 1976. Campaign funds may be raised by direct mail, interest groups, business leaders, fund-raising dinners, and wealthy individuals. The cost of campaigns has soared, with expenditures going toward political consultants, broadcasting, print advertising, staff and office expenses, speechwriting, research, and transportation. The amount of money candidates can raise may dictate the type of campaigns they can run and, to a large extent, the outcome of elections. *See also* FEDERAL ELECTIONS CAMPAIGN ACTS, p. 166; POLITICAL ACTION COMMITTEES, p. 175; POLITICAL CAMPAIGNING, p. 176; PUBLIC FINANCING, p. 180.

Significance   Campaign finance legislation in the United States has sought to regulate political donations and campaign disbursements as well as to require disclosure of both donations and disbursements. The Federal Election Campaign Act of 1971 set limits on campaign expenditures for media advertising and required full disclosure of funds received and spent by political campaigns. The act served to curb many of the abuses brought to public attention by the Watergate scandal and spurred new legislation in 1974. The 1974 amendments aimed at establishing limits on all forms of campaign expenditures but were subsequently ruled unconstitutional by the Supreme Court as a violation of free expression. The 1976 amendments established further limits on campaign contributions: a candidate for federal office may not receive more than $1,000 from a single individual or $5,000 from a committee that supports several candidates.

The problem with campaign finance legislation has been the difficulty of its enforcement, often due to the myriad loopholes that candidates and donors have been able to exploit. Public financing was viewed as an antidote to the escalating costs of presidential campaigns, but it failed to win acceptance for financing congressional campaigns. Many observers believe that only candidates with considerable means, or access to such means, can win seats in Congress. However, all is not lost for those candidates who cannot raise large campaign warchests. It has been observed that spending does not produce as many votes in general elections as in primaries; that it increases voter turnout; that challenger spending is more important than incumbent spending; and that beyond a certain spending threshold, additional money has little effect. But with big money flowing into campaigns via political action committees, spending levels remain extremely high as candidates pursue their elusive electoral advantage. As Jess Unruh, a longtime California politico, opined: "Money is the mother's milk of politics."

Characteristics of Congress Members   The dominant traits of members serving in the House and Senate. Characteristics of members of Congress influence voter perceptions at election time and affect members' attitudes and actions once elected. These characteristics include education, age, social background, religion, race, sex, and prior political experience. While the theory of descriptive representation suggests that members of Congress should "mirror" their constituency, this is not reflected in the composition of Congress. Congress members are recruited from high strata of society, and characteristics such as race and sex may become negative campaign issues in many races. The lack of minority representation in Congress—for example, blacks, Hispanics, and women—evidences its stratified composition, a fact that many critics decry as a serious failing in a representative democracy. *See also* CONGRESSIONAL BLACK CAUCUS, p. 213; CONGRESSIONAL HISPANIC CAUCUS, p. 214; CONSTITUENCY, p. 165; REPRESENTATION THEORY, p. 182.

Significance   Characteristics of members of Congress may vary slightly from session to session, but the overall composition remains steady. Virtually all members of Congress have attended college and graduated, while a large percentage have education beyond the college level. Much of this additional education is in law schools; nearly half of all members of Congress have law degrees and list their occupations as lawyers. Lawyers traditionally have served in Congress in large numbers; other well-represented occupations include business, banking, real estate, education, and various public service or political positions. In terms of age, most House members (at initial election) are in the forty to forty-four age range, followed by the late forties and late fifties ranges. The predominant social background is middle to upper class, and most are of the Protestant faith. In regards to race and sex, white males predominate in Congress. In 1983 only 4.6 percent of House members were black, and 4.3 percent were female. In the Senate, there were no blacks and only two women. Blacks and Hispanics have sought to maximize their influence through congressional caucuses. A women's caucus has been formed also, but not all women members have joined. Women have historically gained congressional seats through "widow's succession": assuming the seats of their late husbands. Finally, most members of Congress have held state or local offices prior to their election to Congress. Many have been active in the party or held party offices. In short, Congress is overladen with white male lawyers and seriously lacks in minority representation. How these key characteristics are perceived by the voters, and the prognosis for a more balanced Congress, is difficult to determine.

Congressional District   The geographical area represented by a member of Congress. Congressional districts are characterized by legal boundaries established by state legislatures or court decisions. For senators, the entire state is a two-member district, shared by the two senators from that state. House districts are single-member districts, with each state apportioned seats based on its population. Six states (Alaska, Delaware, North Dakota, South Dakota, Vermont, and Wyoming) are represented by only one member of Congress elected "at large" by the voters. The drawing of district lines is dictated by the requirement of "one person, one vote," as set forth by the Supreme Court. Apportionment is determined by Congress; districting is the task of state legislatures. *See also* APPORTIONMENT, p. 159; GERRYMANDERING, p. 169.

Significance   Congressional district lines are, in large part, arbitrary, politically motivated boundaries that create constituencies. That is, district lines may be manipulated to consciously include or exclude voters from a geographical district. Such is the power of gerrymandering: to tilt districts in partisan strength and voter concentration. There are infinite ways to draw district lines in a state and still satisfy the principle of equal representation. Hence, party-controlled state governments seek to draw district lines so as to maximize the number of seats their party can expect to win. As a result, observes political scientist Gary C. Jacobson, congressional districts bear no resemblance to the other natural divisions—a city, county, or state legislative district—that party organizations reflect (Jacobson 1983, 13). Adroit state legislators, with eyes toward Congress, can effectively "carve out" districts for themselves if they so wish.

Virtually all states have been forced to redistrict to achieve equality in their districts. Following each decennial census, the states are required to redistrict to achieve the "one person, one vote" requirement. If a state fails to realize this goal, the federal courts may intervene. Population shifts do not merely reflect migration patterns into and out of a state, but internal population shifts as well. This fact is underscored, for example, by the increase of suburban representation in Congress. Suburban districts lean toward the Republican party, whereas Democratic districts tend to be less affluent, more urban, and often rural. Population disbursement is not a random, arbitrary phenomenon, but congressional districting of these populations is. The factors involved in drawing district lines remain outside the hands of Congress, whose electoral fortunes are contingent upon these decisions. As former Senator Fred Harris suggests, "Having friends in their home-state legislature may be especially important for U.S. Representatives in states which lose House seats."

Congressional Election   The process by which a candidate is selected by popular vote to serve as a senator or representative. Congressional elections have been described as local events with national consequences. Primary elections determine each party's candidate for the general election, then the candidate must campaign anew to win office. Constituents are faced with a plethora of candidates, campaigns, and issues. The decision to vote is based on the strength of party loyalty and identification, perceived political efficacy, candidate appeal, and the nature of the issues themselves. Parties and candidates seek to rally the vote on election day, a difficult feat considering that less than 60 percent of eligible voters usually participate in House and Senate elections. *See also* GENERAL ELECTION, p. 168; PRIMARY ELECTION, p. 179.

Significance   Congressional elections are at the very core of the American system of representative democracy. As English political philosopher Thomas Hobbes wrote in *The Leviathan*, a government is based upon a social contract among the people that authorizes someone to act in their behalf. A congressional election is such an authorization, but only the people who vote are entering into this contract. And by this token, voters also become representatives, acting on behalf of nonvoters to select their representatives. Some people argue that low voter participation in congressional elections indicates a satisfaction with government; others suggest that voters feel helpless to change government; and still others blame sheer apathy as a cause. Regardless of who votes, a candidate must reach the voters at least once during the primary election campaign and, if possible, once again during the general election.

Congressional elections have been described as contributing to a fragmentation of Congress. Each congressperson comes to Washington with an individual mandate, local policy actors thrust onto the national stage. As political scientist V. O. Key opines: "To some extent the affairs of senatorial politics in each state and of congressional politics in each district are governed, not by the great considerations of national politics, but by questions peculiar to the locality" (Ripley 1983, 75–76). The Congress thus becomes the locus of the competing interests of 50 states, 435 districts, and American territories. In the House, seats change every two years, and elections are constantly just around the corner. Change is also a fundamental characteristic of representation, and congressional elections provide the means of bringing about such change. Despite the fact that incumbents usually win, too many potential voters do not vote, hence, the necessary changes may not always be effected. Congressional elections remain the benchmark of American democracy, warts and all.

Congressional Ethics   A written and unwritten code of standards dictating the behavior of senators and representatives. Congressional ethics are mandated by the Constitution, criminal laws, ethics codes, and party rules. The Senate Ethics Committee operates as the Select Committee on Standards and Conduct, which handles investigations previously performed by the Senate Rules and Administration Committee. The House Ethics Committee is the bipartisan Committee on Standards of Official Conduct, a standing committee that is not granted investigative authority. Under the Constitution, members of Congress are accorded "congressional immunity" from arrest during "attendance at the Session of their respective Houses." Each chamber is empowered to punish its members for "disorderly behavior" and may expel a member by a two-thirds vote. A member may also face reprimand, the lightest of punishments, or censure, a stronger disciplinary measure, for violations of ethics requirements. *See also* FEDERAL ELECTION CAMPAIGN ACTS, p. 166; FEDERAL ELECTION COMMISSION, p. 167.

Significance   Congressional ethics and their enforcement have posed difficult problems for Congress. Historically, members of Congress have been reluctant to pass judgment on their fellow members, and service on the ethics committees has not been popular. The slow speed at which the committees move, coupled with their hesitancy to investigate members before criminal proceedings are initiated, has fostered a public view of Congress as unwilling to control itself. Congress, though, has sought to rein in many excesses. The Ethics in Government Act, enacted in 1978, strengthened financial disclosure requirements and provided for court appointment of a special prosecutor in cases of criminal allegations against high-level government officials. The Watergate scandal (which led to charges of criminal wrongdoing against President Richard M. Nixon and several of his top staff aides) in the early 1970s underscored the need to strengthen enforcement of government ethics, and subsequent scandals such as Koreagate (which involved congressional influence peddling to Korean officials) in 1978 and Abscam (an FBI attempt to expose members of Congress prone to criminal misconduct) in 1980 brought continued attention to the ethics responsibility.

Congressional misconduct is not a new phenomenon but has been taken more seriously in recent times. Investigative journalists, such as Jack Anderson, have brought cases of political corruption and abuse of power to the widespread attention of the American public. Law enforcement authorities have also become increasingly aggressive in unearthing congressional corruption, as evidenced by the elaborate Abscam plot to expose congressmen who would be likely to sell their votes and participate in other forms of criminal activity. In the long run, the decision of how to punish a member falls to Congress, and a general belief has been that members should be judged by their constituents rather than their colleagues. The low incidence of expulsions and censures bears witness to this tendency; to others, it represents a feeling that ethical problems in Congress could be much worse.

Constituency   The citizens represented by a member of the House or Senate. Constituents are voters—the life blood of politics. Political scientist Richard F. Fenno, Jr. describes four perceptions by members of Congress of their constituencies: geographic, reelection, primary, and personal (Fenno 1978, 27). The geographic constituency describes the citizenry within a legally bounded space; the reelection constituency encompasses the incumbent's supporters; the primary constituency represents strong supporters; and the personal constituency consists of close friends, advisers, and confidants. Constituents vary widely in terms of party loyalty, identification, and participation; a member must reach the majority of them at election time to win office. Once elected, members must represent that constituency in accordance with their views of representation and, in order to be reelected, must be responsive and sensitive to the needs and wants of their constituents. *See also* PORK BARREL LEGISLATION, p. 283; REPRESENTATION THEORY, p. 182; SAFE-MARGINAL DISTRICT, p. 183.

Significance   Constituency variables include the degree to which constituents know or care about what takes place in Congress. Political scientist Barbara Hinckley distinguishes the "attentive" from the "inattentive" constituent, the former being those individuals and groups within and outside the party who are concerned about what happens in Congress (Hinckley 1978, 49). Attentive constituents, she notes, study and read about candidates, especially incumbents. Members of Congress must pay attention to their constituents, answering their questions, protecting their interests, and gauging their sentiments on matters of public policy. Whether this gauge is based on public opinion polls, or simply an intuitive, personal feeling about constituency attitudes, depends on how accurately a member wishes to reflect their attitudes. Political scientist Randall Ripley suggests that members who come from highly competitive districts are more likely to be concerned about representing their district with greater precision than those from less competitive districts. While there is much room for misinterpretation of constituency attitudes, a member generally has a good degree of latitude in which to take positions, as many constituents do not have strong opinions on many issues. On matters that do concern constituents directly, a congressperson must be careful in choosing a position. Members are always anxious to "bring home the bacon" to their constituents, enjoying the benefits of pork barrel legislation to deliver the goods. The constituency impacts upon the member by articulating their economic interests and monitoring their representative's performance. No matter how representatives view their constituency, they are accountable to the voters at election time.

Federal Election Campaign Acts   Legislation promulgated throughout the 1970s to spell out and enforce campaign laws. The Federal Election Campaign Act of 1971 superseded the Federal Corrupt Practices Act of 1925, which had theretofore enumerated basic campaign finance laws. New amendments were added to the 1971 act in 1974, but Supreme Court action on these new provisions spurred further legislation in the form of the Federal Election Campaign Act of 1976. All of these reforms were undertaken to strengthen enforcement of campaign laws and to eliminate some of the many loopholes available to candidates and donors. *See also* FEDERAL ELECTION COMMISSION, p. 167; PUBLIC FINANCING, p. 180.

Significance   The Federal Election Campaign Act of 1971 represented the first major attempt at campaign reform since 1925. This
legislation placed a limit on campaign expenditures by candidates for
president, vice president, senator, and representative. The spending
limits were directed at media advertising, creating a maximum allowa-
ble expenditure of ten cents per voter (or $50,000, whichever was
greater) for television, radio, newspaper, and magazine advertising. The
act also placed a ceiling on the amount candidates or their families could
contribute to the campaign. Additionally, it required that all contributions over $100 be disclosed, with reports filed throughout the year on all
donations and disbursements. The Federal Election Campaign Act of
1974 comprised a series of amendments to plug loopholes and to prevent
abuses that stemmed from the 1971 act. Spending limits were established
for candidates in presidential primary and general election campaigns,
as well as in House and Senate primary campaigns for the first time.
New features included optional public financing for presidential general election campaigns, coupled with federal matching grants for presidential primary election campaigns. New disclosure provisions were
established, and a new Federal Election Commission was created to
enforce these laws.

These 1974 provisions were challenged in the Supreme Court in 1976
in the case of *Buckley* v. *Valeo*. The legality of contribution limits, public
finance provisions, and disclosure were upheld, but limits on campaign
spending were ruled unconstitutional, violating the First Amendment
guarantee of free expression. Additionally, congressional involvement in
the reappointment of commissioners to the Federal Election Commission was declared unconstitutional, as violating the separation of powers
and appointments clauses. The Federal Election Campaign Act of 1976
reestablished the Federal Election Commission as a six-member panel,
with members being appointed by the president and confirmed by the
Senate. Contribution limits were again revised, but spending limits were
left untouched.

Federal Election Commission (FEC)   Federal agency responsible for the interpretation and enforcement of federal election laws. The
Federal Election Commission (FEC) was created under the Federal
Election Campaign Act of 1974 to enforce its provisions and apply
penalties as needed. As originally constituted, it consisted of six members: two appointed by the president, two by the Senate, and two by the
House. Congressional appointments were subsequently ruled unconstitutional; the Supreme Court held that Congress was improperly
exercising executive powers. This, said the Court, was a clear violation of
the separation of powers and appointments clauses. As a result, the FEC

was reconstituted in 1976 as a six-member panel of presidential appointees, each subject to Senate confirmation. Commissioners serve six-year terms. *See also* CAMPAIGN FINANCE, p. 160; FEDERAL ELECTION CAMPAIGN ACTS, p. 166; POLITICAL ACTION COMMITTEES, p. 175.

Significance   The Federal Election Commission was created out of the need for campaign reform, especially in campaign financing, and the need for those reforms to be enforced. These enforcement powers were subsequently weakened by the 1976 amendments. Their powers include audits, investigations, subpoena of witnesses and information, injunctions, and referral of cases to the Justice Department for criminal prosecution. The commission establishes rules and regulations that may be reviewed or vetoed by Congress within 30 days. The Federal Election Campaign Act of 1976 requires that the FEC issue advisory opinions only on specific fact situations. On general questions, they are limited to applying regulations; provisions which state a "separable rule of law" are open to congressional review.

An important function provided by the FEC is its publication of expenditure reports by candidates and political action committees. Both must file itemizations of expenditures over $200 and reports of total campaign expenditures in accordance with campaign laws. This information (such as which congressional candidates spent the most money, or which political action committees contributed the largest sums to campaigns) is available for public scrutiny. The Federal Election Commission has had a tumultuous history, subject to enormous political pressures from all sides. Many of its goals, as envisioned in 1974, have been altered by the Supreme Court and Congress. It continues to function as the overseer of federal elections, but it is overseen by the Congress.

General Election   The contests following the primary election to fill elective offices. A general election pits the nominees of each party against one another in a head-to-head competition. Candidates work long and hard to reach the voters, often spending vast sums of money to garner the necessary votes. Regardless of how well candidates do in the party primary, their battle is only half won; they must now win the general election. In the primary, their task was to win enough votes from members of their own party to secure the nomination. Now, their task is even greater. First, they must heal the wounds created by the primary, bring the various factions together, and forge a united effort. Second, they must make a serious attempt to reach the large bloc of undecided voters and persuade them to support their candidacy. Third, they must make some effort, depending on the locale, composition, issues, and circumstances, to woo as many of their opponent's backers as possible. The task before them is by no means easy. It will require a near perfect campaign: one that is well organized and conducted from start to finish, and one that addresses the diverse interests and concerns of as large a cross section of the electorate as possible. *See also* CONGRESSIONAL ELECTION, p. 163; POLITICAL CAMPAIGNING, p. 176; PRIMARY ELECTION, p. 179.

Significance   General elections are replete with contradictions. The textbook profile of the typical American voter bears little resemblance to the actual voter of today. Classical democratic theory posits a voter who is informed, involved, and interested in the affairs of government; a voter who is willing to invest the required time and effort to study the candidates and issues; and then, in the solitude of the voting booth, select those individuals who are most qualified to lead. The facts, however, bespeak another type of voter. Today's voters are generally uninformed on political issues. They have a vague sense of what is at stake, but rarely do they understand the nuances and complexities that are involved. Instead, they vote on instinct or whim for the candidates who come closest to mirroring their own views on the two or three select issues of concern to them at the time. More often, they vote based on party affiliation, routinely supporting those candidates who carry their party's banner. On occasion, they will vote on the basis of the candidate's style, charm, appearance, or charisma, associating those qualities with the ability to govern.

The implications of such voting are great. They suggest, more and more, that "the medium is the message"—that public relations packaging and mass media advertising are indispensible tools in winning elective office. Successful candidates must build a broad-based coalition of disparate voters. This, in turn, forces them to avoid issues and eschew stands that might cost them votes. Candidates can ill afford to antagonize those voters who determine victory or defeat. All too often, the wrong candidate is elected—the pied piper who promises the sky and then fails to deliver—making the problem of accountability extremely difficult. Since the voters know little of the issues, or the candidates, they are incapable of holding them accountable for their promises. Winning candidates have a personal mandate, but no mandate to solve the nation's ills.

Gerrymandering   The manipulation of electoral district boundaries, usually engaged in by the majority party in a state legislature, for the political advantage of an incumbent or party. Gerrymandering may produce oddly shaped districts in order to accomplish the intended effect. The term originated in 1812, when a district in Essex County, Massachusetts was described as resembling a salamander. In honor of Governor Elbridge Gerry of Massachusetts, the misshapen district was described as a gerrymander. Two techniques of gerrymandering are "packing" and "cracking." A district is packed when its lines are drawn to concentrate party voters into a safe district. To minimize the partisan concentration of the opposition party, a district may be cracked into more than one district to spread that party's vote. Gerrymandering is possible because of the consistent patterns of voting behavior exhibited by most American voters. *See also* APPORTIONMENT, p. 159; CONGRESSIONAL DISTRICT, p. 162.

Significance   Gerrymandering, unlike malapportionment, does not violate the Constitution or federal law. Lines may be drawn in many configurations to allow equally sized districts. This is regarded as one of the fine arts of the political process. When state legislatures draw district lines, the majority party seeks to maximize the number of congressional and state legislative seats they are likely to win. Thus, by packing and cracking, the legislature can distribute voters into districts of relative partisan strength. Opposition voters may be gerrymandered into a district where their party can win by a large margin, while minimizing the number of districts they can win. Or the opposition party's voting strength may be dissipated by spreading it over a number of districts. In cases where each of the two parties control one of the houses of the state legislature, district lines are likely to be drawn to favor incumbents rather than to alter partisan balance. Indeed, congressional incumbents may sometimes draw the district lines themselves.

Gerrymandering not only redistributes partisan balance but also concentrates or disperses voters by such characteristics as wealth, race, and education. Gerrymandering frequently creates a large number of safe districts that aid the incumbent. However, incumbency has proved important in all districts. Additionally, since United States senators also benefit greatly from incumbency and are not affected by gerrymandering, it is difficult to assess the full impact of gerrymandering on congressional elections.

Incumbent's Advantage   The advantage over a challenger enjoyed by an official seeking reelection. The incumbent's advantage in congressional races is extremely strong; reelection rates of 90 percent for House incumbents are typical, while Senate rates may vary between 60 and 90 percent. In addition to incumbency, party balance and national or state political trends affect election outcomes. The advantages of incumbency include name recognition, ability to raise campaign funds, representation of the majority party, leverage in redistricting, and control over an extensive network of resources available to a member of Congress. *See also* APPORTIONMENT, p. 159; POLITICAL CAMPAIGNING, p. 176; SAFE-MARGINAL DISTRICT, p. 183.

Significance   The incumbent's advantage is not a guarantee of electoral success but has proved to be a formidable roadblock for nonincumbent opponents. In House races, incumbency is a salient factor because many districts reflect a solid one-party constituency. This partisan balance usually translates to victory by the candidate of the majority party. Redistricting plans by state legislatures are often made to accommodate incumbents, resulting in safe districts that are virtually impossible for a challenger to penetrate. Moreover, the constituency knows their legislators—their names, their backgrounds, their records. And to rekindle awareness, an incumbent enjoys the privileges of franking, a paid staff, a WATS telephone line, caseworkers, and the publicity a member of Congress can generate. While the challenger's campaign funds are consumed by these expenses, incumbents may use their resources to fortify communications with the voters, relying extensively on television, radio, and newspaper advertisements. They can disseminate their message concerning what they have done for the district or state—tangible accomplishments versus the promises of the challenger.

To overcome these disadvantages, a challenger must often run several times for the same office, thereby increasing name recognition, expanding support base, improving the campaign organization, and avoiding the pitfalls of earlier campaigns. Incumbent members of Congress have the ability to exploit the national media, while challengers are limited to state and local sources. Despite all this, incumbents must still work extremely hard to keep their seats. There are too many variables, too much unpredictability, to assume certain victory. Indeed, incumbents often simply campaign far better than their opponents and possess records that ensure their reelection.

Lame Duck Congress   The session of Congress between the November elections and the first day the new Congress convenes. A lame duck Congress includes the lame ducks, members who will not return for the next session. Prior to the Twentieth Amendment, the terms of outgoing senators and representatives ended on March 4, four months after the general elections. Criticisms of action taken in the short lame duck session from the November elections to March led to passage of the Twentieth Amendment, which reduced the number and length of such sessions, advanced the presidential inauguration date to January 20, and provided for the convening of the new Congress early in January. *See also* ADJOURNMENT, p. 255; FILIBUSTER, p. 274; LEGISLATIVE REORGANIZATION ACTS, p. 204.

Significance   Lame duck Congress sessions are notable for their lack of productivity. Under the old system, lame duck members could block legislation in the short session until the fixed adjournment date of March 4; senators could easily filibuster a bill for the duration. Moreover, members elected in November would have to wait thirteen months until the following December, to begin the new session. The 1933 ratification of the Twentieth Amendment, written to alleviate this situation, did not come easily. The proposed amendment had been approved by the Senate six times before a Democratic-controlled House finally took favorable action in 1932. Adjournment provisions were established under the Legislative Reorganization Act of 1970, which set July 31 as the date when the regular session adjourned unless otherwise provided by Congress. In election years, Congress is likely to adjourn in early summer to allow sufficient time for campaigning; in other years, Congress frequently adjourns in late summer or fall.

Constitutional amendment proposals have been offered in recent years to limit the number of terms a congressperson can serve, which would create lame duck members comparable to the lame duck president established by the term limitations of the Twenty-second Amendment. Supporters of congressional term limitation claim that Congress would be more representative of the people's needs if the long serving incumbents could be removed from Congress. Opponents of term limitation, however, suggest that a member's legislative ability could be impaired and that the member might feel less accountable and less sensitive to the constituency when voting. Lame duck sessions pose special problems in midyear elections, when the president's party typically loses seats in Congress. This was the case in 1982, for example, when the Republicans lost two dozen seats in the House. During this lame duck session, President Ronald Reagan and the Republican House leadership tried to push through a number of budget cut proposals, but they failed.

Lobbyist   A person acting on behalf of a special interest group that attempts to influence legislation. Lobbyists interact with legislators to achieve mutual benefits. Hundreds of corporations and organizations employ Washington lobbyists, who spend millions annually to influence Washington and public opinion. The main types of lobbying include direct lobbying (appealing directly to members of Congress and their staffs), social lobbying (meeting members at social functions), lobby coalitions (lobbies that join together to pursue shared goals), and grassroots lobbying (appealing to citizens to put pressure on their representatives). Lobbyists are required to register and identify themselves, but Congress has been hesitant to apply strict regulations on lobbies. *See also* CAMPAIGN FINANCE, p. 160; POLITICAL ACTION COMMITTEES, p. 175; PUBLIC FINANCING, p. 180.

Significance   Lobbyists seek to gain support for their goals through direct contact with members of Congress. This arrangement is largely reciprocal: legislators seek out lobbyists to provide expert information on issues and problems of special concern. In addition to this substantive advice, lobbyists may be familiar with the bureaucracy and the legislator's constituency, through the efforts of grassroots lobbying and contact with a vast array of Washington power brokers. This information can be most valuable to a member, and its acquisition stems out of political necessity. The lobbyist has something the member wants, and the latter must pay for it by granting favors. Of course, critics decry the influence inherent in these exchanges, charging that the magnitude of what a congressperson can give far outweighs the information a lobbyist can provide. A lobbyist may be active during all phases of the legislative process: planning strategy, influencing votes, mobilizing support, and drafting speeches and amendments.

Lobbyists are a permanent fixture on Capitol Hill, working long and hard to protect their special interests. For example, the American Medical Association lobbied Congress for years in opposition to Medicare; the United Auto Workers against clean air standards; and the National Rifle Association against gun control. The strongest lobbies in Washington are those which represent large bases of economic power. Former Senator Fred Harris suggests that whether or not such groups control Congress depends on how important and visible the issue is; the less visible and more routine the policy question under consideration, the greater the impact of the special interest group. Politics makes strange bedfellows; the relationship between legislators and lobbyists is a beautiful marriage for some, while a lurid affair for others.

Midterm Election   A congressional election held in the off years, the even-numbered years between presidential elections, such as 1982, 1986, and 1990. Midterm election results have traditionally been regarded as a judgment on the performance of the current president. In the twentieth century, the president's party has consistently lost seats in the House in midterm elections, except in 1934. The term negative voting has been used to describe this phenomenon. Congressional candidates seem to enjoy the advantage of riding on presidential coattails in presidential year elections, taking advantage of a presidential candidate's popularity to win their own elections. If presidential popularity or the state of the economy are weak at midterm, congressional candidates of the president's party may fare badly in the off year. *See also* COATTAIL EFFECT, p. 5; GENERAL ELECTION, p. 168; PRIMARY ELECTION, p. 179.

Significance   Midterm elections give voters an opportunity to signal to a president their satisfaction or dissatisfaction with the president's performance in office. The signal is indirect, though, since the American people are voting for House candidates and for one-third of the Senate seats, but not for the president. If presidential popularity is not the primary stimulant of the vote, other factors may shape the election outcome. Political scientist Barbara Hinckley suggests that voters' perceptions of congressional candidates in midterm elections are shaped first by their perception of events and then by their perception of the party (Hinckley 1981, 129). Thus candidates may become victims of negative voting—votes against the president, the party, and the policies of the government. If indeed the president and the party are unpopular, it may prove difficult for that party to field attractive congressional candidates and to raise money for an effective campaign. The voters may then be faced with weak candidates from the president's party who are unlikely to win.

   Since congressional candidates are seen to benefit from the "pulling power" of presidential coattails during the presidential year elections, Hinckley suggests that the midterm loss of congressional seats is directly related to the amount of presidential popularity in the preceding election. In other words, seats that might not have been won without the coattail effect are lost at midterm. This surge and decline phenomenon is seen as a means of returning party balance to Congress at midterm. However, political scientist Randall B. Ripley believes that the low correlation between the presidential and congressional vote in presidential year elections, coupled with the advantage of incumbency, diminishes this argument (Ripley 1983, 116). Finally, midterm elections are observed by Hinckley to attract a different type of voter than presidential year elections. Midterm voters are described as more habitual, interested, and partisan voters, whereas presidential elections appeal to marginal voters who are "attracted by the excitement of the presidential contest."

Nonvoting Delegates   Representatives of incorporated and unincorporated American territories in Congress. Nonvoting delegates represent the District of Columbia, Guam, Virgin Islands, and American Samoa. A resident commissioner represents Puerto Rico. The resident commissioner and delegates may participate in floor discussion in the House but are not entitled to vote. However, they do vote in the congressional committees to which they are assigned. The resident commissioner is elected to a four-year term, while the delegates are elected to two-year terms. *See also* APPORTIONMENT, p. 159.

Significance   Nonvoting delegates in the House were authorized in the early 1970s. Representation for the District of Columbia was long an issue that confronted Congress and was continually rejected. In 1970 legislation was enacted that provided that the District could elect a delegate who would possess the same powers and privileges of any other House member, save the right to vote on the House floor. In 1971 the District elected Walter E. Fauntroy, a black Baptist minister, who continues to serve as the District's representative. In 1975 a resolution was passed by the House Judiciary Committee, sponsored by Fauntroy, that proposed a constitutional amendment providing for two voting senators and an amount of representatives, based on District population, equal to the number that it would be entitled to as a state. (Based on 1976 population, that would have been two representatives.) When brought to the House floor, the sentiments behind District representation became clear. Proponents claimed that District residents were victims of "taxation without representation," and that as long as residents paid federal taxes, abided by federal law, and served in the armed forces, they were entitled to voting representation. Opponents argued that states were the units making up the federal system, and that only by assuming the responsibilities of statehood should the District be allowed a vote in Congress. The resolution was subsequently defeated, but in 1978 a constitutional amendment was submitted to the states providing for full District representation. The measure passed both the House and Senate, but conservative opposition thwarted ratification by the states.

   The unincorporated territories of Guam, Virgin Islands, and American Samoa were granted nonvoting delegates in 1972. Congress exercises complete jurisdiction over the affairs of the territories, even though most matters are left in the hands of the territorial legislatures. Puerto Rico has perennially struggled with the issue of statehood that would bring with it voting representation in the House and Senate. The question has divided Puerto Rican voters for some time and does not appear to be easily resolved. Alternative approaches would be to maintain the status quo or to opt for independence.

Political Action Committees (PACs)   Groups representing special interests who contribute funds to political campaigns. Political action committees (PACs) were the result of changes in campaign financing laws during the 1970s. In 1970 corporate and union contributions to political campaigns were forbidden. Labor unions, and soon business groups, formed groups to collect voluntary contributions from their members. Business soon overshadowed labor in the size and effectiveness of their political action committees. The Federal Election Campaign Act of 1974 and 1976 contributed further to the development of PACs, and PAC money began to flow to congressional campaigns as well as presidential campaigns. The Federal Election Commission defines PAC money as "separate, segregated funds to be utilized for political purposes." PACs contribute millions of dollars to political campaigns. In 1979–1980, for instance, the real estate industry PAC contributed over $1.5 million to candidates, according to the Federal Election Commission. *See also* CAMPAIGN FINANCE, p. 160; FEDERAL ELECTION CAMPAIGN ACTS, p. 166; FEDERAL ELECTION COMMISSION, p. 167; LOBBYIST, p. 172.

Significance   Political action committees have substantially affected the electoral process and the nature of campaign financing. First, most PAC money has been directed toward incumbents, especially those who possess committee assignments advantageous to the group. PAC managers avoid close elections, preferring to channel their funds to candidates that they are certain will win. Additionally, the use of independent expenditures by PACs for ideological purposes has increased. Single-issue interest groups support or oppose candidates based on their views of selected issues. In 1980 the National Conservative Political Action Committee (NCPAC) spent $4 million to try to defeat six liberal senators. Four lost—George McGovern (D-S.D.), John Culver (D-Iowa), Birch Bayh (D-Ind.), and Frank Church (D-Idaho)—and two won—Alan Cranston (D-Calif.) and Thomas Eagleton (D-Mo.). To blame NCPAC solely for their defeat would be overstating the case, but there was a likely impact.

Political action committees have also affected party authority and party campaign financing. To counter the rise in PAC funding of campaigns, congressional and national parties have sought to increase their own fund-raising efforts. Excessive reliance on PAC money has increased support for public financing of congressional campaigns. The fear of a Congress representing special interests rather than constituencies persists, as PACs and special interest groups increase their influence on elections. Elections have become extremely expensive, and PAC money is increasingly tempting for congressional candidates.

Political Campaigning   The process by which a candidate seeks to win voter support in the bid for elective office. Political campaigning involves the development of a systematic strategy to reach the voters—supporters, potential supporters, and the apathetic—as well as to entice the opponent's backers. A political campaign has one main objective: to muster sufficient votes to win. Campaign resources figure prominently in the process; the cost of reaching voters via television or direct mail is extremely high. The amount of funds that candidates have at their disposal will largely determine the type of campaigns they will be able to wage. Money is not the sole determinant of a successful campaign; candidates can spend more than their opponents and still lose. However, money is a vital resource: one for which there is no real substitute because most other campaign activities are dependent on money. *See also* CAMPAIGN FINANCE, p. 160; FEDERAL ELECTION CAMPAIGN ACTS, p. 166; FEDERAL ELECTION COMMISSION, p. 167.

Significance   Political campaigning begins with a candidate's decision to run. At that point, the candidates must appoint a campaign manager; put together a fund-raising effort; hire a campaign counsel; employ media and campaign consultants; enlist a staff; map out the logistics; organize a research and policy team; hire a pollster; recruit a press secretary; and engage in various other organizational activities. And that is just the beginning. A challenger is faced with many disadvantages in attempting to unseat an incumbent who enjoys such key advantages as money, power, influence, staff, and media access. This poses a difficult but not impossible task. Incumbents seeking reelection must reactivate their public support, emphasizing their qualifications, experience, and record. Campaign techniques vary from race to race, depending on a host of factors. Still, candidates must try to reach the voters by whatever strategy each employs. To do so, they must emphasize such qualities as leadership, competence, strength, compassion, and integrity. The old-fashioned methods of door-to-door canvassing, meeting the voters, shaking hands, and kissing babies have been supplanted by newer, more sophisticated methods. Candidates now depend heavily on media advertising (television, radio, newspaper, and magazine advertisements) to reach the voters. Public opinion polls are commissioned or conducted, and many candidates employ campaign management firms to coordinate the effort.

Increasingly, campaigns have been conducted independently of the party organization, with candidates making the crucial decisions as opposed to party leaders. Concomitantly, candidates seek most of their funding outside the party, soliciting personal, organizational, and corporate contributions to finance their campaigns. Congressional campaigns can run into hundreds of thousands or millions of dollars, and the parties, as well as the candidate, can only provide a fraction of the required funds. What money is raised must be spent wisely, in both the primary and general elections, with the ultimate objective of winning sufficient votes on election day. All is not lost, though, on an unsuccessful campaign—particularly if the candidate harbors future political aspirations. There is always the next election; a candidate may learn from past mistakes and prove more successful in the next round.

Political Folkways   Informal or unwritten norms of conduct in the House and Senate. Political folkways contribute to the effective functioning and organization of Congress. The norms of specialization, apprenticeship, legislative attentiveness, and reciprocity contribute to Congress's decision-making capacities, while the norms of courtesy and institutional patriotism are designed to control conflict. Congressional life is described as a process of conformity, learning what to do and not do, what is accepted and not accepted. Power and influence are elusive goals in Congress, and those who achieve them seek to maintain the status quo. While not all folkways must be adhered to, they are strong influences on the behavior of senators and representatives. *See also* SENIORITY SYSTEM, p. 249.

Significance   Political folkways are like good manners; obey them and be accepted, break them and be scorned. Some congressional norms are not easily broken. The norm of apprenticeship dictates that freshmen members limit their involvement and defer to their seniors. Indeed, the seniority system is so firmly entrenched in both houses as to make a breach of this norm most difficult. The member is effectively told to listen and learn—that power is in silence, in committee, and in interpersonal relationships. These early years in a member's career may be a good period to develop a sphere of specialization and to acquire expertise in an area of special interest to the constituency. Specialization is inherent in the detailed committee and subcommittee work a member must perform and facilitates the decision-making and lawmaking functions of Congress. The norm of legislative attentiveness states that members will attend to their duties and not neglect them in their pursuit of publicity and recognition. Reciprocity is a folkway which promotes mutual respect among members. Members are expected to assist each other and, whenever possible, to trade votes. Whether referred to as bargaining, logrolling, or backscratching, the effect is the same: "you support me, I'll support you." The norm of courtesy translates to verbal deference, whether sincere or insincere. When "the distinguished Senator from California yields to the gentlewoman from Kansas," courtesy is being observed. Additionally, the norm of courtesy requires that members refrain from personal attacks on their colleagues and that political disagreements not be aired in public. Finally, the norm of institutional patriotism involves a respect for the Congress and what it stands for. The integrity of the institution must be upheld; frequently a member refers to his or her chamber as "the greatest deliberative body in the world." To some, political folkways may seem old-fashioned and trite. In practice, they are strong currents against which a nonconformist will not swim easily.

Primary Election   A mechanism for nominating a party's candidates for office. Primary elections, as proposed by the progressives early in this century, were devised to take the candidate selection process away from party bosses and put it in the hands of the voters. The direct primary is used by most states in nominating a congressional candidate; some Republican parties use conventions in Southern states, while other states combine conventions with primaries. The three types of direct primaries are open, closed, and blanket primaries. Thirty-nine states use the closed primary, in which voting is restricted to party members. Eight states use an open primary, in which the voter can request both party ballots, but may only vote on one. Three states—Alaska, Washington, and Louisiana—use blanket or crossover primaries, in which a voter may choose a candidate from one party for one office and a candidate from another party for another office. *See also* CAMPAIGN FINANCE, p. 160; GENERAL ELECTION, p. 168; POLITICAL CAMPAIGNING, p. 176.

Significance   Primary elections are run very much like general elections. Voters cast a secret ballot for the candidates of their choice in accordance with the state's primary laws. State-run primary elections are generally limited to Democratic and Republican party nominees, since only a party whose gubernatorial candidate received a minimum percentage of votes in the previous election may nominate a candidate through primaries. In most states, the candidate who wins a plurality of the votes in a primary election becomes that party's nominee in the general election. Eleven states use a run-off primary when a candidate fails to receive a majority of votes in the regular primary. Many primaries are noncompetitive with incumbents being routinely renominated for office.

Primary elections have been distinguished from general elections in the types of voters who participate. Primary voters are described as older, wealthier, better educated, more politically aware, and more ideologically committed than the general electorate. While primary elections are praised for putting the candidate selection process in the hands of the voters, critics suggest that this is eroding the function of the political party: candidates appeal directly to the public and build their own support independent of party leaders. Finally, primary election campaigns are extremely costly, and if no candidate enjoys an overwhelming advantage, most of the primary campaign tactics must be repeated in the campaign for general election.

Public Financing   Taxpayer-supported funding of political campaigns. Public financing for presidential primary and general election campaigns was the result of campaign finance reforms enacted throughout the 1970s. Public financing of congressional campaigns has not followed suit. Concern over political action committee (PAC) contributions to congressional campaigns led to bills and amendments to provide for public financing, but members of Congress have been resistant to such provisions. The Campaign Contribution Reform Act, passed in the House in 1979, contained public finance provisions which were subsequently dropped by its sponsors. A similar bill in the Senate, reported by the Rules and Administration Committee, was filibustered and killed in the Ninety-fifth Congress. *See also* CAMPAIGN FINANCE, p. 160; POLITICAL ACTION COMMITTEES, p. 175; POLITICAL CAMPAIGN-ING, p. 176.

Significance   Public financing of congressional campaigns is a divisive issue. Proponents suggest that public financing would reduce the advantage of wealthy individuals that contribute large sums of their own money to campaigns. Further, since it has been increasingly difficult to raise the sums necessary to finance an expensive campaign solely from individuals, candidates have been forced to rely increasingly on contributions from political action committees. Public financing, it is argued, would reduce this heavy reliance on PAC funds and would help to stem the escalating costs of congressional campaigns. Opponents of public financing suggest that private financing is a valuable gauge of a candidate's popularity; an equal distribution of public funds would eliminate this barometer. Additionally, opponents contend that public financing would weaken the party system, which has considered funding congressional campaigns itself in order to strengthen its rule. Some contend that public financing would likely protect incumbents by limiting the money that challengers could raise. Generally, the evidence does not support this contention. Incumbents typically have large financial resources available, while challengers often have trouble raising money. Public financing would move them toward equality in this critical area.

This concern led Congress to pass the Federal Election Campaign Act of 1971, which permitted individuals to claim a limited income tax credit for contributions to political candidates. Congress also provided that, beginning in 1973, taxpayers could designate that one dollar of their federal income tax goes to a special campaign fund to be distributed among the candidates running for president in the next election. This law was aimed at minimizing the dependence of presidential candidates on private contributions. In 1974 this option was made part of the standard income tax forms. Many observers have endorsed the proposal and called for a similar system as it relates to the financing of congressional campaigns. To date, the Congress has declined to take action on the recommendation, though there are signs that public financing will soon be extended to congressional campaigns.

Qualifications for Office   Constitutional requirements for membership in Congress. A representative must be twenty-five years of age (when seated), a citizen of the United States for seven years, and an inhabitant of the state from which elected. Custom also dictates that a representative live in the district he or she represents. A senator must be thirty years of age (when seated), a citizen of the United States for nine years, and an inhabitant of the state from which elected. Additionally, no member of Congress may hold any other "Office under the United States" and, under the Fourteenth Amendment, no member who has taken the oath to support the Constitution and has engaged in rebellion against the United States may serve in Congress. *See also* CHARACTERISTICS OF CONGRESS MEMBERS, p. 161.

Significance   Qualifications for office, as prescribed in the Constitution, have been adhered to rigorously. Three senators-elect have been denied seats for lack of qualifications, while ten members-elect of the House have been excluded. One of the most controversial cases in Congress was that of Representative Adam Clayton Powell, Jr. (D-N.Y.). Accused of misuse of public funds, the House in 1967 voted to exclude Powell from the Ninetieth Congress to which he had been reelected in 1966. Powell filed suit, and the case reached the Supreme Court. Chief Justice Earl Warren ruled that Congress had acted improperly in excluding Powell and that "in judging the qualifications of its members Congress is limited to the standing qualifications of the Constitution."

Each chamber is the judge of the "elections, returns, and qualifications" of its members and is empowered to decide any disputed congressional election. Such was the case in the 1974 New Hampshire Senate race between Republican Louis C. Wyman and Democrat John A. Durkin. The race was so close that the Senate could reach no compromise, so the seat was declared vacant and a new election had to be held. The House and Senate are also empowered to expel a member by a two-thirds vote. Expulsions are extremely rare, with the less stringent punishments of reprimand and censure more often meted out.

Although millions of Americans meet the legal requirements to serve in Congress, the real test is that of availability—that is, possessing those qualifications that will be likely to result in victory at the polls.

Representation Theory   The philosophy underlying the role of members of Congress and the service they provide to their constituency. Representation, according to political scientist Hanna Pitkin, can be divided into four categories: formal, descriptive, symbolic, and substantive (Vogler 1983, 53). Representation is the core of the American democratic system; it is, notes Thomas Jefferson, a system by which people elect representatives who will reflect the popular will in government. Senators and representatives each serve different groups: a senator serves the interests of the state; a congressperson serves the regional interests of the district. The view of representation adopted by members may differ markedly from that of their constituents, who may see their representatives' roles very differently. Are they substitutes, stand-ins, for their constituency on the floor of Congress? If not, what is their responsibility to their constituents? Theories of representation describe the different roles members of Congress can play when representing their constituents. *See also* CONSTITUENCY, p. 165.

Significance   Representation by the consent of the governed can be described as formal representation. The delegation of power in one person to reflect the view of many is termed the authorization view, as set forth by Thomas Hobbes in *The Leviathan*. Once elected, the legislator becomes accountable to the people he or she was chosen to represent. Formal representation thus embodies the principles of a representative democracy—namely, elections in which the voters may give or withhold support of their representative. Descriptive representation describes the extent to which legislators accurately reflect the characteristics of their district or state. In single-member districts, one person cannot possibly mirror every constituent, every viewpoint, every characteristic of the electorate. Studies of characteristics of members of Congress by age, race, gender, education, occupation, are by no means parallel to that of the general population. Therefore, the representative must focus on symbolic representation: satisfy constituents as the legislator understands their needs, empathize with their concerns, and be qualified to represent them. The extent to which the representative acts upon this symbolism is described as substantive representation. The representatives may assume the roles of delegates, acting solely on the wishes of their constituencies and forsaking their personal views. Or they may view themselves as trustees or free-agents, entrusted to make decisions to the best of their ability. More likely, they will assume both roles and act as a politico—balancing conflicting positions to take a stand on a particular issue. The bottom line, though, is that a member must represent his or her district sufficiently well to be reelected.

Safe-Marginal District   Areas of varying partisan competitiveness in congressional elections. Safe districts, preferred by incumbents, are strongholds of the majority party whose candidate can expect to win by a healthy margin. Marginal districts are competitive districts, where the winner can be expected to receive less than 60 percent of the vote. Safe districts may be the product of gerrymandered district lines, the political strength of the incumbent, or intense party loyalty. Marginal districts have been observed to be decreasing over time, with the high rate of incumbent candidates being reelected. *See also* CONGRESSIONAL DISTRICT, p. 162; GERRYMANDERING, p. 169; INCUMBENT'S ADVANTAGE, p. 170.

Significance   Safe districts, while relatively secure for an incumbent congressperson, pose more serious challenges in the party primaries. Because the majority party's nominee will likely win the general election, it will probably be more hotly contested than the minority party nomination. However, the incumbent still possesses the considerable advantages that emanate from name recognition and control over substantial resources. According to former Senator Fred R. Harris, three-fifths or less of incumbent representatives won general elections with over 60 percent of the vote prior to 1966. Since then, two-thirds, and occasionally as many as three-fourths, of incumbent representatives have won by that margin. The case of the "vanishing marginals" has been explored by David R. Mayhew, a political scientist who suggests hypotheses of redistricting, skillful use of incumbency, and voter behavior (responding to the incumbency cue) as factors in the increased rate of incumbent success and safe elections (Mayhew 1979, 44–58). Many studies indicate that voters simply vote according to name recognition, and that while as many as 95 percent can recognize their representative's name, only half that number recognize the name of the challenger.

Safe districts, though, are not automatic guarantees of reelection for an incumbent. National political trends influence the relative safety of many districts. For instance, in a strong Democratic year, marginal Democratic seats may be won by larger margins while safe Republican seats become more marginal. Finally, the degree of electoral safety in a district is not always attributable to the majority party but sometimes to the representative personally. Thus, while candidates for other offices in a district may find themselves in close elections or as underdogs, the congressperson succeeds in building his or her own majority based on the service provided to the district. A candidate alone cannot make a district safe; only the voter can do so.

8. Powers of Congress

Advice and Consent   The constitutional power of the Senate to approve presidential treaties and appointments. The advice and consent provision is stated in Article II, Section 2 of the Constitution: "He [the President] shall have Power, by and with the Advice and Consent of the Senate to make Treaties, provided two-thirds of the Senators present concur; and he shall nominate, and by and with the Advice and Consent of the Senate, shall appoint Ambassadors, other public Ministers and Consuls, Judges of the supreme Court, and all other Officers of the United States, whose Appointments are not herein otherwise provided for, and which shall be established by Law; but the Congress may by Law vest the Appointment of such inferior Officers, as they think proper, in the President alone, in the Courts of Law, or in the Heads of Departments."

Whereas Senate consent to the ratification of treaties requires a two-thirds vote, its advice and consent in confirming nominated officers needs only a majority vote. The Senate fulfills this responsibility through consultations between Senate leaders and the president, resolutions delineating its position, or by designating several of its members to participate in treaty negotiations. By and large, the Senate grants the president wide latitude in the appointment of cabinet officers but exercises careful scrutiny over appointments to the Supreme Court, regulatory bodies, and commissions. The Senate takes the view that while its job is to review the qualifications of prospective nominees, it should not—except where the evidence is clear and documented—substitute its judgment for that of the president as to the fitness of candidates for the position in question. *See also* EXECUTIVE AGREEMENT, p. 42; NOMINATION HEARING, p. 244.

Significance   The advice and consent requirement provides a pivotal link between the Congress and the executive branch. The Constitutional Convention bestowed upon the president the power to nominate high level officials but was careful to provide a constitutional check upon unwise appointments. This power is extremely important for several reasons: First, it enables the Congress to influence the policies of top department heads and second, it strengthens the senators' patronage power in their home states, thus enhancing the relationship between the state and federal party systems. This power is likewise important in the area of foreign affairs, where the Senate may block ambassadorial appointments and reject presidential treaties.

   In exercising its power, the Senate has been reluctant to disapprove presidential appointments or treaties. Rather than voting them down, most treaties are killed by refusal to report them out of committee. This reluctance is attributable to three factors (1) the constitutional right of the president to nominate certain designated officials and enter into treaty negotiations with heads of state; (2) the generally high caliber of these candidates and the delicate nature of foreign policy; and (3) the recognition that the president has the right to select individuals who share the administration's goals and objectives and propose treaties which reflect them. This does not mean that the Senate serves as a rubber stamp. It has, on numerous occasions, refused to give its advice and consent. The Senate refused, for example, to confirm President Richard M. Nixon's controversial appointments of Clement F. Haynesworth, Jr. and G. Harrold Carswell to the Supreme Court in 1969 and 1970. The Senate's most famous treaty rejection occurred in 1919, when it rejected President Woodrow Wilson's Treaty of Versailles, which ended World War I and established the League of Nations. In modern times, most international arrangements have taken the form of executive agreements, thus eliminating the need for Senate approval.

Bicameralism   A two-house legislature. Bicameralism developed in the Congress as a result of the Connecticut Compromise, which emerged out of the Constitutional Convention of 1787. This compromise established a balanced legislature for the United States, with a House of Representatives based on population and a Senate organized on the basis of equality between states. The Congress and all state legislatures except Nebraska are bicameral. In a bicameral legislature, a bill must pass in identical language in both houses before it becomes law. The two chambers have similar functions to perform, and they have adopted similar procedures in many cases.

   Some key differences between the two chambers are: all revenue bills must originate in the House; the impeachment process starts in the

House; and the House elects the president if no candidate receives a majority of electoral votes. The House is the larger body, with 435 members who are elected for two-year terms. The Senate gives advice and consent to the president on treaties and foreign policy matters and on presidential appointments. It also tries officials impeached by the House and elects the vice president if no candidate receives a majority of electoral votes. The Senate has 100 members who serve six-year terms. *See also* CONGRESS, p. 189; HOUSE OF REPRESENTATIVES, p. 200; SENATE, p. 207.

Significance   Bicameralism is consistent with the principle of checks and balances. Because a bill can be passed only if both the House and Senate agree on it, the legislative product is usually a result of such compromise. The most striking feature of Congress is that the two houses are elected on different bases by the same voters. Supporters of bicameralism maintain that it is admirably suited to a federal system, allowing representation based on state equality as well as population. This helps to hold together a nation as diverse as the United States. Bicameralism is desirable, it is argued, to avoid hasty legislation. Debate and deliberation in two chambers may result in better legislation.

   Opponents argue that bicameralism is basically superfluous. Bicameralism, they contend, provides an overlapping of lawmaking functions and a duplication of responsibility. (To reconcile differences between the House and Senate versions of a bill often produces an entirely different bill.) Bicameralism, they suggest, represents a waste of time and effort on the part of lawmakers. Unicameralism (a single-house legislature) is considered more economical and efficient. If Nebraska can function with a unicameral legislature, critics maintain, why not other legislatures in the country, and particularly the Congress? A change to unicameralism would not be easy, however, since the Constitution guarantees that no state shall be deprived of its equal representation in the Senate without its consent.

Bipartisanship   Collaboration between the two major political parties, especially in foreign affairs. Bipartisanship takes the form of consultation between congressional leaders of the Democratic and Republican parties. One major problem confronting foreign policymakers in the United States is to create and maintain bipartisan support of America's international commitments. Bipartisanship takes at least two forms, formal and informal. Formally speaking, the Office of Congressional Relations in the Department of State and the White House staff respond to inquiries from legislators and furnish information to congressional committees on foreign policy issues. Department of State and White House staff members call on the Senate Foreign Relations Committee and the House Foreign Affairs Committee to ascertain the views and attitudes of members on specific issues. Then they advise the secretary of state, who in turn advises the president on ways of winning congressional support for his foreign policy objectives. It is through intensive lobbying that the White House and Department of State seek to cultivate support for the administration's foreign policy initiatives. Informally, the president may invite a small group of congressional leaders to attend meetings at the White House and the National Security Council, where they will be briefed on foreign policy and defense issues. These legislators receive information about the crisis and how the president proposes to respond. *See also* DEPARTMENT OF STATE, p. 128; WHITE HOUSE STAFF, p. 138.

Significance   Bipartisanship is elusive and unstable. The emphasis of the various branches of government reflects the principle of separation of powers, which often engenders diffusion and disunity. For example, Democratic President Woodrow Wilson took the leadership in creating a global organization and then fought long and hard with Senate Republicans over United States membership in the League of Nations after World War I. Although he attempted to secure the support of Senate Republicans, he was incapable of creating a working alliance; the United States remained the only major Western power that never joined the League. Except during special emergencies, such as World Wars I and II, the problems associated with achieving a bipartisan consensus on policy issues create major stumbling blocks.

Public controversy, debate in Congress, and discussion in the news media on vital foreign policy and security issues result in dialogue between the legislative and executive branches, leading to policy formulation. By this means, the government tries to reduce division in the country and promote broadbased support. It is assumed that any accepted policy arising out of such a debate will engender unity in foreign relations. Thus, opposition to foreign policy will be minimized, and the nation will support the president. The Vietnam War and the controversy surrounding it can be partly attributed to the fact that the White House failed to concede any presumed legislative right in these matters and acted without regard for the concept of congressional bipartisanship. The Vietnam War experience led Congress to enact the War Powers Act of 1973 by which Democrats and Republicans joined in demanding greater congressional control over presidential deployment of American forces abroad.

Capitol Hill   The legislative seat of the United States government. Capitol Hill also houses many libraries, museums, galleries, and exhibits.

It is called Capitol Hill because it is located on Jenkins Hill, in Washington, D.C. In 1792 the Commissioners of the District of Columbia announced a competition to select an architectural design for the Congress, Library of Congress, and Supreme Court buildings. William Thornton, a physician, artist, and amateur architect, won the award to design the Capitol building. President George Washington wrote him, praising the plan for its "grandeur, simplicity, and beauty of the exterior." Thornton was placed in charge of the construction of the building that began in 1793 when Washington laid the cornerstone. It was built in five major sections, with the north wing constructed first. Congress and Supreme Court occupied the north section when the government moved to Washington from Philadelphia in 1800. During the Civil War, while troops protected the Capitol, its Rotunda functioned as a field hospital. Work on the unfinished dome was halted, and 1,500 cots were set up for wounded soldiers. Improvements of the Capitol continued throughout the nineteenth century. Plumbing, steam heat, and forced air ventilation were introduced by 1865; an elevator was constructed in 1874; and fire protection devices were added in 1881. In 1929 Congress authorized the installation of air conditioning. *See also* CONGRESS, p. 189.

Significance   Capitol Hill has become a renowned landmark. At the time of its inception, it seemed to many people to be an ambitious undertaking. Soon the Capitol became a magnificent monument, and today visitors remain captivated by its majesty. Other than the architecture of the building, the most striking feature noticed by visitors is the apparent formality of the House as contrasted with the informal atmosphere of the Senate; perhaps these conditions relate to the relative size of the two bodies. Starting with President Andrew Jackson in 1829, presidents have been inaugurated on the east front steps of the Capitol. Capitol Hill is not only the seat of the nation's legislature but is also a museum teeming with historic treasures. The portraits and statues of past leaders serve as a constant reminder of their sacrifices and contributions to the development of the nation. Today, the Capitol is one of the great tourist attractions in the world.

Congress   The principal branch of the United States government that enacts laws for the nation. Congress makes laws primarily on the basis of its powers under Article I, Section 8 of the Constitution, which states: "All legislative Powers herein granted shall be vested in a Congress of the United States, which shall consist of a Senate and House of Representatives." The first Congress under the Constitution met in 1789 in the Federal Hall in New York City with 20 senators and 59 representatives. Today, the Senate has 100 members, 2 from each state; the House has 435 representatives, with members elected on the basis of population.

Generally, congressional districts average 500,000 people, with each state entitled to at least one representative. Senators are elected for a term of six years, while representatives are elected for two-year terms. In addition to the 435 members in the House, it has a resident commissioner from Puerto Rico, elected for a four-year term, and one delegate each from the District of Columbia, Guam, Virgin Islands, and American Samoa. These delegates are elected for a term of two years. The resident commissioner and the delegates are nonvoting representatives, but they may vote in their assigned committees.

Congress's main powers include matters concerning the federal budget, taxation, interstate commerce, and foreign affairs, including the power to declare war. Moreover, Congress has the sole power to authorize the allocation of funds and requisite money for government expenditures. The budget preparation and lawmaking functions are carried out through Congress's various committees. There are more than 300 committees and subcommittees in the Congress; these include standing (or permanent committees), joint committees, select committees, and conference committees. The most important committees are the 22 standing committees in the House and the 16 in the Senate. Committees are headed by chairmen, usually selected on the basis of seniority. Other important congressional leaders are the Speaker of the House, President, and President pro tempore of the Senate, majority and minority leaders in the House and Senate, and party whips in both houses. Among the major nonlawmaking functions are (1) confirming presidential nominations for specific appointments; (2) electing president and vice president when no candidate receives a majority of the electoral vote; (3) decisions relating to presidential disability, as well as the president's ability to resume office; (4) acting on the president's nomination to fill a vacancy in the vice presidency; (5) impeaching the president and other federal civil officials; (6) approving amendments to the Constitution; (7) overseeing the functioning of the executive branch; (8) disciplining and expelling members of Congress; and (9) providing various services to constituents. See also BICAMERALISM, p. 186; HOUSE OF REPRESENTATIVES, p. 200; SENATE, p. 207.

Significance   Congress is the elected representative institution charged with reflecting the will of the people. The most important structural feature of Congress is that it consists of two branches, a House of Representatives and a Senate, with more or less equal power. The Senate, however, was designed to serve as a check on precipitous actions of the more popular branch, the House. Congress was originally conceived as a device to represent and check the "irrational behavior" of the people: until 1913 senators were not elected by popular vote, and they acted as a "rationalizing influence" on the House, whose members were elected by the people.

As with other institutions, Congress has changed over the years as the nation has become more democratic. The Congress of the 1960s was unwilling to resist President Lyndon B. Johnson's decision to escalate American involvement in Vietnam. But the Congress of the 1980s is determined not to give a free hand to President Ronald Reagan to deploy United States Marines in Lebanon. Congress, more than any other branch of government, has been subject to serious criticism as it relates to its representation function. Major criticisms have been directed at its over- and under-representation, interest group influence, proliferating committees, excessive party politics, inefficiency, corruption, favoritism, nepotism, unnecessary rules and procedures, financial and sexual scandals, and misuse of power. Still, the United States Congress is one of the most democratic institutions in the world, in which a hundred schools of thought prevail and flourish unrestrained by the executive branch.

Congressional Directory A volume that contains biographical, organizational, and statistical information about the members of Congress and all government departments. The *Congressional Directory* is a "who's who" of the Congress and federal agencies. It includes (1) biographical sketches of members; (2) congressional committees; (3) maps of congressional districts; (4) Executive Office of the President; (5) independent agencies; (6) judiciary; (7) foreign and United States representatives and consular offices; (8) international organizations; (9) press representatives and services; and (10) statistical information. The *Congressional Directory* was first published in 1809 and has been published each subsequent session since (with some exceptions). Directly related to this volume is the *Congressional Staff Directory*, compiled and edited by Charles B. Brownson, which was first published in 1959. It is a companion to the *Congressional Directory* and lists the staffs of all members, the committees and subcommittees of each chamber, and brief biographical sketches of key staff aides. The volume contains committee and subcommittee assignments, top federal officials and their liaison staffs, and an index of individual names. Prior to the publication of the *Congressional Staff Directory*, each April the Government Printing Office makes available an Advance Locator to provide relevant data. Both volumes are available from the Superintendent of Documents, Government Printing Office, Washington, D.C., 20401. *See also* CONGRESSIONAL QUARTERLY, p. 197; GOVERNMENT PRINTING OFFICE, p. 315.

Significance The *Congressional Directory* is an indispensible tool for members and their staffs, citizens and organizations, lobbyists and special interest groups, and academics and students of Congress. This volume contains a wealth of data not easily obtainable elsewhere and provides the reader with immediate information of a practical nature. Given the size of Congress and the complexity of the bureaucratic maze, this information is both helpful and relevant. The *Congressional Directory* is a reliable work, noted for its accuracy and completeness. The information is current and dependable.

There are, however, limits to the volume. For example, members' biographies are supplied by the members themselves, emphasizing those experiences and accomplishments which they seek to publicize. The book is descriptive, as opposed to analytical. No attempt is made to assess members of Congress, government departments, independent agencies, or international organizations. Instead, the *Congressional Directory*, like the *Congressional Staff Directory*, is intended as a guide: a factual, current, thumbnail presentation of vital information relating to the Congress, federal establishment, diplomatic corps, and press services. Despite its limitations, the *Congressional Directory* is an invaluable reference for anyone interested in Congress and/or the federal government.

Congressional Functions   The duties, activities, and services performed by Congress. Congress's functions relate chiefly to its representative responsibilities. These functions span four major areas: lawmaking, oversight, education, and representation. Lawmaking, simply defined, is the development of national policy. The Constitution, in Article I, Section 1 states: "All legislative Powers herein granted shall be vested in a Congress of the United States, which shall consist of a Senate and House of Representatives." The Constitution makes clear that lawmaking is the foremost function of Congress. This function, however, does not belong to Congress alone; it is shared by the executive branch and, to a lesser degree, by the judiciary. In its oversight function, Congress serves as a "watchdog" over the other two branches of government, particularly the executive branch, over which it exercises formal supervision. Its goal is to ensure that both branches faithfully carry out the laws passed by Congress. To exercise this function, Congress established the General Accounting Office, which serves as its official watchdog. The oversight function is also performed by individual members of Congress, as well as congressional committees, which question officials and conduct hearings and investigations. Congress performs its education function by informing the public about key issues and congressional actions that are of special importance. Congress is limited in carrying out this function; because no one official or group of officials can speak for the Congress as a whole, members may voice their individual views. Congress's representation function is exercised by individual members, representing their individual districts and states. The quality of representation depends on the individual attitudes, interests, values, and motivations of the members. Each member, once elected, must define this function in light of the above factors. *See also* CONGRESSIONAL POWERS, p. 196; GENERAL ACCOUNTING OFFICE, p. 149; WATCHDOG COMMITTEE, p. 252.

Significance   Congressional functions span many areas and reflect diverse needs. These fall into two broad areas, institutional and individual. Congress attempts to satisfy both functions, recognizing that the two often conflict. Members' role orientations differ, and for Congress to function smoothly and effectively, it must weigh both functions. This is no mean feat. Members often lack sufficient time to accomplish the numerous tasks expected of them. They must constantly balance constituency and legislative tasks. Former House Speaker Sam Rayburn (D-Tex.) explained it well: "A congressman has two constituencies—he has his constituents at home, and his colleagues here in the House. To serve his constituents at home, he must also serve his colleagues here in the House." Political scientists Roger H. Davidson and Walter J. Oleszek found that when members were asked what functions they should perform in office, they typically emphasized the twin roles of legislator and representative (Davidson and Oleszek 1981, 107). Clearly, members vary in the importance they assign to these roles, as well as the time and energy they expend on them. The most common complaint of members was that constituent demands seriously undermined the time they could devote to lawmaking and other congressional responsibilities.

Congressional Immunity   A constitutional protection enjoyed by members of Congress that excepts them from arrest or prosecution for certain stated actions. The principle of congressional immunity is enunciated in Article I, Section 6 of the Constitution, which reads: "The Senators and Representatives ... shall in all Cases, except Treason, Felony, and Breach of the Peace, be privileged from Arrest during their Attendance at the Session of their respective Houses, and in going to and returning from the same; and for any Speech or Debate in either House, they shall not be questioned in any other place." This principle dates back to the English experience, when the Crown attempted to intimidate and punish the Parliament. At the time the Constitution was promulgated, civil arrests were more common and were the major reason for the inclusion of this provision.

Although stated in absolute terms, the "privilege from arrest" provision has been narrowed over the years, as the courts have excluded various acts and proceedings from the protection of the clause. The courts have held that immunity does not apply in certain instances. For example, it is not applicable to service of process in civil or criminal actions, nor to arrest in any criminal case. The second part of the clause has likewise been narrowed, although immunity has been broadly interpreted, with the phrase "speech or debate" referring to virtually everything a member does in discharging his official duties. For example, a court has ruled that the executive branch may not question a member's motives for making a speech. Another court has held that members are immune from prosecution for their words and legislative deeds on the floor, with one notable exception: namely, Congress's right "to regulate the conduct of its Members." However, another court has ruled that members are immune from libel suits for speeches made on the floor. *See also* CONGRESSIONAL PERQUISITES, p. 194.

Significance   Congressional immunity is no longer the absolute that it was at the nation's founding. The immunity clause has been invoked by members to protect a wide variety of actions, several of which, in the opinion of the courts, do not fall under the protection of the Constitution. For example, according to a 1976 Justice Department ruling, members no longer enjoy immunity from arrest in Washington, D.C. for crimes such as drunk driving or soliciting a prostitute. Prior to that time, a D.C. police officer would stop suspects, discover that they were members of Congress, and release them. This practice ceased after a widely publicized case involving Representative Joe D. Waggonner, Jr. (D-La.), who was arrested for allegedly soliciting a District of Columbia policewoman posing as a prostitute. When the police learned who he was, they released him. Based on the Justice Department ruling, Washington, D.C. police stated that members "and all other elected and appointed federal, state, and local officials are subject to arrest for the commission of criminal offenses to the same extent and in the same manner as all other citizens." The ruling granted one exception: parking violations by private automobiles bearing congressional license plates.

One example where immunity did apply was the much-discussed 1971 case involving Senator Mike Gravel (D-Ak.) who, in his capacity as chairman of the Subcommittee on Public Buildings and Grounds, released selected portions of the classified Pentagon Papers (a history of American involvement in the Vietnam conflict). In this case, the Supreme Court held that Gravel's actions were protected by the immunity clause of the Constitution. The courts have sought to narrow the definition of immunity to apply only to actions that, if punished, could threaten the integrity and independence of Congress.

Congressional Perquisites   Those payments, benefits, or privileges received by members of Congress in addition to their regular income or salary. Congressional perquisites assist members to discharge their official duties and cope with the demands and burdens of public life. In 1789 members received six dollars per working day, from which they had to provide for their own living expenses and other job-related responsibilities. During those early years, members had no staff or expense accounts. As the demands grew, so did members' salaries— although very slowly. As late as 1947, congressional salaries were only $10,000 a year. Today, members receive $69,800.

In addition to their salary, they also receive a large number of fringe benefits, the value of which is difficult to estimate. For example, members possess the franking privilege (the ability to mail official business at taxpayers' expense) and the right to free office space in federal buildings in their home district or state. Members also enjoy a sizable expense allowance that includes office expenses and equipment, telephone and telegraph services, stationery, postage, newsletters, and travel costs. Additional benefits include free office decorations, free storage of files, access to television and radio recording studios at reduced rates, authority to make various patronage appointments, free or low-cost services, discounts at selected stores, and hundreds of free publications. They also receive a health protection package, free emergency care while at work, life insurance, and a generous retirement pension. Members have access to computerized mailing and legislative analysis systems, as well as modern recreational facilities: swimming pools, saunas, masseurs, and gymnasiums. Other benefits include legislative counsels, chaplains, photographers, and Internal Revenue Service advisers. Members have access to congressional dining rooms, barber and beauty shops, and convenient Amtrak and airline ticket offices. They and their staffs are also provided assigned parking spaces. Members are exempt from various laws, including the Civil Rights Act of 1964 and the Equal Employment Act of 1972. *See also* CONGRESSIONAL FUNCTIONS, p. 192; CONGRESSIONAL IMMUNITY, p. 193; CONGRESSIONAL POWERS, p. 196.

Significance   Congressional perquisites have been the subject of widespread criticism, both within and outside the institution. There are those members who wish to increase these benefits and others who believe they should be kept in check. Proponents of increased allowances argue that such perquisites are essential in order to serve their constituents, while opponents contend that many perquisites have little to do with constituent service. Obviously, Congress needs those resources necessary to cope with the large volume of bills introduced each session and the sundry demands made on them and their staffs.

The present system has led to certain abuses, although it is difficult to gauge the actual extent. The most common charges involve nepotism and the misuse of funds. Most experts contend that members are no more likely to abuse such privileges than would the general public in a similar position. Furthermore, there is little evidence to suggest that these abuses are intentional or widespread. Indeed, many abuses arise out of confusion or misunderstanding about the law and its application. Although many perquisites are well deserved, they nonetheless tarnish the reputation of Congress and lessen public confidence in government. Do members enjoy too many perquisites? The answer depends on one's perspective. In the end, it is the Congress, owing to the principle of separation of powers, which sets its own salary and decides what privileges are justifiable.

Congressional Powers   The constitutional authority to carry out the stated functions of Congress. Congress's powers flow from the Constitution and the decisions of the Supreme Court as they relate to those powers. The powers of Congress are stated in Article I, Section 1 of the Constitution: "All legislative Powers herein granted shall be vested in a Congress of the United States, which shall consist of a Senate and House of Representatives." Article I, Section 8 delineates the specific powers of Congress, including the power to (1) lay and collect taxes, duties, imposts, and excises; (2) borrow money; (3) regulate commerce with foreign nations and among the states; (4) establish rules for naturalization and bankruptcy; (5) coin money, regulate its value, and punish counterfeiting; (6) fix the standard of weights and measures; (7) establish post offices and post roads; (8) issue patents and copyrights to inventors and authors; (9) define and punish piracies, felonies on the high seas, and offenses against the law of nations; (10) declare war; (11) raise and support an army and navy and make rules for their governance; (12) provide for a militia, suppress insurrections, and repel invasions; (13) exercise exclusive legislative powers over the seat of government (i.e., the District of Columbia) and over places purchased to become federal facilities (forts, arsenals, dockyards, and "other needful buildings"); and (14) "Make all Laws which shall be necessary and proper for carrying into Execution the Foregoing powers, and all other Powers vested by this Constitution in the Government of the United States or in any Department or Officer thereof." (This is known as the "necessary and proper" or "elastic" clause.) In addition to those powers which relate to Congress alone, the Constitution also grants Congress certain powers which bear directly on the two other branches, among them the power to establish courts inferior to the Supreme Court; impeach and convict the president, federal judges, and other federal officials for high crimes and misdemeanors; conduct investigations; and determine the qualifications of its members.

Although Congress boasts a wide array of powers, they are not unlimited; the Founding Fathers were anxious to prevent any one branch of government from becoming too powerful. For example, Congress may not suspend *writs of habeas corpus*, pass bills of attainder or *ex post facto* laws, impose interstate tariffs, or grant titles of nobility. More importantly, Congress's powers are limited by the First Amendment, which prevents it from encroaching upon the free exercise of speech, press, religion, and assembly, and the Fifth Amendment, which prohibits the taking of life, liberty, or property without due process of law. *See also* CONGRESSIONAL FUNCTIONS, p. 192.

Significance   Congress's powers were uppermost in the minds of the framers of the Constitution, who wrestled long and hard over what powers properly belonged to Congress. In defining Congress's powers, they were careful not to invest all powers in a single institution, fearing that such powers could be abused by a tyrannical or impassioned majority. To ensure that this was not the case, they created a system in which power would be shared among three roughly co-equal branches of government, with the president having the power to veto acts of Congress and the Supreme Court having the power to declare them unconstitutional. Although the Founding Fathers created a system of checks and balances, they clearly intended for Congress to be the dominant branch of government. This proved to be the case for 150 years, except for brief periods (e.g., Presidents Andrew Jackson, Theodore Roosevelt, and Woodrow Wilson wielded considerable power and influence).

Prior to the twentieth century and during a few periods of this century, the major struggles for power were not fought between the Congress and the president but took place *within* the Congress (typically over rules and procedures). These struggles have often centered around great issues, such as slavery, tariff restrictions, domestic improvements, and the regulation of business. Although great leaders have left their mark on Congress, the general trend, particularly in the twentieth century, reveals a penchant for decentralized decision making. This has reduced the power of the congressional leadership, while elevating the power of the individual member. This trend has brought with it new problems as well as new opportunities and has, at times, contributed to an increase in presidential power. Congress is fully cognizant of this fact and has taken deliberate steps (i.e., the 1973 War Powers Act) to curb the powers of the executive.

Congressional Quarterly   A publishing and editorial research organization, serving clients in such areas as government, news, business, and education. Congressional Quarterly provides in-depth coverage of Congress, government, and politics. Founded by Henrietta and Nelson Poynter in 1945, Congressional Quarterly is perhaps best known for its much acclaimed publication, *Congressional Quarterly Weekly Report*. It also publishes a cumulative index to the quarterly. Congressional Quarterly publishes a wide range of books, including political science textbooks, public affairs paperbacks, and reference volumes. In the reference area, it publishes the *CQ Almanac* (a compendium of each session's legislation published in April) and *Congress and the Nation* (a record of governmental action for a presidential term, published every four years). Congressional Quarterly's public affairs volumes are aimed at scholars, journalists, and the public, and provide current information on political issues, trends, and events. Recent titles include *Employment in America*, *How Congress Works*, and *U.S. Defense Policy*. College textbooks are authored by renowned outside scholars and distributed under the CQ imprint. Current works include *American Politics and Public Policy*, *The Court and Public Policy*, and *Interest Group Politics*. In addition, Congressional Quarterly publishes *The Congressional Monitor*, a daily report on the activities of congressional committees; *The Congressional Record Scanner*, an abstract of the daily *Congressional Record*; and *Congress in Print*, a weekly listing of committee reports. Congressional Quarterly publishes several newsletters, among them *Congressional Insight*, a weekly assessment of congressional action, and *Campaign Practices Reports*, a bimonthly report on campaign laws and practices.

It also conducts seminars and conferences on Congress, the legislative process, the federal budget, politics and elections, and other topical issues. Congressional Quarterly's Editorial Research Reports examine subjects beyond the purview of Congressional Quarterly. It also publishes reference materials on newsworthy topics, including foreign affairs, business, education, cultural affairs, national security, and science. All publications are available from Congressional Quarterly, 1414 22nd Street, N.W. Washington, D.C., 20037. *See also* CONGRESSIONAL DIRECTORY, p. 191; CONGRESSIONAL RECORD, p. 199; JOURNAL, p. 203.

Significance   Congressional Quarterly is the best known and most widely respected publisher of books, reports, studies, and newsletters about Congress. Its work has received high praise for currency and reliability. Many of its publications are offered at a nominal price and are available in most major libraries. For scholars and students of Congress, the *Congressional Quarterly Weekly Report* is a vital reference source, one which provides invaluable information about Congress and its activities including committee and floor action. It examines major legislation, members' voting records, and committee testimony. It reprints full texts of presidential press conferences, as well as major presidential statements and addresses. Lobbying activities are reported in depth, including special reports on the relationship between congressional voting and interest group action. Each issue usually features an article on key legislation pending in Congress. Also included are the unofficial returns for congressional elections. This publication is an ideal source of information and an excellent starting place for understanding the workings of Congress. Other valuable Congressional Quarterly publications are the *Almanac of American Politics* and *Politics of America*. These two works contain profiles of each senator, representative, and governor, as well as members' voting records, ratings by special interest groups, and detailed analyses of each state and congressional district. These volumes provide useful information of a descriptive and analytical nature about the Congress and its members.

Congressional Record   The daily printed account of the proceedings in the House and Senate. The *Congressional Record* is published every day that Congress is in session and contains the full proceedings of both houses (including votes). Daily issues are bound every two weeks, and at the conclusion of the session a permanent bound record is made available. The *Congressional Record* was first published in 1873. Prior to that time, the proceedings were printed in the *Annals of Congress* (1789–1824), *Register of Debates* (1824–1837), and *Congressional Globe* (1833–1873). The *Congressional Record* includes debate, statements, and votes. Committee actions are not covered, although their reports to the full body are indicated. Selected aspects of committee and legislative action are featured in the Digest section, and members are permitted to include their "extraneous remarks" in an appendix, known as "Extension of Remarks." The *Congressional Record* is published by the Government Printing Office. *See also* GOVERNMENT PRINTING OFFICE, p. 315; JOURNAL, p. 203.

Significance   The *Congressional Record* is the most complete account of the activities of Congress. Even so, it is not a verbatim account of the proceedings. The rules permit members to "revise and extend" their remarks and insert material not actually presented on the floor (marked by black "bullets"). This procedure serves two functions. First, it permits members to withdraw statements they may have made in the heat of debate or to correct inadvertent errors in the remarks. Second, it saves considerable floor time by allowing members to insert material without having to deliver it. This explains why members' quotes, as reported in the media, may differ from those contained in the *Congressional Record*.

The *Congressional Record* serves several important purposes, one of which bears directly on the courts. Often, the courts will use the *Congressional Record* to determine the intent of legislation. This is not always an easy task, as the *Congressional Record* is an imperfect source of information. Indeed, the published version of the day's proceedings often differs markedly from what was said and done on the floor. A major failing of the *Congressional Record* is that it does not accurately capture the spirit or intent of floor debate. Indeed, many of the statements made on the floor are peripheral or irrelevant to the proceedings. They are frequently presented to an empty chamber, attended by only a handful of members. The *Congressional Record* makes no attempt to distinguish those remarks which are germane to the proceedings from those which are delivered for extraneous purposes. Moreover, many of the "colloquies" between members are actually drafted by staff aides, signed by members, and inserted. Although the *Congressional Record* does differentiate statements presented on the floor from those that are merely inserted, members may circumvent the rule by simply reading the first line of the statement on the floor. This satisfies the rules of Congress and permits a member to give the appearance of actually having participated in the debate or taken a lead role in the proceedings when, in reality, the member might only have read a single line from a prepared speech, attended by a half dozen members. This makes it next to impossible to discern what actually took place on the floor, as well as discover the true intent behind legislation.

House of Representatives   The lower and larger house of the United States Congress. The House of Representatives is generally referred to as the House. Article I, Section 2 of the Constitution provides that House seats shall be assigned to the states mainly on the basis of population, which is done every ten years when the population census is taken. The House is composed of 435 members; representation varies from state to state, but each state is entitled to at least one representative. According to law, there shall be no more than one representative per 500,000 people. In addition, the House has a resident commissioner from Puerto Rico, who is elected for a four-year term, and four delegates, one each from the District of Columbia, Guam, American Samoa, and the Virgin Islands. The delegates are elected for a two-year term. Like the Senate, the House has its own rules and customs and is jealous of its powers and prerogatives. The leadership structure of the House includes the Speaker, the floor leaders and whips of the two major parties, the Rules Committee, and the chairmen of the twenty-two standing committees.

A member of the House must be at least twenty-five years of age, a resident of the state from which he or she is elected (though not necessarily of the district he or she represents), and a citizen of the United States for at least seven years. Members are elected for a two-year term, with no limit on the number of terms they can serve. The terms of all members expire simultaneously so that the House must organize anew every two years (unlike the Senate where only one-third of the members are up for reelection at any one time). The House has three unique functions (1) all money bills must originate in the House; (2) it has the constitutional power to elect the president if no candidate receives a majority of electoral votes; and (3) it may impeach the president and other federal officials. (Refer to the Appendix, Figure 7 for a diagram of the House of Representatives.) *See also* BICAMERALISM, p. 186; CONGRESS, p. 189; REPRESENTATIVE, p. 206; SENATE, p. 207; SENATOR, p. 208.

Significance   House membership was initially set at 435, but this was temporarily raised to 437 during the 1950s with the addition of Alaska and Hawaii to the Union. However, when reapportionment was ordered following the 1960 census, the membership reverted to 435. In the early years of the Republic, the House was the dominant branch of Congress. However, this has changed with the passage of years, as the Senate has assumed more and more power. According to political scientist Walter J. Oleszek, there are a number of important differences between the House and Senate. The House, notes Oleszek, (1) boasts a larger membership; (2) has members who serve two-year terms; (3) operates under less flexible rules; (4) represents a narrower constituency; (5) contains more policy specialists; (6) distributes power less evenly; (7) enjoys less prestige; (8) devotes less time to floor debate; (9) relies on staff more; and (10) receives less press and media coverage, though floor proceedings are televised (Oleszek 1978, 24).

The power to originate money bills in the House is based on the idea that the branch of government closest to the people should control the purse strings. Members of the House are seen as the links between the people and Washington. Moreover, there is a closer link between members of the House and local politicians than is the case with senators. The corruption and lack of ethics of some members unfortunately besmirches the entire House. The recent Abscam scandal resulted in the conviction of six House members for accepting bribes. Most lost in their bid for reelection, while others resigned. Amid complicated legal arguments concerning entrapment, the question of the moral and ethical behavior of the members of the Congress was left unresolved. Some critics went so far as to say that a beleagured administration must sometimes use Abscam-type methods to control the members of the Congress.

Impeachment   A formal indictment or accusation made by the House of Representatives of a civil official for official wrongdoing. Impeachment charges must be based on treason, bribery, or other high crimes and misdemeanors. It is the first stage in a two-step process.

Article II, Section 4 of the Constitution states: "The President, Vice President and all civil Officers of the United States, shall be removed from Office on Impeachment for, and Conviction of, Treason, Bribery, or other high Crimes and Misdemeanors." All civil officials, except members of Congress, are subject to impeachment. The procedure begins with formal charges brought by a member before the House Judiciary Committee, a special investigating committee. A simple majority vote of the House is required to impeach.

The case is then sent to the Senate for trial. When the president is on trial, the chief justice of the Supreme Court presides. A two-thirds vote of the senators present results in conviction and removal from office. The convicted official may then be tried in a court of law. The president is barred from pardoning impeachment convictions. Once convicted, the official is disqualified from holding any office in the future. Throughout American history, there have been twelve impeachments, with only four convictions. Andrew Johnson was the only president to be impeached (in 1868), but he was acquitted in the Senate by one vote. Attempts were also made to impeach President Richard M. Nixon in 1974, but such attempts became moot when he resigned. *See also* CONGRESS, p. 189; HOUSE OF REPRESENTATIVES, p. 200; SENATE, p. 207.

Significance   Impeachment is a complicated way of indicting and trying a civil official for high crimes and misdemeanors. Its purpose is to make possible the punishment of high officials, including the president. Impeachment is a highly politicized and publicized procedure. In reality, an impeachable offense is defined by whatever a majority of the members of Congress believe at a given time. If Congress is controlled by one political party, officials and supporters of the other party may be victimized. The House Judiciary Committee, controlled by the Democratic party, recommended adoption of three articles of impeachment, charging President Nixon with obstruction of justice, abuse of power, and contempt of Congress. Nixon's defenders argued that the committee had been weighted against the president. Nixon was not actually impeached for his alleged involvement in the Watergate scandal, but many political observers believe that he would probably have been impeached and convicted had he not resigned from office. A possible indication of this was provided by President Gerald R. Ford, when he pardoned President Nixon for all federal crimes he might have committed while in office. Resignation does not necessarily prevent Congress from impeaching an official, but in Nixon's case, his resignation closed the matter. Removing an unpopular president before the end of his term is no easy task. However, the fact that powerful officials are subject to removal through impeachment can and must serve as a deterrent to some, when it comes to possibly committing a crime.

Journal   The official minutes of Congress, published at the end of each session. The *Journal* reports the official actions of each chamber but, unlike the *Congressional Record*, does not include a verbatim record of the proceedings. Article I, Section 5 of the Constitution requires that: "Each House shall keep a Journal . . . and from time to time publish the same. . . ." This requirement dates back to the Articles of Confederation, which contained a similar provision. During the Constitutional Convention debate on the subject, James Madison (Va.) argued for giving the Senate discretion in the matter. In a strong dissent, James Wilson (Pa.) maintained that "the people have a right to know what their ·agents are doing or have done, and it should not be in the opinion of the legislature to conceal their proceedings." Members of the Constitutional Convention agreed with Wilson and voted to require each house to publish a *Journal*. In doing so, it excepted the publication of information which, in the opinion of either body, required secrecy. The vote also required publication of the votes of members, although several delegates insisted that "the reasons governing the votes never appear along with them." The *Journal* contains a number of important features, including a "History of Bills and Resolutions," which lists congressional actions by number, title, and action. It also includes a name, subject, and title index. The *Journal* first appeared in 1789. Prior to the publication of the *Congressional Record* in 1873, the floor proceedings were contained in the *Annals of Congress* (1789–1824), *Register of Debates* (1824–1837), and *Congressional Globe* (1833–1873). The *Journal* is available from the Superintendent of Documents, Government Printing Office, Washington, D.C., 20402. *See also* CONGRESSIONAL RECORD, p. 199; DILATORY MOTION, p. 268; SUSPENSION OF RULES, p. 299; UNANIMOUS CONSENT AGREEMENT, p. 303.

Significance   The *Journal* is the oldest written organ of Congress. It is, from Congress's point of view, the official record of both bodies. In actuality, it is an incomplete record, a sanitized description of the actions of Congress, minus the rancor and debate which surrounds the proceedings. In this regard, it is a summary account of the actions of Congress, a record of what Congress did or did not do. Its main value lies in its discussion of the status of legislation, as well as the votes of members. It also contains information on veto overrides.

In both chambers, the daily order of business begins with a prayer and is followed by a reading of the *Journal*. In the House, until a rules change in 1971, members often used the reading of the *Journal* as a dilatory tactic. Prior to the rules change, reading could be dispensed with only by a motion to suspend the rules or by unanimous consent, which required a two-thirds vote. Since then, the Speaker has been authorized to review the *Journal* and approve it. In the Senate, the procedures vary. Senate rules require the full reading of the *Journal* prior to conducting the day's business. However, reading can be dispensed with by unanimous consent. Members seldom object to such a motion.

Legislative Reorganization Acts   Congressional reform measures enacted to modernize the institution, enhance its powers, streamline the legislative process, democratize its rules and procedures, increase the emoluments of members, and strengthen its oversight authority. The Legislative Reorganization Act of 1946, the first of two such acts, originated in the reform efforts following World War II, when the powers of the executive had been increased considerably. In 1945 the American Political Science Association conducted a major study, in which it concluded: "Congress must modernize its machinery and methods to fit modern conditions if it is to keep pace with a greatly enlarged and active executive branch." To achieve these objectives, Congress appointed a Joint Committee on the Organization of Congress. Its final report, which led to the Legislative Reorganization Act of 1946, encompassed a wide variety of proposals, including (1) revamping the committee structure; (2) tightening congressional control over the budget; (3) decreasing the workload of Congress; and (4) bolstering staff assistance. In 1970 Congress enacted a second Legislative Reorganization Act, the first reform law passed since the 1946 act. This measure ignored several major criticisms of Congress: the seniority system, the power of the House Rules Committee, and the two-thirds rule for terminating debate in the Senate. It did, however, include a number of key proposals that gave both houses more information on government finances, safeguarded minority rights, and ensured a review of legislative needs under the aegis of a Joint Committee on Congressional Operations. Among other things, the 1970 act (1) required that teller votes be recorded; (2) insisted that the committees develop and abide by written rules; (3) curtailed the powers of committee chairmen; (4) made public roll call votes held in closed committee sessions; and (5) opened House committee hearings to television cameras. *See also* COMMITTEE SYSTEM, p. 238; CONGRESS, p. 189; SENIORITY SYSTEM, p. 249.

Significance   The Legislative Reorganization Acts were championed by congressional reformers who were dissatisfied with the status quo. These members, Democrats and Republicans, fought long and hard to effect changes in House and Senate rules and procedures. Both Legislative Reorganization acts were instigated by members of the House who, in the words of former Senator Fred R. Harris "want Congress to remedy the injustices in society and to be a dynamic institution for

resolving social problems and improving the quality of American life."
The Legislative Reorganization Act of 1946 represented a major step
forward, but it failed to solve many of Congress's most serious problems
including the distribution of power within the institution and the
unequal balance of power between Congress and the executive.

These failures can be attributed, in large measure, to the inability of
the Joint Committee on the Organization of Congress to reach a consensus about what was required. In the late 1950s, many liberal Democratic
congressmen joined together, with the assistance of many moderate
Republicans and government reform groups, and passed the Legislative
Reorganization Act of 1970. Political scientists Lawrence C. Dodd and
Bruce I. Oppenheimer have argued that while this measure "liberalized
and formalized parliamentary procedure in the committees and on the
floor of the House," it did not "alter the distribution of power positions,
since those positions derive from the majority party" (Dodd and
Oppenheimer 1977, 26–27). Both acts should be viewed as major
achievements, despite the fact that they failed to solve all of the problems
facing Congress. They called attention to serious shortcomings in the
system and proposed concrete, positive steps to remedy them. That they
did not succeed in all areas is understandable. Congress is a conservative
institution that is slow to change and reluctant to alter existing power
relationships.

Power of the Purse   Congress's authority to control government
finances. The power of the purse is delegated to Congress by the
Constitution, giving it the authority to oversee government expenditures. This authority extends to both revenue and appropriation functions. As stated in Article I, Section 9 of the Constitution: "No Money
shall be drawn from the Treasury, but in Consequence of Appropriations made by Law...." New programs must be twice approved: first
through authorization and second through appropriation to allocate
funds to them. Congress has exclusive authority, under Article I, Section
7, to initiate bills to raise revenue. It also has the power to introduce bills
which involve the expenditure of money. Sometimes the amount appropriated is smaller than that authorized. In 1974 the Congress enacted a
comprehensive budget reform measure, the Congressional Budget and
Impoundment Control Act. Since then, the taxing and spending powers
of Congress have been coordinated by budget committees in the House
and Senate. *See also* CONGRESS, p. 189; CONGRESSIONAL POWERS, p. 196;
HOUSE OF REPRESENTATIVES, p. 200; WATCHDOG COMMITTEE, p. 252.

Significance   The power of the purse is a major control exercised by
the legislative branch over the executive branch. Through its twin

powers of authorization and appropriation, Congress is able to maintain tight control over the executive agencies. The threat of cutting funds is sometimes enough to elicit cooperation from the executive branch. Although the executive branch makes detailed budget recommendations, the legislative branch finally determines where the revenue comes from and where it is spent. In a bicameral legislature, like that of Congress, the House exercises initial control over money bills. Nevertheless, the Senate exercises considerable influence over them, as all bills are subject to amendment and final passage by both houses before they are sent to the president for approval.

The Congress, in order to accomplish its watchdog objective, established the General Accounting Office (GAO), to maintain surveillance and audit government expenditures. The GAO is directly responsible to Congress, not the president. As such, it can exercise its powers free from administrative interference and executive reprisals. It may be said, to a certain extent, that the GAO reduces the possibility of corruption and the misuse of public funds. Congress maintains additional checks on the executive branch through its zealous watchdog committee. However, efforts have proved only minimally successful to regain Congress's power over the purse and its various checks on the president. Consequently, Congress has been unable to play its dominant role as the first branch of government.

Representative   A member of the United States House of Representatives. Representatives are also known as members of Congress or congresspersons. They serve a two-year term (which is coterminous), as provided by Article I, Section 2 of the Constitution. A representative must be at least twenty-five years of age, a citizen of the United States for at least seven years, and a resident of the state from which he or she is elected. The House consists of 435 representatives, the members of which are elected on the basis of population, with each district averaging approximately 500,000 people. In the Ninety-seventh Congress (1981–1983), the House included sixteen blacks and nineteen women. Vacancies for representatives are not filled by gubernatorial appointment as is the case in the Senate.

The basic annual salary of a representative is $69,800 (the same as a senator), plus a guaranteed cost of living adjustment and a 15 percent pay raise voted by Congress in 1983. They receive many other benefits such as a personal expense allowance, free office space in Washington and in their districts, and a yearly staff allowance. In addition, representatives receive numerous perquisites, including a travel allowance, franking privileges, retirement benefits, health insurance, hospital and medical care, tax benefits, and research assistance from the Library of

Congress. A favorite method of acquiring extra income is the speech and lecture circuit, with representatives receiving honorariums for addressing campus groups and conventions. It is difficult to calculate the amount of money involved in fringe benefits. In 1982 a Washington research organization, the Tax Foundation, estimated that each member of the House costs the taxpayers $836,000 annually. *See also* BICAMERALISM, p. 186; CONGRESS, p. 189; HOUSE OF REPRESENTATIVES, p. 200; PORK BARREL, p. 283; SENATOR, p. 208.

Significance   Representatives face more difficulties than senators in discharging their official duties, as they are constantly involved in electioneering. They must spend inordinate amounts of time and energy in preparing and campaigning for reelection, because their terms of office expire every two years. In this way, they serve as the most frequent and direct contact between the people and the Congress. Congresspersons need to maintain close contact with the voters, particularly those in their congressional districts.

Frequent contact with the voters is one of the major reasons why more incumbent representatives are reelected than incumbent senators; it is an invaluable political asset that most challengers can seldom overcome. Through pork barrel legislation and regular trips back home, representatives enhance their standing and increase their chances of reelection. Although the Constitution does not require representatives to reside in the district they represent, Americans generally refuse to elect nonresidents. Their insistence upon local residence underscores the belief that representatives serve their own district rather than the entire country.

Senate   The upper and smaller house of the United States Congress. The Senate is based on the principle of equal representation. It is composed of 100 members, two from each state, who are elected to serve for a six-year term with no limit on the number of terms they can serve. Senators were originally chosen by the state legislatures, a practice that was changed in 1913 following the adoption of the Seventeenth Amendment to the Constitution. One-third of the Senate is elected every two years, making it a continuously organized body (unlike the House of Representatives, where elections for all 435 seats are held every two years). The vice president is the presiding officer of the Senate and in his absence a senator known as the President pro tempore ("for the time being") elected from the membership presides.

The Senate is granted powers not accorded to the House. It approves or disapproves certain presidential appointments and treaties. The Senate has the power, under Article II, Section 2 of the Constitution, to give advice and consent to the president on treaty-making and foreign policy matters. The Senate elects the vice president if no candidate receives a majority of the electoral vote. A senator must be at least thirty years of age, a citizen of the United States for at least nine years, and a resident of the state from which he or she is elected. (Refer to the Appendix, Figure 8 for a diagram of the Senate.) *See also* BICAMERALISM, p. 186; CONGRESS, p. 189; HOUSE OF REPRESENTATIVES, p. 200; REPRESENTATIVE, p. 206; SENATOR, p. 208.

Significance   The Senate was originally conceived as a House of Lords, consisting of members that represented the aristocracy and not the masses. In the beginning, senators were not elected by the people but by state legislatures. The Senate, because of its size and term of office, represents an "exclusive club." Yet, many observers believe the Senate is more responsive to national interests and needs than the House because it represents the entire nation rather than local interests. As an institution, the Senate is perceived by many to be the more powerful body of Congress because of its power to confirm presidential appointments and to ratify treaties. Also, the Senate's size enables its members to receive national recognition more easily than the House members. The mere fact that the vice president is the presiding officer of the Senate further adds to its prestige.

While the advice and consent role of the Senate in foreign policy matters has been expanded over the years, its consent function has been found impractical by many presidents beginning with George Washington. The Senate has rejected only nineteen treaties since the nation's founding. The requirement of a two-thirds majority of the Senate for treaty ratification has received sharp criticism. Under this rule, a small minority kept the United States out of the League of Nations after World War I. The framers of the Constitution adopted equal representation of all states in the Senate at the insistence of the smaller states as their condition for its acceptance. As a result, California, with more than 20 million people, has the same number of senators (two) as Alaska, which has less than a half million people.

Senator   A member of the United States Senate. Senators have been directly elected by the people since the adoption of the Seventeenth Amendment to the Constitution in 1913. Prior to that, they were elected by the state legislatures. A senator is elected for a six-year term on the basis of staggered elections every two years. Article I, Section 3 of the Constitution states that the senators "shall be divided as equally as may be into three Classes. The Seats of the Senators of the first Class shall be vacated at the Expiration of the second Year, of the second Class at the Expiration of the fourth Year, and of the third Class at the Expiration of the sixth Year, so that one-third may be chosen every second Year. . . ." A senator must be at least thirty years of age, a citizen of the United States for at least nine years, and a resident of the state from which he or she is elected. Vacancies for senators are filled by gubernatorial appointment. Out of 100 senators in the 1983–1984 session (2 from each state), 98 are men.

The annual salary of a senator is $69,800 (the same as a representative), plus a guaranteed cost of living adjustment. The Congress voted itself a 15 percent pay raise in 1983. Senators can earn additional income via the lecture circuit and talks at college campuses and conventions. In addition, they receive a variety of perquisites, including a personal expense allowance, free office accommodations in Washington and their states, and a staff allowance depending on the size of the state they represent. Senators are entitled to health insurance, hospital and medical care, tax benefits, franking privileges, and research assistance from the Library of Congress. They also receive a generous travel allowance, including thirty-three round trips to their constituency each year and reduced air fares for others, as well as numerous free trips abroad. It is difficult to attach a dollar value to these fringe benefits, but the Tax Foundation, a Washington research organization, estimated in 1982 that each senator annually cost the taxpayers $2.3 million. *See also* BICAMERALISM, p. 186; CONGRESS, p. 189; HOUSE OF REPRESENTATIVES, p. 200; REPRESENTATIVE, p. 206; SENATE, p. 207.

Significance   Senators attract more attention and seem to command a greater degree of prestige than representatives. This is because there are only 100 senators, as opposed to 435 representatives; senators' terms are longer, and they have greater access to the national press. Senators represent more voters than representatives: entire states versus single districts. The framers of the Constitution agreed to the appointment of an equal number of senators from each state at the insistence of the smaller states. As a result, each state has two senators. This disproportionate representation has had its problems, but on the whole it has worked well, to the satisfaction of all concerned. Today, this formula of territorial representation is accepted by many other countries. Senators enjoy a unique distinction in the Congress, as they are empowered to confirm presidential appointments and ratify treaties, often bearing on the most vital national interests. They also enjoy the right of unlimited debate (the filibuster), which is not the case in the House. No legislator in the world enjoys such lavish perquisites and privileges as a United States Senator.

Senatorial Courtesy   A practice in the Senate whereby a senator who belongs to the same political party as the president may veto a federal judicial appointment in the member's home state by indicating that the nominee is "personally obnoxious," thereby killing the nomination. Senatorial courtesy is a time-honored tradition in the Senate, one which dates back to the beginnings of that institution. Although this practice is nowhere mentioned in the Constitution, the Senate adheres to this custom and generally, although not always, accedes to the wishes of the members involved. This tradition is particularly effective as it relates to appointments to a United States District Court but is less applicable in the case of appointments to the twelve circuit courts and the United States Supreme Court, which do not serve individual states. Members often attempt to invoke the same prerogative to block other presidential appointments in their home states, with less effectiveness. For example, Senator Jesse Helms (R-N.C.) unsuccessfully attempted to block the nomination of fellow North Carolinian William J. Bennett as chairman of the National Endowment for the Humanities. As a result of pressure from the White House and his Republican colleagues in the Senate, Helms was forced to withdraw his opposition and subsequently endorsed the nomination. *See also* CONGRESSIONAL POWERS, p. 196; POLITICAL FOLKWAYS, p. 178.

Significance   Senatorial courtesy has long held sway in the Senate, where members zealously guard their powers and privileges. This custom provides senators with an influential, and often decisive, voice in the appointment of federal district judges. Members are directly able to influence the makeup of the courts, ensuring that judges appointed from their home states will reflect, to a large extent, their political interests and philosophy. This practice also contributes to the members' patronage power, providing them with additional appointments that they can dictate or influence.

The principle of senatorial courtesy was dealt a harsh blow in the administration of President Jimmy Carter who, as a candidate in 1976, pledged to make judicial appointments "on a strict basis of merit." Upon his election, he established the United States Circuit Judge Nominating Commission. A thirteen-member panel, it was broadly representative, including minorities, women, and even several nonlawyers. When a judicial vacancy opened up, they were asked to propose five potential candidates to the president within sixty days. President Carter also sought to reform the system of district court appointments, which proved to be more difficult than expected. After Chief Justice Warren E. Burger lobbied Congress for more than three years to create additional judgeships that would reduce the court's workload, the Congress, in 1978, enacted the Omnibus Judgeship Act, providing for a 25 percent increase in the number of judges, including 152 new district court judgeships. This development enabled President Carter to significantly influence the makeup of the nation's court system, so much so that today, approximately 40 percent of all federal judges are Carter appointees. These developments contributed to a weakening of the practice of senatorial courtesy but did not destroy it. It is still operative in the Senate, although not as vibrant as it once was.

Session   Assembly of Congress during which time it meets to conduct regular business. Sessions of Congress convened on the first Monday in December from 1820 to 1834. Under the provision of the Twentieth Amendment to the Constitution, Congress now convenes on January 3. There are two additional types of sessions: special sessions and joint sessions. Special sessions may be convened to conduct any emergency business. Under the constitutional powers of office (Article II, Section 3), the president may convene one or both houses in special session. Congress may convene a joint session (where both houses meet together for a specified purpose) when the president or other dignitaries address the body or when the electoral votes for the president and vice president are to be counted. Article I, Section 4 of the Constitution requires that "The Congress shall assemble at least once in every Year...." Under this provision, the date for convening Congress was originally designated as the first Monday in December, "unless they shall by Law appoint a different Day." As many as eighteen bills were passed, prior to 1820, providing for the meeting of Congress on other days of the year.

Each Congress consists of two regular sessions, the first commencing in January of the odd-numbered year and the second beginning in January of the even-numbered year. For example, the first session of the Ninety-ninth Congress will assemble in January 1985; the second session of the Ninety-ninth Congress will convene in January 1986. The Legislative Reorganization Act of 1970 stipulated that "unless otherwise provided by the Congress," the House and Senate "shall adjourn *sine die* not later than July of each year." In a nonelection year, Congress can recess for up to thirty days in August. If Congress declares war officially, this provision becomes moot. Adjournment is left up to Congress, although the Constitution provides in Article II, Section 3 that if the two houses cannot agree on a date, the president may adjourn Congress until such time as he thinks proper. No president has exercised this authority. *See also* CONGRESS, p. 189; HOUSE OF REPRESENTATIVES, p. 200; SENATE, p. 207.

Significance   Sessions of Congress are held continuously to help solve the difficult problems of the nation and the world. The functions of Congress have increased since the eighteenth century, and Congress has adapted itself to the changing demands of a changing society. At the beginning, Congress met three days a week, working three or four hours in the afternoon. Today, Congress meets five days a week, sometimes into the late evening. Its sessions are held all year, with adjournment during holiday seasons. Any bill introduced during the first session of a Congress can be taken up in the second session. However, when the second session ends, all unfinished business automatically dies. Critics claim that members of Congress waste valuable time in many frivolous activities during the session and are thus unable to complete work on important legislation and other related duties.

9. Congressional Leadership

Congressional Black Caucus   Established in March 1971 to formalize and strengthen the efforts of black House members in advancing the plight of their own race, as well as other underprivileged groups. The caucus is open to all black House members. The Congressional Black Caucus was founded by former Representative Charles C. Diggs, Jr. (D-Mich.), who also served as its first chairperson. Once established, the caucus recruited a permanent staff to work on issues and activities of common concern. It consists of four executive officers: a chairperson, vice chairperson, secretary, and treasurer. All officers are nominated and elected by the caucus. Each caucus member has a subcommittee assignment related to his or her House committee assignment. The caucus is concerned with such issues as full employment, national health care, urban revitalization, rural development, political access, equal educational opportunity, criminal justice reform, urban growth, and improved relations with African nations. *See also* CONGRESSIONAL HISPANIC CAUCUS, p. 214.

Significance   The Congressional Black Caucus employs various tactics to achieve its objectives. It publishes a yearly agenda, setting forth its major legislative goals. It works to implement these goals through establishing close contact with other House members, writing letters to congressional colleagues, and disseminating information to interested individuals and groups. In addition, the caucus sponsors seminars on topics such as full employment, minority enterprise, and affirmative action. It also testifies on proposed legislation, administrative policies, and presidential appointments.

   The caucus works closely with black elected officials at all levels of government. It meets frequently with state and local leaders and attempts to keep them informed on issues that are of special interest to the black community. It also works closely with the major civil rights organizations in Washington, D.C. and throughout the nation. The caucus has accomplished several important objectives. First, it has played a vital role in helping to pass legislation that will greatly benefit black Americans. Second, it has raised the level of political consciousness among American blacks and aroused increased political participation. Third, it has provided a black perspective on issues and problems that directly affect that community.

Congressional Hispanic Caucus   An organization of members of Congress devoted to strengthening the federal commitment to Hispanics and creating an awareness of the needs of the Hispanic community. The Congressional Hispanic Caucus was established in 1976 as a political focal point for Hispanics in the United States. The caucus currently has eight members: Chairman Robert Garcia (D-N.Y.), Edward R. Roybal (D-Calif.), Baltasar Corrado (D-P.R.), Manuel Lujan, Jr. (R-N.M.), Henry B. Gonzalez (D-Tex.), Matthew G. Martinez (D-Calif.), Ron de Lugo (D-V.I.), and Eligio de la Garza (D-Tex.). De la Garza is the highest-ranking member and chairman of the House Committee on Agriculture. In addition, 160 other senators and representatives belong to the caucus as honorary members and are kept informed about the legislative priorities of Hispanics through a series of legislative letters, newsletters, and seminars on current issues. *See also* CONGRESSIONAL BLACK CAUCUS, p. 213.

Significance   The Congressional Hispanic Caucus regards its foremost duty as educational, informing the Hispanic community about the need for participation in the political process and government. It also monitors legislative action as well as the policies of the executive and judicial branches of government to ensure that the needs of Hispanics are met. Additionally, the caucus serves as a research and statistical clearinghouse, compiling and distributing data pertinent to the Hispanic population. The caucus publishes a monthly newsletter, *Avance*, which is distributed free of charge. In 1981 they boasted a mailing list of 15,000 and distributed over 25,000 national directories of major Hispanic elected and appointed officials. During the 1982 National Hispanic Heritage Week, the caucus adopted the theme *Su Voto Es Su Voz*— your vote is your voice. The theme reflects the caucus's mission to stimulate voting and political participation among the nation's Hispanics. The caucus describes itself as dedicated to reversing a national pattern of neglect, exclusion, and indifference suffered for decades by the Hispanic community. Through the education of politicians and the nation, the caucus seeks to accomplish that goal.

Democratic Caucus (House)   Meetings of the House's full Democratic membership. The House Democratic Caucus was largely dormant throughout this century, meeting at the beginning of each new Congress to choose party leaders and ratify the nominations of committee members and leaders chosen by the Democratic Committee on Committees. At the beginning of the Ninety-first Congress, the Democratic Study Group convinced the Speaker of the House to activate the caucus, which led to a party rule that a caucus meeting could be held each month if fifty members demanded a meeting in writing. The House Democratic Caucus has been active in initiating party and procedural reforms, most notably in the committee system and the selection of its chairmen. *See also* DEMOCRATIC/REPUBLICAN COMMITTEE ON COMMITTEES, p. 216; COMMITTEE SYSTEM, p. 238; DEMOCRATIC STUDY GROUP, p. 218; SENIORITY SYSTEM, p. 249.

Significance   For a long time, the House Democratic Caucus was a body that served the interests of older and conservative House members. Although they constituted a minority of the caucus, these members held important power positions distributed by the caucus. In the 1970s, the House Democratic Caucus emerged as a center of reform, spurred by younger members who wanted to gain a foothold in the power structure. Among these reforms was the repeal of the "binding rule" in 1975, which since 1909 had stated that a two-thirds vote of the caucus could bind its members on a floor vote. In 1974 the House Democratic Caucus gave committee members the power to determine the number of subcommittees their committees could have. Many of the changes in the seniority and committee systems originated in a special caucus committee, the Committee on Organization, Study, and Review, headed by Julia Butler Hansen (D-Wash.). The seniority system was altered by making committee chairmen subject to secret ballot voting by the caucus. A House rule was enacted requiring that committee bill drafting sessions be open to the public. It limited a member to one committee chairmanship and guaranteed each Democrat a major committee assignment. Also, it created a "bill of rights" for subcommittees, giving them independence from their full committees. Generally, the role of the caucus in party matters depends on how unified the party is on issues.

Democratic Conference   A caucus of Senate Democrats that functions primarily for organizational purposes. The Democratic Conference meets at the beginning of each new session to select or reconfirm leadership and to approve changes in the rules. Senate Democrats usually have not used the conference as a vehicle to shape policy. The chairman of the conference is selected by virtue of being leader of the party. The floor leader also serves as head of the Steering and Policy Committees. Under Lyndon B. Johnson's (D-Tex.) reign, the Democratic Conference met only infrequently after its organizing session at the beginning of each new Congress. Under the leadership of Mike Mansfield (D-Mont.), the conference became a more significant party forum. Many of the reforms—staffing, open meetings, filibuster change, party leadership selection, committee jurisdictions—were either initiated or discussed in the Mansfield-run conference. *See also* COMMITTEE CHAIRMAN, p. 234; FILIBUSTER, p. 274; SENATE MAJORITY/ MINORITY WHIPS, p. 227.

Significance   The Democratic Conference, whose primary function had been to elect party leaders, acquired an important new function as a result of reforms. Senate Democrats allowed the conference to vote on committee chair positions, which effectively limited the control new Senate committee chairmen had over their committees and which ensured that they would not offend the majority of the Democratic Conference. In addition to the leadership positions of the conference, the secretary of the conference exercises an important role by serving as a geographical and ideological balance to those leadership positions. Robert C. Byrd (D-W.Va.) worked very hard in that position, spending many hours on the Senate floor representing the southern and border states in the leadership. In 1971 he was elevated to party whip, defeating Edward M. Kennedy (D-Mass.). Lyndon Johnson was strongly involved in the choice of party whip and secretary to the conference. He regarded these individuals as lieutenants, from whom he expected complete loyalty and devotion. He tried to reach consensus among his colleagues so that his choices would be confirmed in conference without opposition. His successor, Mike Mansfield, eschewed this activism and let the conference make the selections. The Democratic Conference bears the unmistakable imprint of the leadership style of its party leaders, serving as one of their many vehicles for shaping the flow of Democratic action in the House. Their leadership will effectively determine the scope and direction of the Democratic Conference.

Democratic/Republican Committee on Committees   Party committees that appoint members to committees. The Democratic and Republican Committees on Committees appoint committee members through Senate approval of a list of names submitted by party leaders, a practice adopted in 1846. The Democratic roster is drawn up by their Steering Committee, which serves as their committee on committees. The Steering Committee is chaired by the party leader, who also names the other Steering Committee members. In 1971 the roster became subject to caucus approval. The Republican committee roster is drawn up by the Republican Committee on Committees, which is appointed by the chairman of the Republican Conference, but the party caucus does not vote on committee nominations. The leaders of the two parties offer resolutions on the floor that usually are adopted automatically. *See also* COMMITTEE ASSIGNMENT PROCESS, p. 234; DEMOCRATIC STEERING AND POLICY COMMITTEE, p. 217; REPUBLICAN CONFERENCE (SENATE), p. 224; SENATE MAJORITY/MINORITY WHIPS, p. 227.

Significance   The Democratic and Republican Committees on Committees are a tradition in the Senate which goes back to the Civil War era, when Republicans employed a special panel appointed by the party caucus to make both Republican and Democratic committee assignments. Following the war, Republicans took control of the committee away from the caucus as a whole and gave it to the caucus chairman. Democrats set up a similar committee in 1879, appointed and chaired by the caucus chairman. Each party's committee on committees is different, but both of their decisions are subject to approval by the party conferences and the full chamber. However, approval is usually automatic.

The Senate Democrats, since the 1950s, have employed a rule instituted by Lyndon B. Johnson (D-Tex.) that allows each Democratic senator a first choice of assignments before any other Democratic senator receives a second choice. The Republicans generally base their assignments on seniority. The Democratic Steering Committee is large and broadly representative, growing in size in recent years so as to represent a wider spectrum of the party. The Republican Committee on Committees is somewhat smaller while still striving to achieve regional balance. The party whip is a member of the Democratic Steering Committee but does not serve on the Republican Committee on Committees.

Democratic Steering and Policy Committee   The Democratic committee on committees in the House that makes committee assignments. The Steering and Policy Committee was set up by the House Democratic Conference under the party leadership's control to develop party and legislative priorities. The power to make committee assignments was taken away from the Ways and Means Committee Democrats (who had held that power since 1911) and transferred to the Steering and Policy Committee, composed of party leaders and their nominees, and elected members who represent various regions. In addition to recommending committee assignments to caucus, the Steering and Policy Committee schedules the introduction of new legislation under the leadership of a Democratic Speaker. *See also* COMMITTEE ASSIGNMENT PROCESS, p. 234; DEMOCRATIC CONFERENCE, p. 215; SPEAKER OF THE HOUSE, p. 229.

Significance   The Democratic Steering and Policy Committee has the power to make all committee assignments except for the Rules Committee. The Speaker makes appointments to Rules to prevent the committee from refusing to report legislation favored by the Democratic leadership. The committee has twelve members: the Speaker, the majority leader, the majority whip, chairman of the caucus, eight appointees of the Speaker, and twelve regional representatives. The Democratic members of the House in a specific state, or in several states within a specific region, choose the regional representatives. These representatives serve from one to ten states, with a limit of two two-year terms.

The transfer of committee assignment power from the Ways and Means Committee has greatly enhanced the influence of party leaders. The Democratic leadership has greater influence on the assignment process than does the Republican leadership. Each member has a single vote in the process. Nominations are typically made by a regional representative. When nominees exceed the number of vacancies, the Steering and Policy Committee votes on the applicants, with thirteen votes needed to win a position. The decisions of the committee are brought for approval before the full Senate Democratic Conference, which rarely rejects them.

Democratic Study Group (DSG)   An organization of liberal Democrats in the House. The Democratic Study Group (DSG) is committed to liberal legislation and liberal control of the House. They disseminate information to members on liberal issues and inform members of votes on liberal legislation. The DSG has been described as a party within a party, possessing a whip system, a steering committee, and research capability. The DSG staff issues weekly reports on pending House bills, fact sheets and reports on important issues, and campaign booklets describing how individual House members voted on particular legislation. This information assistance, along with fund-raising assistance, is provided to House Democratic members. *See also* HOUSE OF REPRESENTATIVES, p. 200; LEGISLATIVE REORGANIZATION ACTS, p. 204; REPUBLICAN WEDNESDAY GROUP, p. 226.

Significance   The Democratic Study Group was founded in 1959 to offer liberal alternatives to legislation proposed by conservative Republicans and southern Democrats in the House. During the 1960s, they helped shape New Frontier and Great Society legislation and supplied important votes for passage of education, civil rights, and social welfare legislation. The title Democratic Study Group was selected by House liberals for its neutrality; they were, at inception, an informal group, seeking not to be viewed as directly challenging the House leadership. Many of the House procedural and party reforms, initiated during the 1960s with DSG involvement, solidified into the 1970 Legislative Reorganization Act.

The DSG has provided House Democrats with much valuable research and has served as a vehicle to allow liberal Democrats to present themselves as a united bloc. The DSG has been active in providing nonincumbent Democratic candidates with funds and research information and has conducted orientation programs for freshmen Democrats, making it possible to mobilize these junior members in support of reforms adopted by the group. The list of DSG members is kept secret; they do not officially issue public stands on particular bills. The House Republicans also have a study group, the Republican Wednesday Group, founded in the 1970s as a counterpart to the DSG. It provides many of the same services to its members as the DSG.

House Majority Leader   The floor leader of the majority party in the House. The House majority leader is second in command to the Speaker. He or she serves as the Speaker's principal deputy, leading their party during floor debates and voting, formulating its legislative program, and participating in strategy sessions with the Speaker. The majority leader then steers the program through the House, making sure the committees have reported out important bills, and helps to establish a legislative schedule. In the absence of a strong House Speaker, the power of the majority leader may increase. While House and party rules do not spell out the duties of the majority leader, the job traditionally has included the duties of party floor defender and party spokesman. By custom, the majority leader does not chair any committees. *See also* HOUSE MINORITY LEADER, p. 221; SPEAKER OF THE HOUSE, p. 229.

Significance   The House majority leader, like the Speaker, is usually an experienced legislator. Jim Wright (D-Tex.) served for twenty-two years on the Public Works and Transportation Committee before he became majority leader in 1977. Although the Speaker may virtually designate the choice of the majority leader, election for this position occurs every two years by secret ballot of the party caucus. To be selected a majority leader, a congressperson must meet these six basic criteria (1) ideological acceptability to the party; (2) political acumen and skill at forging a winning majority; (3) deftness at speaking for and representing the party; (4) experience as a legislative leader and effective politician; (5) ability to work with all segments of the party and reconcile differences among competing factions; and (6) willingness to challenge the opposition party and articulate the policies and programs of his or her party. House Democrats usually promote their whip to majority leader and majority leader to Speaker when these positions become open. Of the fourteen majority leaders since 1910, seven went on to become Speaker, four relinquished the position when their party became the minority party, two ran for the Senate, and one died. The majority leadership is an excellent training ground for the Speakership, since the two work so closely together on the floor of the House. The majority leader, aided by the assistant floor leader and whip, serves as the eyes and ears of the Speaker in the information network of the House. The majority leader helps to establish the legislative schedule by securing unanimous consent agreements from the membership. If a member objects to the leader's proposal to consider a specific bill, the majority leader may circumvent the obstacle by putting the issue to a majority vote on the floor.

House Majority/Minority Whips   The assistant majority and minority leaders in the House. The House majority and minority whips' job is to promote party discipline and attendance at votes. The Democratic whip is appointed by the majority leader in consultation with the Speaker; the Republican whip is elected by Republican members. At the request of the floor leader, the whip conducts polls to determine members' attitudes toward a proposed bill or section of a bill. In this information-gathering role, the whip provides the leader with the best possible information to decide whether proposed legislation may be headed toward success or failure on the House floor. *See also* HOUSE MAJORITY LEADER, p. 219; SPEAKER OF THE HOUSE, p. 229.

Significance   The House majority and minority whips head up a large network that gathers intelligence and counts votes. The Democratic whip organization consists of the chief whip and assistant whips who are selected on a regional basis by state delegations. The Republican whip organization consists of a chief whip, a deputy whip, regional whips, and area whips. The Republican whips have been more successful than Democratic whips in controlling their members, due to the liberal/conservative split within the Democratic party. Whips make telephone calls and establish personal contact with members in gathering information for the leadership. The accuracy of this information is vital, as it may spell victory or defeat for the legislation being considered. To serve effectively in this position, the whip must (1) thoroughly understand the legislative process; (2) develop close and intimate relations with the members; (3) be able to explain the party's position to colleagues; (4) be adept at persuading members to embrace the party line; (5) do research and have a good sense of timing; and (6) have an intuitive understanding of the institution and its members. Occasionally, the two-party whip organizations have pooled their information in order to assess the overall mood of the House toward particular legislation. The whip system is vital in bringing a bill to a vote at the right time. When that time comes, House whips will usually stand by the doors to the floor, signalling arriving members to vote yea (thumbs up) or nay (thumbs down) on a particular bill. House whips also prepare weekly "whip notices" that notify members of the upcoming floor agenda.

House Minority Leader   The floor leader of the minority party in the House. The House minority leader, as the titular leader of the party, holds its most important job. House Republicans divide their major party positions among several members, unlike the Democrats, and the minority leader emerges as the most influential. Minority leaders' duties are similar to those of the majority leaders, except that they have no power to schedule legislation. They serve as party spokesmen, promote party unity among colleagues, and act as "field generals" on the floor. The minority leader monitors the progress of bills through committees and subcommittees, consulting with ranking minority members on the committees and encouraging them to follow adopted party positions. When the minority party occupies the White House, the minority leader will usually be the president's spokesman in the House. If the minority party becomes the majority, the minority leader is likely to become Speaker. *See also* HOUSE MAJORITY LEADER, p. 219; SPEAKER OF THE HOUSE, p. 229.

Significance   The House minority leader is faced with a variety of special problems, unlike the majority leader. First, he or she lacks the votes necessary to translate the minority party's programs into law. Second, the minority leader is disadvantaged in terms of staff, space, and control over investigatory funds. Third, he or she is forced to play the role of critic, often becoming cast in a negative light. Should the minority party prove unable to wrest away votes from the majority party, the minority leader is forced into one of three postures: cooperation with the majority party, partisan opposition, or advocacy of positive alternatives to the party in power. None of these, however, are mutually exclusive; most minority leaders adopt one or more of these strategies. Minority leaders become the target of members' frustration because of these obstacles; therefore, they are more likely to voluntarily retire or be removed than majority leaders. Of the eleven minority leaders in the twentieth century, two were ousted by their party, and another was denied the Speakership nomination; only three have advanced to the Speakership. Gerald R. Ford held the post of minority leader from 1965 to 1973 before resigning to become vice president. Like the majority leader and the Speaker, the minority leader is usually an experienced legislator and is instrumental in formulating legislative strategy. To be effective, the minority leader must forge coalitions with the opposition party while standing strongly for the minority party's policies.

President Pro Tempore   The presiding officer of the Senate in the absence of the vice president, as provided for in the Constitution. The President pro tempore ("for the time being") is usually the senator of the majority party with the longest continuous service and is third in line behind the vice president and Speaker of the House in the succession to the presidency. The pro tem has the same powers as the vice president when the pro tem is in the chair but may appoint a substitute replacement and also, as a member of the Senate, may vote on all matters. Presidents pro tem hold the office for as long as they serve in the Senate and as long as their party maintains majority control over the Senate unless the Senate decides to elect a different member to the post. Election to the position of President pro tempore usually follows straight party lines. *See also* CONGRESSIONAL BUDGET OFFICE, p. 311; SPEAKER OF THE HOUSE, p. 229; VICE PRESIDENT, pp. 135, 231.

Significance   The President pro tempore has been regarded as an honorary position for a senior member. The task of presiding over the Senate is not particularly demanding, and any authority vested in the position is effectively neutralized when the chair is regained by the vice president, who is often of a different party and who can intercede in behalf of that party. However, in the position as a senior member of the party, and often the chairman of an important committee, the leadership may consult with the pro tem on the policies and actions of the party.

Influential Presidents pro tempore of the twentieth century include Arthur H. Vandenberg (R-Mich., 1947–1949), who was also chairman of the Foreign Relations Committee, and Richard B. Russell (D-Ga., 1969–1971), chairman of the Appropriations Committee. In 1977 the Senate created the position of Deputy President pro tempore for any member of the Senate who had held the office of president or vice president of the United States. Only Hubert H. Humphrey (D-Minn.) ever filled that slot. The President pro tempore, along with the House Speaker, chooses the director of the Congressional Budget Office.

Presiding Officer   The chief officer holding the chair in the House or Senate. The presiding officer of the Senate is the vice president. According to the Constitution, the vice president "shall be President of the Senate, but shall have no vote, unless they be equally divided." In his absence, a President pro tempore presides, also provided for in the Constitution: "The Senate shall choose ... a President pro tempore, in the absence of the Vice President, or when he shall exercise the office of the President of the United States." Additionally, the task of presiding over the Senate may fall to any Senate member, usually a junior majority senator, for a half-hour each day. No presiding officer of the Senate has the power of the Speaker of the House, who presides over that chamber. The Speaker may step down from the chair and appoint a Speaker pro tempore to preside over the House and also appoint another Speaker to preside when the Committee of the Whole House is in session. *See also* COMMITTEE OF THE WHOLE, p. 236; PRESIDENT PRO TEMPORE, p. 222; SPEAKER OF THE HOUSE, p. 229; VICE PRESIDENT, pp. 135, 231.

Significance   The presiding officer is entrusted with various powers in each chamber. While the presiding officer of the Senate has many of the formal powers of the Speaker of the House, such as recognizing members to speak and interpreting rules, the office has no real authority or influence. The Senate places its power in its floor leaders, who schedule legislation and coordinate floor activity. The vice president seldom presides over the Senate, and the President pro tempore is likely to be involved with chairing a major committee. The position of presiding officer in the Senate is regarded as a symbol of authority, toward which debate is directed, and as a voice for the Senate parliamentarian. Since Senate rules are less strict than House rules, such as unlimited debate, and because the chamber is smaller, the task of presiding over the Senate does not compare in scope with that of the Speaker of the House. The Speaker wields considerable authority from the chair and may share this authority with the floor leaders. Most Speakers aim to exercise their power within parliamentary limits while helping their own party whenever possible. The position of Speaker has evolved since the 1800s from being largely ineffectual to one of great power and national attention.

Republican Conference (House)   Internal Republican organization, roughly equivalent to the Democratic Caucus, which seeks to maximize that party's influence, as well as influence the direction of public policy. The Republican Conference has undergone a less turbulent history than its Democratic counterpart and has played a less significant role in influencing House rules and procedures. The

Democratic Caucus's influence derives, in large measure, from the fact that the Democrats have controlled the House for an extended period of time. By and large, battles within the group have centered around who would lead the Democratic majority and what faction(s) would prevail on policy matters. The Republican Conference lacked these motivations. Moreover, most House Republicans seem satisfied with the rules of the conference as they impact on various policy questions. As a result, the Republican Conference has focused most of its criticism on the Democratic Caucus, which, in its view, has attempted to make binding decisions for the whole House, affording Republicans little opportunity to participate in the deliberations. *See also* DEMOCRATIC/REPUBLICAN COMMITTEE ON COMMITTEES, p. 216; REPUBLICAN WEDNESDAY GROUP, p. 226.

Significance   The Republican Conference views its role differently than its opposite, the Democratic Caucus. Unlike the latter, which has battled over rules changes and the seniority system, the Republican Conference has avoided such skirmishes. The drama, rancor, and debate that have often characterized the Democratic Caucus have been noticeably lacking in the Republican Conference. However, there have been fierce struggles within the group and among House Republicans, particularly over the position of floor leader. The Republican Conference meets regularly during the session; members participate in briefings and discuss issues of special interest. It rarely takes a vote on major legislative proposals and avoids punitive sanctions.

Because the Republicans are presently the minority party in the House, ranking minority members are unable to exercise influence over positions taken by committee chairpersons. In addition, the Republican minority is rarely able to thwart the will of a determined Democratic majority. Still, House Republicans are deeply interested in the methods used to select its ranking committee members. Like the Democrats, they have officially modified the seniority rules by allowing, since 1971, the full membership of the House Republican Conference to vote (by secret ballot) on all nominations for ranking minority members proposed by the Republican Committee on Committees. Despite this fact, the Republican Conference has not overthrown any ranking minority members.

Republican Conference (Senate)   A meeting of all Senate Republicans. The Republican Conference elects its own chairman and meets periodically to consider institutional and policy matters of special importance. Although the conference will attempt to reach consensus on an issue, its position is not formally binding. On many occasions, however, the members support the position of the group. This is best illustrated by the action of the conference on the 1964 civil rights act, when the group went on record in support of the measure. On the final roll call, thirty Republicans voted for the bill, and none opposed it. Typically, the Republican Conference will meet from six to eight times a year. It holds both formal and informal meetings. In its formal meetings, it often discusses organizational matters as they relate to Senate Republicans. For example, in 1965 the conference met several times on the proposed rules change in the seniority system as it pertained to committee assignments. It also meets on various occasions to consider major legislative initiatives. Generally, 60 to 70 percent of the Senate Republicans attend the meetings—more members attend if the matter is of vital importance. *See also* DEMOCRATIC/REPUBLICAN COMMITTEE ON COMMITTEES, p. 216; REPUBLICAN CONFERENCE (HOUSE), p. 223; REPUBLICAN WEDNESDAY GROUP, p. 226.

Significance The Republican Conference is both active and influential, particularly when key rules changes are being considered or when an important bill is scheduled. The success of the conference depends on several factors, including (1) the abilities of the leadership; (2) the nature of the issue; (3) the size of the Republican contingent; (4) the division of opinion among the members; and (5) whether there is a Republican president in the White House. The conference chairman plays a salient role in the proceedings, in most cases avoiding to ask colleagues for commitments, knowing that to do so could jeopardize the chairman's personal effectiveness and that of the group. Instead, the chairman and supporters attempt to persuade dissident members on the merits of the issue but avoid putting them in a position where they must vote in a way that could embarrass them politically or compromise their beliefs.

The conference is most likely to meet when there are clear differences on a pending bill. An attempt is made to reach agreement, if such an agreement is possible, prior to floor action. Wherever possible, the chairman tries to reduce conflict and minimize the possibility of party wrangling. Any member of the conference may request a meeting and will, in most cases, prove successful. On those occasions where a meeting is not possible, the chairman will attempt to satisfy the wishes of the member. Usually, meetings are requested by several members, at which time they will express themselves on the issue at hand. Once they have done so, the conference is open for general discussion, and all members are free to express their opinions. These meetings are characterized by their openness and candor and serve to harness the conflicting views and political ambitions of members.

Republican Wednesday Group   An organization composed of liberal Republicans in the House. The Republican Wednesday Group, which meets on Wednesdays, seeks to influence the more conservative House leadership and to discuss and analyze legislative issues. Like its counterpart, the Democratic Study Group, the Republican Wednesday Group sprang from a desire for constructive opposition. Membership is by invitation, with the basic criterion being a moderate or liberal political orientation. The members pay no dues; the group is financed through contributions. *See also* DEMOCRATIC STUDY GROUP, p. 218.

Significance   The Republican Wednesday Group was formed in 1963, when Republicans were the minority party in the House and Democrats occupied the White House. The idea for this group was proposed on a Wednesday afternoon in the office of F. Bradford Morse (R-Mass.), and the group grew steadily over the years. This growth produced division among the members as to the role of the group, and a researcher, Douglas Bailey, was hired to coalesce the group. In addition to the members' ideologies as a criterion for membership, the group attempts to have varied geographic representation among its members, as well as members from most of the standing committees. The Republican Wednesday Group meets on Wednesday afternoons at 5:00 P.M. when Congress is in session. The members take turns as host, with the host serving as chairman. They discuss pending legislation, committee matters, and other issues. The group is informal, relaxed, and designed to foster communication among members rather than promote an activist faction or bloc. It has no whip system; rather, it focuses on the preparation of studies. These studies have included reports on air safety, crime, and education. In 1970 the Republican Wednesday Group began preparing legislative summaries highlighting important points in major bills. Occasionally, small study groups are set up to study issues in more depth. The Republican Wednesday Group has thrived as a forum for the exchange of ideas among members and the advancement of new party ideas.

Senate Majority Leader   Head of the majority party in the Senate. The Senate majority leader is that chamber's most influential officer, serving as a leader on the floor and as the leader of the Senate. (Neither the vice president nor President pro tempore hold substantive powers over Senate proceedings.) The majority leader controls the legislative schedule and can nominate members to party committees, appoint ad hoc study groups, influence the committee assignment process, and recommend substantive and procedural reforms. Duties also include serving as party spokesman and key strategist. The majority leader performs a gatekeeping function when a bill, after the committee stage, seeks to gain access to the floor. *See also* COMMITTEE ASSIGNMENT PROCESS, p. 234; DEMOCRATIC CONFERENCE, p. 215; PRESIDENT PRO TEMPORE, p. 222.

Significance   The Senate majority leader, a position nowhere mentioned in the Constitution, evolved from the party post of conference (caucus) chairman around the turn of the century. Although long viewed as being largely ineffective, there have been strong majority leaders, among them Republican Majority Leader Henry Cabot Lodge (R-Mass.), who emerged during the era of World War I, and Democratic Majority Leader Joseph T. Robinson (D-Ark.), active during the New Deal era. More recently, Lyndon B. Johnson's (D-Tex.) reign as majority leader (1954–1960) is regarded as a masterful example of leadership, persuasiveness, and compromise—all important qualities in an effective floor leader. Senate Democrats have concentrated significant power in their majority leader as opposed to Senate Republicans. The Democratic floor leader also serves as the chairman of the Senate Democratic Conference, chairman of the Steering Committee (affecting committee assignments), and chairman of the Policy Committee (developing party positions on legislation). Senate Republicans fill these posts with different members.

The majority leader controls the access of a bill to the Senate floor, usually consulting with the party's Policy Committee and minority leader before setting the schedule for the floor. Once a bill is passed by a committee, though, the majority leader rarely attempts to keep the legislation off the floor. Democrats generally want the majority leader to control the floor, to keep floor activities moving, and to promote party cohesiveness. However, they also want the latitude to pursue their goals in committees and subcommittees. Johnson's majority leader successors, Mike Mansfield (D-Mont., 1961–1977) and Robert Byrd (D-W. Va., 1977–present), are viewed as less forceful, more mindful of their colleagues, in the development of their leadership roles.

Senate Majority/Minority Whips   Assistant to the majority and minority leaders in the Senate. Senate majority and minority whips generally perform the same functions as their House counterparts, but the task is considered less demanding and not performed as effectively as in the House. The Democratic whip is often referred to as the assistant majority leader, assisting in managing the floor and developing party consensus. Both Democratic and Republican whips have assistant whips, often first-term congressmen; the assistant whip position serves as a means of socializing these new members. *See also* DEMOCRATIC

CONFERENCE, p. 215; SENATE MAJORITY LEADER, p. 226; SENATE MINORITY LEADER, p. 228.

Significance   The Senate majority and minority whips have had a more difficult time than their House counterparts in promoting party unity. At times, Senate whips have openly defied stands taken by their party leaders. This has occurred in part because the Senate Democratic and Republican Conferences elect their floor leaders and whips and have sometimes been forced into regional logrolling to secure agreement on their selections; thus, Senate leaders have become hesitant to share power with the whips. Senate whips also have had a more difficult time being elected to higher party positions. Historically, majority whips have not gained the position of Senate majority leader as often as House majority leaders have gained the position of Speaker. In recent decades, several Democratic whips failed to attain the position of majority leader. But succession from party whip to floor leader has emerged in recent years, with four of the last five Democratic and two of the last three Republican floor leaders serving first as the party whip.

While the party whip's job has been described as peripheral and not influential, the whip's degree of persuasiveness may effectively determine his or her real power. But an inability to work with the party leadership may hinder the scope of that influence. Although the job of whip can be frustrating and mechanical at times, competition for these positions is keen. Candidates start early and attempt to line up as many political favors as possible. Once members declare themselves candidates for the job, they campaign vigorously for the necessary votes to win. In the process, they take advantage of past favors rendered and are quick to promise future help in exchange for support. To win, they must be aggressive and affable; candidates who are either distant or aloof are sure to lose.

Senate Minority Leader   Head of the minority party in the Senate. The Senate minority leader is elected biennially by secret ballot of party colleagues. The job includes summarizing minority criticism of the majority party's legislation, mobilizing support for minority party positions, and acting as Senate spokesman for the president if both are of the same party. The minority leader consults continually with the majority leader, while at the same time exercising a watchdog role over the majority party along with party colleagues, seeking to frustrate majority actions and formulate alternative proposals. He or she must see that party colleagues are on the floor to vote, especially on matters on which the party has taken a position. The minority leader usually is not involved in committee hearings or bill drafting but must be prepared to deal with legislation as it comes out of the committees. If the minority party supports the bill, the minority leader's job is to garner enough votes to secure passage. If they oppose it, he or she must work to defeat it. *See also* SENATE MAJORITY LEADER, p. 226.

Significance The Senate Minority Leader, as party spokesman, must represent that party well. By tradition, the Republican party has almost always selected a senior conservative member as its floor leader. Moderates and liberals, virtually always a minority within Republican ranks, have had to settle for lesser party positions such as party whip. Everett McKinley Dirksen (R-Ill.), during his ten-year service as party leader from 1959 until his death in 1969, fit the senior conservative mold. He exercised strict, formal party leadership and came to be regarded as a national institution. Dirksen was succeeded by Hugh Scott (R-Pa.), who brought with him a moderate-liberal philosophy that often cast him in opposition to the conservative positions taken by Presidents Richard M. Nixon and Gerald R. Ford. Scott retired at the end of the Ninety-fourth Congress and was replaced by Howard Baker (R-Tenn.) in a heated contest against favored Senate Minority Whip Robert Griffin (R-Mich.). The Democratic administration of President Jimmy Carter demanded an articulate spokesman for the Republican party, and Baker filled the bill. Baker became majority leader when the Republican party gained control over the Senate in 1980.

Speaker of the House The presiding officer of the House. The Speaker is elected by the members, according to the constitutional mandate that "the House shall choose their Speaker." Although not required to be a member of the House, all Speakers have been members. The Speaker has the power of recognition and the power to rule on points of parliamentary procedure. He or she influences the scheduling of legislation, refers bills to committees, appoints House members of conference committees, and selects the chairman of the House Committee of the Whole. The Speaker is second in line behind the vice president to succeed to the presidency and is regarded as near the president as a national figure, exercising the most powerful leadership role in either branch of Congress. By custom, Speakers are not assigned to any committee. They may participate in debate and may vote, but most recent Speakers have voted only to break a tie. *See also* COMMITTEE OF THE WHOLE, p. 236; COMMITTEE SYSTEM, p. 238; CONFERENCE COMMITTEE, p. 240; HOUSE MAJORITY LEADER, p. 219.

Significance The Speaker of the House is the chief strategist in that chamber, scheduling House activities and controlling them to guarantee success for the party. The speaker may hold up voting on legislation until sufficient support has been garnered or may remove a bill from the calendar if the necessary support is lacking. Legislative discretion, coupled with the Speaker's control over the House information network, gives considerable influence to this office. Influence is also gained as a result of the Speaker's personal prestige, abilities of persuasion, support among colleagues, and personal legislative expertise. This expertise is a basic prerequisite for office, as the Speaker historically has had lengthy service in the House, usually a minimum of eight to ten terms. Of the thirteen members (eight Democrats and five Republicans) who have served as Speaker in this century, nine have held the office of majority or minority leader. Once elected, the Speaker is almost always reelected as long as the Speaker's party remains in control of the House. Sam Rayburn (D-Tex.) holds the record for Speaker, having served in that position for seventeen years. House Speaker Thomas P. (Tip) O'Neill (D-Mass.) served as a member for twenty-four years and was majority leader in the Ninety-third and Ninety-fourth Congresses before being elected Speaker in 1977.

Tuesday-to-Thursday Club   A phrase used to describe the work-week of members of Congress who depart Washington for their district or state on Thursday evening not to return to the Capitol until Tuesday morning. The Tuesday-to-Thursday Club consists primarily of House members from the Northeast, liberals more than conservatives, who use the time to reestablish contact with their families and constituents. The primary reason for such trips is political: the need to cement ties with the voters, campaign supporters, financial donors, and the local press. This has produced a situation where votes taken in the middle of the week, typically on domestic matters, have a more liberal flavor than those taken Friday through Monday. This has forced the leadership of both houses to schedule major legislation on those days when members will be present. This is not always an easy task, as Congress is overwhelmed with work and finds it difficult to conduct business in a smooth and timely manner even when members are present Monday through Friday. *See also* CAPITOL HILL, p. 188; CONSTITUENCY, p. 165; POLITICAL CAMPAIGNING, p. 176.

Significance   The Tuesday-to-Thursday Club reflects the practical realities of American politics: the need for representatives to maintain close contact with the voters and high visibility back home. The penalty for not doing so is defeat at the polls, a fact which most members try hard to avoid. While it is easy to understand the desire of members to return home, this practice has profound consequences for the legislative process. It puts extraordinary pressure on party leaders to schedule legislation around the wishes and conflicts of election-minded members. In 1980 Senator Barry M. Goldwater (R-Ariz.) expressed his disdain for this custom, observing: "I personally am getting a little tired of having to jam the work of this Senate into three days to take care of the senators who are running for reelection, and I happen to be one of them. But my getting home is not as easy as going to New Hampshire or to Kentucky or to some other state that is literally next door."

While many members may dislike the present system, they recognize that their continued tenure in Congress depends upon such trips and that until a viable alternative is proposed, it would be unwise to curtail this practice. All members must decide for themselves how much time to actually spend on the Hill. Many representatives who live within a 500 to 600 mile radius of the Capitol reside at home, commuting to Washington during the Tuesday to Thursday period and returning home every weekend. For example, House Ways and Means Chairman Daniel Rostenkowski (D-Ill.) is reported to have spent only nine weekends in Washington during his first twenty-two years in Congress. Many such members spend little time on the Hill, preferring to avoid the Washington social and political scene. Other members, for various reasons, become deeply involved in such activities, going from one function to another. However, most members eschew both extremes, spending as much time in Washington as family and politics permit.

Vice President   Constitutional president of the Senate. The vice president is the chief presiding officer of the Senate but usually presides only on ceremonial occasions and may vote only to break a tie. The vice president is first in line in the presidential succession; the Twenty-fifth Amendment provides that in the event of the death, removal from office, or resignation of the president, the vice president shall become president. As presiding officer of the Senate, the vice president has powers to recognize members for debate and introduction of bills, decide points of order, appoint senators to conference committees and select committees, maintain decorum, and administer oaths and affirmations. The Senate, however, is not inclined to delegate any real power or authority to the vice president since he is a nonmember. *See also* CONFERENCE COMMITTEE, p. 240; SELECT (OR SPECIAL) COMMITTEE, p. 248; VICE PRESIDENT, p. 135.

Significance   The vice president serves more as an emissary than a leader in the Senate. One of the most important tasks is to function as a liaison between the president and his party in the Senate. This role is an important factor initially in a presidential candidate's selection of a running mate; this factor affected John F. Kennedy's selection of Lyndon B. Johnson (D-Tex.) to run as his vice president. A vice president who is an experienced legislator can effectively lobby senators on behalf of administration policies. Former Republican Representative George Bush (R-Tex.) and former Senator Walter F. Mondale (D-Minn.) possessed these capabilities. Vice President Bush attends the weekly meetings of Republican committee chairmen and the luncheons of the Republican senators which follow these meetings to convey the president's position on various issues. The role as presiding officer of the Senate was skillfully portrayed in Allen Drury's *Advise and Consent* (1959), in which the vice president was reduced to maintaining order, exchanging quips with the members, and "looking good" for the gawkers in the galleries.

10. The Committee Structure

Ad Hoc Committee   A panel that considers bills that overlap the jurisdiction of several committees. Ad hoc committees are created by the Speaker of the House with House approval. The Senate has no provision for the establishment of such committees. Members of ad hoc committees are chosen from those committees which have legislative jurisdiction over the bill in question. The process of creating ad hoc committees was provided for in committee reform amendments adopted in 1974, along with provisions for multiple referral of a bill. *See also* REFER TO COMMITTEE, p. 246; SPEAKER OF THE HOUSE, p. 229.

Significance   Ad hoc committees represent one of the many discretionary options available to the Speaker when referring legislation to committee. They often serve to expedite important legislation. In 1977 House Speaker Thomas P. (Tip) O'Neill (D-Mass.) created an Ad Hoc Energy Committee to consider the energy proposals of President Jimmy Carter's administration. Specific parts of the package had been referred to the Interstate and Foreign Commerce, Ways and Means, Banking, Finance and Urban Affairs, Government Operations, and Public Works and Legislation Committees. Members of each of these committees made up the ad hoc committee. Speaker O'Neill knew that the fragmentation of the bill into multiple committees would result in the breakdown of the package, so he appointed members friendly to the Carter bill to the ad hoc committee. The bill passed through the House largely intact, as a result of this maneuver. The referral of legislation can be a strategic decision; a well-chosen ad hoc committee may prove to be an effective vehicle for ensuring passage of legislation. The recognition and utilization of bases of support is paramount in the legislative process, and ad hoc committees provide a means of coordinating this needed support.

Committee Assignment Process   The system of placing members of Congress on various congressional committees. Committee assignments are made by enactment in each house, but the job of reviewing requests and making assignments falls to each party's committee on committees in each chamber. These assignment panels use formal and informal criteria to choose committee members. Their selections must then be approved by each party's caucus and confirmed by election by the full House or Senate. *See also* COMMITTEE CHAIRMAN, p. 234; COMMITTEE ON COMMITTEES, p. 235; COMMITTEE SYSTEM, p. 238; SENIORITY SYSTEM, p. 249.

Significance   The committee assignment process has been described as a political mini-campaign. Members seek to be placed on committees which suit their individual needs and priorities. There are three main reasons for members seeking specific assignments, notes political scientist Richard F. Fenno, Jr. These include (1) the desire to help their constituents and thereby improve their chances for reelection; (2) the desire to exercise influence within the chamber; and (3) the desire to help formulate public policy in certain areas (Jewell and Patterson 1977, 189).

While numerous factors, including seniority, influence the committee assignment process, a member's preference for a particular assignment is considered the most important. House members from farm areas, for example, often seek assignment to the Agriculture Committee, while those from urban areas lean toward the Banking, Currency, and Housing Committee. But while members are lobbying for assignments, special interest groups are also lobbying for those members friendly to their interests. The party leadership may also exert influence, seeking to reward cooperative members with choice assignments. Lyndon B. Johnson (D-Tex.), as Senate Democratic leader, played an active role in selecting committee members; as head of the Steering Committee, he chose new members who would support him. Choice assignments include membership on the House Ways and Means Committee or the Senate Finance Committee, two powerful and influential committees. Less desirable assignments often include the Senate Ethics Committee and the House District of Columbia Committee. Not all assignments work to the benefit of members, as evidenced by Representative Shirley Chisholm's (D-N.Y.) assignment to the House Agriculture Committee, a committee far removed from the concerns of her Brooklyn constituency.

Committee Chairman   The top leadership position on a committee. The committee chairmanship was long a product of the seniority system, in which the member of the majority party who had served the longest on the committee became chairman. Committee chairmen rose to a level of virtually absolute power before changes were made that limited their role and scope of power. Their authority, though, is evident in their broad set of responsibilities, such as establishing priorities and managing the affairs of the committee. A chairman's formal powers, coupled with the support and cooperation of the committee's members, will effectively determine the sphere of the chairman's influence. *See also* COMMITTEE ASSIGNMENT PROCESS, p. 234; COMMITTEE SYSTEM, p. 238; SENIORITY SYSTEM, p. 249.

Significance   The committee chairman is a key figure in the legislative process, as are the committees. His formal powers include setting and controlling the committee's agenda; scheduling, allocating the time for and delaying hearings when necessary; and hiring and firing minority staff, among others. A chairman's disposition toward particular legislation can determine its eventual outcome. The chairman often has the most information and understanding of the bills brought before the committee. Wilbur D. Mills (D-Ark.) amassed great influence in Washington as chairman of the House Ways and Means Committee and was regarded as a leading expert on tax policy. While longevity of service produced chairmen of considerable knowledge, the seniority system for selecting chairmen came under attack as new members sought to increase their influence in Congress. The most significant change came with the introduction of secret ballot elections of committee chairmen by parties in both chambers. Restrictions were applied that limited leadership on more than one committee. These changes made chairmen accountable to their colleagues and necessitated a spirit of cooperation and cohesion among the chairman and committee members.

An effective chairman is regarded as one who does not use power arbitrarily but seeks to achieve consensus among colleagues and is sensitive to their needs. Further, a chairman must cooperate with other chairmen and subcommittee chairmen, utilizing these bases of support to the best advantage. While seniority is still a major factor in determining committee chairmanships, it is not a cloak under which the chairman can wield unbridled power, as success will be weighed in the context of the committee's overall strength and effectiveness. Chairmen are no longer immune from challenges to their authority; in 1975 three incumbent chairmen were voted out of office in the House. But a just and fair chairman may indeed hold significant power for a long time.

Committee on Committees   Panels of each party in the House and Senate that place members on the various committees. The committee on committees takes on a different form within each party. The

House Republicans create their committee on committees with one representative from each state having Republican members in the House. Each member has a vote equal in number to the Republican representatives their state has in Congress. The House Democrats elect a Steering and Policy Committee to determine standing committee assignments. The Senate Republican committee on committees is a panel of approximately fourteen members appointed by the caucus chairperson. The Senate Democrats employ a Steering Committee as their committee on committees, with appointments made by the floor leader. *See also* COMMITTEE ASSIGNMENT PROCESS, p. 234; DEMOCRATIC/ REPUBLICAN COMMITTEE ON COMMITTEES, p. 216; SENIORITY SYSTEM, p. 249.

Significance   The committee on committees' job of assigning members to committees varies with each new Congress. Members who are reelected can keep their assignments or change them if they wish. Incoming freshmen members apply for their first assignments. The committees will seek to accommodate the members' preferences for committee assignments while balancing the personnel needs of the committee and the wishes of committee and party leaders. They will consider the members' party loyalty and their ideological orientation. While seniority long governed the assignment process, it is not the sole arbiter of that decision. Factors that influence the committee assignment process include interpersonal relations, geography, reelection needs, seniority, ideology, and expertise. Democratic Committee rosters of nominations in the House and Senate are subject to caucus approval. The House Republican caucus does not vote on nominations; the Senate Republican Conference only votes on the ranking Republican member in each committee.

Historically, the party caucuses automatically ratified the committee's nominees, but in the 1970s they became more actively involved in the process. When the committee on committees meets, it is usually known which assignments are available. The members seeking assignments may elect to lobby the members on the committee on committees and make their preferences known, or they may simply put in a request and then wait for the committee to decide. The committees keep in mind the various norms and customs in play and endeavor to achieve balance and harmony on the standing committees so that they will function effectively.

Committee of the Whole   A procedure for considering bills in the House with different rules and customs than the regular proceedings.

The term Committee of the Whole is derived from Committee of the Whole House on the State of the Union, which considers Union Calendar bills (those involving the appropriation or expenditure of money) and Committee of the Whole House, which considers bills on the Private Calendar (those involving individuals). Upon adoption of a rule, the House resolves itself into the Committee of the Whole for preliminary consideration of a bill. The Committee of the Whole requires a quorum of 100 members, as opposed to a majority of the House. The Speaker appoints a chairman, usually of the majority party, to preside. The bill goes to the floor for general debate. The committee chairman mentioned in the bill is the bill's spokesman, while the ranking minority member mentioned in the bill manages the opposition. The bill is amended under the five-minute rule and when action is completed, the Committee of the Whole "rises," or dissolves, the Speaker regains the podium, and the adopted amendments are reported to the House and acted on. *See also* AMENDMENT, p. 256; BILL, p. 259; ELECTRONIC VOTING, p. 270; FIVE-MINUTE RULE, p. 275.

Significance   The Committee of the Whole is a method for expediting consideration of a bill. Today, almost all important bills are considered by the Committee of the Whole, with those not on the appropriate calendar considered on motion. Critics contend that because of the small quorum requirement, important decisions are made by a minority of representatives. The amendment process effectively determines the shape of legislation that reaches the House. When the rules are used effectively, strategic amendments may give the bill's sponsors key advantages. By sweetening a proposal to attract the support of additional members, the chances for a bill's success may be greatly improved.

Prior to 1970, there was no way to know how members voted because their votes were not recorded. Recorded teller votes were taken following the Legislative Reorganization Act of 1970, which also authorized electronic voting. This made the members of the Committee of the Whole more publicly accountable and increased their voting participation. Legislators could improve their attendance records by calling for many recorded votes. Floor managers can monitor the voting and move quickly to seek additional support if needed. Members, not always familiar with what they are voting for, will take cues from influential members and must take their own views, their party's views, and their constituent's views into consideration when casting a vote.

Committee Staff   A body of assistants that provide technical support to the various legislative committees. Committee staffs are relied on for their subject matter expertise and competence. They are designed to free the Congress from overreliance on research studies produced by executive agencies. The major functions of committee staffs include organizing hearings, conducting investigations, drafting bills and amendments, and working on conference committees. The 1946 Legislative Reorganization Act permitted committees to hire their own staffs, and their growth since then has been rapid. Since many of the staff members are appointed by the chairman or ranking minority member of a committee, these positions have often been doled out on a patronage or spoils system basis. However, most agree that staff assignments are made more on competence than patronage, as evidenced by the large number of staff members holding advanced college degrees. Because senators generally serve on more committees than do representatives, Senate staffs are larger and more heavily relied upon than House staffs. *See also* COMMITTEE CHAIRMAN, p. 234; COMMITTEE STAFF, p. 309; COMMITTEE SYSTEM, p. 238; LEGISLATIVE REORGANIZATION ACTS, p. 204; SUBCOMMITTEE, p. 251.

Significance   Committee staffs possess a virtually self-determined sphere of influence. A staff member may be as inclined as a committee member to initiate legislation; policy decisions are based on the results of their research, analyses, and investigations. This influence has been noted by those who refer to a "government by staff": unelected individuals who dictate the flow of policy legislation. Still, staff members are bound by the rules and norms of their committees. They are expected to be loyal to their chairmen and deferential to the committee members. Norms govern that staff members should remain in the background and refrain from advocacy. However, staffs differ in style and temperament. Anonymity is not popular among staff members who would like to be recognized for their hard work and expertise. But their role is to do the work and utilize their expertise to benefit the committee. Committee staffs are employed in varying degrees by committee and subcommittee chairmen and ranking minority members but may also often be diverted to noncommittee work. While the need for staff support increases, this expansion threatens to mushroom into an unmanageable bureaucracy. Studies have urged the pooling of staff members and the removal of party lines in staff assignments to counteract this expansion.

Committee System   A network of legislative groups that scrutinizes proposed legislation and oversees executive agencies and their administration of policy. The committee system is an expansive, influential part of the legislative process. Committees facilitate the duties of members of Congress through their varied powers and functions, and they serve to control the congressional agenda. Committees guide the path of legislation from its introduction to its eventual conclusion. Committees have been described as little legislatures, each one an independent group with self-determined rules, procedures, and power bases.

The four principal types of committees are (1) standing (or permanent) committees, permanent panels with specified jurisdiction over stated policy areas; (2) select (or special) committees, temporary panels of the House or Senate which investigate a particular problem; (3) joint committees, temporary panels comprised of members of both the House and Senate which study specific problems; and (4) conference committees, formed by members of the two chambers when a single bill is passed in different forms in the House and Senate. The committee system is further characterized by subcommittees, specialized subgroups of full committees. *See also* COMMITTEE CHAIRMAN, p. 234; CONFERENCE COMMITTEE, p. 240; JOINT COMMITTEE, p. 242; SELECT (OR SPECIAL) COMMITTEE, p. 248; STANDING (OR PERMANENT) COMMITTEE, p. 250; SUBCOMMITTEE, p. 251.

Significance   The committee system has resulted in what some call government by committee or government by subcommittee. Such is a committee's power to influence the nature and direction of legislation, since they consider virtually every bill that is introduced. The complexity of legislation before Congress has made specialized knowledge vital, and the committees serve as a vehicle for this support. While the scope of legislation may be broad, the intricate details must be examined at close range. The committees consider, evaluate, and recommend action on the legislation that falls under their jurisdiction.

Committees also serve as points of access to those outside the legislative system—interest groups and private individuals. The committees' public hearings allow for expression of these viewpoints. This combination of critical examination and feedback provides a mechanism for members of Congress to gauge the policy implications of their actions. Committees also provide a means of advancing members' political careers, offering opportunities to showcase their knowledge and expertise and to influence public policy. Members' needs and goals are clearly important motivations in their quest for committee assignments which will be most beneficial to them. Committees are not merely tangled webs through which legislation must pass, but bodies which act as lawmakers, investigators, consultants, specialists, and negotiators. While the spheres of influence of the committees may vary—from the broad scope of the Senate Foreign Relations Committee to the narrower focus of the Senate District of Columbia Committee—they each serve to address an important area of policy concern.

Conference Committee   An ad hoc joint committee composed of members of the House and Senate that meets to resolve differences and disagreements on a bill. The temporary conference committee becomes necessary when bills are passed in differing forms in both chambers, and compromise cannot otherwise be reached. According to the Constitution, the president cannot sign any legislation unless it is in the exact same language from both houses. The steps involved in the conference committee process include (1) the request for a conference; (2) the selection of conferees; (3) conference committee bargaining; (4) conference committee report; and (5) House and Senate consideration of the report. Once the report is made, it must be completely accepted or rejected. A majority vote of the House and Senate conferees is required for agreement to be reached. Upon approval, the committee disbands. *See also* BICAMERALISM, p. 186; COMMITTEE SYSTEM, p. 238.

Significance   Conference committees were once mysterious bodies, meeting in secret to resolve House-Senate differences. Under public pressure, the conferences were held openly beginning in 1975. Some members criticized these "sunshine" rules, suggesting that detachment from constituency pressures was required in order to effectively reach compromise. Some were concerned that members would pander to the galleries and their constituents, making long speeches and stretching out the proceedings. Proponents of open conferences denied that public scrutiny would disrupt the process. Conference committees were also criticized for rewriting bills arbitrarily, producing virtually new legislation. Reform measures were adopted in 1946 and 1970 which limited conferees to the language and concerns of the bill in question. House rules were adopted which provided that nongermane amendments added to a bill in conference by the Senate could be voted on separately at a member's request and approved by majority vote.

Almost all important legislation passes through conference committees. The bargaining process is where compromise can often be reached. Some amendments are added to bills simply as bargaining tools that can be traded away for more important concessions. Often, members of Congress prefer to sidestep the conference process in order to expedite passage of a bill, especially toward the congressional adjournment date, when the legislation will die if agreement is not reached. The conference committee system underscores the nature of a bicameral legislature, where give-and-take, logrolling, and compromise become the necessary tools for achieving a common goal.

Congressional Investigation   A tool of legislative committees to probe into the affairs of government. Congressional investigations fall into the domain of a nonlegislative inquisitorial power of Congress. The power of Congress to conduct investigations was assured in the Supreme Court case of *McGrain* v. *Daugherty* (1927), rising out of the Teapot Dome scandal, in which the authority of the Senate to probe into the official conduct of a former attorney general was upheld. Congressional investigations may be conducted by standing or special committees, subcommittees, or by the House and Senate as a body. The general purposes of congressional investigations are to gather information relevant to enactment of legislation; to oversee the management of administrative agencies and executive departments; and to settle questions concerning the actions of individual members of Congress. A congressional investigation is considered valid if it falls within the purview of the legislative branch, not encroaching on executive, judicial, or state powers, and if constitutional guarantees are not violated. The Congress may issue subpoenas to summon witnesses, books, and papers, and may issue warrants of arrest for noncompliance. Senate committees regularly spend more money on investigations than do House committees. *See also* COMMITTEE SYSTEM, p. 238; OPEN HEARING, p. 245; WATCHDOG COMMITTEE, p. 252.

Significance   Congressional investigations underscore the powers of Congress. On several occasions, the courts have been forced to limit these powers. The expanded use of investigations has made them an important political issue. While the Constitution assigned "all legislative powers herein granted" to Congress, factors such as the rights of witnesses were also subject to constitutional protection. This disparity was evident in the 1948 House Un-American Activities Committee's investigations of communism, wherein the right of the committee to seek information collided with the witnesses' loss of rights of privacy and self-incrimination. The House followed with fair play rules and reforms to establish new measures of conduct for investigation committees, while the Senate offered their own suggestions for reform. But the actions taken by committees are in large part determined by their members. While the process may be well-used or abused, it provides a means of gathering important information for legislators and the public. The gathering process may meet many obstacles—a president's supposed right of executive privilege during an investigation into the executive branch, or a witness's invocation of the Fifth Amendment as protection from self-incrimination. But these tools serve as checks and balances between the various branches and participants and will long be open to interpretation, dispute, and debate.

Discharge Petition   A method of relieving a standing committee of their control over a bill by forcing them to report it out. In the House, a discharge petition can be prepared after a bill has been in committee for thirty days or after a resolution has been held up for seven days by the Rules Committee. Once the discharge rule has been invoked, the appropriate house clerk prepares the petition for members' signatures. If a majority of signatures is obtained, the members' names are published in the *Congressional Record*. The measure is put on the Discharge Calendar for seven days prior to a member offering a discharge motion. Discharges are privileged business on the second and fourth Mondays of the month. If the motion is rejected, the bill is not eligible for discharge in that session. If it prevails, a member who signed the petition can move for immediate consideration of the bill. Senators may also introduce discharge petitions that are considered the next day. If approved, they may start consideration of the the bill the following day. *See also* COMMITTEE SYSTEM, p. 238; *CONGRESSIONAL RECORD*, p. 199.

Significance   Discharge petitions have not been especially successful in either chamber. In the House, only 25 of 860 discharge petitions gained enough signatures to be put on the Discharge Calendar from 1910 to 1973, and only two became law. In the Senate, only six petitions were successful from 1789 to 1966, with only one becoming law. The petition process serves as a threat to committees who are holding up legislation. The seven-day period after its appearance on the Discharge Calendar allows the committee enough time to report out the the bill before the possibility of it being taken from them by the House. Committees may also keep track of the number of signatures being collected on the petition to determine the extent of the threat. Discharge petitions are rarely pushed, though, because members are dependent on the committees for guidance and interpretation of the legislation. Also, they realize that the same procedure could be used against a committee on which they serve. Members may sometimes sign a discharge petition to satisfy interest group or constituent demands that they are making an effort to move a measure to the floor, but this is often with the assurance that the petition will lack enough signatures to force any action. It is extremely difficult to gain a majority of signatures, as evidenced by the weak record of previous discharge motions. Some, notably the majority leaders, see the process as a violation of legislative norms and an obstacle to the proper flow of business, while minority leaders praise the system as a democratic weapon for fighting committee domination.

Joint Committee   A special panel composed of members of the House and Senate set up temporarily to study a particular problem. Joint committees are created by statute or resolution which determine their size. They are usually composed of an equal number of senators and representatives. The chairmanship and vice chairmanship rotate between the two houses in each new Congress. When a senator is chairman, a representative is vice chairman, both from the majority party. Joint committees function to study and investigate legislation, oversee administrative agencies, and perform routine activities. There are three types of joint committees: standing, select, and conference. Joint committees generate policy studies in particular areas and report them to Congress and appropriate standing committees. With the exception of the Joint Committee on Atomic Energy, legislation is not referred to joint committees. *See also* COMMITTEE SYSTEM, p. 238; CONFERENCE COMMITTEE, p. 240; SELECT (OR SPECIAL) COMMITTEE, p. 248; STANDING (OR PERMANENT) COMMITTEE, p. 250.

Significance   Joint committees ideally provide a means of coordination between the House and Senate. The passage of important legislation can be expedited through shared resources and manpower. However, factors such as party rivalry and party advantage may often create friction in such joint ventures. Senators, with heavier committee assignments than their House counterparts, eschew joint committee work. The presence of senatorial staff members at joint committee meetings can be a source of resentment for some House members. House members may also feel handicapped in joint hearings because their Senate colleagues enjoy greater prestige. Each chamber is protective of its own prerogatives, and the fundamental differences of the two bodies in attitudes, procedures, and interests can be formidable roadblocks to effective cooperation. While some joint committees, such as Printing, Library, and Disposition of Executive Papers, are routine and custodial in nature, others are broader in scope. The Joint Economic Committee has become permanent, conducting studies and holding hearings on important national and international economic issues. The Joint Committee on Taxation, composed of senior members of the House Ways and Means Committee and the Senate Finance Committee, is also permanent and works closely with tax-writing committees. While interparty, interhouse differences may hinder the joint committee process, it is a necessary fusion in the context of a bicameral legislature.

Joint Referral   The concurrent referral of a bill to two or more committees in cases of overlapping jurisdiction. Joint referrals are one of three types of multiple referrals. The other two types are sequential referrals (the bill is considered by one committee and then passed on to the next) and split referrals (parts of a bill are sent to separate committees for consideration of the subsection which falls under their jurisdiction). In 1977 the Senate authorized multiple referrals upon joint motion by the majority and minority leaders. In 1975 the House authorized the Speaker to make multiple referrals or to create an ad hoc committee to study a bill that overlapped committee jurisdictions. Often the subject matter of legislation is so complicated that a single committee's jurisdiction is not broad enough to encompass it. *See also* AD HOC COMMITTEE, p. 233; COMMITTEE SYSTEM, p. 238; REFER TO COMMITTEE, p. 246.

Significance   Joint referrals, as well as other multiple referrals, have become necessary because a piece of legislation may have repercussions in many areas. In addition to the problem of overlapping jurisdictions, there may be a new problem area that does not fall into a clearly defined policy jurisdiction. While House and Senate leaders may exercise discretion in the referral process, certain committees may not want to be bypassed on referrals, and they will assert their jurisdiction over bills. The multiple referral process serves to circumvent one committee's dominance over a bill.

With the additional obstacles a bill must face in multiple committees come increased opportunities for negotiation and compromise. Clearly, the more committees that are involved with a bill, the more chances exist that it will be significantly altered or killed. However, multiple committees may water down a bill to make it politically palatable to the chamber. For instance, the Federal Election Campaign Act of 1971 was referred to three Senate committees: Commerce, Rules and Administration, and Finance. The nature of the legislation (limits on campaign contributions) was not attractive to many members, yet they had to adopt some reforms. While a single committee was unlikely to come up with legislation that would be supported by the full Senate, the process of multiple referrals enabled the building of a broad-based consensus which ensured its passage.

Nomination Hearing   A tool of legislative oversight by which the Senate approves or rejects executive appointments. Senate confirmation of presidential appointments is mandated by the constitutional "advice and consent" provision. Nomination hearings are held by committees and subcommittees; some are routine in nature, such as those involving military officers, while others may produce exhaustive investigations, as in the cases of top government positions. The nominees' qualifications, policy viewpoints, physical health, and financial status are all subject to Senate scrutiny.

Once the nomination hearing is completed, the subcommittee votes and sends their recommendation to the full committee. The nomination is either approved or rejected by the committee, or no action is taken. Once the nomination reaches the Senate floor, it is most often approved, but not without frequent heated debate or political maneuvering. Nomination hearings make a nominee's views public record and nominees may be called back later to account for these statements. To ensure cooperation by the nominee, the Senate Democratic Conference in 1973 required committees to secure a pledge from the nominee before sending their name to the Senate for action. *See also* ADVICE AND CONSENT, p. 185; SENATORIAL COURTESY, p. 209.

Significance   Nomination hearings vary according to the sphere of influence of the Senate over the position to be filled. While potential cabinet secretaries may be closely questioned, the Senate usually defers to the president's right to select appointees, since the president dictates their term of service and seeks individuals who are loyal and supportive of administration policies. Confirmations of career civil servants and military officers are usually performed routinely without particular discretion. In the cases of positions whose terms extend beyond that of the president, such as Supreme Court justices or commissioners of regulatory agencies, the Senate has exercised more discretion. In 1968 the Senate blocked the confirmation of Supreme Court Justice Abe Fortas as chief justice, and in 1973 it blocked the confirmation of Robert H. Morris, President Richard M. Nixon's nominee to the Federal Power Commission.

The Senate's main area of influence is evident in appointees who serve the national government within a particular state, such as federal district judges. These appointments are usually bound by the custom of "senatorial courtesy." Traditionally, the president chooses a nominee who is acceptable to the senator from the state in which the office is situated, provided the senator belongs to the same party as the president. The rule of courtesy is a strong one but not an automatic guarantee of confirmation. In 1965, for example, President Lyndon B. Johnson's nomination of Francis X. Morrissey for a federal district judgeship in Massachusetts, with Senator Edward M. Kennedy's (D-Mass.) active support, was met by Senate opposition, and the nomination was withdrawn. Morrissey, a long-time friend of the Kennedy family, was proclaimed "unfit for the office" by several members, so President Johnson, with Kennedy's approval, withdrew the nomination.

Open Hearing   A legislative hearing that is open to the public and the press. The decision to hold an open hearing is made by the committee or subcommittee chairman prior to voting on a bill. House and Senate rules provide that hearings will be held publicly, unless the committees vote to close them because of their sensitive nature. In recent years virtually all hearings have been open, except for those involving national security or in which charges are made against an individual. Hearings are usually characterized by witnesses, chosen by the committee chairman, who read prepared statements. A witness will then be questioned by committee members, often in order of their seniority. Each member is given a limited amount of time to ask questions, and then the next witness is called. After the hearings, the bill is "marked up" in sessions that are also held publicly, and a report is prepared if the full committee votes to send the bill to the House or Senate. *See also* CLOSED DOOR SESSION, p. 264; MARK-UP SESSION, p. 279.

Significance   Open hearings are praised by their advocates for serving to present the public with the facts and providing a means for obtaining information, although some critics maintain that the hearings are orchestrated too carefully. The chairman's selection of witnesses depends on his support for or opposition to a bill, shifting the advantage to one side or the other. Opponents cite misinformation, lack of representation, and bias as other flaws of open hearings. Committee members, while ideally expected to remain impartial protectors of the public interest, play their roles in these hearings based on constituent demands and interest group pressures. A lobbyist presenting testimony may be working in tandem with a sympathetic congressperson who has prepared the lobbyist for the expected questioning. The member might view this role as an administration loyalist, cooperating closely with an administration witness. It is not unexpected that interest group concerns and administration witnesses will present testimony that is going to serve their own best interests. What the open hearings produce are information, opinions, and policy perspectives, serving to educate the public. Each actor is playing a role before an audience, and while the system may be viewed as propagandistic, it provides an arena for public participation and scrutiny.

Refer to Committee   The process whereby a bill which has been introduced by a member is directed to the appropriate committee for consideration. A bill is technically referred to committee by the Speaker of the House or the presiding officer of the Senate, but the parliamentarians normally discharge the duty. Custom and rule govern the referral of a bill to the committee that has jurisdiction over its subject matter. The jurisdiction, of the standing committees are outlined in House Rule 10 and Senate Rule 25. However, discretion may be involved in cases of overlapping or ambiguous jurisdiction. In many cases, bills may be referred to more than one committee. Once a bill has been referred to committee, the committee chairman can assign it to a subcommittee or consider it in the whole committee. Hearings (open or closed) are held, the bill is analyzed and then marked up, or amended. The committee perhaps may introduce a clean bill of their own. The full committee then votes on its recommendations to the House or Senate, thus "ordering a bill reported." *See also* BILL, p. 259; CLEAN BILL, p. 263; COMMITTEE SYSTEM, p. 238; OPEN HEARING, p. 245.

Significance Nearly all bills are referred to committee. House members may not appeal a referral decision unless it is erroneous; the Senate may appeal by majority vote, but disagreements are usually informally resolved before the legislation is introduced. With the increasing complexity of legislation, bills often fall in the jurisdiction of more than one committee.

Careful drafting coupled with favorable referral decisions in the House and Senate may effectively prevent a bill from being sent to a committee where it is sure to be killed. Since only those bills which receive a favorable committee report are considered by the House or Senate, the first step of referral may often be a critical one. In 1963 a civil rights bill was referred to the Senate Commerce Committee, chaired by a supportive Warren G. Magnuson (D-Wash.), rather than to the Senate Judiciary Committee, chaired by James O. Eastland (D-Miss.). Since the bill dealt with public accommodations, it fell within the purview of the commerce clause, thereby preventing referral to the southern-dominated Judiciary Committee, where it might have received hostile treatment.

Select Committee on Committees A legislative panel set up by each house to study and suggest reforms in the committee system. A Select Committee on Committees was created in the House in 1973, headed by Richard Bolling (D-Mo.), which held hearings and issued a report of reform recommendations in the committee system. In 1977 the Senate acted on the matter, creating a Select Committee on Committees chaired by Adlai E. Stevenson (D-Ill.). The Senate subsequently adopted approximately 60 percent of the recommendations that the select committee proposed. The House again created a Select Committee on Committees in 1979, headed by Jerry Patterson (D-Calif.), which focused on a narrower range of reforms than did its predecessor, including the creation of a standing committee on energy. *See also* COMMITTEE CHAIRMAN, p. 234; COMMITTEE SYSTEM, p. 238; DEMOCRATIC CAUCUS (HOUSE), p. 215.

Significance Select committees on committees have had a difficult time initiating committee reforms and realignments. Because many of the proposals brought forth in the hearings concerned rules regarding chairmanships, assignments, and jurisdiction, they met with significant opposition from those who stood to lose any power or influence. The Bolling Committee proposed to eliminate some standing committees and consolidate others in their Committee Reform Amendments of 1974. This threatened the powers of important committees and chairmen. Bolling sought support for his committee's proposals in the House Democratic Caucus. There, a heavily modified and weakened version was drafted by the Democratic Caucus Committee on Organization, Study, and Review and was subsequently approved by the House.

The Stevenson Committee was more successful at initiating reform along these same lines, mostly because they ensured a more equitable distribution of the workload for junior members. The Patterson Committee was wholly ineffective, with its proposals soundly rejected by the House. Committee realignment is a delicate process, requiring the support of the members and interest groups who are sensitive to any loss of power or influence. The select committees on committees do suggest, though, that the Congress is cognizant of the need for reform and is willing to tackle this difficult assignment.

Select (or Special) Committee   A temporary panel set up by the House or Senate to investigate a particular problem. Select committees are also known as special committees. These committees are created by resolution and usually disband after their report has been filed. Select committees usually have no legislative authority but can study and investigate a problem and make recommendations. After Congress has adjourned, select committees have the power to meet to administer oaths, subpoena persons and records, and perform other similar duties. *See also* COMMITTEE SYSTEM, p. 238; CONGRESSIONAL INVESTIGATION, p. 240; STANDING (OR PERMANENT) COMMITTEE, p. 250.

Significance   Select committees are similar in nature to standing (or permanent) committees, supplementing that system by investigating problems beyond their purview. They often perform specific duties in cases of overlapping committee jurisdiction. Select committees also can accommodate the needs and talents of their members. Senator Sam Ervin (D-N.C.) was thrust into national prominence by his position on the Senate Select Committee on Presidential Campaign Activities which investigated Watergate. Select committees serve special interest groups, providing them with a point of access in the committee system. They have been compared with third parties in a two-party system, affording access to those not being served by the standing committee system. While select committees do not challenge the standing committees' dominance, they play an educational and informative role, perhaps setting in motion ideas for future legislation based on their recommendations. Although select committees are generally temporary in nature, some, such as the Permanent Select Committee on Aging in the House and the House and Senate Select Committees on Small Business, have extended beyond the life of one Congress, later becoming standing committees. Select committees on space and aeronautics became standing committees in both houses, dealing in an area that crossed jurisdictional lines of existing standing committees. And while select committees do not generally report legislation, the Senate Select Committee on Intelligence was given legislative authority over the Central Intelligence Agency in 1976.

Seniority System　A process of choosing leaders based on length of service and party affiliation. Congressional seniority refers to length of service in Congress; committee seniority is based on consecutive years of service on a committee. The seniority system was long the primary determinant in the selection of committee chairmen and assignment to important committees. It has been traditionally relied upon as an arbitrary criterion for doling out perquisites. Favored by the older members and attacked by the young, committee seniority as the chief factor for choosing chairmen was phased out in the 1970s. Still, even though the parties are more involved in the selection process now, most chairmen are indeed senior members; the tradition remains philosophically and practically entwined in the distribution of power and privilege in Congress. *See also* COMMITTEE ASSIGNMENT PROCESS, p. 234; COMMITTEE CHAIRMAN, p. 234; COMMITTEE SYSTEM, p. 238; SAFE-MARGINAL DISTRICT, p. 183.

Significance　The seniority system has been described as sacrosanct or an iron law. Its proponents praise the system because it rewards long service, provides for experienced and knowledgeable leadership, and seems the fairest of other methods of selection. Committee seniority has been the focus of considerable criticism, as members from one-party areas (notably the Deep South) dominated chairmanships for years. Consequently, the system serves to penalize members from highly competitive states and districts. Younger members, anxious to establish their own power bases, feel disadvantaged by the seniority system because longevity, not ability and skill, counts the most. Over the years, both the Democratic and Republican parties have sought to modify the system, proposing age limits or year limits that a chairman can serve on a committee.

Reforms in the 1970s weakened the committee seniority system, specifically the adoption of secret ballot voting for chairmen. Seniority today is regarded as one of many factors of influence in the committee assignment process and the choice of a chairman. Since most congressional seats are safe and incumbents are reelected, there are more members of Congress with long careers than there are chairmanships to be filled. Political scientist Barbara Hinckley suggests that the seniority system reinforces party strength and provides stability and predictability in the distribution of power and influence (Hinckley 1971, 111). However, a system that generates power and influence for some at the expense of others will likely remain open to criticism and further reform as members vie to establish themselves in the political arena.

Standing (or Permanent) Committee   A permanent panel created by House and Senate rules with specific policy jurisdictions. Standing committees are the most important class of committees, since they consider virtually every legislative measure introduced by members of Congress. They are generally the only committees that may report bills. Once a bill is referred to committee, the committee members may consider and report it to the House or Senate with or without amendments, rewrite the bill, reject it, or fail to act on it. The committee chairman may also refer the bill to subcommittees for consideration, again provided for by House and Senate rules. The size of standing committees is determined by each house. Generally, party ratios in committees correspond to the party ratio of the full chamber. (Refer to the Appendix, Figure 9 for a table of the standing committees in the Senate and House of Representatives.) *See also* COMMITTEE ASSIGNMENT PROCESS, p. 234; COMMITTEE CHAIRMAN, p. 234; COMMITTEE SYSTEM, p. 238; LEGISLATIVE REORGANIZATION ACTS, p. 204.

Significance   Standing committees are highly respected by members of Congress for their specialized knowledge; thus their recommendations tend to be followed. Standing committees select from the great mass of proposed legislation to determine which merit floor consideration. Once in committee, a bill's success or failure depends largely on the committee chairman's disposition toward it. The chairman may ensure that no action is taken on a bill, effectively killing it. Standing committees have been described as the burial ground of most legislation. Early congresses were characterized by large numbers of standing committees. The Legislative Reorganization Act of 1946 pared down the number of such committees, grouping related policy areas into consolidated committees and organizing House and Senate committees along somewhat similar lines. In the Ninety-seventh Congress, there were sixteen standing committees in the Senate and twenty-two in the House. The broad influence of such standing committees as the House Ways and Means Committee and the Senate Foreign Relations Committee make them attractive committee assignments for members of Congress. The House distinguishes three exclusive committees—Rules, Ways and Means, and Appropriations—on which members may have only one assignment. The Senate classifies ten major committees—Appropriations, Agriculture, Armed Services, Banking, Finance, Labor, Foreign Relations, Commerce, Judiciary, and Public Works—on which all senators have at least one assignment. The permanence and scope of standing committees ensure their powerful and important role in the legislative process.

Subcommittee   A subgroup of a large standing, select, or joint committee. Subcommittees perform much of the daily lawmaking and oversight functions of Congress. They are centers of specialization and may be further divided into even smaller subcommittees in certain instances. Subcommittees allow members of Congress to focus their attention on complex and technical governmental problems. Appropriations subcommittees provide a vehicle for careful scrutiny of detailed budget requests, for example. Subcommittees offer leadership opportunities for younger members in a committee system dominated by the senior members. Members may pursue their own interests and gain prestige and influence. Subcommittees may operate virtually autonomously of their full committees, hiring their own staffs and drafting their own legislation. *See also* COMMITTEE ASSIGNMENT PROCESS, p. 234; COMMITTEE CHAIRMAN, p. 234; COMMITTEE STAFF, pp. 237, 309; COMMITTEE SYSTEM, p. 238.

Significance   Subcommittees have proliferated over the years as complex problems required increased policy specialization. The decentralization and dispersal of power from committees to subcommittees is regarded as democratic on the one hand, while discouraging unification and increasing fragmentation on the other. Questions about jurisdiction become more sensitive at the subcommittee level, with increased arguments over which issues fall in which subcommittee's domain. Party leaders must contend with separate and competing centers of power, each with differing sources of loyalty. Each subcommittee possesses its own set of rules and customs, providing great diversity in an already diverse legislative system.

Subcommittees have become increasingly institutionalized, with House Democrats leading the way in strengthening the autonomy of subcommittees. In 1971 the House Democratic Caucus adopted a rule that no member could serve as chairman on more than one subcommittee. They adopted a subcommittee "bill of rights" in 1973 and later adopted a rule whereby all committees of more than twenty members must have at least four subcommittees. This led to the creation of subcommittees in the Ways and Means Committee for the first time, weakening the dominance of Chairman Wilbur D. Mills (D-Ark.), who had previously abolished subcommittees. By the end of the 1970s, subcommittees possessed adequate staff, budget, and jurisdiction to function as powerful and influential bodies. Despite the surge in sub-committee activism, though, studies found that some never held meet-ings, and others met infrequently. In addition, there have been abuses of the subcommittee system by chairmen who filled positions with less than qualified personnel. At their best, subcommittees accom-modate a multiplicity of individuals and viewpoints that reflects an increased representativeness in Congress. At their worst, subcommit-tees reflect a burgeoning fragmentation and bureaucratization that serves to impede effective congressional decision making.

Watchdog Committee   A legislative committee that monitors the executive branch to see that it is carrying out its congressional mandate. Watchdog committees are designed to promote active participation in the administrative decision-making process. Special and standing com-mittees perform investigations of the executive branch. Periodic reports may be required from executive agencies concerning their overall per-formance or their administration of a particular program. Watchdog committees may also audit expenditures by the executive branch. The Legislative Reorganization Acts of 1946 and 1970 required that each committee exercise "continuous watchfulness" over the administration of policy that fell within the subject matter jurisdiction of that commit-tee. *See also* CONGRESSIONAL INVESTIGATION, p. 240; LEGISLATIVE REORGANIZATION ACTS, p. 204.

Significance   Watchdog committee functions vary in each chamber. Most of the standing committees in the House must report their over-sight activities at the end of each Congress. There are fewer guidelines in the Senate, but Senate committees have become more active in oversee-ing administrative conduct. Watchdog committees sprang forth in the House following passage of the House Committee Reform Amendments in 1974. Each committee with more than fifteen members is required to set up an oversight subcommittee or to carry out their own oversight duties. The oversight subcommittees are given the same jurisdiction as the full committee. In the Senate, oversight tends to be performed by subcommittee staff members. Watchdog or oversight functions are not particularly popular with members of Congress, who primarily see themselves as lawmakers and not bound up in overseeing the administration of these laws. Many times the scope and goals of the legislation are broad and unclear, sometimes ambiguous. This makes it difficult and time-consuming to investigate their implementation. Also, some members see oversight duties as unglamorous, taking time away from other activities which may be more personally beneficial to them. While watchdog functions are considered severely neglected, they remain of critical importance. Lawmaking is not an end in itself, and as political scientist David B. Truman notes, "Administration of a statute is an extension of the legislative process" (Truman 1953, 439).

11. Rules and Procedures

Adjournment   The conclusion of a congressional session. Adjournment marks the end of Congress's annual session. The 1970 Legislative Reorganization Act prescribes that "unless otherwise provided by the Congress," the Senate and House "shall adjourn *sine die* not later than July 31 of each year" or, in the event of a nonelection year, take a 30-day recess in August. This requirement may be abrogated if "a state of war exists pursuant to a declaration of war by Congress." Congress formally concludes its work with *sine die* (without setting a date for reconvening in that session) adjournment. During a session, Congress may establish an agreed-upon adjournment date; neither body may adjourn for more than three days without the concurrence of the other house. In 1973 Congress revived a process dormant for twenty-five years when it authorized the leadership to reconvene both bodies during adjournment. The decision to recess (take short breaks, usually tied to holidays) or adjourn falls upon the leadership and requires unanimous consent or a majority vote.

Congress is a full-time legislative body, meeting and working throughout the calendar year. Adjournment not only brings the session to its formal conclusion but serves several other important functions as well. During the period when Congress is not in session, members generally spend time in their state or district rekindling family ties, meeting with constituents, delivering speeches, appearing before groups, and studying pending legislation. Members also use the time to strengthen their political ties with the voters, often using this period for campaign purposes. *See also* POLITICAL CAMPAIGNING, p. 176.

Significance   Adjournment has important legislative repercussions. Congress is anxious to conclude its work prior to adjournment. The last

255

days preceding adjournment are hectic and, at times, confusing. Members attempt to push through bills and amendments that failed to be acted upon during the session. As adjournment approaches, there is a flurry of activity as Congress tries to dispose of as much unfinished business as possible. This provides members with an opportunity to push through legislation that might not win approval if it were considered earlier in the session. Members are anxious to adjourn and at times will vote for measures that they might not have supported otherwise. Moreover, there is little time to study legislation with care, and members will often approve measures with little discussion or debate.

The Congress works extremely hard. Members spend the better part of the year on Capitol Hill, with only occasional trips back to their state or district. These trips are short in duration and crowded with obligations. It is difficult for members to gauge voter sentiment or cement political ties on these short trips. As a result, members look forward to an extended break. Despite the importance of their work in Washington, most members recognize that their future depends on reelection. They cannot afford to become isolated from the voters or give the impression that they are out of touch with their constituents. The adjournment period affords them an opportunity to reestablish those vital contacts that their reelection depends upon.

Amendment   A legislative action to delete, alter, or revise a bill or an act. Amendments are introduced for several reasons. Some are proposed in response to interest group, executive branch, or constituent demands. Others are intended to spark public interest, hinder legislative action, exhibit member concern, or test sentiment for or against a bill. Some amendments are of a technical nature, while others represent substantive changes. There are three main types of amendments: committee amendments, riders, and previously noted amendments. The rules permit four forms of amendment, once a bill is pending on the floor (1) an amendment itself; (2) an amendment to the amendment; (3) a substitute amendment; or (4) an amendment to the substitute. Both the Senate and House provide opportunities to amend a bill prior to passage. The Senate provides myriad opportunities. The House, however, can limit amendments by adopting a closed rule. This is done by the Rules Committee, which establishes agreed-upon limits. Amendments offered by the committee take precedence over those proposed by individual members.

In the Senate, it is common practice to hold a number of roll calls on amendments prior to the final vote. The House employs a different procedure for disposing of amendments; it is called the Committee of the Whole. Proposed amendments are introduced, debated, and acted on. Members may request a vote on individual amendments. Should the House reject an amendment in the Committee of the Whole, it may not be revived in the House. Once the Committee of the Whole concludes its business and reports the results to the House, the chamber takes a single vote to officially adopt all previously-approved amendments. *See also* COMMITTEE OF THE WHOLE, p. 236; RIDER, p. 292.

Significance   Amendments reflect a wide variety of member motivations. Some members may vote for an amendment, although they may prefer the bill as written, because such an amendment is vital in order to secure sufficient votes for passage. They are willing to compromise, knowing that the amended version of a bill is better than no bill at all. Other members will vote against an amendment where it considerably weakens the bill, believing that such a compromise represents an unwise concession to a particular individual or group and thus deceives the public. Opponents of a measure may propose a "killer amendment," one that is so opprobrious that it is certain to undermine the bill and make final passage unlikely. Members who have little interest in the issue may vote for or against the bill depending on how they view the amendment, whether the amended bill is preferable to no bill at all. Much depends on member attitudes and whether the majority can garner the requisite votes without having to agree to an amendment(s). Where such votes are lacking, the majority will, at times, reluctantly agree to support an amendment which weakens the bill but is crucial to its adoption. The floor managers play a critical role in this process. They must be able to count votes and distinguish between members who are for, against, or undecided on the bill. If they misjudge the sentiment of the chamber, they could doom the bill to defeat or acquiesce to changes which are unnecessary or undesirable. This is a difficult task, as member attitudes are often in a state of flux.

Appropriation Bill   A measure which allocates funds for agencies or programs already authorized by Congress. An appropriation bill is passed following formal authorization by Congress of the measure under consideration. No funds may be appropriated until a bill has been authorized. At that point, the authorization legislation establishes the funding level. The Constitution states that "all bills for raising revenue shall originate in the House of Representatives." This provision has generally been interpreted to encompass appropriation (spending) bills as well. All other legislation may originate in either chamber. Congress affects the administration of government programs in three ways. First, it dictates the amount of money for an agency or program. Second, members on the Appropriations Committees control the manner in which agencies and programs are administered. Third, committee members are able to influence programs by indicating to agency officials that unless they provide a particular service or eliminate one, their appropriations may be reduced or eliminated.

In government, money is power. The Appropriations Committees are able to shape government policy as a result of their power over the purse strings. This power enables them to play a unique role in shaping the goals and objectives of those agencies that are dependent on their support. *See also* AUTHORIZATION BILL, p. 258; COMMITTEE SYSTEM, p. 238.

Significance   Appropriation bills are vital to the success or failure of any legislation. The political process guarantees that the Appropriations Committees will affect considerably the content and direction of a bill. This role leads to inevitable tension between the Appropriations Committees and the substantive committees that may have very different views on the legislation and the appropriate funding level. This tension is reduced in the Senate, where members of the Appropriation Committee also serve on a variety of other committees. This makes them more sensitive to the needs of the members, as well as cognizant of the consequences should they approve major cuts in key programs. Moreover, the Senate committee is less inclined than its House counterpart to support budget reductions.

The members of the Appropriations Committees do not operate in a vacuum. They are influenced by the goals and expectations of their colleagues, who have definite views on the appropriate role of these committees. Should the Appropriations Committees violate the wishes of their colleagues, they are likely to face institutional sanctions by the full membership. It is rare for the House or Senate to exact such sanctions; this perhaps attests to the satisfaction of the two houses with the actions of the committees.

Authorization Bill   Legislation that approves a program, articulates its goal, and establishes a monetary ceiling for funding the program. Authorization is the first of the two-part budgetary process, as outlined in the Congressional Budget and Impoundment Control Act of 1974. The authorization committees review measures that authorize the continuation of government agencies and programs and also determine the appropriate level of funding. They establish funding ceilings which prescribe the maximum amounts the appropriations committees can approve. The appropriations committees, however, are not required to approve the stated maximums. Agencies typically request far more than they receive, knowing that they will receive less than they request. All standing committees are designated as authorization committees, with the exception of the appropriations, budget, and housekeeping committees. *See also* APPROPRIATION BILL, p. 257; STANDING (OR PERMANENT) COMMITTEE, p. 250.

Significance Authorization bills establish the rules governing federal agencies, propose appropriate funding levels, and are forwarded to the president for either a signature or a veto. No federal agency may receive public monies unless and until Congress approves the necessary authorization. Authorizations may be annual, multi-year, or permanent, although recent trends indicate a penchant for annual authorizations. This type of authorization permits the Congress to more carefully monitor the performance of the agencies in question, thus enabling the Congress to better discharge its oversight functions. For example, the Congress, under the 1971 Foreign Assistance Act, voted to place the Department of State and the United States Information Agency under annual authorization. This move reflected the Congress's desire to make these entities more accountable and responsible to the people's elected representatives. Many members believe that the federal agencies have grown so large and complex that it is virtually impossible to assess their effectiveness. This is particularly evident at budget time, when Congress must review the requests of the various agencies.

Most members have scant understanding of the agencies in question and are often unable to evaluate their requests intelligently. The problem is complicated by multi-year authorizations, when Congress is required to approve funds for agencies for extended periods of time. Members often vote blindly, or with great dispatch, on massive budgetary requests—often not understanding what they are approving. This places Congress in the position of giving rubber-stamp approval to agency requests that may or may not reflect the will of Congress. To reverse this trend, Congress more and more often requires the agencies to justify their requests and show tangible evidence that their goals have been met. An agency which cannot provide such evidence may find Congress not only unwilling to approve additional appropriations, but unwilling to approve the existing funding level.

Bill A legislative proposal to effect a new law or alter or abolish an existing one. Bills take many forms: general or special, public or private. Once a bill is approved by both houses (in identical language) and signed by the president (or enacted by overriding a veto), it becomes law. Bills may only be introduced by members of Congress. In the House, members introduce a bill by delivering it to the clerk or by placing it in a box called a hopper. No formal recognition is required to introduce a bill.

This process is different in the Senate, where members introduce bills during what is referred to as the morning hour. Once a bill is introduced, it is numbered (in order of introduction), referred to the appropriate committee by the parliamentarian, labeled with the sponsor's name, and forwarded to the General Printing Office, where copies are printed and distributed for study and action. Members may introduce as many bills on as many subjects as they wish. Bills may bear the names of several sponsors or cosponsors.

Thousands of bills are introduced each session of Congress, although only a small percentage of these reach the floor, and an even smaller percentage become law. Those bills that fail in committee die with the congressional session they were introduced in and must be reintroduced in the following session in order to be considered. Once a bill has been approved by the appropriate committee, it is sent to the floor, where it must be voted on. If passed, it is forwarded to the other body for consideration. If it wins approval there, the bill is sent to the president to be signed into law. (Refer to the Appendix, Figure 10 for a diagram of how a bill becomes law.) *See also* COMMITTEE SYSTEM, p. 238; GOVERNMENT PRINTING OFFICE, p. 315; MORNING HOUR, p. 280; PRIVATE BILL, p. 285; PUBLIC BILL, p. 287.

Significance   Bills vary in their importance and impact. Some bills receive serious consideration, while others fail to elicit interest or support. Obviously, the Congress cannot treat all bills similarly. Whether or not a bill is seriously considered depends on many factors, among them (1) the nature of the bill; (2) the groups affected by the bill; (3) the influence of the bill's sponsor(s); (4) the cost of the bill to the taxpayers; (5) the impact of the bill on members' states or districts; (6) the degree of support the bill enjoys with the leadership, president, and executive agencies; (7) the level of public interest in the bill; (8) the extent to which the bill departs from existing policies and practices; (9) the attitudes and actions of influential individuals and groups regarding the bill; and (10) the intrinsic merits of the bill.

Since most bills are doomed to the legislative graveyard, it is necessary for a bill's supporters to lay the groundwork for a favorable outcome. Bills are not passed on their merits alone. A great many good bills are introduced each session of Congress. Success lies in building a solid base of support for the bill, attracting colleagues, party leadership, affected groups, the president, government agencies, and the general public. This support must be manufactured and nourished. Members must believe that it is in their interest—and that of their constituents—to support a bill. It is rare that members will go out on a limb to support a bill that does not enhance their political standing. The bills that pass are those that promise the greatest dividends for the greatest number of members.

Calendar of Business (General Orders)   The Senate calendar to which all legislation is assigned. The Calendar of Business is one of two Senate calendars; the other is the Executive Calendar, which lists nominations and treaties. Generally, bills are introduced in the Senate in one of two ways (1) by making a motion to call up a bill on the calendar, to be followed by a vote; or (2) by unanimous consent. Once a bill has been reported by a committee, it is assigned to the appropriate calendar to await action by the majority leadership. Scheduling takes place following consultation between the majority and minority leaders and other pertinent senators. The Senate rules permit bills to be shifted from the Executive Calendar to the Calendar of Business, following the requisite consultation.

The Calendar of Business lists a wide variety of bills: public, private, appropriations, taxation, authorizations. Bills are listed in chronological order, based on their reporting date. Once a bill is listed on the Calendar of Business, any senator may move to have it removed from the calendar for general discussion and debate. If this action is backed by the leadership, as well as a majority of the Senate, the measure will, in all likelihood, reach the floor. Conversely, a senator may propose a blocked measure as a nongermane amendment to almost any bill. Finally, a senator may threaten a filibuster or an objection to all unanimous consent requests until the desired measure is scheduled for floor consideration. *See also* BILL, p. 259; FILIBUSTER, p. 274; GERMANE AMENDMENT, p. 276; MORNING HOUR, p. 280; UNANIMOUS CONSENT AGREEMENT, p. 303.

Significance   The Calendar of Business ensures the orderly consideration of legislation. The Senate, unlike the House, has greater flexibility when it comes to calling up bills to the floor; no committee like the House Rules Committee exists in the Senate. The rules permit any senator, at almost any time, to offer a motion to consider a bill. A motion of this kind requires a simple majority to pass. The motion may be made during the morning hour, at which point no debate is allowed, or at other times, when it is subject to debate—and a possible filibuster. Most routine bills receive swift approval; controversial bills, however, may be defeated at this stage of the proceedings.

The authority for scheduling floor action falls on the majority leader, who, with the assistance of the majority Policy Committee and after consultation with the minority leader, decides which measures will be considered. The leadership attempts to satisfy the wishes of individual senators, on whose support they depend, so they rarely block important measures from reaching the floor. The calendar is more than a record-keeping device; it has profound policy implications. It governs, to a large extent, what legislation will be considered and when. With the thousands of bills introduced each session, the various calendars are instrumental in ensuring equity and order. Members must be able to predict when legislation will be called up, so they can study bills that they will be asked to vote on. Their time is extremely limited and must be employed efficiently. A calendar affords both sides—proponents and opponents—an opportunity to marshall their forces and prepare for the battle ahead.

Calendar Wednesday   A method for ordering a bill to the House floor that has been stalled by the Rules Committee. Under the Calendar Wednesday procedure, committees may be called in alphabetical order for the express purpose of bringing bills from the House or Union Calendars (with the exception of privileged bills) to the floor. House rules limit debate to two hours. The Committee of the Whole considers bills called up from the Union Calendar and debates amendments under the five-minute rule. Measures considered under the Calendar Wednesday procedure must be completed in the same legislative day. As a result, the bill is subject to dilatory action by its opponents. This rule is disregarded during the last two weeks of the legislative session and may be forsaken by a two-thirds vote. The Calendar Wednesday procedure was adopted in 1909 to weaken the scheduling power of Speaker Joseph G. Cannon (R-Ill.), who often wielded his power in dictatorial ways. *See also* COMMITTEE OF THE WHOLE, p. 236; FIVE-MINUTE RULE, p. 275.

Significance   Calendar Wednesday is a cumbersome procedure, owing to several intrinsic limitations. First, since the committees must be called in alphabetical order, those at the bottom of the list may have to wait for upwards of fifteen to twenty weeks. Second, opponents of a bill may resort to a variety of delay tactics, using the same-day requirement to kill the bill. Third, a committee may only call up one bill, thus having to wait until all committees have been called before calling up other measures. Fourth, the chairman is the only person authorized to call up a bill reported by the committee. During the period from 1950 to 1974, the Calendar Wednesday procedure was used successfully only twice: the Fair Employment Practices Act (1950) and the Area Redevelopment Act (1960). The procedure is quite uncommon and represents a significant departure from accepted custom. It has, however, been used to call up controversial bills stalled in the Rules Committee. Its limitations, though, make it difficult to employ. For instance, it was used to bring up several important pieces of civil rights legislation. However, since the committees are called alphabetically—and committee chairmen can only call up one bill at a time—a chairman predisposed against a bill could, if he wished, call up another measure, thus delaying consideration of the more controversial bill.

Central to the smooth operation of the House is the Rules Committee. Although the Rules Committee generally works closely with the majority leadership, it can and occasionally does act in a capricious manner, thwarting what appears to be majority will. In recognition of this fact, the House, on more than one occasion, has sought to curb the committee's powers, but it is quite unlikely that the House will approve additional limitations. Indeed, it has generally opposed attempts to bypass the Rules Committee and weaken the powers of committee chairmen. Still, Calendar Wednesday is a procedural tool that, if used with caution and restraint, can enhance the movement toward democratic reform in the House.

Clean Bill   A measure that has been significantly reworked by a committee so as to bear little resemblance to the original version. A clean bill replaces the original version. Once a clean bill has been drafted, it is assigned a new number and reported to the chamber for action. If the new bill is not substantially different from the original version, the measure is reported with amendments. When a bill is reported to the floor, the Senate or House must approve, modify, or reject the amendments proposed by the committee before the bill can be voted on. One advantage of a clean bill is that the various amendments offered by the committee do not have to be individually approved but can be approved en masse. A clean bill is a combination of what remains of the original measure and any amendments that have been added as a result of committee action. *See also* AMENDMENT, p. 256; BILL, p. 259; COMMITTEE SYSTEM, p. 238.

Significance   Clean bills are often significantly different in content and language, intent and impact, than the original measure. Often a clean bill represents a watered-down version of the original measure. The nature of politics is, of course, the art of compromise. Committees must not only report out bills that they support, but they must report out bills that will win the support of the full body. Most committees are reluctant to recommend measures that stand little chance on the floor. Most members agree that some bill is better than no bill at all; a bill's supporters must be willing to make concessions if they hope to win sufficient votes for passage. To make it politically palatable to a majority of members, a committee will often rewrite a bill. Whether or not a bill is drastically rewritten depends, in large part, on the attitude of the chairman. If the chairman enthusiastically supports the bill as originally written, it is unlikely that the measure will be significantly altered. If, however, the bill is opposed by the chairman or a large cross-section of the committee, it is highly probable that the measure will undergo major alteration. If the chairman or committee members are undecided or indifferent to the bill, then the outcome will largely depend on the views of others, such as key committee members, the entire membership, special interest groups, executive departments, and the general public.

Closed Door Session   A meeting that is closed to the public and the press. Closed door sessions were commonplace prior to 1973, at which time the House approved new rules designed to reduce the number of these meetings. The rules provided that all committee, subcommittee, and other official meetings be open, unless a majority of the committee in open session voted to close them. At that time, hearings were open to the public and the press, but most mark-up sessions were closed. The new rules permitted interested citizens and, more importantly, the press to view these sessions, observe the conduct of the members, and monitor their votes on important amendments and other legislative matters.

In 1975 the House voted to open up the process further by requiring that conference committee sessions be open. The Senate voted likewise later that year. That same year the Senate followed the House's lead and voted to require all standing, select, or special committees or subcommittees to meet in open session, including bill-drafting sessions. However, committee members could vote (by majority action) to close the meeting, but only on the limited grounds specified in the new rule. The Senate adopted more stringent requirements than the House, designating a limited number of acceptable reasons for meeting in closed door session. Also that year, the Senate joined the House and voted to open conference committee sessions. *See also* CONFERENCE COMMITTEE, p. 240; MARK-UP SESSION, p. 279.

Significance   Closed door sessions were the rule in the Senate when the nation was founded. Embracing the practice of the Congress of the Confederation, the Senate originally convened behind closed doors. In 1790 several state legislatures petitioned the Senate to meet in open session, as a means of ensuring greater accountability and responsibility. The Senate refused, voting down the request in four successive years. Finally, in 1794, the Senate voted to open its doors, upon completion of the galleries. This move admitted the public but did not include the press, who were finally admitted in 1802, after the Capitol had moved to Washington, D.C. Today, most but not all meetings are open to the public and the press.

Discussions of classified or top secret information are held in closed door sessions. In these cases, the committee chairman requests the public, press, and most Senate aides to leave the chamber and galleries. The Senate will, on such occasions, later release a censored transcript of the proceedings. The Congress recognizes that, as the people's representatives, they are obligated to conduct the nation's business in the open. The percentage of closed door meetings has steadily declined. In 1954, for example, 41 percent of all committee meetings were held behind closed doors. This percentage remained constant through 1972 and then dropped to 16 percent in 1973. Closed door sessions have become even less common since then, with less than 5 percent conducted behind closed doors in 1980.

Cloture (Rule 22)   A device used in the Senate to end a filibuster, other than by unanimous consent. Cloture requires that three-fifths of the full Senate (60 votes if there are no vacancies) vote in the affirmative in order to terminate debate. For most of its history, the Senate required that two-thirds of the members present and voting were needed to invoke cloture. The rules were changed in 1975 to make prolonged debate less likely. The process works as follows: a cloture motion must be filed by sixteen senators, then a cloture vote is scheduled two days after the motion has been filed. Once the motion is adopted, each senator is allotted one hour for debate purposes on the bill and on all amendments and motions pertaining to it. At this point, no new amendments may be introduced. The only amendments that may be considered are those that were introduced prior to cloture. Amendments held not to be germane to the bill, as well as motions aimed at delaying final action, are out of order. The three-fifths rule applies expressly to routine Senate business. Where the measure under consideration would result in a change in the standing rules of the Senate, a two-thirds vote of members present and voting is required. There is no limit on the number of possible cloture attempts. *See also* DEBATE, p. 267; FILIBUSTER, p. 274.

Significance   Cloture reflects the Senate's impatience with prolonged, drawn-out debate, a realization that unlimited debate could paralyze the Senate and render it incapable of conducting the nation's affairs. Recent years have witnessed a sizable increase in the number of cloture attempts. Correspondingly, there has been a marked increase in the number of successful cloture votes. In the decade following its adoption in 1917, cloture was used successfully on several occasions. However, from 1928 through 1961 there were few cloture attempts, none of which succeeded. This changed in the 1960s, when the Senate voted to shut off filibusters on three major civil rights bills. The number of cloture votes increased dramatically in the 1970s. From 1971 through 1974, more cloture votes were held than during the entire period from 1919 to 1970, with nearly one-half proving successful.

Cloture has been used to pass a number of important pieces of legislation, including the Voting Rights Act (1965); Open Housing (1968); the Military Draft (1971); Equal Job Opportunity (1972); United States-Soviet Arms Pact (1972); Public Campaign Financing (1974); Common Site Picketing (1975); and New York City Aid (1975). Cloture is invoked to block a threatened filibuster or stop one that is underway. Clearly, cloture is a vital parliamentary tool: one that is used to block small groups of senators from frustrating the majority will and jeopardizing the institutional consensus. Without such a procedure, the Senate would find it impossible to resolve controversial matters or take action on the large number of bills before it.

Consent Calendar   The House calendar on which noncontroversial bills are placed. The Consent Calendar lists measures which are deemed routine, such as the appointment of a staff assistant for the chief justice of the Supreme Court. Bills placed on this calendar are called on the first and third Mondays of each month. Following the reading of the *Journal*, the Speaker requests the clerk to call those bills that have appeared on the Consent Calendar for three legislative days, by order of their appearance. When a measure is called the first time, any member may raise an objection. If an objection is made, the bill is placed back on the Consent Calendar to be read the next day that the calendar is called. If there are three objections the second time, the bill is taken off the Consent Calendar. If there are less than three objections, the measure is passed by unanimous consent without debate. Amendments are generally limited to those recommended by the reporting committee. *See also* READINGS OF BILLS, p. 289.

Significance   The Consent Calendar serves a variety of purposes, chiefly to expedite the flow of legislation. A large percentage of bills introduced in Congress are of a routine nature, not warranting prolonged floor debate. For such measures, the Consent Calendar is an effective vehicle. The Consent Calendar is supervised by six official objectors, evenly divided among the two major parties. They are appointed by the majority and minority leaders and function as their unofficial spokespersons. The objectors' role is to monitor legislation placed on the Consent Calendar, so as to ensure that these measures satisfy the rules of the House. For example, bills may be removed from the Consent Calendar if they call for expenditures in excess of $1 million, if they constitute a significant departure from existing domestic or international policy, or if they are substantive in nature or too controversial. The authors of such bills are encouraged to contact potential objectors at least twenty-four hours prior to Consent day, in order to resolve any differences which may exist. Members who fail to follow this requirement, or who place upon the Consent Calendar bills which are clearly inappropriate, are likely to jeopardize their passage and perhaps incur the enmity of their colleagues. The authors of bills typically sound out their colleagues and attempt to anticipate any likely objections. Most members are eager to avoid a confrontation and will go to great lengths to satisfy whatever objections may exist.

Debate   Formal discussion among senators and representatives on the floors of the Senate and House. Debate differs markedly in the two chambers. The Senate is casual in its rules, and by tradition it adheres to free and unlimited debate. The House is more rigid in limiting debate, as it seeks to keep the body moving at a forward pace. House debate on a bill begins with debate on the rule, which may be discussed for up to one hour. The House resolves into the Committee of the Whole for general debate upon the entire bill. Unless otherwise stipulated, a bill may be debated for one hour by each member. Under suspension of the rules, debate is limited to forty minutes; under the five-minute rule, five minutes. Debate may be ended by a motion to move the "previous question." Senate debate, once restricted by the "previous question" procedure, no longer is subject to that constraint. The rule of unlimited debate in the Senate makes possible the filibuster, an obstructionist technique to prevent passage of a bill. *See also* COMMITTEE OF THE WHOLE, p. 236; DILATORY MOTION, p. 268; FIVE-MINUTE RULE, p. 275; SUSPENSION OF RULES, p. 299.

Significance   Debate in the two chambers takes on various forms and serves different purposes throughout the legislative process. General debate in the House is characterized by formal speeches rather than a brisk interchange between members. This allows members to send signals to undecided members, as well as messages to constituents and interest groups. The text of the debate becomes public record, available to executive departments, agencies, and the courts. Debate is a mechanism whereby members can communicate with, influence, and often obstruct each other. The flow of House debate is directed by the floor manager, who has priority recognition from the chair during debate. In the Senate, debate on a bill usually begins with prepared speeches by the floor managers. The text may be delivered to only a handful of other members or inserted directly into the *Congressional Record* without ever being delivered.

While Senate debate is often regarded as dull or lackluster, exciting debates may flare up during consideration of critical issues of national concern. Once the communicative function of debate has been served, it may then be used as a means of delaying or thwarting a vote. A bill may be subject to filibuster on the motion to take up the legislation, as well as during consideration of the bill. Whether this curtailment of debate is a positive or negative characteristic of the Senate is debatable in itself. The House is subject to its own brand of filibustering: dilatory quorum calls and roll-call votes designed to stall the proceedings. Overall, debate is a strategic device above and beyond the simple talk on the floor. The decision to speak before one's colleagues is subject to legislative norms of conduct and the political exigencies of future campaigns. Members take great care to manicure their remarks before they become part of the public record; the *Congressional Record* bears witness to the members' control over the text of debates and proceedings.

Dilatory Motion   An action, based on an alleged technical violation, made for the express purpose of squandering time and postponing action. Dilatory motions are prohibited by the rules, but their enforcement depends on the presiding officer, who may or may not entertain such motions. Key dilatory motions include (1) extensive quorum calls; (2) the reading of amendments; (3) the introduction of nongermane amendments; and (4) the use of the filibuster or extended debate. In any legislative battle, timing is of critical importance; dilatory motions are aimed at forestalling action and preventing a vote.

Motions of this type may be made at several points in the legislative process. The reading stage, for example, is a propitious time to employ such tactics. Members may also object to a unanimous consent request that would eliminate the reading of sections, titles, or amendments. A bill's opponents may draft lengthy amendments, not because they stand a serious chance of passage, but because they may impede business. These tactics are used sparingly by members; they invite reprisals by others who frown upon their use. Legislation can be blocked in numerous ways. Members who are determined to prevent a vote can request roll calls on amendments of an insignificant nature. One of the most common dilatory tactics is the quorum call. Repeated quorum calls can result in long delays and postpone action for an indefinite period of time. The Senate, with its tradition of unlimited debate, permits members to filibuster. *See also* FILIBUSTER, p. 274; GERMANE AMENDMENT, p. 276; MARK-UP SESSION, p. 279; QUORUM, p. 287; ROLL-CALL VOTE, p. 293; UNANIMOUS CONSENT AGREEMENT, p. 303.

Significance   Dilatory motions are frequent and effective. However, controversy exists over what constitutes such a motion. For example, there is often disagreement over whether a motion is intentionally dilatory or whether it is germane in nature. Dilatory motions are often used with masterful effectiveness. On other occasions, they are counterproductive and produce negative repercussions. Members must weigh the short-term and long-term consequences before employing such motions. For example, during a 1977 House debate on amendments to the Clean Air Act, Congressman Henry A. Waxman (D-Calif.) raised repeated objections to requests that the sections of the bill be considered as read, arguing that reading was essential "because the chairman of the subcommittee (that considered the bill) is not here right at the moment...." In response to this action, Representative Gene Snyder (R-Ky.) opined: "There is not anything we can do about prolonging the reading of the [Clean Air Act], but when other important bills come up requiring prompt action, other members can object to dispensing with the reading and can require that they be read." This threat or potential threat encourages members to be reasonable and act with restraint; they know that their actions can and will be used against them in the future. While members may sympathize with a colleague's objections, they generally take the view that dilatory motions serve to undermine majority rule, bring the institution into disfavor, and encourage small minorities to extort questionable concessions from the majority.

Discharge Rule   An action that relieves a committee of jurisdiction over a matter falling within its purview. Discharge is an uncommon procedure, particularly in the Senate, where it has occurred only fourteen times in the history of that body, most recently in 1964. The practice is more common in the House, although sufficiently rare as to be noteworthy. The rules of the House state that if a standing committee does not report a bill within thirty days after referral, any member may file a discharge motion. This is accomplished through a discharge petition, which requires the signatures of a majority of the House (218 members). Once the required signatures have been collected, there is a mandatory seven-day waiting period. Then, on the second and fourth day of each month (except during the last six days of a session), any member who has signed the petition may make a motion to report the bill. Debate is limited to twenty minutes. If the motion is adopted, the bill in question will receive prompt consideration.

The procedure is slightly different as it relates to the Rules Committee. If the committee fails to report the bill in seven days, any member may move to discharge the committee from further action. In the case of a noncontroversial measure, the committee may be discharged upon unanimous consent of the House, thereby precluding the need for a petition. In the Senate, this procedure is referred to as a discharge motion. This is a special motion that any senator may make to relieve a committee of a bill. The motion is treated in much the same manner as other Senate business, and it is subject to the approval or disapproval of the membership. *See also* COMMITTEE SYSTEM, p. 238; STANDING (OR PERMANENT) COMMITTEE, p. 250.

Significance   Discharge is a difficult and complex procedure, one that is rarely employed, and then only in exceptional cases. Congress believes that discharge procedures undermine the committee system and weaken institutional stability. The leadership can prevent such motions by several means—and they will do so if the motions threaten to disrupt the institution or produce legislation of a questionable nature. There are times, however, when a committee refuses to acquiesce to the will of the leadership and/or a majority of the membership. In such cases, procedures exist whereby a committee may be discharged from further consideration of the bill. The procedures used in these instances depend on the type of legislation involved. These devices are difficult to execute, but if the House is in agreement, it will not hesitate to resort to the discharge. Still, the House is reluctant to exercise the discharge rule, as the Rules Committee plays a pivotal role in maintaining institutional stability. When the committee has acted unreasonably or capriciously, the House leadership has taken steps necessary to discharge the committee. As a result of past actions, the House has voted to curb some of the powers of the Rules Committee. In recent years, however, the House has been reluctant to press for further reforms, perhaps owing to the increased responsiveness of committees and the democratization of procedures.

Electronic Voting   A system that electronically tallies and records members' votes. Electronic voting was first authorized by the 1970 Legislative Reorganization Act and took effect in 1973. To vote, members insert their personalized card (similar in size to a credit card) into one of the more than forty voting stations throughout the House floor and press one of three buttons: Yes, Nay, or Present. Votes are displayed on panels above the Speaker's rostrum and on the other House walls. This system is also used to establish whether or not a quorum is present. Should the system fail, members vote by traditional means. Members have fifteen minutes to respond to quorum calls or vote on legislation before the House. When a series of votes are called for (where several bills are brought up under the suspension of the rules provision), members are given only five minutes in which to vote. The leadership monitors the vote by watching the consoles which are positioned on the majority and minority sides of the House chamber. *See also* QUORUM, p. 287; ROLL-CALL VOTE, p. 293; SUSPENSION OF RULES, p. 299.

Significance   Electronic voting has had a significant impact—both positive and negative—on House proceedings. Clearly, this procedure has reduced the amount of time necessary to vote, thus affording members additional time for other matters. On the other hand, it has also increased the number of recorded votes taken each session. This has resulted in various scheduling conflicts and forced members to excuse themselves from committee meetings and other activities in order to vote. It is not uncommon to hear members bemoan the increasing number of unnecessary or frivolous recorded votes on trivial matters. Other members disagree, arguing that electronic voting enables them to improve their attendance records simply by requesting recorded votes on innocuous matters. The floor managers are particularly strident in their criticism of the system: not so much of electronic voting, but of the burgeoning number of recorded votes. This method of voting has decreased the time necessary to vote from thirty minutes to fifteen minutes. This means that the floor managers have one-half the time to coordinate their efforts and organize their forces. This problem is compounded by the fact that members can slip into the chamber, insert their card in the voting machine, and exit quickly without being noticed by the floor managers. To lessen the problem, both sides station monitors at the doors, who provide information to the members and notify the leadership of any problems that might ensue.

Still, problems persist. For example, the reduction in time has meant that floor leaders are less able to analyze the vote, consider alternative proposals, contact key members, or buttonhole disappearing colleagues. This places an additional burden on the floor managers, who must now spend more time on these matters, prior to floor action, contacting, informing, and convincing party members to support the leadership's position. Although not easy, and certainly more time-consuming, the problems attendant with electronic voting are manageable. The system serves a valuable function—notably, reducing the amount of dead time—and affords members increased opportunities to attend to more important matters.

Enacting Clause   The opening phrase of a bill that makes it law, once it is approved by both houses in identical language and signed by the president. The enacting clause begins: "Be it enacted by the Senate and House of Representatives of the United States of America in Congress assembled. . . ." A successful motion to strike the enacting clause kills the measure. Several motions are given preferred status over other floor business, one of which is a motion to strike the enacting clause. The process in both bodies is fairly similar. In the House, for example, a measure is considered rejected if the chamber approves a motion to strike the enacting clause. This motion is relevant at any time during the amending process. As a privileged motion, it must be voted up or down before the House proceeds with further action on the bill. This motion may only be made once, unless the bill is significantly altered by the acceptance of major amendments. The decision rests with the chair, who is empowered to decide whether or not to entertain a point of order against a motion to strike. *See also* AMENDMENT, p. 256; BILL, p. 259; PRIVILEGED LEGISLATION, p. 286.

Significance   The enacting clause is the operative part of a bill. Therefore a motion to strike this clause, particularly where the chamber is sharply divided, is sure to engender interest and excitement. It is employed by a bill's proponents as well as its opponents. If executed wisely, it has great psychological value, as evidenced by a 1974 battle in the House over a hotly debated committee reform bill. Representative Richard Bolling (D-Mo.), the bill's floor manager, stunned his opponents by encouraging them to offer a motion to strike the enacting clause. He hoped that the motion would be so convincingly defeated that it would produce a decided psychological advantage for his side, thus ensuring passage of the bill. Bolling's strategy worked. Representative Joe D. Waggonner (D-La.), a leader of the opposition, was forced to admit that his side simply lacked the votes necessary to approve the motion. Admitting defeat, at least for the moment, he observed: "It might be made at a point in time when we think there is a chance for it to succeed." Surprisingly, a proponent of committee reform, disheartened over the debate, later offered a motion to strike the enacting clause, which was soundly defeated. Most members did not want the measure abruptly killed.

Engrossed Bill/Enrolled Bill   A bill passed by one house (engrossed) or by both houses and signed by their presiding officers (enrolled bill). Engrossment/enrollment describes the status of legislation and its proximity to passage. The lawmaking process differs markedly in the two chambers. In the House, once the amendments have been considered, the question is on engrossment and third reading (by title only) of the bill. This is the stage when members can offer a motion to recommit. If the recommital motion fails, the bill moves to final passage. That vote, which depends on House sentiment, may be followed by a *pro forma* motion to reconsider and then by a motion to lay the motion on the table. The bill can then be said to have been approved by the body. As long as a motion to reconsider is pending, a bill cannot be sent to the Senate. At this point, the bill formally becomes an act, although it is still referred to as a bill. When the engrossed copy of the bill wins House approval, it is certified by the clerk, printed on blue paper, and sent to the Senate for action.

In the case of the Senate, once all amendments have been disposed of, the bill is ready for engrossment and third reading (usually by title only, although if demanded, it must be read in full) and followed by a vote on final passage. A motion to reconsider may be offered by any senator on the winning side, or one who did not vote, within two days of the vote. If adopted without a recorded vote, any senator may make the motion. In fact, a *pro forma* motion to reconsider is usually made and quickly tabled, in order to move to final passage. Recommital motions are seldom employed in the Senate, owing to the increased flexibility of the amending process in that body. Once the bill has been passed by both houses, the original papers are sent to the enrolling clerk of the chamber in which the measure originated. The clerk then prepares an enrolled bill, printed on parchment paper. After the bill has been certified as correct by the Secretary of the Senate or the Clerk of the House (depending on where the measure originated), it is signed first by the Speaker of the House (regardless of where it originated) and then by the President of the Senate. From there it is sent to the president for his signature. *See also* BILL, p. 259; RECOMMITAL MOTION, p. 290.

Significance   Enrollment/engrossment are clear terms to describe a convoluted process. Rarely does the process work as smoothly or harmoniously as that described above. Invariably, problems develop which make passage a complex and drawn-out affair. The legislative process is laden with unforeseen mines that can explode at any given moment, causing injury or death to the bill. This is especially true with bills of a controversial nature. In the end, every bill that passes must go through the process of enrollment/engrossment, guaranteeing that it has received due consideration by both houses. The final bill rarely expresses the exact language or provisions of the chamber where it originated. Both bodies reflect different points of view, constituencies, different ideological perspectives, priorities, and different goals and objectives. For a bill to win approval in both houses, members must be willing to make concessions and compromises if they hope to secure approval. This is not always easy, as the two bodies often have very different views of what the final bill should contain. Still, engrossment/enrollment ensures that a bill will receive ample consideration, that it will embody the creative wisdom of both houses, and that it will reflect a broad consensus. In the end, that is what lawmaking is all about.

Executive Session   A meeting of House and Senate committees, or the entire chambers, that only members of each may attend. Executive sessions are also referred to as closed, or closed-door sessions; the public and the press are barred from attendance. Such sessions have fallen into disuse with the advent of "sunshine" rules adopted in both chambers in the 1970s to open committee meetings to the public. Prior to these reforms, committees were free after hearings to mark up bills in the secrecy of executive sessions. While virtually all doors are now open, there continue to be instances when committee meetings will be closed. In the Senate, for example, matters involving national security, criminal charges, committee staff, trade secrets, or identification of informants justify a closed hearing. *See also* COMMITTEE SYSTEM, p. 238; MARK-UP SESSION, p. 279.

Significance   Executive sessions, whether they are hearings, mark-ups, or conferences, highlight the conflict over Congress's desire for secrecy versus the public's right to know. Advocates of executive sessions contend that such secrecy may encourage a witness to speak more forthrightly, keep the lure of publicity away from the proceedings, and ensure that secretive information not be disclosed. In the Senate, a committee has the option to make its own rules regarding secrecy and thus open or close a session. In the House, all committee meetings are open unless the majority of a committee votes to close the session. Some observers maintain that all executive sessions should be open to the public. Even when a session such as a mark-up is open, some complain that decisions have already been reached by negotiations prior to the meeting. Indeed, if a closed session enhances committee decision making and promotes free and open discussion, there is an argument to be made against disturbing this process. However, if the legislative process is not facilitated by closing a session, if closed sessions are simply a matter of preference or habit, then the argument is weakened. It is difficult to gauge the practical as opposed to the theoretical merits of open versus closed executive sessions. Many open sessions are well-choreographed, nonspontaneous proceedings which provide to the public only that information which the members want them to know. Rather than opening doors, meetings of this kind raise deep and disturbing questions. The dynamics of decision making in Congress are complex and transitory; public access into that shadowy domain, while illuminated by "sunshine" rules, is still in the twilight stage.

Filibuster   A tactic to delay Senate action, used by a minority to frustrate the will of the majority by attempting to talk a bill to death. Filibusters have characterized the Senate since its inception. Senators can filibuster at various points in the legislative process. The filibuster can be used to block bills, amendments, and conference reports. Its strength lies in the Senate rules that provide for unlimited debate. It is one of several devices used to kill a bill; others that can also be used during a filibuster include the extensive use of roll calls, quorum calls, and amendments.

The device itself is very simple. A senator or group of senators have the right to debate a bill as long as they wish, or until the Senate sees fit to shut off debate. The process begins with a member rising and asking to be recognized. The senator may speak for an unlimited period of time—on any subject. When a members tires, he or she may yield the floor to an ally on the bill. The speaker may not sit down or walk off the floor without unanimous consent. The process continues until one of three things occurs: the filibusterers give up, the majority agrees to table the bill, or the Senate votes for cloture. For many years, the filibuster was used by Senate conservatives to block liberal legislation. The record for the longest filibuster belongs to Strom Thurmond (R-S.C.), who spoke for twenty-four hours and eighteen minutes in opposition to the 1957 Civil Rights Act. *See also* AMENDMENT, p. 256; CLOTURE, p. 265; QUORUM, p. 287; ROLL-CALL VOTE, p. 293.

Significance   The filibuster is one of several parliamentary devices used to kill legislation. It reflects the Senate's long-standing pride in individualism and commitment to protecting the rights of a minority, however small. The filibuster has far-reaching implications. The Senate cannot consider other important legislation so long as the filibuster continues. To prevent the Senate from coming to a halt, the rules permit the majority leader to move for action on other less controversial measures while the filibuster is postponed. Opponents of a bill may use the filibuster to accomplish one or more objectives (1) to kill the bill; (2) to win concessions from the majority; or (3) to focus public attention on the bill in question.

Proponents of the filibuster argue that it prevents poor legislation from being passed; it protects the rights of the minority against an unreasonable majority; it enhances discussion and debate; and it dramatizes the issues for the public. Opponents of the filibuster are equally strident in their condemnation. They contend that the filibuster undermines majority rule; brings the Senate into public disfavor; and permits a small group of recalcitrant senators to wring concessions from a determined majority. In the end, support for, or opposition to, the filibuster depends on the bill in question and whether one is for or against it. Increasingly, liberals as well as conservatives have used the filibuster to accomplish their policy objectives, regardless of the arguments for or against.

Five-Minute Rule   A House rule that allows any member to speak for five minutes on any amendment offered in the Committee of the Whole. The rule states: "Any member shall be allowed five minutes to explain any amendment he may offer . . . after which the Member who shall obtain the floor shall be allowed to speak five minutes in opposition to it, and there shall be no further discussion thereon." This procedure permits members to say whatever they wish, as long as it is germane to the bill under consideration. During this period, members often move to "strike the last word" of an amendment. Most major House bills reach the floor after consideration by the Rules Committee, which assigns each bill a rule specifying limits on debate. Once the bill has been granted a rule, the majority leadership schedules the adoption of the rule in the full House. This is considered *pro forma*. Upon passage, a motion is made to resolve the House into the Committee of the Whole. Measures assigned an open rule are subject to amendment and debate. These amendments are governed under the five-minute rule. *See also* COMMITTEE OF THE WHOLE, p. 236; STRIKE THE LAST WORD, p. 297.

Significance   The five-minute rule is designed to facilitate and limit debate. Time limitation rules are extremely important, as they prevent undue delay. Without such limitations, members could speak indefinitely, tying up the House for long periods of time. Despite the five-minute rule, members may, if they wish, debate amendments at length. This is accomplished through the unanimous consent provision, by members yielding their time to one another, and by a motion to "strike the last word" or "to strike the requisite number of words." Technically these are amendments, but, since they are not aimed at altering the bill under consideration, they are allowed. Their purpose is to prolong debate. Despite these maneuvers, debate is limited—and must be—if the institution is to function smoothly and expeditiously. Should the floor manager wish to terminate debate, he or she may make such a motion, requesting that debate cease at a specified time. Motions to limit or close debate are usually approved. Members are well aware of the myriad demands on their time and are not eager to wile away time in needless discussion.

Germane Amendment   An amendment that is relevant to the subject matter of a bill. Germane amendments are those which bear directly on the bill under consideration. In the House, amendments must be germane to the bill at hand, although, occasionally, nongermane amendments may be entertained. The Senate is more prone to accept nongermane amendments, owing to the increased flexibility of their rules. These measures are large in number and far-reaching in scope. The House has steadfastly opposed nongermane amendments, arguing that they undermine the committee process and permit important bills, often of a controversial nature, to be approved with minimal discussion (House rules only permit one hour of debate on conference reports). The majority of House bills are considered under an open rule. This permits germane amendments to be offered from the floor. In granting a rule, the Rules Committee may limit the number of permissible amendments or forbid them altogether. Senate unanimous consent agreements do not limit amendments, except those that expressly prevent nongermane amendments. *See also* AMENDMENT, p. 256; RIDER, p. 292; UNANIMOUS CONSENT AGREEMENT, p. 303.

Significance   Germane amendments are difficult to define and, at times, are sufficiently questionable as to provoke deep controversy. In the House, for example, certain amendments are technically relevant but significantly extend government policy beyond the narrow intent of the measure. These amendments have been increasingly employed by the conservative bloc within the House, which has made masterful use of the limitation rider on appropriation bills. According to congressional analyst Alan Murray, these riders have "forced the full House to vote on politically sensitive issues. Riders clog the appropriations process. They lead to hours and days of debate on non-fiscal matters that make it virtually impossible for Congress to complete action on money bills before the beginning of the government's fiscal year ..." (Murray 1980, 3251).

The use of nongermane amendments has also led to a feud between the House and Senate. In the past, the House was often forced to accept nongermane Senate amendments or else jeopardize passage of the bill, that frequently included many provisions that had originated in the House. This led to a great deal of rancor in the House. For example, in 1970 former Rules Committee Chairman William Colmer (D-Miss.) expressed his frustration this way: "I have chafed for years about the other body violating the rules of this House by placing entirely foreign, extraneous, and nongermane matters in House-passed bills" (Oleszek 1978, 191). The dispute came to a head in the early 1970s, when the House, in approving a rules change, took steps providing for separate votes on the nongermane parts of conference reports. This reduced the number of nongermane Senate amendments to conference reports. House conferees may now request that certain nongermane amendments (that would, regardless, be voted down in the House) be set aside in conference. The new procedures have served to significantly limit the introduction of nongermane amendments on the Senate floor.

Legislative Veto   A procedure allowing either the Senate, the House, or both chambers to review proposed executive branch regulations or actions and reject or alter those that they disagree with. The legislative veto originated in the last days of President Herbert Hoover's administration, as a means to curb the excesses of an "imperial presidency" and a plethora of low-profile regulatory agencies that were thwarting the will of Congress. The legislative veto may take many forms but typically works as follows: Congress authorizes the president to act (for example, to sell arms abroad) while reserving for itself the power to overrule any sale it may not like. For the most part, the legislative veto has served as a trump card, one that Congress could play should the president exceed his constitutional powers. While Congress approved forty-one new provisions in 1980 alone, over the past five years it actually vetoed only thirty-one measures, most of which were minor. In practice, the legislative veto has served to stimulate compromise between the Congress and the president, both of whom recognize the dangers inherent in these actions. *See also* BILL, p. 259.

Significance   The legislative veto was, until recently, a source of constitutional friction. However, in July 1983 the United States Supreme Court, by a 7–2 vote, declared the legislative veto unconstitutional in *Immigration and Naturalization Service* v. *Chadha*. The Court's ruling, considered by many a legal landmark, appeared to strike down veto provisions that Congress had attached to nearly 200 laws. Chief Justice Warren E. Burger, speaking for the majority, wrote: "The veto ... doubtless has been in many respects a convenient shortcut. But it is crystal clear ... that the framers (of the Constitution) ranked other values higher than efficiency." According to Burger, the Constitution requires that all legislative actions must not only pass both houses of Congress, but must also be presented to the president for approval. The difficulty with the legislative veto, maintained Burger, was the lack of the "presentment" procedure. However, Justice Byron White in a strong dissent wrote: "I have not spoken orally in dissent in many years, but this is no ordinary case. It is probably the most important case that the court has handed down in many years." White proceeded to sharply criticize his colleagues for, as he stated, "in one fell swoop," radically altering the constitutional balance between the executive and legislative branches by striking down an instrument that most Americans know little or nothing about: the legislative veto. He went on to observe: "Only within the last half-century has the complexity and size of the federal government's responsibilities grown so that the Congress must rely on the veto to ensure its role as the nation's lawmakers."

The consequences of the Court's ruling remain to be seen. It will probably be several years before the full impact can be gauged. However it will, in all likelihood, alter the way Congress does business and, to an extent, force Congress to write tighter laws. At this point, it is not clear whether the 200 or so statutes themselves—or merely their veto provisions—are unconstitutional. Major laws which could be affected include the War Powers Act of 1973, Congressional Budget and

Impoundment Control Act of 1974, Military Appropriation Authorization Act of 1975, National Emergencies Act of 1976, and Nuclear Nonproliferation Act of 1976. Despite these Court-imposed restraints, Congress has not been rendered helpless. It retains the power of the purse; it can call hearings to scrutinize, probe, and embarrass agency heads; and it can assume greater responsibility in making difficult policy decisions, rather than deferring to administrative rulemakers.

Mark-up Session   A meeting where committee members rewrite portions of a bill, insert new provisions and delete others, wrestle over the bill's language, and arrive at a consensus on the final version of the legislation. Mark-up sessions are dominated by the committee chairman, who is charged with securing approval for the bill on the floor and managing the debate. During the mark-up session the chairman has several duties, including keeping the committee on track, securing unanimous consent on certain key sections, attempting to resolve differences through compromise, and sensing when to expedite or delay action. Indeed, the bill's passage on the floor will largely depend on the chairman's ability to pacify the diverse interests of the committee and avoid a sharp split among the members.

Prior to the reforms of the 1970s, mark-up sessions took place behind closed doors. At the end of the hearings, the chairman would simply announce that the committee would retire into executive session, where they would attempt to work out whatever differences or disagreements existed. The only persons present at these sessions were staff and committee members, and the process was characterized by frank exchanges between the members and a good deal of legislative bargaining. This ended in the 1970s, when the new rules required the House and Senate to hold mark-ups in open sessions, thereby permitting the public, lobbyists, and the press to witness the proceedings. *See also* AMENDMENT, p. 256; COMMITTEE CHAIRMAN, p. 234; EXECUTIVE SESSION, p. 273; FILIBUSTER, p. 274.

Significance   Mark-up sessions underscore the importance of strategy. These sessions provide proponents and opponents of a bill an opportunity to shape its final form and affects its chances for final passage. Opponents, for example, may attempt to add amendments to the bill that would strengthen its provisions but weaken its chances on the floor. Proponents, on the other hand, may offer amendments to weaken the bill in mark-up, knowing that such amendments will make it more palatable to the full body, on whose support the bill depends. Often opponents will offer a plethora of amendments, attempting to make the bill overly complicated or unworkable and hoping to mobilize opposition by the executive branch agencies. They may also resort to filibustering with the intent of forestalling committee action. The success of a bill in mark-up is largely dependent on the willingness of committee members to compromise, to accept less than they may desire in order to arrive at a consensus.

Although mark-up sessions are now held in public, there is still considerable controversy surrounding the process. Veteran members harken back to the days when the committee actually redrafted the bill in mark-up session. Now, they complain, most of the real work is done in advance of the session, with mark-ups merely serving to formalize and legitimize decisions already reached in private discussions. Newer members point out that the present system fosters more open discussion and requires the members to do in public what they may say in private, thereby promoting increased accountability and responsibility.

Morning Hour   The time allocated at the outset of each legislative day in the Senate for the consideration of regular business. The morning hour technically includes the first two hours of a session following an adjournment, as distinguished from a recess. It can be concluded earlier if the morning business has been dispensed with. Typical morning hour business includes: messages from the president; the presentation of petitions and memorials; communications from the heads of departments; messages from the House; speeches inserted in the *Congressional Record*; reports of standing and select committees; brief speeches; and the introduction and referral of bills and resolutions. During the first hour, no motions may be made to consider any bill on the calendar, except by unanimous consent. During the second hour, motions can be made but must be resolved without debate. Senate rules permit committees to meet while the Senate is in the morning hour. *See also* ADJOURNMENT, p. 255; DISCHARGE RULE, p. 269; UNANIMOUS CONSENT AGREEMENT, p. 303.

Significance   The morning hour, although a fixed two-hour period each legislative day, may be restricted or changed by the leadership with the unanimous consent of the Senate. For example, former Majority Leader Mike Mansfield (D-Mont.) once remarked: "There will be no morning hour tomorrow for the conduct of morning business, unless it occurs late in the afternoon." Discharge motions may be made only during the morning hour. This period serves a number of important purposes, chiefly that it expedites matters that require minimal attention at the time and serves to inform the members of matters that will require their attention in the future. It enables the Senate to dispose of routine business without becoming bogged down in endless hours of debate and discussion. It also keeps the members abreast of recent actions and pending legislation. The Senate has before it, at any one time, a significant number of matters that require its prompt attention. It is always running behind schedule, and legislative sessions grow longer with each passing year. Increasingly, the Senate finds it difficult to attend to the myriad matters that fall within its purview, thus requiring it to act with dispatch. This may be appropriate for minor matters but poses severe problems when applied to matters of major importance. The morning hour is an effective vehicle for disposing of regular business, thereby leaving the Senate additional time for more critical issues.

Omnibus Bill   A conglomerate bill containing one or more previously rejected private measures. Omnibus bills include provisions that have been passed over by the House, owing to the opposition of an official objector or any other member. Bills that have been passed over are routinely returned to the House Committee on the Judiciary. The committee will, upon reviewing the measure, decide whether or not it still favors the legislation. If so, it may include one or more of the bill's provisions in another measure, referred to as an omnibus bill. The rule, as originally approved by the House in 1935, provides that on the third Tuesday of each month, after the disposal of business on the Speaker's table that requires reference only, the Speaker may direct the clerk to call the bills and resolutions listed on the private calendar. Preference is given to omnibus bills that contain provisions previously objected to on a call of the private calendar. These bills are read for amendment, paragraph by paragraph; no amendments are permitted except those that strike out or reduce the amounts of money stated or provide limitations. Provisions that are stricken from an omnibus bill may not be reconsidered for the duration of the session in any other omnibus bill. If an omnibus bill is approved, the bill is divided into the individual bills and resolutions that comprise it, and these original bills and resolutions are coupled with any amendments approved by the House (and engrossed, when necessary). It then proceeds through the legislative process as if such bills and resolutions had been adopted by the House separately. The procedure in the Senate closely resembles that of the House. In either body, a single objection to a particular measure within an omnibus bill is sufficient to strike that particular provision. *See also* AMENDMENT, p. 256; BILL, p. 259; PRIVATE BILL, p. 285.

Significance   Omnibus bills reflect the conviction that various desirable measures may have received short shrift, owing to the objection of a single member, and thus deserve another hearing. This rule serves a valuable purpose: it provides the House or Senate an opportunity to vote on a bill that may enjoy widespread support. Since it is relatively easy to defeat a private bill when it is first called, this procedure ensures that the objector embodies the prevailing view of the chamber. Members may object to a private bill for several reasons: (1) it may be philosophically objectionable; (2) it may encroach on their personal turf; (3) it may threaten a political interest in their state or district; (4) it may be ill-advised and/or politically unpopular; (5) it may benefit a particular interest or group; or (6) it may have been introduced by a member who is personally disliked. These reasons may be valid from the viewpoint of a single member but may not be valid from the vantage point of the entire chamber. Omnibus bills afford the members an opportunity to rise above the objections of a single member and act in what they believe is the best interest of the entire nation.

Pair   A "gentlemen's agreement" that members of Congress make to cancel out the effect of absences on recorded votes. Pairing provides that a member who expects to be absent during a vote pairs with another member of the opposite viewpoint, both of whom agree not to vote. Pairing permits two members who share opposite views on the subject to cancel out each other's vote, without actually voting. Pairs are not counted in the vote total, but the members' names are published in the *Congressional Record*, along with their position (if known) had they been present to vote. If the issue at hand requires a two-thirds vote, then a pair requires two members who favor the measure and one who opposes it. There are three types of pairs (1) a general pair (members are listed without any indication as to how they might have voted); (2) a specific pair (indicates how the two absent members would have voted, both for and against); and (3) a live pair (matches two members, one present and one absent). *See also* CLOTURE, p. 265; *CONGRESSIONAL RECORD*, p. 199; FILIBUSTER, p. 276.

Significance   Pairing is permitted in both the Senate and House, either in "live" or "dead" pairs. In a live pair, the member in attendance casts a vote but then withdraws it to vote "present," announcing that he has a live pair with a colleague, and indicating how each would have voted on the issue. In a dead pair, both members are absent for the vote. Their stands are printed after each recorded vote.

Pairing can have an important impact on congressional voting, particularly if the issue is close. This was the case in the debate over an antibusing amendment which occurred in the Ninety-seventh Congress. In that debate, several senators made unsuccessful attempts to end a filibuster led by Senator Lowell P. Weicker, Jr. (R-Conn.). The antibusing forces could marshall only fifty-nine votes—one short of the sixty required to invoke cloture. Senator Claiborne D. Pell (D-R.I.), who objected to filibusters, stated that he would vote for cloture. A supporter of the filibuster approached Pell and convinced him to form a live pair. This union made it possible for the supporter to go on record against cloture, while Pell could claim that he opposed it. However, this marriage of convenience did not affect the vote on cloture. By pairing his vote, Pell failed to provide the necessary sixtieth vote, and the cloture petition was defeated. Pairing serves the institutional objectives of Congress, as well as the personal objectives of the members. Members can avoid having to vote, but claim later that had they been present, they would have voted in a particular way. It also enables members to be absent for crucial votes and yet appear to have played a part in the proceedings.

Pork Barrel   The appropriation of public monies by Congress for local projects, often of questionable importance, in order to improve a member's political standing at home. Pork barrel assumes many forms: federal buildings, dams, military installations, grants, and sewage treatments plants, to list only a few. Most members, regardless of seniority or philosophy, recognize the value of securing pork barrel legislation. Former Representative Michael (Ozzie) Myers (D-Pa.) expressed it this way: "It's a big pie down in Washington. Each member's sent there to bring a piece of that pie back home. And if you go down there and you don't—you come back without milkin' it after a few terms . . . you don't go . . . back." Although bluntly stated, Myers' observation underscores an important political fact: pork barrel is a potent tool for securing reelection. As a result, many members in both houses request committee assignments that will enable them to "bring home the bacon." In the Senate, for example, the main pork barrel committees are Appropriations, Interior, Public Works, and Post Office and Civil Service.

The longer members serve in Congress, the more adept they become at dipping into the pork barrel. Most voters care little whether the project is needed. Regardless of its merits, it is viewed as an economic boon to the state or district. Despite Congress's affinity for pork barrel, there are limits to how much it can spend. Most government outlays are determined by fixed formulas written into the law or by federal agencies that designate project locations and award government contracts. However, in the public works area, where monies are targeted for specific locales, Congress is able to specify the precise location of these projects through legislation. *See also* COMMITTEE SYSTEM, p. 238.

Significance   Pork barrel exists because it serves the political needs of members. It is made possible through legislative logrolling, whereby members support each other's pet projects. Members recognize that their political fortunes will climb if they can deliver projects such as new courthouses, highways, inland waterways, and nuclear plants. It is interesting to note that, despite the 1981 budget-cutting fervor in Congress following the election of President Ronald Reagan, the Congress demonstrated little interest in cutting back on pork. Many of the President's most strident supporters, the same individuals who led a fierce assault on such domestic programs as welfare and food stamps, were apparently quite willing to overlook the waste, fat, and mismanagement associated with pork barrel. When presidents attempt to cut these projects, they are likely to incur the wrath of Congress, eager to seek retribution. This was the case in 1977, when President Jimmy Carter provoked bitter protest with his "hit list" of water projects slated for cancellation. His efforts met with strong opposition in the House and Senate; members chastised him for insensitivity, aloofness, and heartlessness in assaulting this all-American phenomenon known as pork barrel.

Previous Question   A motion that, when adopted, closes debate and forces a vote on the measure under consideration. A motion calling for the previous question serves a variety of purposes, chiefly to limit debate and prevent additional amendments. This motion is applicable in the House but not in the Senate. If the previous question is moved and carried prior to debate on a subject that is debatable, then the rules dictate that forty minutes be set aside for purposes of debate (with each side given twenty minutes to present its case). Once the Committee of the Whole has finished its work, it "rises." At this point, the Speaker resumes the chair, and the chairman of the Committee of the Whole formally presents the amended bill to the full House, stating that the committee has completed its work on the bill. If the previous question has been ordered, which is a routine practice, the House will vote on those amendments reported by the Committee of the Whole. Unless a previous question motion were made, the House could debate the bill for an endless period of time and offer myriad amendments. Members may demand a roll-call vote on any amendment approved by the Committee of the Whole. If no member requests a vote on any amendment, then the House votes on all amendments en masse by a *pro forma* voice vote. Members may not request another vote on an amendment rejected in the Committee of the Whole unless it is part of a motion to recommit. *See also* AMENDMENT, p. 256; COMMITTEE OF THE WHOLE, p. 236; FILIBUSTER, p. 274; RECOMMITAL MOTION, p. 290; SUSPENSION OF RULES, p. 299; UNANIMOUS CONSENT AGREEMENT, p. 303.

Significance   A previous question motion is aimed at reducing the possibility of prolonged debate—a distinct possibility in the Senate, which allows the filibuster. With 435 members in the House (plus four delegates and one resident commissioner), it is necessary for that body to avoid becoming bogged down in interminable debate. Many members relish the opportunity to speak on issues of national and local importance, particularly those issues that affect their constituencies and electoral fortunes. The previous question motion ensures that the House will not fall victim to endless hours of speechmaking that could bring its operation to a grinding halt. This motion is also employed to prevent amendments from being introduced that could cripple or weaken the bill under consideration. It may be used by a bill's supporters or opponents, who may view the possibility of unlimited debate as detrimental to their position. A previous question motion is one of several parliamentary procedures that can be used to hasten the flow of legislative business, among them unanimous consent and suspension of the rules.

Private Bill   A law intended to rectify a particular problem that public laws either created or ignored. Private bills date back to the first Congress. Typically, one to two thousand private bills are introduced each session. These measures have been challenged, both in Congress and in the courts, on constitutional grounds. Proponents contend that such measures are rooted in sound legal principles, notably the First Amendment to the Constitution, which gives individuals the right to petition Congress for a redress of grievances. They also cite: Article I, Section 8, Clause 1, which authorizes Congress to pay the nation's debts; Article I, Section 8, Clause 4, which authorizes Congress "To establish an uniform Rule of Naturalization, and uniform Laws on the subject of Bankruptcies throughout the United States"; and Article I, Section 9, Clause 8, which requires the consent of Congress for acceptance of a gift or title from a foreign state by a government employee.

Opponents counter that private bills are, both in theory and fact, unconstitutional. They maintain that they violate the separation of powers and the equal protection clause; that these bills are, in reality, bills of attainder. The courts have dismissed the latter claims, holding private bills to be constitutional, as employed by Congress. Still, the debate rages on. Private bills are utilized to solve several types of problems, chiefly claims and immigration cases. There are five categories of private bills: (1) private claims cases; (2) immigration and naturalization bills; (3) private bills to avert deportation; (4) nationality bills; and (5) miscellaneous private bills. *See also* PUBLIC BILL, p. 287.

Significance   Private bills have historically proved a thorn in the side of Congress, which has taken several steps to decrease their number and limit their scope. The first significant step in this direction was passage of the Legislative Reorganization Act of 1946, which eliminated three important categories of private bills: those that settle tort claims, those that authorize construction of bridges, and those that correct military records. In each case, the act established alternative means to deal with these matters. In recent years, the Congress has taken additional steps to curtail their use. It has broadened the discretionary authority of federal administrative agencies to handle unusual or difficult problems. It has also established and expanded the jurisdiction of the United States Court of Claims, in order to curb the introduction of private bills. Clearly, many members resent the disproportionate amount of time and effort expended on such matters. There is also a growing realization of the potential for abuse which these measures represent.

Privileged Legislation   Selected legislation that may be called up on the floor once the required waiting period has been satisfied. Privileged legislation consists primarily of "power of the purse" measures originating from the House Appropriations, Ways and Means, and Budget Committees, as well as such other housekeeping committees as the Administration and Rules Committees. Privileged legislation, unlike other legislation, may bypass the Rules Committee and, generally, the Committee of the Whole. House rules stipulate that six standing committees have direct access to the floor for selected measures. The committees and types of bills that qualify for immediate debate include (1) Appropriations (general appropriations bills); (2) Budget (budget resolutions under the Congressional Budget and Impoundment Control Act of 1974); (3) House Administration (printing resolutions and expenditures of the House contingent fund); (4) Rules (rules and the order of business); (5) Standards of Official Conduct (resolutions recommending action with respect to the conduct of a member, officer, or employee of the House); and (6) Ways and Means (revenue-raising bills). *See also* COMMITTEE OF THE WHOLE, p. 236; STANDING (OR PERMANENT) COMMITTEE, p. 250.

Significance   Privileged legislation receives special status in the Senate and House. Scheduling is primarily a party matter in the two houses. In the House, privileged legislation (general and supplemental appropriation bills, conference reports, revenue bills, vetoed bills, and Senate bills with House amendments) can be called up at almost any time on the motion of a member. In the Senate, the procedure varies, with party leaders deciding when such motions will be made. The rules reflect the view that certain legislation—usually bills dealing with money matters—should be able to bypass the bureaucratic maze of the Rules Committee and receive immediate attention. These measures, in the opinion of Congress, are sufficiently different from other legislation that they should be treated as such. Priority matters of this kind can thus be more expeditiously considered and disposed of, thereby ensuring prompt consideration and action. This rule speeds up the legislative machinery and guarantees such matters a timely hearing.

Public Bill   A bill dealing with matters of general concern to the public. Public bills, if approved, become public laws. In the House, public bills are placed on either the Union Calendar or House Calendar for consideration; in the Senate, all major bills are placed on the Calendar of General Orders. Once a public bill has been passed and signed by the president or passed over a veto, it is assigned a number by the archivist of the United States. There are two series of laws, one for public bills and one for private bills. Each is identified by a law number, beginning with the number 1 for each two-year term of Congress and by the Congress in which they were approved; for instance, Public Law 5 approved by the Ninety-sixth Congress becomes PL 96–5. Starting in 1936, the Library of Congress began publishing a *Digest of Public General Bills*. Published five times a year, the *Digest* includes all public bills considered by Congress. If a bill is not included in the *Digest*, it may be considered a private bill. *See also* PRIVATE BILL, p. 285; VETO OVERRIDE, p. 304.

Significance   Public bills are not always easily distinguished from private bills. In the House, the distinction is outlined in *Precedents of the House of Representatives*: "A private bill is a bill for the relief of one or several specified persons, corporations, institutions, etc., and is distinguished from a public bill, which relates to public matters and deals with individuals only by classes." In cases where the distinction is difficult to make, the Speaker of the House may render an opinion. In the Senate, the distinction has been raised on the floor when private-claim amendments were attached to general appropriation bills. Such an amendment is subject to a point of order unless it carries out existing law. Prior to 1969, presidents vetoed more private bills than public bills; for example, President Harry S Truman vetoed 83 public bills and 167 private bills. After 1969, beginning with President Richard M. Nixon, more public bills were vetoed than private bills. Since the time of the Truman administration, Congressional Quarterly has divided presidential vetoes into public bills and private bills. The status of the bill depended on its inclusion in the *Digest of Public General Bills*.

Quorum   The minimum number of members who must be present in order to transact business. The quorum requirement is stated clearly in the Constitution, which specifies that "a majority of each [house] shall constitute a Quorum to do Business. . . ." In the Senate, this means 51 members; in the House, 218. A quorum is 100 in the Committee of the Whole House. Despite the fact that only a simple majority is required, it is often difficult to obtain a quorum. To do so, the leadership must at times resort to lobbying, cajoling, pleading, and maneuvering in order to summon the requisite number. There are many reasons for this, chief of which is that most of the important business of Congress takes place off the floor—in committee, in the members' offices, in meetings with constituents, lobbyists, and organizations. Members are extremely busy. Their time is limited, and they are plagued by numerous responsibilities. Members recognize that most key decisions are made prior to a bill reaching the floor. As a result, they prefer to expend their time and energy in other areas. This is particularly evident when one observes the floor proceedings or attends a committee session. Rarely will there be more than a few dozen members in attendance. It is important, however, that members answer quorum calls, as their lack of attendance will be recorded and reported and, at times, used against them—particularly when it comes time for reelection. *See also* DILATORY MOTION, p. 268.

Significance   Quorum calls serve a number of important functions. Despite their importance, they are disliked and at times difficult to execute. Although at times a quorum may not exist, both chambers presume that a quorum exists and daily business proceeds uninterrupted, until a member challenges the lack of a quorum. When the issue is raised in the Senate, for example, the secretary of the Senate is directed to call the roll. At this point, buzzers sound and bells ring and, if the quorum goes "live," senators drop what they are doing and head to the floor. If they do not, they are recorded as absent. When members arrive, they may only stay long enough to be counted as present before returning to whatever they were doing prior to the call.

Quorum calls play an important part, both positive and negative, in the legislative process. They can either advance or retard the flow of business. Quorum calls are used, at times, as a dilatory tool—to delay a key vote or stall for additional time—in order to influence the outcome of a vote. On other occasions, quorum calls are designed to waste time or frustrate a particular outcome. Most members dislike quorum calls and feel inconvenienced when they are requested. They resent the necessity of breaking away from other more important work, only to come to the floor to hear a speech or vote on an innocuous measure, particularly for repeated quorum calls. Members are discouraged from requesting such calls, but like other rules, these informal understandings are often violated, at times for no apparent reason. Obviously, the public expects—and has a right to expect—their representatives to be present for important votes. After all, it is for that purpose that they were elected. It could be disastrous for the nation if a handful of members could, in the absence of a quorum, conduct the nation's business and make the vital decisions of the day.

Readings of Bills   Recitations of bills by the appropriate clerk in the Senate and House. Readings of bills are designed to ensure that each member is familiar with the measure at hand. Although parliamentary law dictates that a bill be read three times before it may be passed, this procedure is often bypassed. A bill technically has its first reading when it is introduced and printed, by title, in the *Congressional Record*. The second reading occurs when floor consideration begins, where bills are read for amendments. The third reading takes place prior to final passage after action has been completed on amendments. Rarely are bills read in their entirety; unanimous consent agreements usually expedite the procedure. However, readings of bills can be used as dilatory tactics in some instances. *See also* AMENDMENT, p. 256; BILL, p. 259; CONGRESSIONAL RECORD, p. 199; UNANIMOUS CONSENT AGREEMENT, p. 303.

Significance   Readings of bills are governed by House Rule 21 and Senate Rule 14. House rules require a bill or joint resolution to be read three times; verbatim readings are dispensed with by unanimous consent, but a member may delay the proceedings by requesting a full reading of the title or section of a bill. The first reading occurs when the bill is introduced and referred to committee; the bill's number and title are printed in the *Congressional Record*. The second reading occurs in the Committee of the Whole. The Rules Committee determines how bills will be read for amendment, either by title or by section. An amendment must be offered after a section has been read and before the clerk reads the following section. Unanimous consent is required to offer an amendment to a previous section once reading on the succeeding motion begins. The floor manager may request unanimous consent that the entire bill be considered as read, in which case amendments may be offered at any point. During this stage, members may delay the proceedings by objecting to unanimous consent requests to dispense with readings by introducing amendments designed to stall action by being read in their entirety. After action is completed on the amendments, the Speaker announces that "the question is on engrossment and third reading of the bill." The bill is automatically read by title, in accordance with House rules, thus making the question *pro forma*. Prior to a rules change in 1965, a member could demand that the bill be read in full.

In the Senate, bills and resolutions must be read twice, on different days, before they can be referred to committee. This rule is rarely followed, as unanimous consent agreements are used to circumvent it. The rules also dictate the reading of amendments by the Senate clerk, but again, this practice is usually dispensed with, owing to unanimous consent agreements, unless members wish to deliberately delay the proceedings. The third and final reading of the bill is ordered by the presiding officer after the floor manager announces that there are no further amendments. Unlike in the House, a senator may request a full reading of the bill, but this is rarely done. Finally, if any senator objects to the second reading of a House-passed bill, the bill goes directly onto the calendar, bypassing the committee stage.

Recommital Motion   A privileged motion, sanctioned and protected by the rules, to return a bill to the committee that reported it out, for further consideration. A motion to recommit may instruct the committee to report the bill out again with certain amendments or at a future date. Most recommital motions, however, simply call for further study by the reporting committee. If approved, a motion to recommit usually spells the death of the bill. This motion provides the minority party or opponents to the bill one final opportunity to modify or defeat the bill. Recommital motions apply only in the House, not in the Committee of the Whole. A motion to recommit must be made by an opponent to the bill. The Speaker, in recognizing the member, gives preference to the minority party. *See also* COMMITTEE OF THE WHOLE, p. 236; COMMITTEE SYSTEM, p. 238.

Significance   Recommital motions are of two types (1) a simple or straight motion, where the bill is sent back to committee with no instructions, or (2) a motion to recommit with specific instructions to the committee. Prior to 1970, the rules prohibited debate on a recommital motion. This was changed by the Legislative Reorganization Act of 1970, which authorized ten minutes of debate on recommital motions with instructions. If passed, a simple motion to recommit kills the bill, although it may be returned to the House later in the session. Recommital motions with instructions typically require the committee to report "forthwith." If the motion is approved, the committee chairman immediately reports back to the House in accordance with the instructions, and the bill, as modified, is again before the House in a matter of moments. Motions to recommit rarely prove successful, but this depends, to a large extent, on the size of the minority party. In addition, since the minority party is now able to call for recorded votes on matters of special interest, recommital motions have become less important. If the motion to recommit fails, the Speaker moves for final passage on the whole bill. Normally, final passage is by recorded vote. Where the outcome is clear and the members are anxious to dispose of the matter, the bill may be adopted by a voice vote.

Resolution   A measure that deals with rules and procedures or expresses the will of one or both houses on issues of current interest. Resolutions take many forms and serve many functions. A simple resolution, the most common form, deals with matters that fall within the purview of one house. It is not sent to the other body for its approval nor is it signed by the president. These measures are not binding. Joint resolutions (designated H J Res or S J Res), unlike simple resolutions, must be approved by both houses (in identical language) and by the president, and have the force of law. They closely resemble bills but generally concern a single issue or item, for example, an emergency appropriation bill. Joint resolutions are also used as vehicles for proposing constitutional amendments. These require the approval of two-thirds of both houses. They do not require the president's signature but become law after they have been ratified by three-fourths of the states. Concurrent resolutions (designed H Con Res of S Con Res) deal with matters that affect the operations of both chambers, for example, fixing the time of adjournment. They require the approval of both bodies but do not require the signature of the president and do not have the force of law. The president may not veto a concurrent resolution, as it is not "legislative in character and effect." These resolutions are commonly used to make or amend rules binding on both houses. *See also* BILL, p. 259.

Significance   Resolutions are both symbolic and substantive. They deal with institutional matters, as well as policy questions. For example, Congress often uses joint resolutions in the area of foreign affairs. Occasionally, it uses such resolutions to bypass the Senate's two-thirds majority requirement for treaty matters, for example, the annexation of Texas and Hawaii. These resolutions are also used in cases involving limited questions, such as the approval of a single appropriation for a specified purpose. In 1964 Congress approved the Tonkin Gulf Resolution, which gave President Lyndon B. Johnson the authority to take whatever steps were necessary to protect American troops in Southeast Asia. This resolution became the subject of considerable controversy, owing to widespread public disaffection with the Vietnam War and the questionable circumstances under which the resolution was approved. In 1970 Congress conducted a fullscale investigation of the Tonkin Gulf incident and voted to repeal the resolution.

Concurrent resolutions deal with institutional concerns and are not legislative in nature. Still, there is considerable controversy over what matters are legislative and what matters are not. For example, Congress adopted a concurrent resolution in 1937 authorizing President Franklin D. Roosevelt to reorganize the executive branch. This raised congressional eyebrows, as some members questioned whether this action was legislative in character and thus subject to a presidential veto. In the end, it was agreed that it was not legislative, inasmuch as the president, by virtue of signing the legislation, would legitimize the action. This did not end the controversy. Congress has sought to resolve the issue in later reorganization plans by including provisions permitting it to disapprove such plans by a simple resolution of either house.

Rider   A provision tacked onto a popular bill that is not germane to its purpose. A rider's sponsor hopes it will pass because it is attached to a bill that enjoys widespread support. Riders are especially common in the Senate, where nongermane amendments are permitted. The House expressly prohibits such amendments, but the rules are sufficiently vague and/or contradictory as to permit riders. Riders have been used on numerous occasions to win support for controversial measures that stood little chance of passage if introduced on their own. It stands to reason that riders are more apt to slip through if they are tacked onto bills that are extremely popular. This practice makes for interesting, if not strange legislation. For example, the House passed a measure in 1980 which established new nutritional requirements for infant formulas while increasing federal penalties for marijuana trafficking. The bill was made possible by a rider that secured passage of both items. *See also* GERMANE AMENDMENT, p. 276.

Significance   Riders have become increasingly common in Congress, as members wrestle with issues that are both controversial and, at times, quite unpopular. Under the rules, any member may challenge the relevance of an amendment by raising a point of order on which the presiding officer must rule. Although many measures are clearly incidental to a bill's purpose, they are not challenged for a variety of reasons, among them legislative oversight, popular support, or Rules Committee waivers. In the case of appropriations bills, there are two main types of riders: limitation riders and legislative riders. The former restrict the use of funds appropriated by the bill but are considered, for all intent and purposes, germane. As such, they are permissible in both houses. The latter alter existing laws or expand the responsibilities of government agencies. They are forbidden, by and large, in the case of money bills in both bodies. The rules, however, can and are often waived under the unanimous consent provision or by a two-thirds vote of the members.

Despite the fact that riders are more commonplace in the Senate, House members proposed a record high number of riders to appropriation bills in 1980 (67 were offered, with 75 percent adopted). These riders encompassed a wide variety of social goals and regulatory procedures. Riders were proposed to prohibit abortion, exempt the Iranian hostages from income taxes, call a halt to the decennial reapportionment of House seats, and prohibit a withholding tax on interest and dividend income. In recent years—particularly since the election of President Ronald Reagan—House conservatives have instigated such amendments with increasing frequency, relying extensively on the limitation rider on appropriations bills. This procedure has, in the words of political analyst Alan Murray, "forced the full House to vote on politically sensitive issues" (Murray 1980, 3251). This was particularly evident in House debate over the Treasury and Postal Service appropriations bill in 1980. In more than two days of debate, less than one hour was devoted to discussion of money matters; most of the debate focused on a score of controversial riders—measures which would prohibit government purchases of typewriters from communist countries, halt the Internal Revenue Service from revoking the tax-exempt status of private schools designed to avoid integration, and rescind authorization of withholding tax on interest income.

Roll-Call Vote   A system of voting in which each member's vote is separately recorded. Roll-call votes permit members to vote in one of three ways: yes, nay, or present (if they do not wish to vote). Senate members may request a roll-call vote more easily than their counterparts in the House. In both chambers, roll-call votes can be demanded by one-fifth of those present (a minimum of eleven is required). It is uncommon, however, for a senator to be denied a roll-call vote. In the Senate and in committees, the clerk calls the names of the senators, who vote as described above. The roll may be called several times in order to accommodate late members. The process is different in the House, owing to its use of electronic voting. Here, members' votes are displayed above the press gallery situated behind the Speaker's desk. Members simply insert their personalized, plastic identification card into one of the more than forty voting stations located in the chamber and press one of the three buttons. The same system is used to establish quorums. *See also* CONGRESSIONAL RECORD, p. 199; ELECTRONIC VOTING, p. 270; QUORUM, p. 287.

Significance   Roll-call votes, as distinguished from voice votes, have a profound impact on members—who know, after all, that their votes will be recorded and publicized. This system of voting is highly visible; it is difficult, if not impossible, to say one thing and vote another. A southern

Democratic congressman, for example, may be able to support his party's leadership on a pro-union bill at the committee stage, whereas to do so on the floor may be politically hazardous in his home district.

The outcome of most roll-call votes is known in advance and yields few surprises. Predictions made by floor managers and party leaders are generally accurate. Roll-call votes are particularly important when the vote may be close or when members are undecided. In such cases, members may not vote the first time their name is called, preferring instead to assess the possible outcome and determine how other members have voted. This may provide the information necessary to vote when their name is called a second time. Where the outcome is known beforehand, members are more likely to vote on the basis of expediency and personal interest than they might if their votes could affect the final result. Roll-call votes are not only recorded and reported by the clerks of the two houses, but they are printed in the *Congressional Record*. Moreover, Congressional Quarterly, an independent congressional research organization, publishes the members' votes each year and analyzes their records on the basis of such issues as party loyalty. This information is especially useful to scholars, interest groups, and interested citizens who rely on such information for academic and political purposes.

Rule   The conditions under which a bill may be amended, debated, and voted on in the House. Rules comprise four main types: open, closed, modified closed, and waivers of points of order. Most bills are considered under an open rule that permits germane amendments to be offered from the floor, and also prescribes a fixed period for debate before amendments may be proposed. A closed rule, or "gag" rule, prohibits floor amendments, although occasional exceptions are granted to the reporting committee with the approval of the House. This rule is rarely assigned and is viewed as an impediment to the legislative process and a violation of democratic custom. Proponents contend that the closed rule is necessary, particularly in the case of complex legislation and legislation subjected to heavy interest group pressure. The modified closed rule, or complex rule, permits amendments to particular parts of a bill, but not others. All three rules may permit a substitute bill to be considered and/or a waiver on any point of order that may be made against the bill or any of its provisions. *See also* GERMANE AMENDMENT, p. 276; RIDER, p. 292.

Significance   Rules are granted by the House Rules Committee. They have important policy and procedural implications and determine, to a considerable extent, the shape and scope of legislation, as well as its chance for passage. In granting rules, the Rules Committee considers the wishes of the bill's author, as well as that of the House leadership. Most bills are assigned an open rule. This reflects the popular belief that members should have the right to propose relevant amendments that could, if adopted, strengthen the measure. This rule benefits organized minorities who can plead their case on the floor and lobby for votes sufficient to add or delete provisions that reflect their political objectives. The committee, however, grants some bills a closed rule. For example, the Ways and Means Committee typically requests—and receives—a closed rule. Committee members contend that this is particularly necessary in the case of tax legislation, that, because of the complexity of the tax code, should not be subject to amendment. This legislation, they argue, is of such a complex nature that floor amendments would only confuse the issue and further complicate what is already a complicated matter. Closed rules are also granted to package specific proposals, thus requiring the House to vote for or against the entire package. A popular measure that contains unpopular provisions "locked in" under the closed rule, can also ensure passage of unpopular riders.

Special Order   A measure that grants permission to members to speak on a particular subject that is not presently before the House. These measures are normally scheduled for Friday afternoon. Special orders are the province of the Rules Committee, which follows an elaborate process in granting such requests: (1) a request is made by a committee for a special order to debate a bill on either the House or Union Calendars at a particular time under specified conditions; (2) the Rules Committee holds hearings on the request, and committee members testify both for and against the special order; (3) a decision is reached as to whether a special order or rule should be granted and, if so, what it should contain; and (4) the Rules Committee decides among several options in issuing a special order. Obviously, their decision is influenced by the nature of the original request. The possible options include (1) an open rule, setting the time and length of debate and permitting amendments; (2) a closed rule, also setting the time and length of debate but permitting only committee amendments; (3) a modified closed rule, permitting amendments on specified sections of the bill; and (4) waivers of points of order. Any of these rules may permit a substitute bill to be voted on and/or a waiver on any point of order that may be raised against the bill or any of its provisions. *See also* RULE, p. 294.

Significance   Special orders play a pivotal role in the legislative process. New members will often use the allotted time to practice for the actual debate in which they will participate. As one member stated: "Get a special order and have a few of your friends participate with you. Get the feel of being in the well of the House.... Practice in the somewhat stilted language of yielding to other colleagues ... so that when you do get into the real legislative fight it isn't all new" (Tacheron and Udall 1966, 196).

Special orders also permit members to raise issues of national importance and stimulate a meaningful dialogue on the issues involved. In the 1960s, for example, antiwar members used special orders to call attention to the wrongness of American participation in the Vietnam conflict. To initiate the debate, a group of congressmen led by Representatives Benjamin S. Rosenthal (D-N.Y.) and Andrew Jacobs, Jr. (D-Ind.) took a series of special orders aimed at keeping the House in session all night, when they rose to denounce the war. Because they took steps to publicize their move, they ensured that the galleries would be full. Indeed, people were lined up four abreast, waiting to hear the debate. Congressman Wayne Hays (D-Ohio), a hawk on the war issue, requested sufficient quorum calls to break up the session. However, the media, in response to the evening's events, gave full coverage to the views of the antiwar dissidents, as well as Hays, further stimulating public interest and discussion about the war.

Statute   A law passed by Congress. Statutes take two main forms: public laws and private laws. These are numbered consecutively in each session of Congress. Simple, concurrent, and joint resolutions are not considered statutes. A measure passed by one house is called an act. Laws are published three ways: (1) Slip Laws: each law is published separately for immediate reference in the documents room of both houses, or by subscription or purchase from the Superintendent of Documents. The Officer of the Federal Register, General Services Administration, prepares the slip laws, furnishes marginal citations to laws mentioned in the text, and includes historical information on the bill's passage; (2) Statutes at Large: a bound volume of laws is prepared by the General Services Administration for each session of Congress, called the *Statutes at Large of the United States*. Laws are listed in chronological order, coupled with useful reference material on the effect of the statutes on earlier laws and the legislative history of each statute; (3) *United States Code*: this document includes a consolidation and codification of the general and permanent laws arranged according to subject matter. The current status of laws is outlined, with amendments. However, not all the language from the amendments appears in the *United States Code*, as it does in *Statutes at Large*. The Code is prepared by the House Judiciary Committee. New editions are published every six years, with cumulative supplements released after each session of Congress. *See also* BILL, p. 259; PRIVATE BILL, p. 285; PUBLIC BILL, p. 287.

Significance Statutes are laws and, as laws, they must be constitutional. In the end, the courts determine the constitutionality of statutes passed by Congress. They do this by examining legislative intent, revealed by reviewing a statute's legislative history including committee reports, floor debates, and conference reports. If the documents reveal consideration of a problem by Congress, the courts are able to weigh the intent of Congress and thus apply the law to the case before it. However, a court only looks to legislative history if the statute's meaning is unclear. The court must follow certain rules in interpreting the history of a statute. It cannot ignore the words of the law in determining the intent of the law. With the use of unambiguous words, the legislation should speak for itself. Should the Congress disagree with the court's interpretation of a statute, it has a simple alternative: It can enact new legislation clarifying its intent.

Strike the Last Word   A procedure whereby House members are permitted to speak for a stated period on a measure under debate. The motion to strike is a relatively easy device to employ. A member is recognized by the chair by moving to "strike the last word" of the bill or to "strike the requisite number of words" of the bill. The motion is *pro forma*, usually requiring no vote. Although these procedures technically are amendments, their intent is to extend debate, not to alter the bill under consideration. House debate on amendments is limited to five minutes for supporters and five minutes for opponents. However, members may secure additional time by introducing *pro forma* amendments of the kind described above. Unlike the Senate, amendments to House bills must be germane, not only to the bill at hand but also to the specific section to which they are offered. *See also* AMENDMENT, p. 256; BILL, p. 259; FILIBUSTER, p. 274; FIVE-MINUTE RULE, p. 275.

Significance The motion to strike is a procedural device used to expedite the proceedings and minimize the possibility of protracted debate, owing to the size of the House (435 members, plus four delegates and one resident commissioner). During this five-minute period, members are free to express their views, so long as they are pertinent to the measure under consideration. When members move to strike the last word, they are indicating, by and large, that they merely wish to discuss, rather than support or oppose, the amendment being debated. Despite the five-minute limitation, members can, by resorting to this device, extend the time allotted for debate. In essence, the motion to strike is the

House equivalent of the filibuster. By coordinating their efforts, opponents of a bill can speak almost indefinitely. Debate can be stopped by one of two means: when members have exhausted their comments, or when the floor manager, by vote of the House, shuts off debate. The motion to strike guarantees that the members will be able to express their views on the bill or the amendment being discussed. Unlike the Senate, which enjoys the right of unlimited debate, the House must, of necessity, limit such discussion. Obviously, this is a source of frustration for members who wish to speak but cannot because of the five-minute rule. The motion to strike affords these members an opportunity to speak at length on the measure being debated, thereby ensuring adequate discussion of the issues. The House will give considerable rein to members who feel compelled to speak but will, when necessary, enforce the five-minute limitation.

Substitute   An amendment, motion, or entire bill proposed in place of pending business. A substitute, if adopted, kills the original measure by supplanting it. The House first considers committee amendments on the floor. These are subject to further amendments, as are all amendments, up to the second degree. Members may not propose an amendment to an amendment to an amendment, as this would constitute an amendment to the third degree. Although the rules forbid such amendments, it is quite possible for four amendments in the first and second degree to be pending at the same time: an amendment to the bill, an amendment to the amendment, a substitute for the original amendment, and an amendment to the substitute. If the members approve the substitute, the fourth vote technically occurs on the amendment as amended by the substitute. The substitute, if approved, entirely replaces the original.

The process is markedly different in the Senate. Usually the Senate, by unanimous consent, approves all the committee amendments together, especially if they are extensive. It then specifies that the amended bill is to be "considered as the original text for the purpose of further amendment." This facilitates amending the bill on the floor. The rules permit substitute amendments, providing that both the committee-approved version of the bill and the substitute measure are subject to amendment at the same time. Members may propose the text of one bill as a substitute for another. *See also* AMENDMENT, p. 256; CONFERENCE COMMITTEE, p. 240; ENACTING CLAUSE, p. 271.

Significance   Substitutes are commonplace in Congress, as members frequently attempt to kill bills with which they disagree. Whether or not a substitute passes depends on (1) the nature of the substitute; (2) its popularity within and outside Congress; (3) the strength of support that exists; (4) the position of the leadership; (5) the attitudes of special interest groups; and (6) the degree of public interest and pressure. If a substitute enjoys the support of the leadership, as well as bipartisan approval, it is likely to be adopted.

The converse is equally true. Occasionally, a substitute is offered as a compromise and stands a good chance of passing if the proponents of the original version lack sufficient votes for adoption. The leadership will often agree to a substitute, knowing that they simply do not have the votes necessary for passage and believing that, in certain cases, the substitute is preferable to no bill at all. A conference committee has considerable flexibility when one chamber takes a bill from the other and, rather than approving it with amendments, strikes out everything after the enacting clause and inserts an entirely new version of the measure. This is called an "amendment in the nature of a substitute." In such cases, the conference committee can review both versions and actually draft a third version, provided, of course, that it is a germane modification of either the House or Senate bill.

Suspension of Rules   A time-saving procedure to expedite consideration of a bill and bring it to a vote. Suspension of the rules is commonplace in the House, where any member may make such a motion. Once recognized by the Speaker, who is in charge of the suspension procedures, the member states: "I move to suspend the rules and pass the bill. . . ." A two-thirds vote of those present is required for passage. Debate on the bill is limited to forty minutes, and no floor amendments are permitted. If the motion fails to secure the necessary two-thirds vote, the bill may be considered under regular procedures. Prior to 1975, motions to suspend the rules were entertained only on the first and third Mondays of the month (following the call of the Consent Calendar) and during the last six days of the legislative session, when Congress was faced with a large number of bills to be voted on. In 1975 the rules were changed. It was agreed to double the number of days that the suspension motion could be invoked, thereby adding the first and third Tuesdays of the month. The rules were changed again in 1975, over the opposition of many Republicans, to permit the Speaker to entertain such motions every Monday and Tuesday. The Republican minority saw this as a Democratic attempt to hasten legislation through the House. Suspension of the rules is reserved, by and large, for non-controversial measures. Its primary purpose is to speed up the passage of legislation. *See also* AMENDMENT, p. 256; CONSENT CALENDAR, p. 266.

Significance   Suspension of the rules is a potent tool in the hands of a skillful Speaker. This legislative shortcut enables the Speaker to place certain bills on the suspension calendar. This permits the measure to bypass the Rules Committee and go directly to the floor for consideration. At times this procedure is used to circumvent a committee chairman who opposes the bill, thereby minimizing his influence. The Speaker alone decides whether or not to recognize members who wish to offer suspension motions. The Speaker's decision often hinges on the nature of the bill—whether or not it is controversial. For example, in 1976 Congressman Donald M. Fraser (D-Minn.) authored a bill, unanimously approved by the House International Relations Committee, to condemn human rights violations by both the North and South Korean governments. Fraser moved to have the measure considered under the suspension rule. However, Speaker Carl Albert (D-Okla.) refused, contending that the bill was too controversial. On occasion, major legislation is passed under the suspension rule. In 1977, following a particularly inclement winter, President Jimmy Carter requested emergency powers to meet the nation's energy crisis. Following one day of hearings and a day of mark-up by the House Interstate and Foreign Commerce Committee, the House passed the Emergency Natural Gas Act of 1977, which was approved by a substantial majority, under suspension of the rules.

Table a Bill   A motion to either delay or kill a bill. It is not debatable in either chamber. The Senate, however, employs different language than the House. In the Senate the motion is worded to allow a bill to "lie on the table," perhaps to be picked up at a later time. This wording is less final than the House phrase ("lay on the table"), leaving the possibility for future action, if desired. In most cases, once a bill is tabled it is unlikely that it will be revived, at least in its present form, unless sentiment changes. The motion is often used to kill a controversial bill, as opposed to voting on the bill directly. In this case, it can be invoked to mask a policy objective. Theoretically, when members vote to table a bill they are simply voting to postpone immediate consideration of it. In practical terms, this procedural device is often a way of disposing of the matter without having to take a stand on its merits or demerits. *See also* BILL, p. 259.

Significance   Tabling a bill is an important procedural tool, one which can have far-reaching implications. Senate Minority Leader Robert Byrd (D-W.V.) explains it this way: "It obfuscates the issue, and makes possible an explanation by a senator to his constituents, if he wishes to do so, that his vote was not on the merits of the issue. He can claim that he might have voted this way or he might have voted that way, if the Senate had voted up or down on the issue itself. But on a procedural motion, he can state he voted to table the amendment, and he can cite any number of reasons therefore, one of which would be that he did so in order that the Senate would get on with its work or about its business."

This procedure underscores the fact that it is generally more difficult to pass a bill than to defeat it. There are innumerable ways to prevent a measure from becoming law; one is to table the bill. As Minority Leader Byrd points out, this maneuver provides members an opportunity to kill a measure—leaving open the possibility that they may choose to revive it—while not having to defend what may be an unpopular vote. A delay of this kind may afford one side or the other sufficient time to garner the necessary votes when the bill is reintroduced in the future. After all, it is better to postpone action, when you do not have the votes, than to lose the vote.

Teller Vote   A method of voting in the House, where members pass down the center of the aisle to be counted, the yeas first and then the nays. Teller votes, prior to 1971, recorded only vote totals, not individual votes; no record was kept of individual votes. The Legislative Reorganization Act of 1970 provided that teller votes could be recorded if twenty or more members demanded a record vote. This not only stimulated increased citizen awareness of members' voting records but encouraged greater attendance in the Committee of the Whole. Under this procedure, tellers with clerks were appointed to record members' votes. When this procedure was first instituted, members were required to write their names on red and green cards that they handed to the tellers. Once electronic voting was installed in 1973, the recorded vote simply became known as a "recorded vote." In 1979 the House voted to increase the quorum required to demand a recorded vote from twenty to twenty-five, or one-fourth of a quorum, replacing the previous one-fifth requirement. The rule change also applied to teller votes and to recorded votes requested when members are sitting as the House. *See also* COMMITTEE OF THE WHOLE, p. 236; ELECTRONIC VOTING, p. 270; QUORUM, p. 287.

Significance   Teller votes have long been a subject of controversy and debate. Prior to 1971, the rules forbade recorded votes in the Committee of the Whole. This was particularly important, since critical amendments were often decided by the committee. Teller votes were the only means of scrutinizing members' votes in this forum. Proponents of unrecorded votes have argued that this system promotes compromise and protects the public interest. When votes are recorded and subjected to the scrutiny of the press, they contend, members often vote in a manner calculated to enhance their public image or electability with the voters.

Members are more reluctant to vote by their conscience, knowing that their votes will be publicized and discussed.

Although voting was secret, it was not totally secret. Reporters and citizen activists monitored teller votes and reported the results. The press, however, found it difficult to identify many members, particularly those who scurried past the tellers. This led to the rise of gallery spotters—individuals who represented groups and organizations that had a special interest in the issue being considered. Their job was to recognize and record members as they voted. This process was far from perfect; many errors were made and reported in the press. In 1970 the House voted to permit recorded teller votes. This move reflected their disaffection with the spotters, their dislike of the existing system, bipartisan reform efforts, and widespread citizen pressure. The change itself, however, was brought about by the Democratic Study Group (DSG), an ad hoc group composed of about 235 moderate-to-liberal members in 1978 who campaigned hard to generate public support for the change. The DSG proved successful in convincing the House that a recorded teller vote was in the members' best interests, as it would stimulate increased floor attendance and make them less susceptible to the charge of absenteeism.

Twenty-One Day Rule   A procedure that allows the House to bypass the Rules Committee in bringing legislation to the floor. The 21-day rule was promulgated in 1949 but revoked two years later. The procedure, applicable on the second and fourth Monday of each month, was designed to unblock legislation stalled in committee. Under the rule, bills could be brought directly to the floor if the Rules Committee failed to grant clearance within twenty-one calendar days from the date a resolution to call up the bill had been filed by the legislative committee. Authority rested with the Speaker to recognize a member who wished to invoke the rule, thus making it difficult, if not impossible, for a measure to be called up unless it enjoyed the backing of the Speaker.

In 1965 the Congress modified the rule, employing it eight times during the Eighty-ninth Congress. This, too, was short-lived; the membership rescinded the rule in the subsequent Congress. Pressure for the rule dissipated in 1966, following the reelection defeat of Rules Committee Chairman Howard W. Smith (D-Va.), who used his great powers to block legislation which he opposed. The House considered a 31-day rule in 1971, but it was rejected by a vote of 233 to 152. The 21-day rule has been used sparingly in recent times, owing to the reduced authority of the Rules Committee, which was stripped of several of its powers following the political demise of Chairman Smith. House liberals and moderates have shown little interest in the rule, due to the more progressive nature of the committee since the reforms were instituted. *See also* COMMITTEE CHAIRMAN, p. 234; DISCHARGE RULE, p. 269.

Significance   The 21-day rule was an outgrowth of congressional dissatisfaction with the conduct of the House Rules Committee under Chairman Smith from the mid-1930s through the early 1960s. As chairman, Smith used the committee in ways that incensed House liberals and moderates. In response to his authoritarian leadership, the House enacted the 21-day rule. The rule was modified several times but failed to accomplish the results that were achieved with the defeat of Chairman Smith. While in force, it accomplished little in the way of progressive change and met with a slow but sure death. Its lack of use reflects its cumbersome nature and the changing political realities that made it unnecessary.

Unanimous Consent Agreement (Time-Limitation Agreement)

A Senate accord that determines when important bills will be considered and limits debate on amendments, debatable appeals or motions, points of order, and final passage. Unanimous consent agreements are aimed at expediting the flow of legislative business. A major goal of such agreements is to minimize the likelihood of a filibuster. Obviously, this is not always possible. In such cases, members may resort to filibustering, a practice strongly frowned upon. In some cases, the failure to reach agreement may facilitate compromise, as members recognize the negative consequences of prolonged debate. The Senate's unanimous consent agreements correspond to special orders from the House Rules Committee. These agreements waive the rules of their respective bodies, and each requires the approval of the members—in one case by majority vote, in the other by unanimous agreement. The main difference is that whereas senators and staff draft unanimous consent agreements privately, the Rules Committee considers requests for special orders in public session. *See also* DEBATE, p. 267; FILIBUSTER, p. 274; GERMANE AMENDMENT, p. 276.

Significance   Unanimous consent agreements are of two main types: simple and complex. Simple agreements are proposed on the floor by any senator and typically concern routine matters or noncontroversial actions. These are made orally and are, with few exceptions, accepted without objection. For example, members routinely ask permission for aides to accompany them on the floor. Permission is sought to hold committee hearings while the Senate is in session. Simple agreements may also rescind quorum calls, add or delete the names of cosponsors of bills, include various materials in the *Congressional Record*, or limit the time allotted for roll-call votes. Complex agreements are quite different. Typically, they establish guidelines for the consideration of important measures. They are made orally, usually by the leadership, and are recorded in writing once they are agreed to by party leaders and influential senators. They serve many purposes: to decide the order in which bills will be considered; to identify the time when legislation is likely to reach the floor; and to establish rules for debate, including the requirement that amendments be germane to the bill in question. Prior to 1975, unanimous consent agreements were negotiated during floor debate on the measure. They were used, for the most part, to spare the Senate from unnecessary parliamentary wrangles. Today, these agreements are resolved in advance of floor debate, agreed to by the members, and distributed in writing to all senators. Regardless of the type, unanimous consent agreements promote institutional harmony, facilitate legislative action, increase members' knowledge, encourage political accommodation, and expedite floor proceedings.

Veto Override   A mechanism that allows Congress to reverse a presidential veto and enact a bill into law. A veto override requires a two-thirds vote of those present and voting in the Senate and House. The Supreme Court ruled in 1919 that two-thirds of a quorum was sufficient for a successful override, rather than two-thirds of the entire chamber's membership. A quorum must be established by roll-call vote. Each chamber is posed the question: "Shall the bill pass, the objections of the president to be contrary notwithstanding?" If the override vote is passed in one house, the measure is sent to the other house. If the veto is again overridden by a two-thirds vote, the bill becomes law without the president's signature. If the vote fails, the veto is upheld and the bill dies. The vote to override a veto begins with the chamber in which the bill originated, in accordance with the Constitution. The chamber is not obliged to initiate an override attempt. Party leaders may recognize that there is insufficient support to marshal a two-thirds majority to override, and therefore they will not schedule a vote. *See also* QUORUM, p. 287; ROLL-CALL VOTE, p. 293.

Significance   Veto overrides provide a strong link in the legislative-executive relationship. The veto is a powerful presidential weapon; the president can often muster the support of at least one-third of the members of either house on his behalf. The proponents of vetoed legislation are all too cognizant of this advantage and must carefully consider any attempt to override the veto. The threat of a presidential veto may well influence the nature of the legislation passed by the chamber; the president may indicate that if certain sections of a bill are contrary to his wishes, he will veto the bill. The options available are either to compromise or to assess the possibility of an eventual override.

The success record of veto overrides is dismal; from the presidencies of George Washington to Jimmy Carter, only 3 percent of presidential vetoes were overridden. Still, the president must also be aware of the mood of Congress and the public before initiating a veto. A president does not like to have his veto overridden, especially by a Congress of his own party. In 1980 Jimmy Carter was the first president since Harry S Truman to have this occur; first, on a debt-limit bill, that included a section killing an import fee he had imposed on foreign oil and, second, on a bill to increase salaries of doctors at veterans hospitals. If the president thinks that his veto has public support, he will likely exercise the veto, and it will probably be sustained by Congress.

12. Congressional Staffs and Specialized Offices

Administrative Assistant (AA)   A top aide on the personal staff of a member of Congress. The administrative assistant (AA) supervises the member's Washington and district offices, coordinating the member's movements between the two. Considered the most influential member of the staff, the AA serves as the member's alter ego, representing him or her at meetings, social functions, and in negotiations with colleagues, constituents, and lobbyists. In addition to managing the affairs of the member's office, the administrative assistant is often closely involved with the election and reelection campaigns of the member. The authority granted to AAs varies with each member, but the AA is usually regarded as the member's most trusted aide and confidant. *See also* PERSONAL OFFICE STAFF, p. 322; PERSONAL OFFICE SUPPORT STAFF, p. 323.

Significance   The administrative assistant is often a close personal friend of the representative or senator he or she works for and has contributed strongly to the member's election or reelection campaign. Studies show that the average AA holds a bachelor's degree, is approximately forty years of age, and has a background in law, political science, or journalism. Administrative assistants often have worked in state and local politics prior to Capitol Hill employment and are familiar with the member's home district prior to coming to Washington. At election time, the AA will usually spend time in the home district, often working on the campaign staff. In the Washington office, the AA manages the office, hires and fires staff, distributes the workload, determines the office budget, doles out perquisites (including parking and office space), and controls the access of individuals to the member.

An AA must be politically astute, understanding the mechanisms of Congress and its members, while keeping a close eye on the member's constituents and the impact of legislation on them. The administrative assistant's control over office resources, staff, and access to the member, provides the AA with considerable influence over office policy. The administrative assistant must be able to counterbalance the constant demands made on a member's time to ensure maximum efficiency and to make certain that each and every piece of information which leaves the member's office is accurate and appropriate. Experience, political savvy, attention to detail, and a keen eye for organization are the earmarks of a successful AA. Deficiencies in any of these areas may cause embarrassment or trouble for the member.

Caseworker   A member of a congressperson's personal staff that deals with problems involving constituents. The caseworker assists constituents in dealing with executive agencies and federal departments. Constituents may phone, visit, or write to their congressperson requesting help in such matters as locating lost social security checks or obtaining veteran's benefits. The caseworker puts the constituent in touch with the relevant person or persons, helping to expedite the trek through the federal bureaucracy. Casework is seldom initiated by the congressional office; it almost always stems from a constituent's request. The position is generally regarded as an ombudsman or middleman role. The caseworker fields complaints and questions and refers them to the appropriate individual or agency. *See also* CONSTITUENCY, p. 165; PERSONAL OFFICE STAFF, p. 322; PERSONAL OFFICE SUPPORT STAFF, p. 323.

Significance   Caseworkers must first obtain key information before bringing a request to an agency or department. The case must first be checked for facts, often involving a meeting or conversation with the constituent. Privacy Act clearance must then be obtained, and the caseworker must select the most appropriate source of help for the constituent. Once the source is located, a letter is usually sent from the member along with the constituent's letter. A progress report is later sent to the constituent, and the case is followed through to resolution. Many congressional offices have several caseworkers, each handling cases in a specific area, such as the military, social security, or housing. This specialization allows the caseworker to develop expertise in a particular subject and to cultivate contacts with members of particular agencies and departments. If a matter may be resolved simply by a telephone call, the Congressional Liaison Office may handle the matter.

It has been suggested that pork barreling and casework are two areas which are pure profit for the member. Casework has burgeoned over the years in order to increase the member's visibility and electoral support. Some have criticized constituency casework as unfair and biased, since all citizens may not have equal access to their member's office. Also, casework may be performed with favoritism toward political supporters and friends. Finally, administrative agencies may spend so much time responding to congressional requests that it hampers their own effective administration of laws. Clearly, though, the member's job is to serve constituents, and the casework process is the means by which members perform that service.

Committee Staff   Professional and clerical staff of committees and subcommittees. Committee staff have four basic functions (1) administrative (chief clerk); (2) substantive (professional aides); (3) political (staff director and chief counselor); and (4) public relations (press officer). Clerical staff provide office support while professional staffers engage in drafting legislation, investigating, researching, policymaking, and oversight. Professional staffs were created to offset excessive committee reliance on research provided by executive agencies. The Legislative Reorganization Act of 1946 allowed committees to hire four professional staff members and six clerical workers; the Legislative Reorganization Act of 1970 increased the number of professional staffers to six for each standing committee. *See also* COMMITTEE STAFF, p. 237; COMMITTEE STAFF AIDES, p. 310; COMMITTEE SYSTEM, p. 238; LEGISLATIVE REORGANIZATION ACTS, p. 204; STAFF DIRECTOR, p. 325.

Significance   Committee staff are governed by a basic set of norms including limited advocacy, loyalty to the committee chairman, deference, and anonymity. Neutrality and anonymity are often difficult to maintain among ambitious staff members. Because their attention is focused on a narrow policy area, committee staff often acquire great expertise at the expense of personal recognition, but to the invaluable benefit of Congress. Committee staff organization has been described as falling into three categories (1) hierarchical, where the staff director is the main link between the staff aides and the chairman; (2) egalitarian, where all the staff members share equal access to the member; and (3) supervisorial, a structure whereby the professional and clerical aides are supervised jointly by the staff director and chief clerk. Committee staff positions are considered more prestigious than personal staff positions because they are regarded as more substantive and less political. As committees and subcommittees have proliferated, so has the growth rate of committee staff.

Because the committee system is so vital to the effective functioning of Congress, the committee staff member is a vital part of the legislative machinery. Committee staff contribute to public policy through innovative research, the formulation of ideas for legislation, and the identification of potential problem areas and possible solutions. Quite often staff members possess previous experience in executive branch jobs and in other committee staff positions. Because committee staff are in a position to shape the policy agenda, these positions are often coveted posts in Washington.

Committee Staff Aides   Committee staff members that work with the members of committees to generate and shape legislation and to provide staff support. Committee staff aides may be professional or clerical staffers. Professional committee staff aides are usually highly trained specialists, often recruited from the executive branch and other government agencies. Their previous experience is coupled with advanced education; many staff aides hold college degrees, often law degrees. They are often young and live in or around Capitol Hill— Washington, D.C., Maryland, and Virginia—as opposed to personal staff aides, who tend to come from the member's home district. The functions of professional committee staff aides include organizing hearings, conducting investigations, drafting bills and amendments, writing reports, preparing for floor action, assisting conference committees, and working with lobbyists and special interest groups. Clerical committee staff aides perform such duties as organizing the office, arranging for hearing rooms, and keeping track of financial expenditures. *See also* ADMINISTRATIVE ASSISTANT, p. 307; CAPITOL HILL, p. 188; COMMITTEE STAFF, pp. 237, 309; COMMITTEE SYSTEM, p. 238; PERSONAL OFFICE STAFF, p. 322; STAFF DIRECTOR, p. 325.

Significance   Committee staff aides generally perform many of the same activities as their personal office staff counterparts, but the frequency with which they engage in these functions varies. Professional committee staff aides have been described as fitting into two roles: supervisor and companion. The supervisor works with other committees and oversees the clerical and professional staff workers. The companion works with the members in hearings, mark-ups, conferences, and executive sessions. The influence of committee staff aides depends on the responsibilities delegated to them by the member and the staff director and the time that committee members can spend overseeing their work. The titles that may be given to professional staff aides are wide-ranging: research specialist, legal counsel, professional staff member, research analyst, staff consultant, and more. Clerical staff aides may be known as staff assistants, research clerks, administrative assistants, staff members, etc. Prestige is often attached to particular titles and can affect interstaff relationships. In many cases, the distinction between professional and clerical staff aides becomes hazy. Because the Legislative Reorganization Acts allowed a specified number of permanent professional and clerical staff assistants, the number allowed may not fit the needs of the committee, causing a readjustment of the roles the aides must play. There is no specific definition of how staff aides are to function from office to office; their roles, responsibilities, influence, and importance vary, but all must work to keep the committee's work flowing smoothly and evenly.

Congressional Budget Office (CBO)   An agency that assists Congress in the analysis of the federal budget. The Congressional Budget Office (CBO) was the product of the Congressional Budget and Impoundment Control Act of 1974, which established House and Senate Budget Committees as well as the CBO. The Congressional Budget Office works with these committees in analyzing budget options and in preparing budget resolutions. It is administered by a director, appointed for a four-year term by the Speaker of the House and the President pro tempore of the Senate, in consultation with the chairpersons of the House and Senate Budget Committees. The CBO is required to make staff and resources available to all congressional committees, with priority given to the Budget Committees. The Congressional Budget Office assumed the functions and staff of the Joint Committee on Reduction of Federal Expenditures, which was abolished. *See also* COMMITTEE CHAIRMAN, p. 234; COMMITTEE SYSTEM, pp. 237, 309; PRESIDENT PRO TEMPORE, p. 222; SPEAKER OF THE HOUSE, p. 229.

Significance   The Congressional Budget Office is responsible to all members of Congress. Although first priority goes to the Budget Committees, assistance is provided to the Appropriations and Revenue Committees, authorizing committees, and members seeking budgetary information. Specific responsibilities of the CBO include economic forecasting and fiscal policy analysis; cost projections; annual reports on the budget; and special studies. The Congressional Budget Office provides the Congress with the experts and computers needed to analyze the president's budget. The CBO has not been a passive provider of research to Congress but has pursued an activist stance under the leadership of current director Alice Rivlin. Rivlin has stated that the CBO's role is to work for the entire Congress and not just the Budget Committees. She has argued for an analytical independence for the CBO, not merely a bookkeeping function.

The Congressional Budget Office has offered its own alternative budget to the one prepared for the president by the Office of

Management and Budget, seeking to maintain objectivity in its economic models and forecasts. In its support role to Congress, the CBO will analyze the impact of budget cuts on a member's home district. It analyzes the budgetary effect of all new authorizations in accordance with House and Senate rules. The impact report of the Congressional Budget Office is included in the committee report. Often the budgetary impact statement is negotiated in advance by the committee staff and the CBO staff. While not all legislative and executive branch personnel will agree with the economic assumptions used by the Congressional Budget Office in arriving at its projections and forecasts, the CBO uses the best available information in providing budgetary data.

Congressional Page   A youth who serves as messenger and/or floor assistant to members of Congress. Congressional pages are patronage appointees, ranging in age from fourteen to eighteen years old. Their term as page may range from six months to a year, while some have stayed on as long as three years. Congressional pages attend a special school during the week and perform their jobs on Capitol Hill after classes. Their duties include answering phones, running errands, delivering messages, and distributing information. The pay is high for this age bracket (over $750 per month in 1982), making the position a coveted one. Prior to 1971, all pages were male. The Senate was the first chamber to allow female pages, followed by the House in 1973. House pages must be sixteen or seventeen when they begin to serve, while Senate pages must be at least fourteen but not more than sixteen. *See also* CAPITOL HILL, p. 188.

Significance   Congressional pages are selected by individual members of Congress under the patronage system. As such, charges of discrimination have occasionally been levelled when qualified youths were not appointed. Congressional pages adhere to a strict schedule when attending school and working on the Hill, but problems have persisted when the pages were not under close supervision. While some members may take a close interest in looking after their pages, others leave the pages on their own to tend to their individual needs. In 1982 this matter became explosive when charges were made concerning sexual misconduct and drug-related activity among pages and members of Congress. The sensational charges served to highlight some serious problems and flaws in the page system. Recommendations to remedy the ills of the system included raising the age requirement of pages, supervising their activities more closely, providing chaperones, housing them in dormitories as opposed to fragmented housing arrangements, and centralizing the responsibility for the pages in a particular individual, such as the sergeant-at-arms. The reportage of the so-called page scandal underscored the long hours pages must work, the strict demands made on their time, and the internal pressures pages face in Congress. The Congress, which is extremely sensitive to such negative portrayals, will doubtlessly alter the system to confront these types of problems. The page system may ideally be a rich and rewarding experience for privileged youths to experience first-hand the workings of Congress. Closer attention will now have to be paid to the page system to restore it to this ideal ground.

Congressional Research Service (CRS)   The research branch of Congress in the Library of Congress. The Congressional Research Service (CRS) provides research for Congress and its members that is objective and nonpartisan. Prior to the Legislative Reorganization Act of 1946, the CRS was known as the Legislative Reference Service, created in 1914 to provide information to Congress. Until the Legislative Reorganization Act of 1970, the Congressional Research Service did mostly bibliographic and research work. After 1970 the CRS was given greater responsibilities and was mandated to work closely with congressional committees to analyze and evaluate legislative proposals and policy alternatives. The Congressional Research Service is divided into ten divisions: Library Services, Congressional Reference, American Law, Economics, Education and Public Welfare, Environmental Policy, Foreign Affairs, Government and General Research Division, Science Policy Research, and Senior Specialists. Requests for information may be placed by telephone, by letter, or in person. Inquiries about specific facts are handled by the Quick Reference Division. *See also* LEGISLATIVE REORGANIZATION ACTS, p. 204; LIBRARY OF CONGRESS, p. 318.

Significance   The Congressional Research Service provides a wide range of research services in its role as a support agency to Congress. In addition to evaluating legislative proposals and alternatives, the CRS works with the committees in estimating the results of proposed legislation, identifying expiring programs at the beginning of each new Congress, and suggesting possible policy areas that the committees might consider. Upon request by committee staff, the Congressional Research Service will analyze Supreme Court cases, proofread committee reports, recommend amendments, critique legislation, and suggest possible witnesses for committee hearings. The CRS also provides research reports for Congress on internal procedural and organizational questions, such as committee jurisdictions and the rules of each chamber. The Congressional Research Service also prepares law indices and digests, and provides an index of newspaper articles on almost any issue. Congressional inquiries to CRS are kept strictly confidential, and all work prepared by its staff is screened carefully for objectivity, accuracy, and professionalism.

While the Congressional Research Service aims to maintain nonpartisanship, its work may still be subject to political exploitation and partisan usage. A staff member may work closely with a CRS researcher to produce a politically effective and advantageous report. However, if a member demands that a research study support a particular point of view, the report will be marked Directed Writing. Further, the Congressional Research Service refuses to perform historical analyses of campaign opponents for members. Whatever the impact of research biases and political input, the CRS is generally regarded as fair and objective and is an indispensable tool to the effective functioning of Congress, its members, staff, and committees.

General Accounting Office (GAO)   An agency created by the Budget and Accounting Act in 1921 to oversee the expenditures of the executive branch. The General Accounting Office (GAO) functions to assist on request the Congress, its committees and its members, in the performance of legislative and oversight responsibilities. The GAO is regarded as the watchdog of bureaucratic waste, fraud, and abuse. It conducts investigations of federal government programs, including legal, accounting, auditing, and claims settlement functions. The General Accounting Office is headed by the comptroller general of the United States, appointed by the president for a single fifteen-year term. He is assisted by the deputy comptroller. The GAO is authorized to audit nearly all departments and agencies of the federal government, except certain funds relating to intelligence activities. The comptroller general oversees the accounting systems of federal agencies, approving and reviewing them. The legal work of the GAO is centered at the headquarters office in the Office of the General Counsel. *See also* COMMITTEE SYSTEM, p. 238; GENERAL ACCOUNTING OFFICE (GAO), p. 149.

Significance   The General Accounting Office provides a critical information base to Congress regarding its oversight of the executive branch. GAO audits may uncover administrative problems that may be brought to the attention of Congress. When Congress seeks information concerning a federal program that requests additional funds, the General Accounting Office may conduct an investigation. It may make recommendations to promote more effective operations of a program. GAO staff act as consultants to the House and Senate Appropriations Committees and have been involved in such activities as monitoring federal election campaigns and reviewing Medicare and Medicaid programs. The scope of the General Accounting Office's activities has increased as the Congress delegated them new responsibilities.

The GAO is intended to be nonpartisan, as evidenced by the long term of the comptroller general. But the agency has been criticized by some for conducting politically motivated investigations. However, the GAO is considered to be extremely careful in its handling of studies and investigations, so as to avoid the appearance of partisanship. Its neutral stance has allowed the agency to be entrusted with many controversial tasks. Their reports on government waste, fraud, and inefficiency have provided the Congress with the needed information to make intelligent and informed budgetary decisions. Further, GAO reports have freed the Congress from overreliance on executive branch and special interest group research as a source of primary information. With many of the oversight responsibilities of Congress handled by the committees and subcommittees and their staffs, the General Accounting Office provides expert assistance on critical financial and budgetary matters.

Government Printing Office (GPO)   The office responsible for the printing and binding orders placed by Congress and various departments and agencies of the federal government. The Government Printing Office (GPO) was created in 1861 to provide printing services for the House and Senate, executive and judicial departments, and Court of Claims. The GPO is overseen by the congressional Joint Committee on Printing, which acts as its board of directors. The public printer is appointed by the president with the advice and consent of the Senate and must be a practical printer versed in the art of bookbinding, as required by law. After each daily session of Congress, the Government Printing Office publishes the *Congressional Record*, which is printed and delivered the following morning. All transcripts of debates must reach the GPO by 9:00 P.M. to be included in the following day's *Record*. The Government Printing Office also runs bookstores in Washington, D.C., as well as across the country. Almost all GPO publications are distributed free to Congress, government agencies, private organizations, and the general public. *See also* CONGRESSIONAL RECORD, p. 199.

Significance   The Government Printing Office is recognized as one of the largest and best equipped printing plants in the world. The GPO maintains an expansive distribution and sales operation and supplies paper, ink, and other such items for government activities on order. The Government Printing Office often contracts out work to outside commercial suppliers, inviting bids on many printing and binding services, and maintaining liaison between the ordering agency and the contractor.

Publication of the *Congressional Record* requires a large percentage of the GPO's staff and resources. The text of the daily floor debates in the House and Senate is compiled each night and, regardless of the length of the floor proceedings, the *Record* must be prepared and ready for distribution the following morning. The Government Printing Office prides itself on never missing its morning delivery deadline.

GPO publications often serve as the backbone for much academic and scholarly research, covering the gamut of political and policy issues. The Government Printing Office attempts to make these publications available in many places and provides indexes of available material: the bimonthly *GPO Sales Publications Reference File* (PRF) and the *Monthly Catalog of U.S. Government Publications*. The distribution of documents is handled by the Superintendent of Documents. In short, the task of translating the word of Congress to the printed page falls to the Government Printing Office and, as long as Congress never runs short of something to say, the GPO will never run short of material to print.

Investigative Staff   Committee staff personnel hired specifically for investigative work. Investigative staffs have increased over the years as new oversight subcommittees were created and the number of subcommittees in general grew. Funding for investigative staff is provided yearly through resolutions approved by the administration committee of each chamber. Investigative staff are regarded as temporary, but often many of the aides have been on a committee for a long time. While all committee staff members possess investigative and oversight responsibilities, investigative staff provide the specialized knowledge necessary to effectively carry out an investigation. *See also* COMMITTEE STAFF, pp. 237, 309; CONGRESSIONAL INVESTIGATION, p. 240.

Significance   Investigative staff do much of their own research, in addition to utilizing the resources of such agencies as the Federal Bureau of Investigation and General Accounting Office when necessary. The research may involve going through files and records before a public hearing and providing much of the information which will be used in the course of the hearing. Expert investigative staffs are vital to committees whose primary function is to conduct hearings and investigations. Such hearings must be well-conceived, prepared, and executed, with the background of the case fully explored and the witnesses selected with great care in order to maximize their contribution to the investigation. As is the case throughout Congress, the committees seek to avoid overreliance on information and data provided by executive branch agencies and special interest groups, preferring to rely on their own expert staff.

During the Watergate era, the Senate Watergate committee boasted a staff of 64, including 17 attorneys; the House Judiciary Committee's impeachment inquiry staff in 1974 totalled almost 100 members, including 43 attorneys. The maze of complex and technical legalities involved in conducting an investigation requires trained investigators that are familiar with the law, government records, and the investigative procedures of Congress. With much of the oversight responsibility of Congress delegated to its subcommittees, and most often their staff members, investigative expertise and background are critical in the fulfillment of this function.

Legislative Assistant (LA)   A personal staff member that handles the office's legislative functions. The legislative assistant (LA) works with the members in committees, drafting legislation, writing speeches, analyzing bills, and attending committee sessions. Many offices have a chief legislative assistant, aided by general legislative assistants, each possessing specialized knowledge in a particular area, such as economics or foreign policy. A large number of LAs possess degrees in law or political science, and many of them are lawyers. Since the Senate may hire more legislative assistants than the House, Senate LAs tend to be more specialized than their House counterparts. *See also* AMENDMENT, p. 256; BILL, p. 259; PERSONAL OFFICE STAFF, p. 322.

Significance   The legislative assistant must be able to follow the cycle of legislation from beginning to end. After a bill is drafted and introduced, the LA must monitor floor activity, interact with appropriate committee members, interest groups, and party leaders, and keep track of when the legislation will reach the chamber for a vote. When a member poses a floor challenge to a bill, the legislative assistant must work to make the amendment successful: forging coalitions, determining support for the amendment, writing statements for floor discussion, and obtaining cosponsors for the amendment. All the while, the LA must be prepared to field questions concerning the legislation from constituents, special interest groups, reporters, and members of other office staffs. Most importantly, the legislative assistant must always be keenly aware of the impact of any bill or amendment on the member's home district. At election time, the LA may serve such political functions as writing speeches, meeting with constituents, and determining and researching key policy issues.

Studies have shown that legislative assistants tend to be younger than administrative assistants, with training and experience more directly related to the functioning of Congress than AAs. They are less likely to come from the member's home state or district than administrative assistants and generally have shorter tenures with the member. Lawyers might find the experience of serving as an LA enough to establish their credibility and move into more lucrative jobs in Washington. In short, the position of legislative assistant is a visible one, and the competent LA must be in a constant state of preparedness, ready to deal with the numerous cogs and components in the legislative machinery.

Library of Congress   One of the world's largest repositories of information. The Library of Congress serves dual roles: to assist the Congress and to serve as the national library of the United States. The Joint Committee on the Library oversees the library's service to Congress. In 1802 the position of Librarian of Congress was established. According to law, the librarian "shall be appointed by the President, and with the advice and consent of the Senate. He shall make rules and regulations for the government of the library." The Library of Congress performs research work for the members and committees of Congress, providing much information via SCORPIO, its computer data system. On request, the library will supply members of the two houses with published materials relating to specific problems, reading lists, analyses of literature, reports on policy issues, expert staff service, and will occasionally write speeches. *See also* CONGRESSIONAL RESEARCH SERVICE, p. 313.

Significance   The Library of Congress houses tens of millions of items: books, pamphlets, manuscripts, music, photographic negatives, prints, slides, maps, and much more. Reading materials are available in hundreds of languages. Some of the library's treasures include the Gutenberg Bible, the Declaration of Independence, the Bill of Rights, and the Gettysburg Address. The library is divided into four reference units: Research Department, Reader Services Department, Law Library and, most important to Congress, the Congressional Research Service. Since 1870 the library has been responsible for copyrights, which are now registered by the Copyright Office. Nearly all books published possess a Library of Congress card.

The Library of Congress has received criticism for inefficient research and staff. But the scope of its collections and the wide range of services provided make the Library of Congress a national treasure. One problem which has plagued the library is overcrowded conditions and lack of space, as their acquisitions increase. While members of Congress may complain about deficiencies in library service, they have generously appropriated funds to the library over the years. Also contained within the Library of Congress is the American Folklife Center, which sponsors programs to support, preserve, and present American folklife through archives, research, field projects, performances, and publications; the Center for the Book, designed to heighten public interest in the role of books and printing; and the National Preservation Program, which provides technical information related to the preservation of library and archived material. As these programs suggest, the Library of Congress may justly be described as the Library of the People.

Majority/Minority Staff   Staff members selected by the committee chairman or ranking minority member with regard to partisan affiliation. The majority and minority staffs consist of individuals who share the political and policy orientations of the committee leadership. Since the chairman usually prevails in placing staff members on a committee, most committee staff are from the majority party. The Legislative Reorganization Act of 1970 provided that minority members of House committees could hire three full-time minority staff members on most committees. In 1975 the Senate allowed junior members to hire staff aides, cutting into the power base held by senior members who previously controlled all committee staff. The party leadership allocates staff funds for the different committees among majority and minority positions. *See also* COMMITTEE CHAIRMAN, p. 234; COMMITTEE STAFF, pp. 237, 309; COMMITTEE SYSTEM, p. 238; FILIBUSTER, p. 274; LEGISLA-TIVE REORGANIZATION ACTS, p. 204.

Significance   The majority and minority staff are under the direct control of the committee leadership. The committee chairperson hires and fires majority staff, while the ranking minority member hires and fires minority staff. Majority committee staffs consist largely of lawyers who are responsible for setting up hearings, drafting bills and amendments, establishing the committee's agenda and priorities, and working out the floor strategy for legislation reported out of committee. Minority staffers are involved in developing policy alternatives, mapping out their strategy, and gathering research and information.

The minority staff members often function as obstructionists, working to kill legislation offered by the majority party. They use the tools of threatening filibusters and preventing quorums to block majority action. Since the minority party cannot initiate hearings, these devices enable them to address some of their policies and legislative priorities. The majority staff are mainly regarded as the legislation writers, while the minority staff provide an informational role for the minority members. Some have suggested that committee staffing should be a nonpartisan process, while others maintain that professionalism may supplant partisan considerations in the retention of a staff member. Provisions for minority staffing have surfaced repeatedly in the Congress over the years, as members strive for a measure of partisan equilibrium in the critical ground of committees.

Office Manager   A personal staff member that handles the daily chores of running a senator's or representative's office for the administrative assistant. Office managers may share supervisory responsibilities with the administrative assistant, overseeing the work done by the receptionist, the clerks, and the interns. The office manager performs such duties as acquiring office equipment, telephones, stationery, and supplies; paying bills; handling accounting functions; preparing budgetary projections; and monitoring interns. They are responsible for coordinating the workload of the secretarial personnel, making sure that the mail and other daily duties are handled in a timely and efficient manner. *See also* ADMINISTRATIVE ASSISTANT, p. 307; PERSONAL OFFICE STAFF, p. 322.

Significance   Office managers usually have worked their way up the office ladder to reach this position. Often they have begun as secretaries or in other clerical positions. The typical office manager has been described as female, possessing many years of experience on Capitol Hill in a number of positions. Having begun as a secretary, the office manager has usually handled casework functions and has contacts among staff in both the executive and legislative branches. This experience, coupled with a working familiarity with office procedures, enables the office manager to bring good judgment and political expertise to the job. In some offices, the administrative assistant may perform the functions of the office manager, but in most instances, the workload is too great and must be delegated to a manager. The office manager consults frequently with the administrative assistant, reviewing the monthly clerk-hire allowance, preparing documents for the member's signature, and analyzing ledgers. In order for the office to function smoothly, close supervision of the flow of work is necessary. Filing systems must be kept current and organized. Most importantly, the office manager must see that deadlines are met. The interns and the staff must be kept busy and productive, and the office manager must supervise, scrutinize, and synthesize the resources of the member's office.

Office of Legislative Counsel   An office of trained legal staff in the House and Senate that assists members in drafting and redrafting legislation in the appropriate language. The Office of Legislative Counsel was created in 1919 under the Revenue Act of 1918 and was originally called the Legislative Drafting Service. The House and Senate each has its own staff and chief counsel, who is appointed by the Speaker of the House in the House and the President pro tempore in the Senate. The Office of Legislative Counsel is nonpartisan, and all communications between the office and the members are held in confidence. *See also* BILL, p. 259; COMMITTEE STAFF, pp. 237, 309; COMMITTEE SYSTEM, p. 238; LEGISLATIVE REORGANIZATION ACTS, p. 204.

Significance   The Office of Legislative Counsel possesses the expertise necessary to draft legislation in accordance with the appropriate statutory language of the United States Code. Lawyers analyze and research precedents, compare bills with existing laws and for conflicts with the Code, and provide details such as the date when the legislation will go into effect. Extensive legal research may be necessary in carrying out these functions, and the staff must have the specialized knowledge to perform these duties. After drafting a bill, representatives of the Office of Legislative Counsel may attend committee mark-up and conference sessions, working closely with the committee staffs. Sometimes lawyers are assigned to work with a particular committee or subcommittee for such a long period that they in effect serve as a member of the committee staff.

The Senate utilizes the Office of Legislative Counsel under the basic authority as set forth in 1918, while the House expanded the function following the Legislative Reorganization Act of 1970. Title V of the act provided that the House Legislative Counsel would assist both committees and committee members "at the direction of the Speaker, performing on behalf of the House any legal services which were within the capabilities of the office." While the Office of Legislative Counsel drafts bills and suggests alternatives, there has been a trend toward members of Congress introducing legislation drafted by executive branch agency and special interest group experts. Indeed, the Office of Legislative Counsel works closely with executive agencies, special interest groups, committees and committee staffs, and all the players in the legislative process. The office is respected for its knowledge and expertise and provides an essential function throughout the lifespan of legislation.

Office of Technology Assessment (OTA)   An agency established to assist Congress in evaluating scientific and technical proposals for legislation. The Office of Technology Assessment (OTA) was the product of PL 92–484, which amended the National Science Foundation Act of 1950 to provide Congress with an additional support mechanism. The OTA began operations in January of 1974. The primary function of the Office of Technology Assessment is to conduct long-range studies of the "social, biological, physical, economic, and political effects of technological issues." The OTA is mandated to serve congressional committees and not individual members. It is governed by a bipartisan Technology Assessment Board, which consists of six senators, six representatives, and the OTA director, who is appointed by the board for a six-year term. The Office of Technology Assessment is also guided by an advisory council and maintains liaison with the National Science Foundation and the Congressional Budget Office. The policy areas of the OTA include energy, exploratory assessments, food, health, materials, oceans, research and development, transportation, and world trade. *See also* CONGRESSIONAL BUDGET OFFICE, p. 311; CONGRESSIONAL RESEARCH SERVICE, p. 313; GENERAL ACCOUNTING OFFICE, pp. 149, 314; LIBRARY OF CONGRESS, p. 318.

Significance   The Office of Technology Assessment conducts studies that assess the beneficial and adverse consequences of various technologies, along with analyses of alternative policies. Requests for OTA assessments may be initiated by (1) the chairman of any standing, select, or joint committee of Congress, acting individually or at the request of the ranking minority member or a majority of the committee members; (2) the Technology Assessment Board; or (3) the OTA director, in consultation with the board. The Office of Technology Assessment may utilize the resources of the Library of Congress, such as the Congressional Research Service. The OTA's services may be used by the General Accounting Office. The Congressional Budget Act requires the OTA to assist the Congressional Budget Office on matters concerning federal science and technology programs.

    The Office of Technology Assessment handles many complex requests and will often use consultants or contract its work to outside sources for much of the research. The OTA has the authority to undertake projects on its own but is frequently overwhelmed with requests that tax its staff and resources. It has been suggested that OTA reports, utilized by congressional committees and objective in nature, are vulnerable to political attack if their findings or implications come into conflict with congressional attitudes. The ideal of policy neutrality is difficult in the political arena, but the Office of Technology Assessment strives to provide the best possible information in the complex area of gauging the impact of science and technology in the United States and around the world.

Personal Office Staff   The office staff of the individual members of Congress. Personal office staff are responsible for activities including administration, legislation, research, press relations, correspondence, oversight, and constituency service. A personal staff worker reports directly to the individual member of Congress and is paid by the member. Salaries come from a clerk-hire fund, with monies deposited in each member's account each year by the federal treasury. In the Senate, the size of the staff is determined by the member's state's population— the larger the state, the larger the staff. In the House, each representative is allowed eighteen full-time employees and four temporary ones. Personal staffs can be divided into the categories of Washington staff and home district staff. Washington staff workers are mainly engaged in political and issue-related activities, while home district staff workers often have been engaged in the member's election campaigns. *See also* CONSTITUENCY, p. 165.

Significance   Personal office staff characteristics vary from office to office, but several attributes are common. Personal staff workers are frequently from the home state of the member they work for, have strong party preferences, are highly educated, and possess specialized training, skills, and expertise. The scope of duties includes managing the office, keeping the member's daily schedule, typing, answering the phone, and most importantly, handling the flood of mail received by congressional offices. The duties may be divided among personnel or shared by the staff. One of the aims of office organization is the creation of an efficient work routine, performed in the most effective way possible so as to leave the member with as much time as possible to concentrate on legislative matters. The power or influence of personal staff workers is closely related to the amount of access they have to the member. Their job security lies solely with the member, who may hire and fire them at will—and there is no guarantee of a job once a member leaves office. In many cases, a personal staff position may serve as a stepping stone for higher positions for young, well-educated professionals, while other staffers may transfer among several offices on Capitol Hill and move into executive branch and federal agency jobs. An effective personal staff is critical to congresspersons during their campaign for office as well as in the successful functioning of their term of office. Successful constituency service, coupled with well-handled press relations and well-drafted speeches, may significantly enhance a member's political future. The personal staff members are working for that future as well as their own.

Personal Office Support Staff   Office workers on the personal staffs of senators and representatives. Personal office support staff positions may include receptionist, clerk typist, computer operator, legislative correspondent, appointments secretary/scheduler, research assistant, and federal grants assistant. These positions are overseen by the administrative assistant and the office manager, and some of the duties may overlap with the work of the caseworker, legislative assistant, and press assistant. While the titles and responsibilities of these jobs may vary from office to office, each represents a facet of work that must be handled for each congressperson. In many offices, the title of staff assistant encompasses any number of these duties and more. The larger the office staff, the more likely the specialization evident in staff titles and positions. *See also* ADMINISTRATIVE ASSISTANT, p. 307; CASEWORK-ER, p. 308; LEGISLATIVE ASSISTANT, p. 317; OFFICE MANAGER, p. 320; PERSONAL OFFICE STAFF, p. 322; PRESS ASSISTANT, p. 324.

Significance   The personal office support staff is responsible for handling the daily workload of the office. The receptionist answers the phones, greets constituents, lobbyists, visitors, and job seekers, opens and distributes the mail, relays messages to staff members, and may handle constituent requests for documents and publications. The legislative correspondent answers the mail, forwarding appropriate inquiries to a legislative assistant who is responsible for a particular policy area. Since the average congressional office receives hundreds or thousands of letters per week, the mail must be opened, sorted, routed, and researched before it can be answered. The legislative correspondent may coordinate this process. The appointments secretary or scheduler is responsible for planning the member's time. Usually there are two schedulers: one for the Washington office and one for the home district office. Members begin their days with an agenda given to them in the morning that outlines the day's activities. The scheduler must keep the staff and the member aware of hearings, mark-ups, meetings, receptions, luncheons, appointments, and leave sufficient time for the handling of other daily duties. The computer operator processes replies to correspondence via computer terminals and word processors. A data base of computerized letter responses must be kept maintained and updated to keep the flow of mail running smoothly. House offices usually possess one computer operator, while Senate offices may have a number of staff assigned to such tasks. The secretaries and clerks type, file, take dictation, and handle the routine duties of the office. Some offices have specialists in federal grants, a duty usually handled by a top staff member, such as the administrative assistant. Finally, many offices now employ research assistants, who assist the staff in gathering information and preparing relevant reports.

Press Assistant   A congressional personal staff worker that handles press relations for the member. The press assistant may also be known as a press secretary, communications specialist, or information director, among other titles. The job of the press assistant is to communicate the programs and policies of the member to the various media—television, newspaper, radio, etc. Press assistants usually possess expertise in the media, coming from journalism backgrounds or prior experience in radio, television, or newspaper work. Press assistants function to portray a positive image of the member via the mass media and to generate all types of press coverage whenever possible. *See also* PERSONAL OFFICE STAFF, p. 322.

Significance   The press assistant is involved in all facets of mass communications: writing press releases, speeches, radio shows, television spots, newsletters, newspaper columns, and editorials. The press assistant must keep the press and the public informed on the impact of legislation on the home district, and the role that the member plays in it. Thus, the press assistant must cultivate close contacts with the national and local press and promote the member as the lead person or mastermind behind beneficial legislation, or as the strong opponent of detrimental legislation. Television is one of the most vital media for spreading the member's message, and often the press assistant will train the member in the use of the TelePrompTer (electronic cue cards) to facilitate smooth and effective speechmaking. The press assistant keeps the staff on the lookout for any opportunities to get the member on television, such as personal interviews. Research shows that press assistants often come from the member's home state, possessing valuable contacts with state and district television, radio, and press people. A press assistant not from the home state may have some difficulty in dealing with members of the local media. Someone more familiar with the home state may be able to exploit these contacts more masterfully. In addition to writing various materials for the members, such as editorials planted in newspapers to support the member's legislation, the press assistant also monitors press clippings relevant to the legislation. Effective use of the mass media is critical for any member of Congress, and the press assistant must be capable of utilizing the many news media in the most efficient and broad ways possible.

Staff Director   An assistant and personal representative of the committee chairman. The staff director oversees the path of legislation through the committee process, establishing links with other members, staff aides, interest groups, federal agency officials, and other key participants in the legislative process. In some offices, the title of chief counsel may denote the head of the staff, but there is usually a staff director on those committees. The administrative management functions of the committee staff are handled by the chief clerk, and press relations are handled by a press officer. Because power may be decentralized on committee staffs, the roles and responsibilities of these top positions may come into conflict. While staff directors in different offices may perceive and carry out their roles differently, their basic responsibility is to manage the committee staff and to carefully guide legislation through committee. *See also* COMMITTEE CHAIRMAN, p. 234; COMMITTEE STAFF, pp. 237, 309; COMMITTEE SYSTEM, p. 238.

Significance   The staff director aids the committee chairman in planning the committee program and in organizing staff and resources to carry it out. He or she serves as a liaison between the staff and the members of Congress who, in many cases, may never meet, depending upon the organizational structure of the office. Staff directors usually possess great experience on Capitol Hill, and their knowledge of how congresspersons make decisions enables them to anticipate reactions to programs and policies and to weed out those that will likely prove unsuccessful. Staff directors recognize political exigencies and priorities, enabling them to predict what legislation is likely to receive the committee's attention. The staff director also monitors the quality, organization, and impact of reports and studies, reviewing all these materials for acceptability and technical competence, perhaps suggesting revisions or alternative ways of presenting the information to enhance the attractiveness of the committee staff work. Finally, the staff director is responsible for the distribution of the workload among professional staff members, the progress of the work, and its culmination. Once a bill is introduced, the staff director seeks to mobilize public opinion behind the legislation and to develop the necessary support and coalitions at the committee, floor, and conference levels. The increasing importance attached to congressional committees makes the staff director a powerful and influential actor in the legislative process.

APPENDIX

Fig. 1 *Appendix* 329

The Electoral Vote

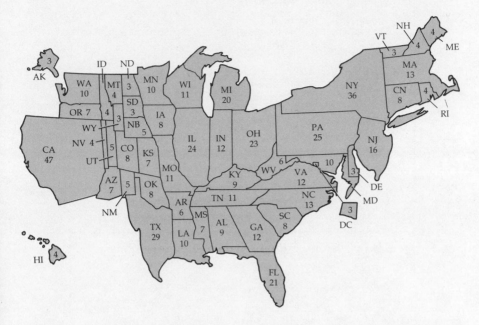

The Nomination Game

Players.* Any number can play, but only the following have any real chance to win, and they should be handicapped accordingly:

- *Incumbent president:* Start at square 7 (don't neglect to take square 7's bonus points for frequent meetings with key party leaders).
- *United States senators:* Start at square 3 (take bonus points).
- *Governors or members of Congress:* Start at square 3. *Former occupants of these roles:* Start at square 2.

Goal. To win a majority of convention delegates at the party's summer national convention. The final tally of these delegates will be made in a big amphitheater in a major city sometime in July or August. Winner must make a speech.

Rules. In the early versions of this game, there weren't many rules. The main one was "Don't lie, cheat, steal, or get caught." New rules have been added because too many players were caught violating the old rule. Hire a good lawyer to help you avoid rules legally.

Strategies. You're on your own here. Things that work for one player flop for another. Remember that you have only three resources: time, money, and organization. Where you decide to use them is up to you.

Ready to Play? Select a token, roll one die, and move according to instructions.

*Note: Although anyone can play, possible players are warned that no one has ever won this game who was not white, middle-aged (or older), Protestant or Catholic, and male. For each handicap, allow other players two turns before starting at square 1.

Fig. 2   *Appendix*   331

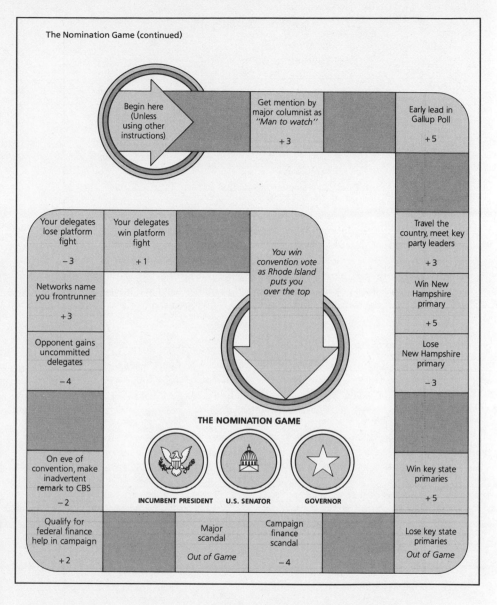

The Nomination Game (continued)

Begin here (Unless using other instructions)

Get mention by major columnist as "Man to watch" +3

Early lead in Gallup Poll +5

Your delegates lose platform fight −3

Your delegates win platform fight +1

You win convention vote as Rhode Island puts you over the top

Travel the country, meet key party leaders +3

Networks name you frontrunner +3

Win New Hampshire primary +5

Opponent gains uncommitted delegates −4

Lose New Hampshire primary −3

THE NOMINATION GAME

INCUMBENT PRESIDENT   U.S. SENATOR   GOVERNOR

On eve of convention, make inadvertent remark to CBS −2

Win key state primaries +5

Qualify for federal finance help in campaign +2

Major scandal *Out of Game*

Campaign finance scandal −4

Lose key state primaries *Out of Game*

Source: Robert L. Lineberry, *Government in America: People, Politics and Policy*, 2d ed., © 1983 by Robert L. Lineberry. Reprinted by permission of Little, Brown and Company.

Presidential Vetoes

President	Total Vetoes	Regular Vetoes	Pocket Vetoes	Vetoes Sustained	Vetoes Overriden
Washington	2	2	0	2	0
J. Adams	0				
Jefferson	0				
Madison	7	5	2	7	0
Monroe	2	1	1	1	1
Jackson	12	5	7	12	0
Van Buren	0				
W. H. Harrison	0				
Tyler	10	6	4	9	1
Taylor	0				
Fillmore	0				
Pierce	9	9	0	4	5
Buchanan	7	4	3	7	0
Lincoln	6	2	4	6	0
A. Johnson	28	21	7	13	15
Grant	92	44	48	88	4
Hayes	13	12	1	12	1
Garfield	0				
Arthur	12	4	8	11	1
Cleveland (1885–1889)	414	304	110	412	2
B. Harrison	44	19	25	43	1
Cleveland (1893–1897)	170	42	128	165	5
McKinley	42	6	36	42	0
T. Roosevelt	82	42	40	81	1
Taft	39	30	9	38	1
Wilson	44	33	11	38	6
Harding	6	5	1	6	0
Coolidge	50	20	30	46	4
Hoover	37	21	16	34	3
F. Roosevelt	631	371	260	622	9
Truman	250	180	70	238	12
Eisenhower	181	73	108	179	2
Kennedy	21	12	9	21	0
L. Johnson	30	16	14	30	0
Nixon	43	24	19	38	5
Ford	66	48	18	54	12
Carter	22	9	13	21	1
Reagan (as of August 1, 1982)	7	6	1	7	0

Source: Ross K. Baker, Gerald Pomper, and Carey McWilliams, *American Government.* Copyright © 1983 by Macmillan Publishing Company.

Fig. 4   *Appendix*   333

Major Parties' Popular and Electoral Vote for President

(F) Federalist; (D) Democrat; (R) Republican; (DR) Democrat Republican; (NR) National Republican;
(W) Whig; (P) People's; (PR) Progressive; (SR) States' Rights; (LR) Liberal Republican; Asterisk (*)—See notes.

Year	President elected	Popular	Elec.	Losing candidate	Popular	Elec.
1789	George Washington (F)	Unknown	69	No opposition		
1792	George Washington (F)	Unknown	132	No opposition		
1796	John Adams (F).	Unknown	71	Thomas Jefferson (DR)	Unknown	68
1800*	Thomas Jefferson (DR)	Unknown	73	Aaron Burr (DR)	Unknown	73
1804	Thomas Jefferson (DR)	Unknown	162	Charles Pinckney (F)	Unknown	14
1808	James Madison (DR).	Unknown	122	Charles Pinckney (F)	Unknown	47
1812	James Madison (DR).	Unknown	128	DeWitt Clinton (F)	Unknown	89
1816	James Monroe (DR)	Unknown	183	Rufus King (F)	Unknown	34
1820	James Monroe (DR)	Unknown	231	John Quincy Adams (DR). . . .	Unknown	1
1824*	John Quincy Adams (DR) . . .	105,321	84	Andrew Jackson (DR)	155,872	99
				Henry Clay (DR)	46,587	37
				William H. Crawford (DR)	44,282	41
1828	Andrew Jackson (D)	647,231	178	John Quincy Adams (NR)	509,097	83
1832	Andrew Jackson (D)	687,502	219	Henry Clay (NR)	530,189	49
1836	Martin Van Buren (D).	762,678	170	William H. Harrison (W)	548,007	73
1840	William H. Harrison (W)	1,275,017	234	Martin Van Buren (D)	1,128,702	60
1844	James K. Polk (D)	1,337,243	170	Henry Clay (W).	1,299,068	105
1848	Zachary Taylor (W).	1,360,101	163	Lewis Cass (D)	1,220,544	127
1852	Franklin Pierce (D)	1,601,474	254	Winfield Scott (W)	1,386,578	42
1856	James C. Buchanan (D)	1,927,995	174	John C. Fremont (R)	1,391,555	114
1860	Abraham Lincoln (R)	1,866,352	180	Stephen A. Douglas (D)	1,375,157	12
				John C. Breckinridge (D)	845,763	72
				John Bell (Const. Union).	589,581	39
1864	Abraham Lincoln (R)	2,216,067	212	George McClellan (D)	1,808,725	21
1868	Ulysses S. Grant (R)	3,015,071	214	Horatio Seymour (D).	2,709,615	80
1872*	Ulysses S. Grant (R)	3,597,070	286	Horace Greeley (D-LR)	2,834,079	. . .
1876*	Rutherford B. Hayes (R)	4,033,950	185	Samuel J. Tilden (D)	4,284,757	184
1880	James A. Garfield (R)	4,449,053	214	Winfield S. Hancock (D)	4,442,030	155
1884	Grover Cleveland (D)	4,911,017	219	James G. Blaine (R)	4,848,334	182
1888*	Benjamin Harrison (R)	5,444,337	233	Grover Cleveland (D)	5,540,050	168
1892	Grover Cleveland (D)	5,554,414	277	Benjamin Harrison (R)	5,190,802	145
				James Weaver (P)	1,027,329	22
1896	William McKinley (R)	7,035,638	271	William J. Bryan (D-P)	6,467,946	176
1900	William McKinley (R)	7,219,530	292	William J. Bryan (D)	6,358,071	155
1904	Theodore Roosevelt (R)	7,628,834	336	Alton B. Parker (D).	5,084,491	140
1908	William H. Taft (R)	7,679,006	321	William J. Bryan (D)	6,409,106	162
1912	Woodrow Wilson (D)	6,286,214	435	Theodore Roosevelt (PR)	4,216,020	88
				William H. Taft (R)	3,483,922	8
1916	Woodrow Wilson (D)	9,129,606	277	Charles E. Hughes (R).	8,538,221	254
1920	Warren G. Harding (R)	16,152,200	404	James M. Cox (D)	9,147,353	127
1924	Calvin Coolidge (R).	15,725,016	382	John W. Davis (D)	8,385,586	136
				Robert M. LaFollette (PR). . . .	4,822,856	13
1928	Herbert Hoover (R).	21,392,190	444	Alfred E. Smith (D).	15,016,443	87
1932	Franklin D. Roosevelt (D) . . .	22,821,857	472	Herbert Hoover (R)	15,761,841	59
				Norman Thomas (Socialist). . .	884,781	. . .
1936	Franklin D. Roosevelt (D) . . .	27,751,597	523	Alfred Landon (R)	16,679,583	8
1940	Franklin D. Roosevelt (D) . . .	27,243,466	449	Wendell Willkie (R).	22,304,755	82
1944	Franklin D. Roosevelt (D) . . .	25,602,505	432	Thomas E. Dewey (R)	22,006,278	99
1948	Harry S. Truman (D)	24,105,812	303	Thomas E. Dewey (R)	21,970,065	189
				J. Strom Thurmond (SR)	1,169,021	39
				Henry A. Wallace (PR)	1,157,172	. . .
1952	Dwight D. Eisenhower (R) . . .	33,936,252	442	Adlai E. Stevenson (D)	27,314,992	89
1956*	Dwight D. Eisenhower (R)	35,585,316	457	Adlai E. Stevenson (D)	26,031,322	73
1960*	John F. Kennedy (D)	34,227,096	303	Richard M. Nixon (R).	34,108,546	219
1964	Lyndon B. Johnson (D).	43,126,506	486	Barry M. Goldwater (R)	27,176,799	52
1968	Richard M. Nixon (R).	31,785,480	301	Hubert H. Humphrey (D)	31,275,166	191
				George C. Wallace (3d party) .	9,906,473	46
1972*	Richard M. Nixon (R).	47,165,234	520	George S. McGovern (D) . . . ,	29,170,774	17
1976*	Jimmy Carter (D).	40,828,929	297	Gerald R. Ford (R)	39,148,940	240
1980	Ronald Reagan (R).	43,899,248	489	Jimmy Carter (D).	35,481,435	49
				John B. Anderson (independent)	5,719,437	. . .

1800—Elected by House of Representatives because of tied electoral vote.
1824—Elected by House of Representatives. No candidate polled a majority. In 1824, the Democrat Republicans had become a loose coalition of competing political groups. By 1828, the supporters of Jackson were known as Democrats, and the J.Q. Adams and Henry Clay supporters as National Republicans.
1872—Greeley died Nov. 29, 1872. His electoral votes were split among 4 individuals.
1876—Fla., La., Ore., and S. C. election returns were disputed. Congress in joint session (Mar. 2, 1877) declared Hayes and Wheeler elected President and Vice-President.
1888—Cleveland had more votes than Harrison but the 233 electoral votes cast for Harrison against the 168 for Cleveland elected Harrison president.
1956—Democrats elected 74 electors but one from Alabama refused to vote for Stevenson.
1960—Sen. Harry F. Byrd (D-Va.) received 15 electoral votes.
1972—John Hospers of Cal. and Theodora Nathan of Ore. received one vote from an elector of Virginia.
1976—Ronald Reagan of Cal. received one vote from an elector of Washington.

Source: *The World Almanac & Book of Facts*, 1983 edition. Copyright © Newspaper Enterprise Association, Inc., 1982, New York, NY 10166.

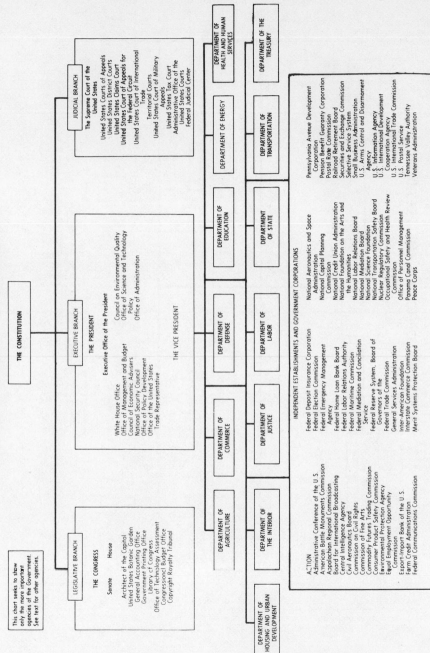

THE GOVERNMENT OF THE UNITED STATES

This chart seeks to show only the more important agencies of the Government. See text for other agencies.

THE CONSTITUTION

LEGISLATIVE BRANCH

THE CONGRESS

Senate   House

Architect of the Capitol
United States Botanic Garden
General Accounting Office
Government Printing Office
Library of Congress
Office of Technology Assessment
Congressional Budget Office
Copyright Royalty Tribunal

EXECUTIVE BRANCH

THE PRESIDENT

Executive Office of the President

White House Office
Office of Management and Budget
Council of Economic Advisers
National Security Council
Office of Policy Development
Office of the United States Trade Representative

Council on Environmental Quality
Office of Science and Technology Policy
Office of Administration

THE VICE PRESIDENT

JUDICIAL BRANCH

The Supreme Court of the United States

United States Courts of Appeals
United States District Courts
United States Claims Court
United States Court of Appeals for the Federal Circuit
United States Court of International Trade
Territorial Courts
United States Court of Military Appeals
United States Tax Court
Administrative Office of the United States Courts
Federal Judicial Center

DEPARTMENT OF AGRICULTURE

DEPARTMENT OF COMMERCE

DEPARTMENT OF DEFENSE

DEPARTMENT OF EDUCATION

DEPARTMENT OF ENERGY

DEPARTMENT OF HEALTH AND HUMAN SERVICES

DEPARTMENT OF HOUSING AND URBAN DEVELOPMENT

DEPARTMENT OF THE INTERIOR

DEPARTMENT OF JUSTICE

DEPARTMENT OF LABOR

DEPARTMENT OF STATE

DEPARTMENT OF TRANSPORTATION

DEPARTMENT OF THE TREASURY

INDEPENDENT ESTABLISHMENTS AND GOVERNMENT CORPORATIONS

ACTION
Administrative Conference of the U S
American Battle Monuments Commission
Appalachian Regional Commission
Board for International Broadcasting
Central Intelligence Agency
Civil Aeronautics Board
Commission on Civil Rights
Commission of Fine Arts
Commodity Futures Trading Commission
Consumer Product Safety Commission
Environmental Protection Agency
Equal Employment Opportunity Commission
Export-Import Bank of the U.S.
Farm Credit Administration
Federal Communications Commission

Federal Deposit Insurance Corporation
Federal Election Commission
Federal Emergency Management Agency
Federal Home Loan Bank Board
Federal Labor Relations Authority
Federal Maritime Commission
Federal Mediation and Conciliation Service
Federal Reserve System, Board of Governors of the
Federal Trade Commission
General Services Administration
Inter-American Foundation
Interstate Commerce Commission
Merit Systems Protection Board

National Aeronautics and Space Administration
National Capital Planning Commission
National Credit Union Administration
National Foundation on the Arts and the Humanities
National Labor Relations Board
National Mediation Board
National Science Foundation
National Transportation Safety Board
Nuclear Regulatory Commission
Occupational Safety and Health Review Commission
Office of Personnel Management
Panama Canal Commission
Peace Corps

Pennsylvania Avenue Development Corporation
Pension Benefit Guaranty Corporation
Postal Rate Commission
Railroad Retirement Board
Securities and Exchange Commission
Selective Service System
Small Business Administration
U.S. Arms Control and Disarmament Agency
U.S. Information Agency
U.S. International Development Cooperation Agency
U.S. International Trade Commission
U.S. Postal Service
Tennessee Valley Authority
Veterans Administration

Source: *The United States Government Manual 1982/83.* Washington, D.C.: Office of the Federal Register, 1982, p.792.

Fig. 6 *Appendix* 335

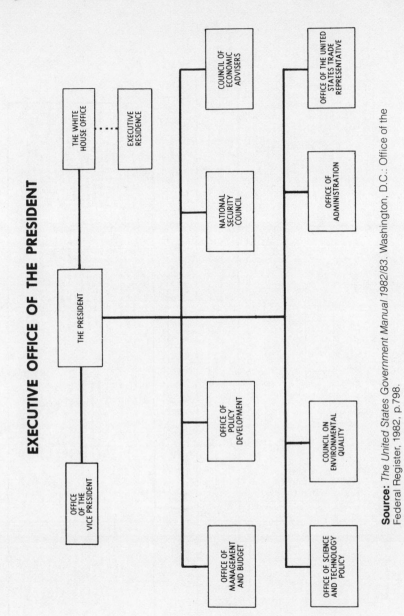

EXECUTIVE OFFICE OF THE PRESIDENT

OFFICE OF THE VICE PRESIDENT

THE PRESIDENT

THE WHITE HOUSE OFFICE

EXECUTIVE RESIDENCE

OFFICE OF MANAGEMENT AND BUDGET

OFFICE OF POLICY DEVELOPMENT

NATIONAL SECURITY COUNCIL

COUNCIL OF ECONOMIC ADVISERS

OFFICE OF SCIENCE AND TECHNOLOGY POLICY

COUNCIL ON ENVIRONMENTAL QUALITY

OFFICE OF ADMINISTRATION

OFFICE OF THE UNITED STATES TRADE REPRESENTATIVE

Source: *The United States Government Manual 1982/83.* Washington, D.C.: Office of the Federal Register, 1982, p.798.

HOUSE OF REPRESENTATIVES

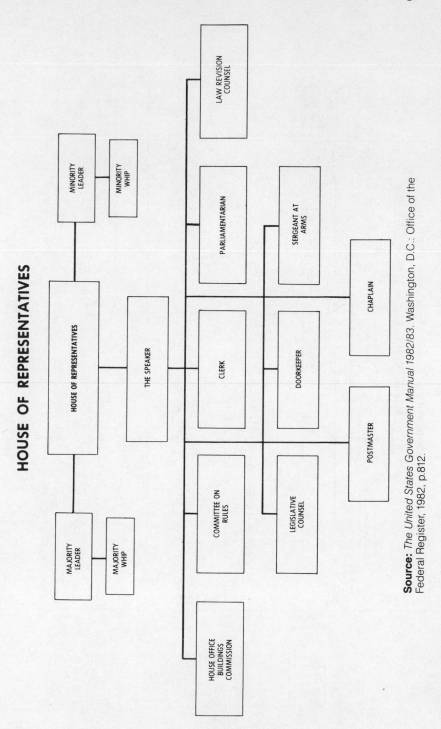

Source: *The United States Government Manual 1982/83.* Washington, D.C.: Office of the Federal Register, 1982, p.812.

Fig. 8 *Appendix* 337

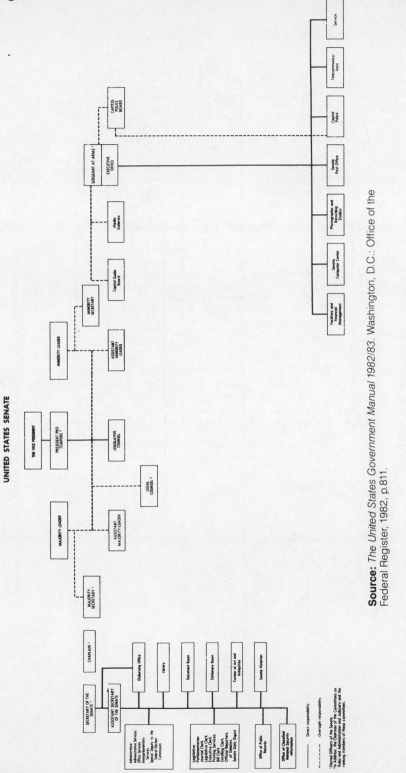

UNITED STATES SENATE

Source: *The United States Government Manual 1982/83.* Washington, D.C.: Office of the Federal Register, 1982, p.811.

Standing Committees in the Senate and in the House

Senate Committees	House Committees
Agriculture, Nutrition, and Forestry	Agriculture
Appropriations	Appropriations
Armed Services	Armed Services
Banking, Housing, and Urban Affairs	Banking, Finance, and Urban Affairs
Budget	Budget
Commerce, Science, and Transportation	District of Columbia
Energy and Natural Resources	Education and Labor
Environment and Public Works	Energy and Commerce
Finance	Foreign Affairs
Foreign Relations	Government Operations
Governmental Affairs	House Administration
Judiciary	Interior and Insular Affairs
Labor and Human Resources	Judiciary
Rules and Administration	Merchant Marine and Fisheries
Small Business	Post Office and Civil Service
Veterans' Affairs	Public Works and Transportation
	Rules
	Science and Technology
	Small Business
	Standards of Official Conduct
	Veterans' Affairs
	Ways and Means

Source: Robert L. Lineberry, *Government in America: People, Politics and Policy*, 2d ed., © 1983 by Robert L. Lineberry. Reprinted by permission of Little, Brown and Company.

Fig. 10   *Appendix*   339

How a Bill Becomes Law

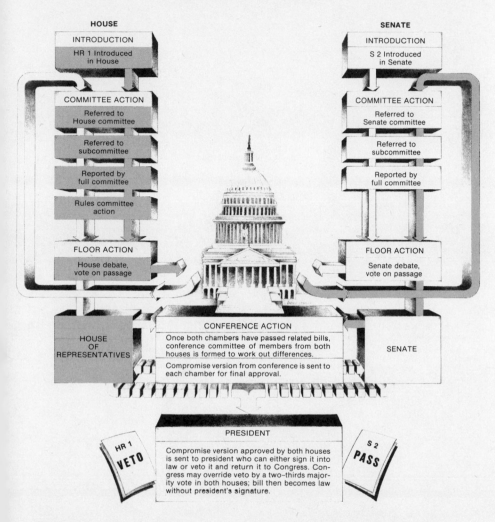

HOUSE

INTRODUCTION
HR 1 Introduced in House

COMMITTEE ACTION
Referred to House committee
Referred to subcommittee
Reported by full committee
Rules committee action

FLOOR ACTION
House debate, vote on passage

SENATE

INTRODUCTION
S 2 Introduced in Senate

COMMITTEE ACTION
Referred to Senate committee
Referred to subcommittee
Reported by full committee

FLOOR ACTION
Senate debate, vote on passage

HOUSE OF REPRESENTATIVES

CONFERENCE ACTION
Once both chambers have passed related bills, conference committee of members from both houses is formed to work out differences.
Compromise version from conference is sent to each chamber for final approval.

SENATE

PRESIDENT
Compromise version approved by both houses is sent to president who can either sign it into law or veto it and return it to Congress. Congress may override veto by a two-thirds majority vote in both houses; bill then becomes law without president's signature.

HR 1 VETO

S 2 PASS

NOTES

1. The President and the Electorate

1. Ross K. Baker, Gerald M. Pomper, and Wilson C. McWilliams, *American Government* (New York: Macmillan Publishing Co., Inc., 1983), 255.

2. Powers of the President

1. Richard E. Neustadt, *Presidential Power* (New York: John Wiley and Sons, 1960), viii.

3. The Presidents

1. *Durham Morning Herald*, February 21, 1983, 2A.

2. *Encyclopedia Americana* (Danbury, CT: Grolier Inc., 1981), 674.

4. Presidential Leadership

1. Louis Fisher, *Presidential Spending Power* (Princeton: Princeton University Press, 1975), 3.

2. Harold D. Lasswell, *Politics: Who Gets What, When, and How* (Cleveland: The World Publishing Co., 1958).

3. Richard E. Neustadt, *Presidential Power: The Politics of Leadership* (New York: John Wiley and Sons, 1960), viii.

4. Walter F. Mondale, *The Accountability of Power: Toward a Responsible Presidency* (New York: David McKay Co., 1975), 67.

5. Theodore Roosevelt, *An Autobiography* (New York: Scribner's, 1913), 357.

7. The Congress and the Electorate

1. Gary C. Jacobson, *The Politics of Congressional Elections* (Boston: Little, Brown and Co., 1983), 13.

2. Randall B. Ripley, *Congress: Process and Policy* (New York: W. W. Norton and Co., Inc., 1983), 75–76.

3. Richard F. Fenno, Jr., *Home Style: House Members in Their Districts* (Boston: Little, Brown and Co., 1978), 27.

4. Barbara Hinckley, *Stability and Change in Congress* (New York: Harper and Row, 1978), 49.

5. Barbara Hinckley, *Congressional Elections* (Washington, DC: Congressional Quarterly, 1981), 129.

6. Randall B. Ripley, *Congress: Process and Policy* (New York: W. W. Norton and Co., Inc., 1983), 116.

7. David J. Vogler, *The Politics of Congress* (Boston: Allyn and Bacon, Inc., 1983), 53.

8. David R. Mayhew, "Congressional Elections: The Case of the Vanishing Marginals," in *The Congressional System: Notes and Readings*, ed. by Leroy N. Rieselbach (North Scituote, MA: Duxbury Press, 1979), 44–58.

8. Powers of Congress

1. Walter J. Oleszek, *Congressional Procedures and the Policy Process* (Washington, DC: Congressional Quarterly, 1978), 24.

2. Lawrence C. Dodd and Bruce I. Oppenheimer, "The House in Transition," in *Congress Reconsidered*, ed. by Lawrence C. Dodd and Bruce I. Oppenheimer (New York: Praeger, 1977), 26–27.

10. The Committee Structure

1. Malcolm E. Jewell and Samuel C. Patterson, *The Legislative Process in the United States* (New York: Random House, 1977), 189.

2. Barbara Hinckley, *The Seniority System in Congress* (Bloomington: Indiana University Press, 1971), 111.

3. David B. Truman, *The Governmental Process* (New York: Alfred Knopf, 1953), 439.

11. Rules and Procedures

1. Alan Murray, "House Finding Bill Riders Become Potent Policy Force," *Congressional Quarterly Weekly Report* (November 1, 1980), 3251.

2. Walter S. Oleszek, *Congressional Procedures and the Policy Process* (Washington, DC: Congressional Quarterly, 1978), 191.

3. Donald G. Tacheron and Morris K. Udall, *The Job of the Congressman: An Introduction to Service in the U.S. House of Representatives* (Indianapolis: Bobbs-Merrill, 1966), 196.

INDEX

Cross-references to dictionary entries are located in the text at the end of each definition paragraph. Page references in BOLD type indicate dictionary entries.

Hayes, Lucy Webb, 70, 99
Hayes, Rutherford B., 10, 41, **70–71**, 72, 75, 99
Hayes, Sophia Birchard, 70
Haynesworth Clement F., Jr., 186
Hays, Wayne, 296
Health and Human Services, Department of. *See* Department of Health and Human Services
Health Care Financial Administration, 123
Hearings, open, 245–246
Hearst, Patricia, 44
Helms, Jesse, 210
Hepburn Act, 77
Highways, 129–130
Hinckley, Barbara, 166, 174, 250
Hinckley, John W., 138
Hispanic Caucus, Congressional. *See* Congressional Hispanic Caucus
Hobbes, Thomas, 163, 182
Hoffa, Jimmy, 44
Home Owners Loan Corporation, 84
Hoover, Herbert, 81, **82–83**, 106, 110, 116, 277
Hoover, Hulda Minthorn, 82
Hoover, J. Edgar, 28
Hoover, Jesse Clark, 82
Hoover, Lou Henry, 82
House, **200–201**, 330
   Administration Committee, 286
   apportionment of seats in, 159
   Appropriations Committee, 251, 257–258, 286, 314
   and bicameralism, 186–187
   bills in, 259–260, 263–264
   Black Caucus, 213–214
   Budget Committee, 286, 311
   Calendar, 262, 287, 295
   Clerk of the, 273
   closed door session of, 264–265
   Committee on Committees, 224, 235–236
   Committee on the Judiciary, 281
   Committee on Organization Study and Review, 215
   Committee Reform Amendments of 1974, 252
   committees, 234, 238–239, 243, 248–249, 249–250, 250–251, 338–339
   Committee of the Whole, 236–237, 256–257, 267, 275–276, 284, 288, 289, 290, 301
   Consent Calendar, 266–267
   debate in, 267–268, 297–298
   Democratic Caucus, 215, 223–224, 248, 251–252

Democratic Study Group, 218–219, 226
discharge rule, 269–270
and election of president, 10
Ethics Committee (Committee on Standards of Official Conduct), 164
executive session of, 273–274
five-minute rule in, 275–276
floor managers, 271
Foreign Relations Committee, 188
functions of, 192–193
hearings by, 245–246
Hispanic Caucus, 214
impeachment powers of, 201–202
legislative veto by, 277–279
Judiciary Committee, 202, 296, 317
majority leader, **219–220**
majority/minority whips, **220–221**
minority leader, **221–222**
Permanent Select Committee on Aging, 249
Private Calendar, 237
privileged legislation, 286–287
qualifications for office in, 181–182, 200–201, 206–207
quorum of, 287–289
quorum calls in, 268
readings of bills in, 289–290
Republican Caucus, 236
Republican Conference, 223–224
Republican Wednesday Group, 219, 226
resolutions, 291–292
revenue bills, 257
rules, 286, 294–295, 299–300
Rules Committee, 204, 217–218, 251, 256, 262–263, 269–270, 277, 286, 289, 292, 294–295, 300, 302–303, 376
Rule 10, 246
Rule 21, 289
salary of members of, 206
Select Committee on Committees, 247–248
Select Committee on Small Business, 249
seniority system, 249–250
Speaker, 190, 200–201, 218–223, 229–230, 233, 237, 244, 246, 284, 287, 289, 290, 299–300, 302–303, 311, 321
Speaker pro tempore, 223
staff, 237–238
Standards of Official Conduct, 286
Steering and Policy Committee, 217–218, 236
subcommittees, 251–252
suspension of the rules, 267